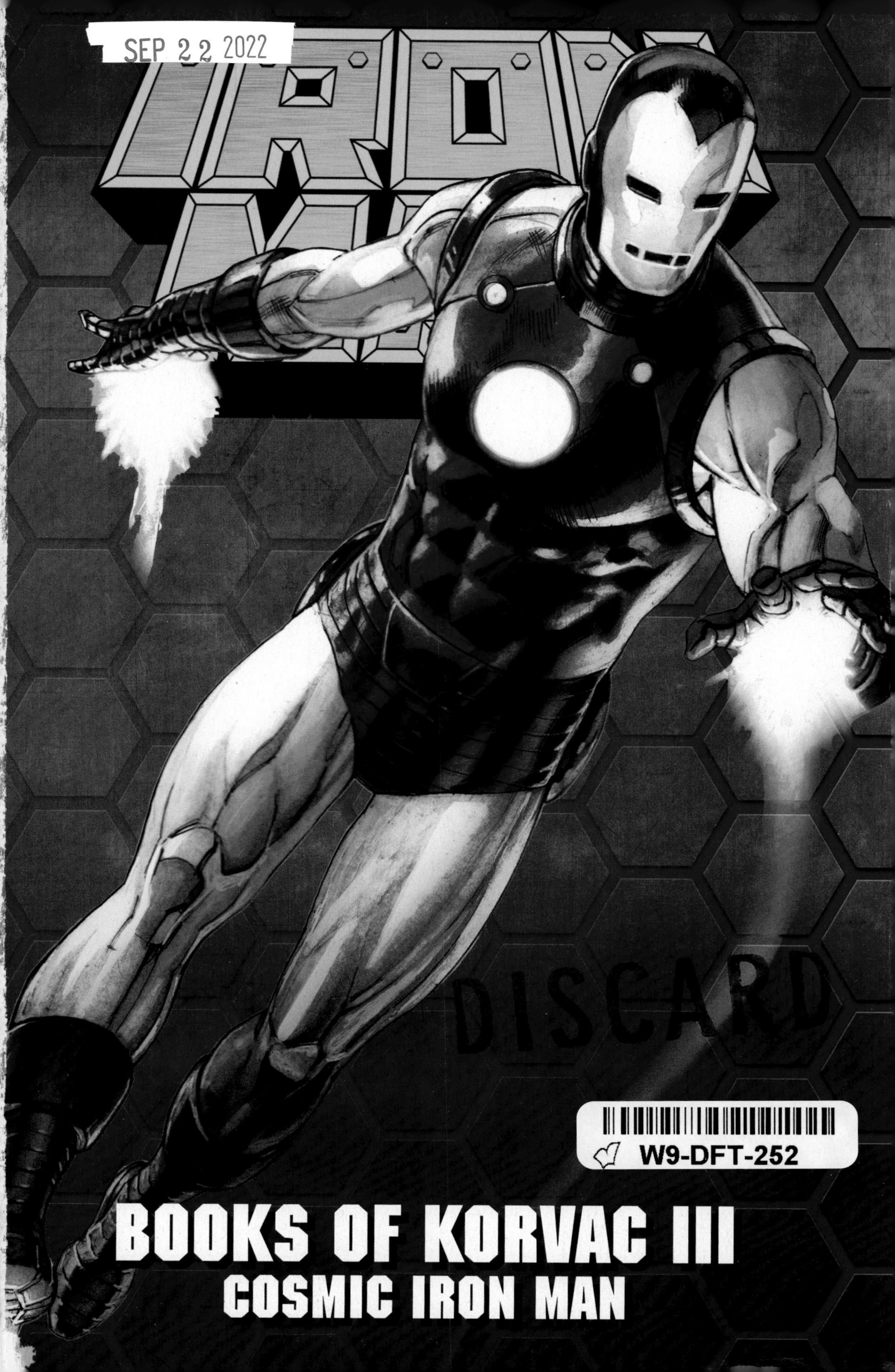

BOOKS OF KORVAC III
COSMIC IRON MAN

Korvac, resurrected in an android body, seeks to boost his powers to godlike levels by stealing cosmic energies from *Taa II*, Galactus' worldship. Iron Man assembled an eclectic team of heroes, including Hellcat, to pursue Korvac off-planet.

While en route in space, Iron Man was mysteriously teleported away to an alien planet inhabited by individuals from across the galaxy, including the armored hero Avro-X. There, they managed to form a peaceful community overseen by Tony's old foe Stilt-Man. But their tranquil existence was revealed to be a lie engineered by Stilt-Man, who was secretly responsible for stranding everyone on the planet.

After Iron Man and Avro-X defeated Stilt-Man, the cosmic entity known as the Living Tribunal appeared. The Tribunal revealed that only Iron Man could prevent an upcoming imbalance of cosmic proportions and teleported Tony and Avro-X to *Taa II*—which immediately activated the worldship's defense systems!

BOOKS OF KORVAC III
COSMIC IRON MAN

CHRISTOPHER CANTWELL
WRITER

ANGEL UNZUETA (#12, #14, #17),
CAFU (#13-14, #19),
IBRAIM ROBERSON (#15, 17),
JULIUS OHTA (#16)
& LAN MEDINA (#18)
ARTISTS

FRANK D'ARMATA
COLOR ARTIST

VC's JOE CARAMAGNA
LETTERER

ALEX ROSS
COVER ART

MARTIN BIRO
ASSISTANT EDITOR

**ALANNA SMITH
& ANNALISE BISSA**
ASSOCIATE EDITORS

TOM BREVOORT
EDITOR

IRON MAN CREATED BY STAN LEE, LARRY LIEBER, DON HECK & JACK KIRBY

COLLECTION EDITOR: **DANIEL KIRCHHOFFER**
ASSISTANT MANAGING EDITOR: **MAIA LOY**
ASSOCIATE MANAGER, TALENT RELATIONS: **LISA MONTALBANO**
DIRECTOR, PRODUCTION & SPECIAL PROJECTS: **JENNIFER GRÜNWALD**

VP, PRODUCTION & SPECIAL PROJECTS: **JEFF YOUNGQUIST**
BOOK DESIGNERS: **SARAH SPADACCINI** with **STACIE ZUCKER**
SVP PRINT, SALES & MARKETING: **DAVID GABRIEL**
EDITOR IN CHIEF: **C.B. CEBULSKI**

IRON MAN VOL. 3: BOOKS OF KORVAC III — COSMIC IRON MAN. Contains material originally published in magazine form as IRON MAN (2020) #12-19. First printing 2022. ISBN 978-1-302-92627-4. Published by MARVEL WORLDWIDE, INC., a subsidiary of MARVEL ENTERTAINMENT, LLC. OFFICE OF PUBLICATION: 1290 Avenue of the Americas, New York, NY 10104. © 2022 MARVEL. No similarity between any of the names, characters, persons, and/or institutions in this book with those of any living or dead person or institution is intended, and any such similarity which may exist is purely coincidental. **Printed in Canada.** KEVIN FEIGE, Chief Creative Officer; DAN BUCKLEY, President, Marvel Entertainment; JOE QUESADA, EVP & Creative Director; DAVID BOGART, Associate Publisher & SVP of Talent Affairs; TOM BREVOORT, VP, Executive Editor; NICK LOWE, Executive Editor, VP of Content, Digital Publishing; DAVID GABRIEL, VP of Print & Digital Publishing; MARK ANNUNZIATO, VP of Planning & Forecasting; JEFF YOUNGQUIST, VP of Production & Special Projects; ALEX MORALES, Director of Publishing Operations; DAN EDINGTON, Director of Editorial Operations; RICKEY PURDIN, Director of Talent Relations; JENNIFER GRÜNWALD, Director of Production & Special Projects; SUSAN CRESPI, Production Manager; STAN LEE, Chairman Emeritus. For information regarding advertising in Marvel Comics or on Marvel.com, please contact Vit DeBellis, Custom Solutions & Integrated Advertising Manager, at vdebellis@marvel.com. For Marvel subscription inquiries, please call 888-511-5480. Manufactured between 3/25/2022 and 4/26/2022 by SOLISCO PRINTERS, SCOTT QC, CANADA.

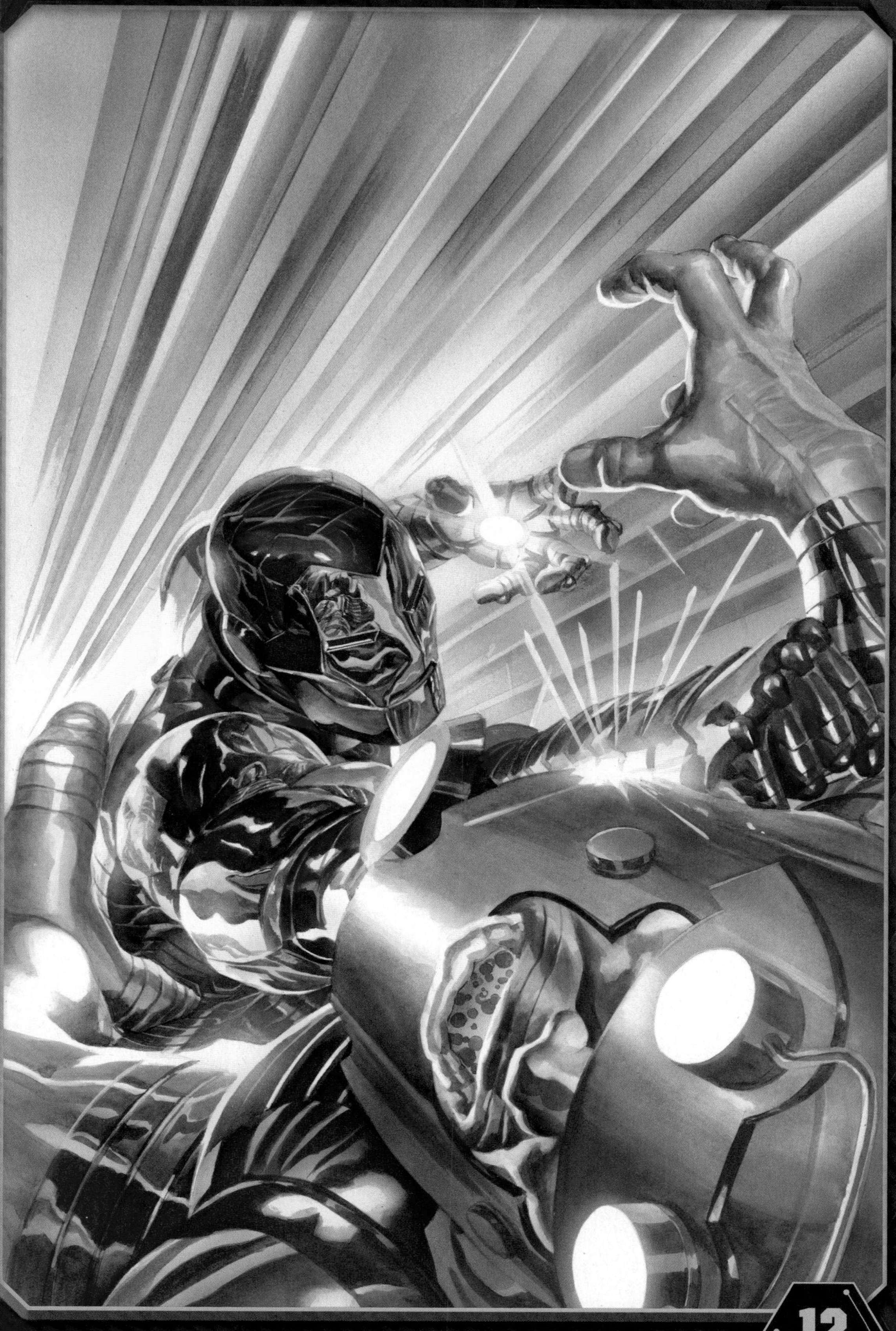

12

LET US NOW CROSS OVER

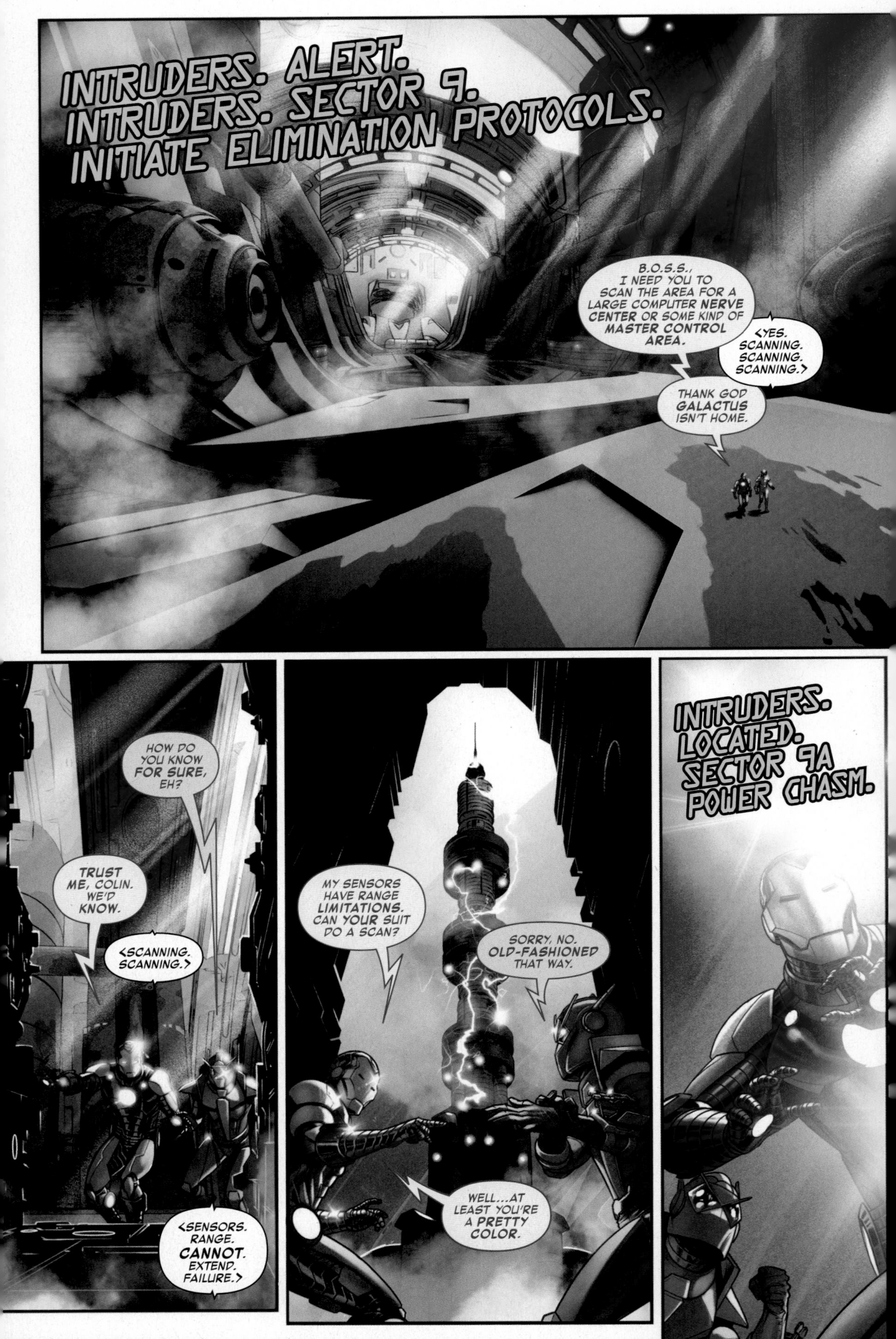
INTRUDERS. ALERT.
INTRUDERS. SECTOR 9.
INITIATE ELIMINATION PROTOCOLS.
B.O.S.S., I NEED YOU TO SCAN THE AREA FOR A LARGE COMPUTER NERVE CENTER OR SOME KIND OF MASTER CONTROL AREA.
<YES. SCANNING. SCANNING. SCANNING.>
THANK GOD GALACTUS ISN'T HOME.
HOW DO YOU KNOW FOR SURE, EH?
TRUST ME, COLIN. WE'D KNOW.
<SCANNING. SCANNING.>
<SENSORS. RANGE. CANNOT. EXTEND. FAILURE.>
MY SENSORS HAVE RANGE LIMITATIONS. CAN YOUR SUIT DO A SCAN?
SORRY, NO. OLD-FASHIONED THAT WAY.
WELL...AT LEAST YOU'RE A PRETTY COLOR.
INTRUDERS. LOCATED. SECTOR 9A POWER CHASM.

TZCHOEOWW
TZCHOEOWW
TZCHOEOWW

THIS WAY!

SSHHKNCK

DEAD END!

NOT NECESSARILY...

TONY!

COLIN, GET OUTTA THERE--

KAEFFFSSV

AGGNH...

NNNGH... I'M...ALL RIGHTY-TIGHTY... JUST A TICKLE...

GOOD. NOW WATCH THESE DRONES UP AHEAD.

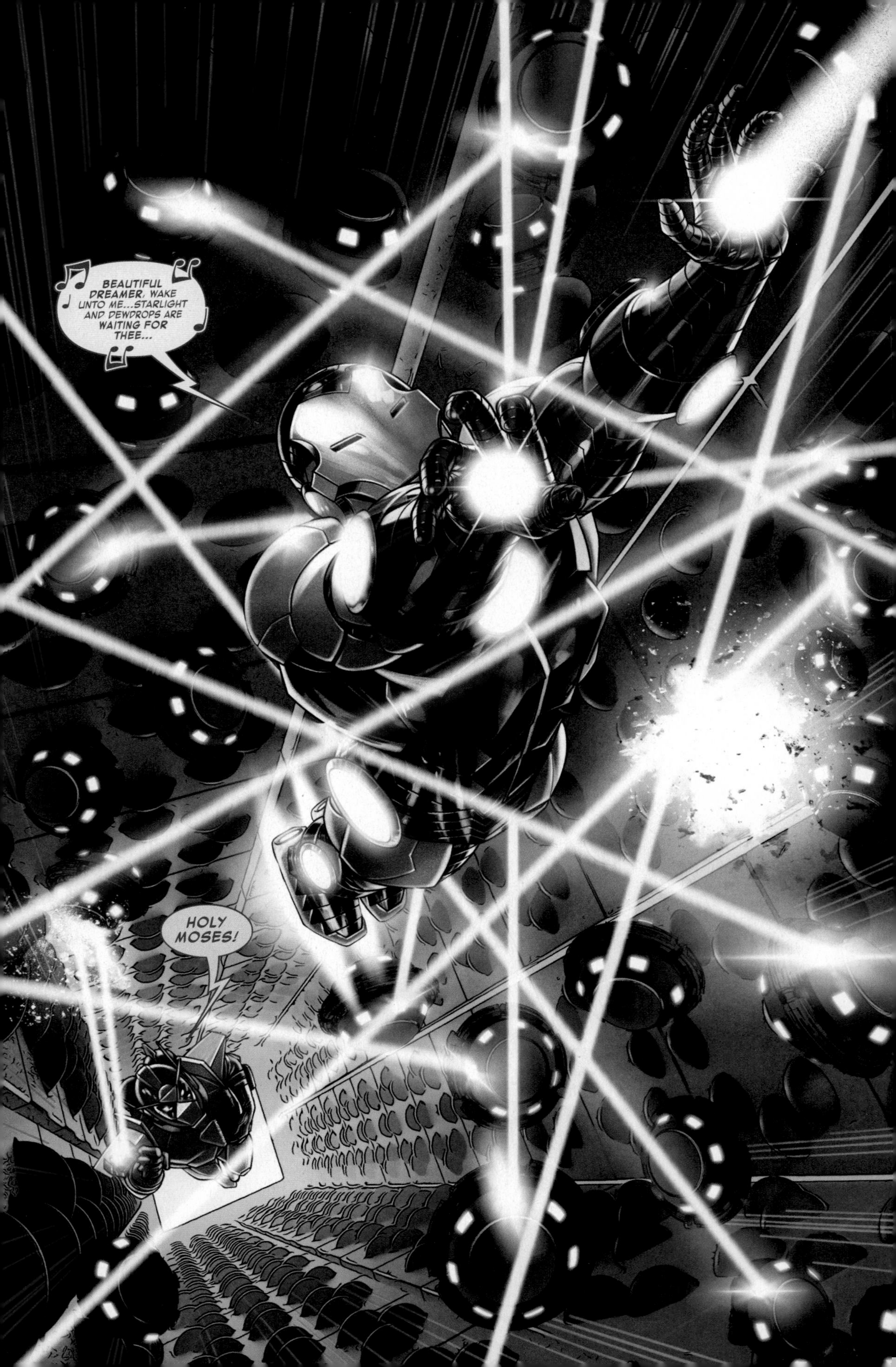
BEAUTIFUL DREAMER, WAKE UNTO ME...STARLIGHT AND DEWDROPS ARE WAITING FOR THEE...
HOLY MOSES!

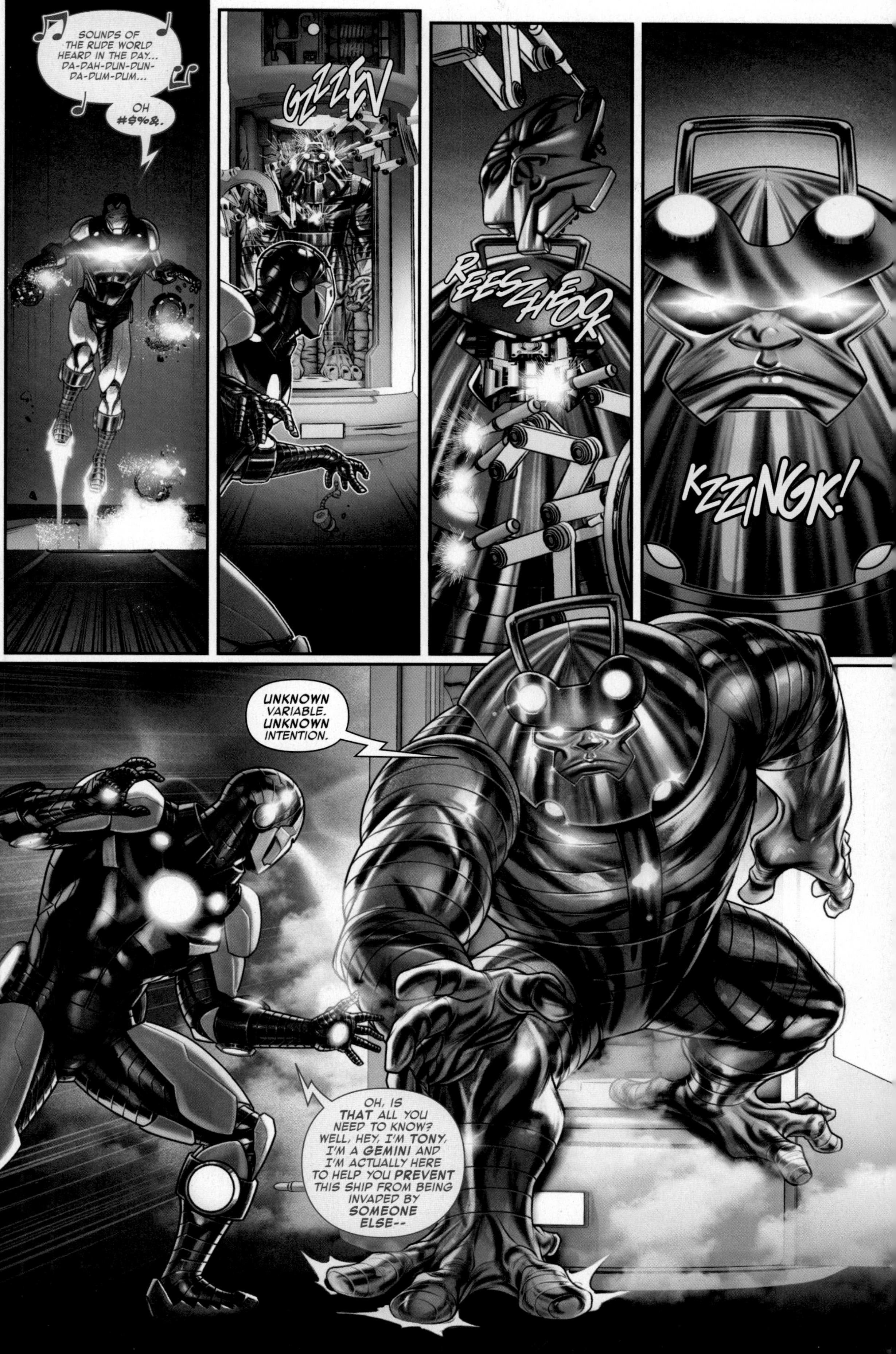
SOUNDS OF THE RUDE WORLD HEARD IN THE DAY... DA-DAH-DUN-DUN-DA-DUM-DUM...
OH #$%&.
GZZZEV
REESZHEOOK
KZZINGK!
UNKNOWN VARIABLE. UNKNOWN INTENTION.
OH, IS THAT ALL YOU NEED TO KNOW? WELL, HEY, I'M TONY, I'M A GEMINI AND I'M ACTUALLY HERE TO HELP YOU PREVENT THIS SHIP FROM BEING INVADED BY SOMEONE ELSE--

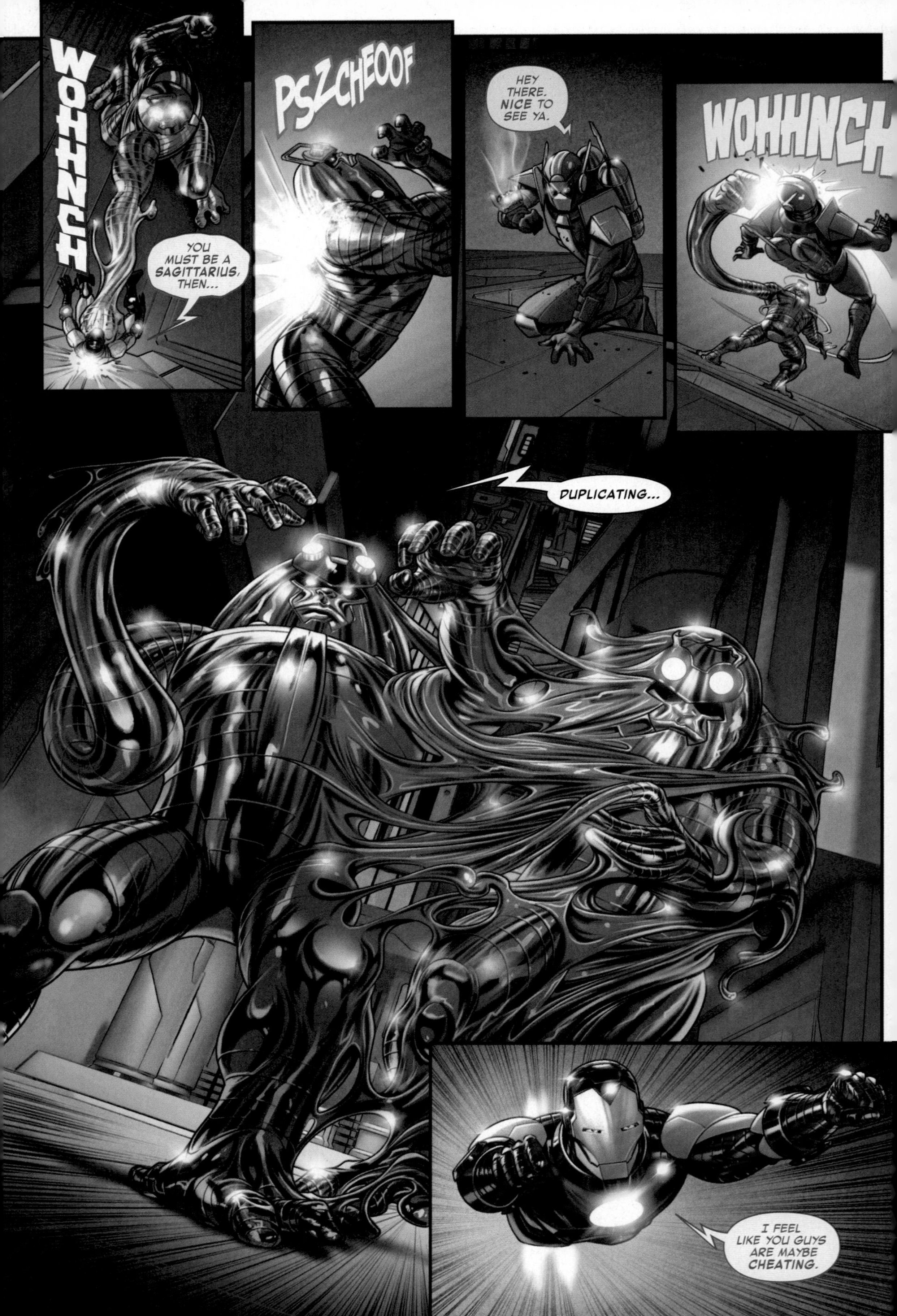
WOHHNCH
YOU MUST BE A SAGITTARIUS, THEN...
PSZCHEOOF
HEY THERE. NICE TO SEE YA.
WOHHNCH
DUPLICATING...
I FEEL LIKE YOU GUYS ARE MAYBE CHEATING.

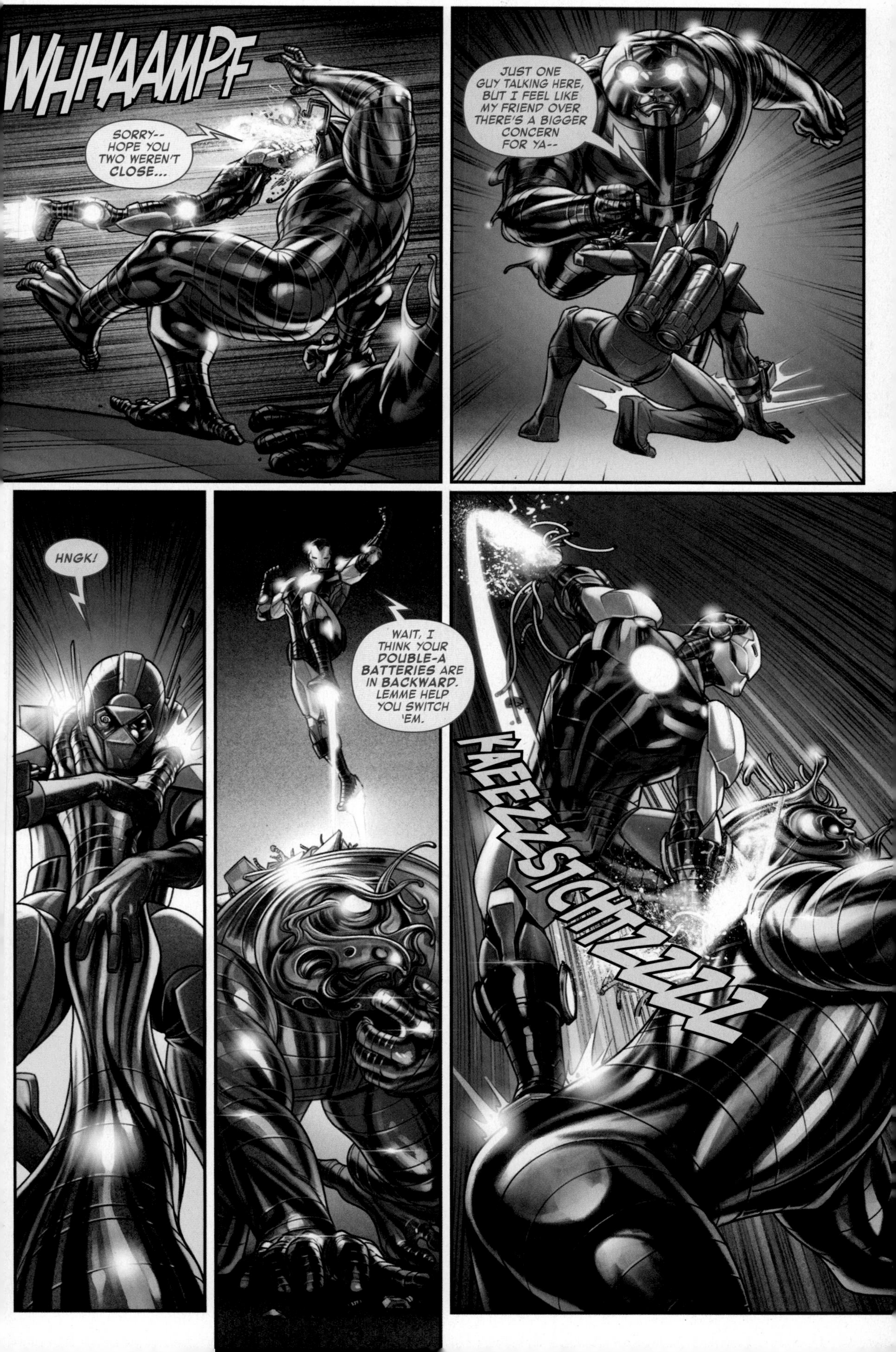

WHHAAMPF
SORRY-- HOPE YOU TWO WEREN'T CLOSE...
JUST ONE GUY TALKING HERE, BUT I FEEL LIKE MY FRIEND OVER THERE'S A BIGGER CONCERN FOR YA--
HNGK!
WAIT, I THINK YOUR DOUBLE-A BATTERIES ARE IN BACKWARD. LEMME HELP YOU SWITCH 'EM.
KAEEZZSTCHTZZZZ

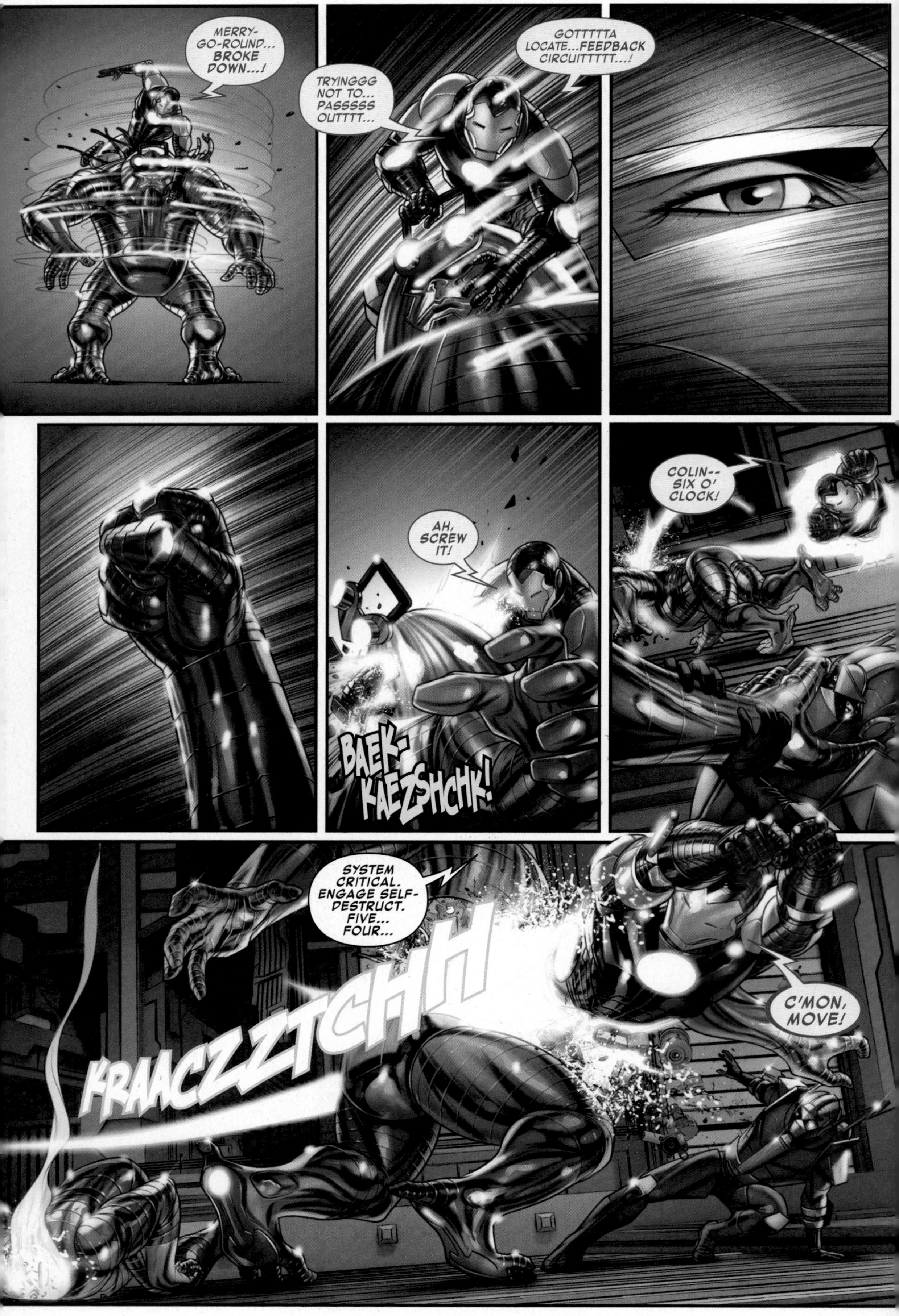
MERRY-GO-ROUND... BROKE DOWN...!
TRYINGGG NOT TO... PASSSSS OUTTTT...
GOTTTTTA LOCATE...FEEDBACK CIRCUITTTTT...!
AH, SCREW IT!
BAEK-KAEZSHCHK!
COLIN--SIX O' CLOCK!
SYSTEM CRITICAL. ENGAGE SELF-DESTRUCT. FIVE... FOUR...
KRAACZZTCHH
C'MON, MOVE!

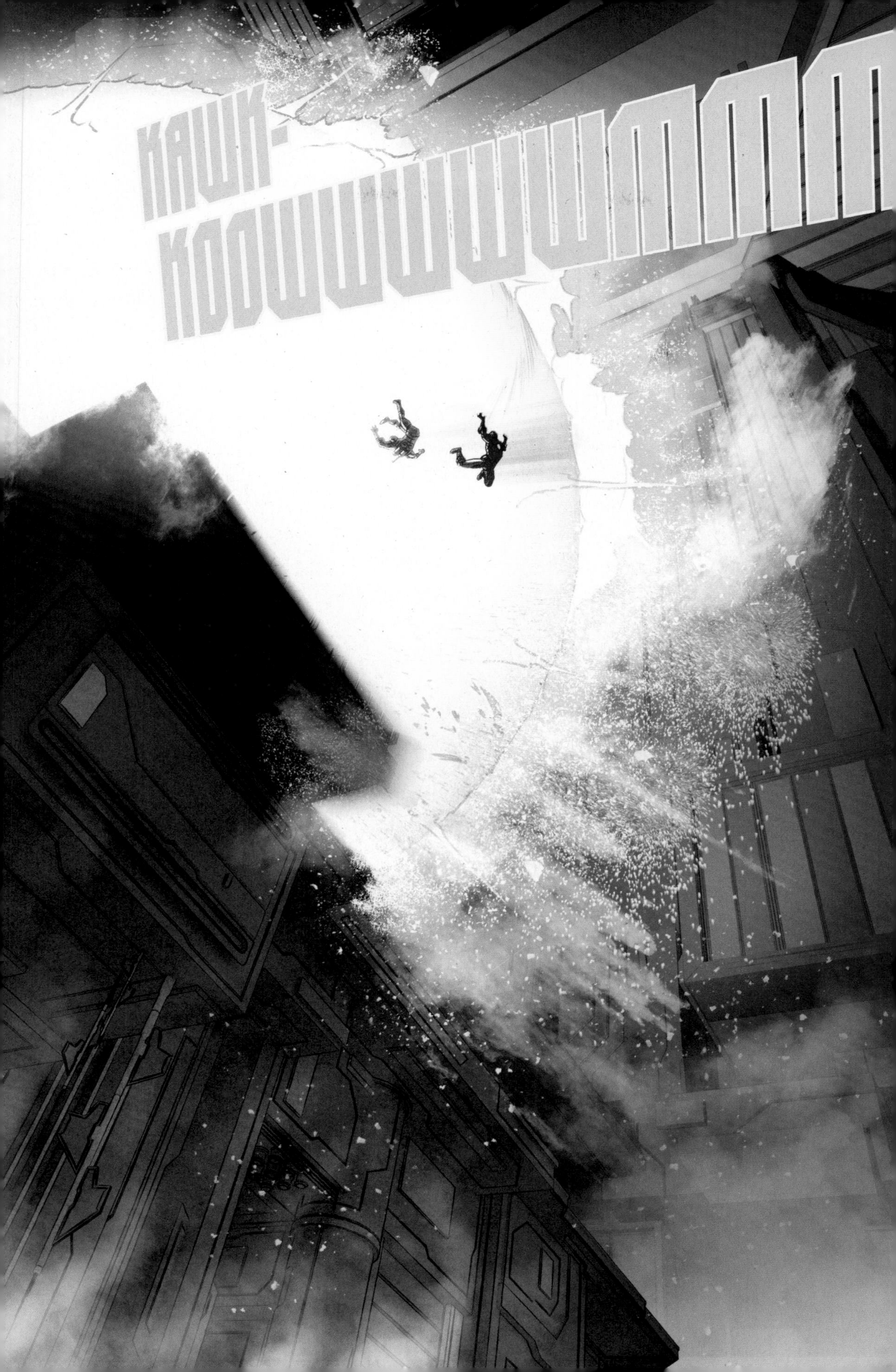
KAWK-
KOOWWWWWMMM

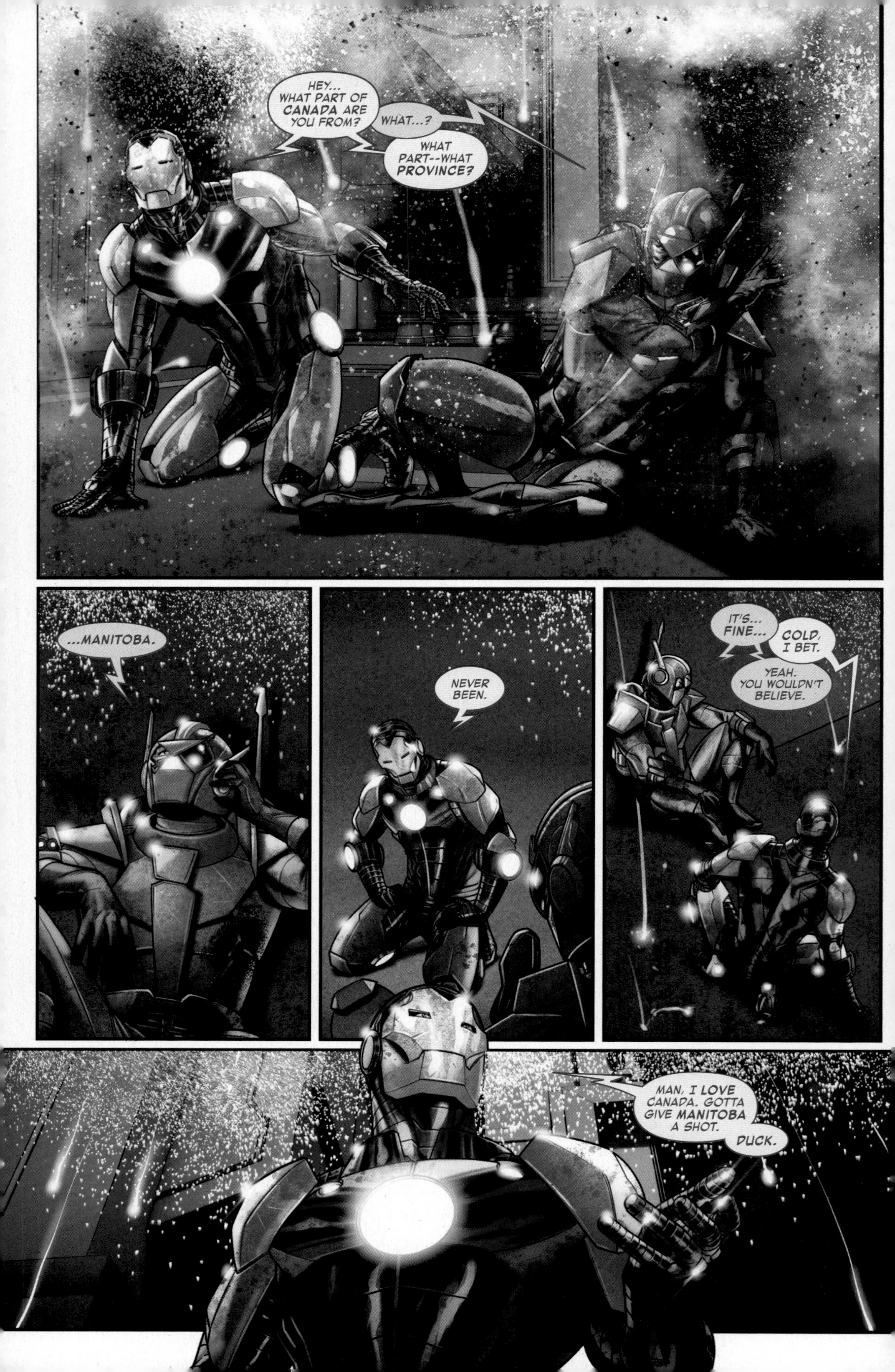
HEY... WHAT PART OF CANADA ARE YOU FROM?
WHAT...?
WHAT PART--WHAT PROVINCE?
...MANITOBA.
NEVER BEEN.
IT'S... FINE...
COLD, I BET.
YEAH. YOU WOULDN'T BELIEVE.
MAN, I LOVE CANADA. GOTTA GIVE MANITOBA A SHOT.
DUCK.

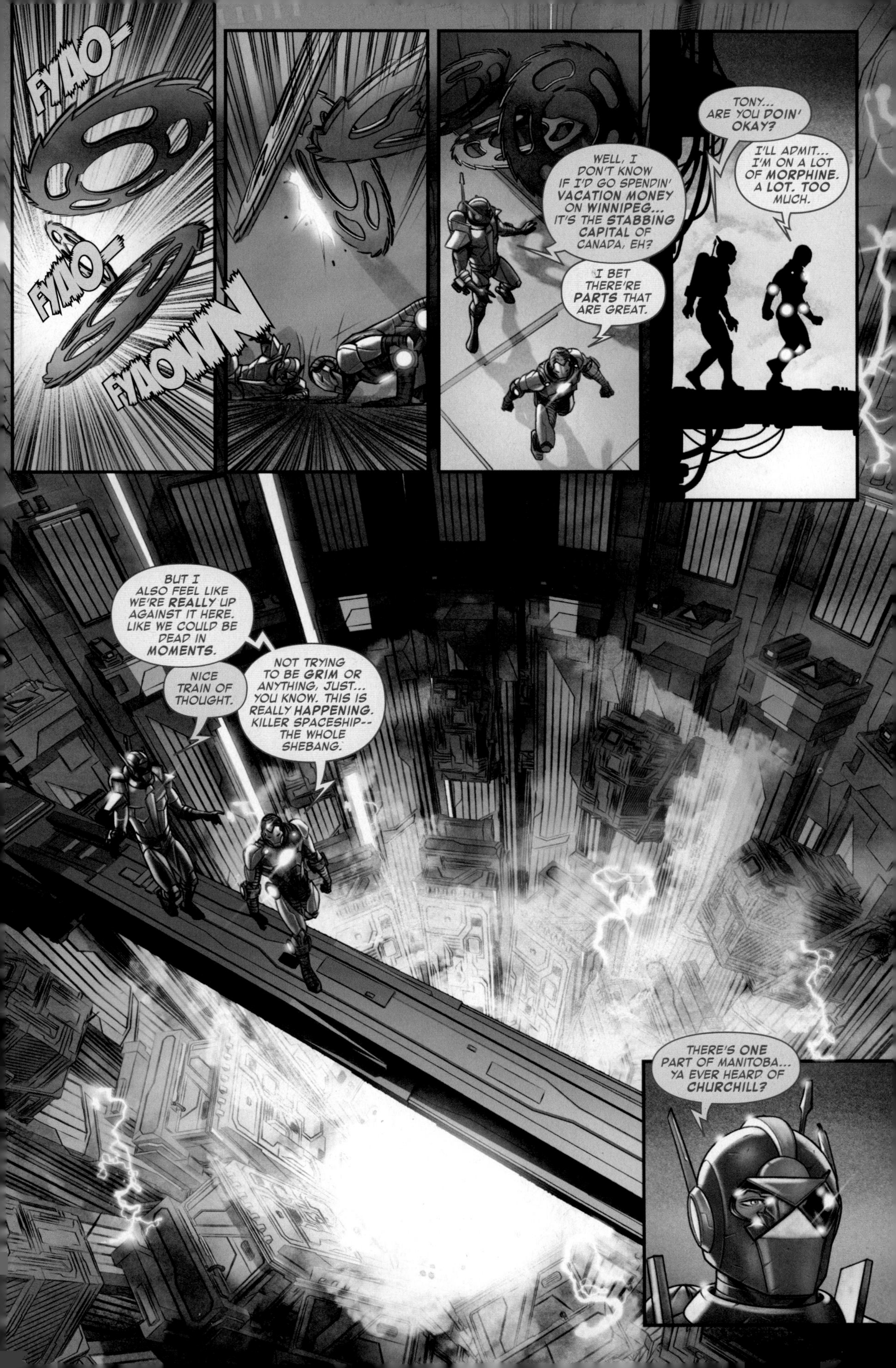
FYAO-
FYAO-
FYAOWN
WELL, I DON'T KNOW IF I'D GO SPENDIN' VACATION MONEY ON WINNIPEG... IT'S THE STABBING CAPITAL OF CANADA, EH?
I BET THERE'RE PARTS THAT ARE GREAT.
TONY... ARE YOU DOIN' OKAY?
I'LL ADMIT... I'M ON A LOT OF MORPHINE. A LOT. TOO MUCH.
BUT I ALSO FEEL LIKE WE'RE REALLY UP AGAINST IT HERE. LIKE WE COULD BE DEAD IN MOMENTS.
NOT TRYING TO BE GRIM OR ANYTHING, JUST... YOU KNOW. THIS IS REALLY HAPPENING. KILLER SPACESHIP-- THE WHOLE SHEBANG.
NICE TRAIN OF THOUGHT.
THERE'S ONE PART OF MANITOBA... YA EVER HEARD OF CHURCHILL?

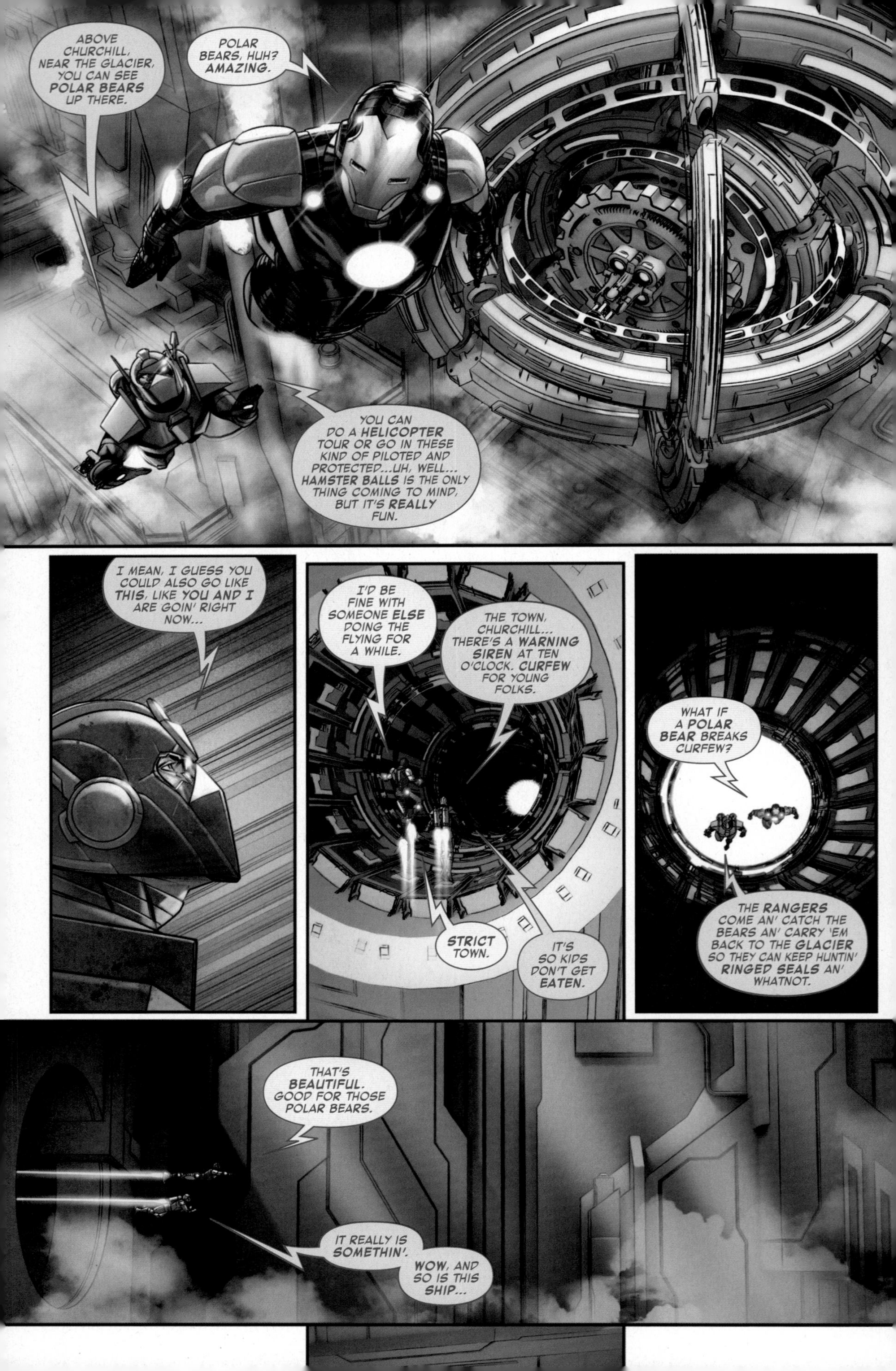
ABOVE CHURCHILL, NEAR THE GLACIER, YOU CAN SEE POLAR BEARS UP THERE.
POLAR BEARS, HUH? AMAZING.
YOU CAN DO A HELICOPTER TOUR OR GO IN THESE KIND OF PILOTED AND PROTECTED...UH, WELL... HAMSTER BALLS IS THE ONLY THING COMING TO MIND, BUT IT'S REALLY FUN.
I MEAN, I GUESS YOU COULD ALSO GO LIKE THIS, LIKE YOU AND I ARE GOIN' RIGHT NOW...
I'D BE FINE WITH SOMEONE ELSE DOING THE FLYING FOR A WHILE.
THE TOWN, CHURCHILL... THERE'S A WARNING SIREN AT TEN O'CLOCK. CURFEW FOR YOUNG FOLKS.
STRICT TOWN.
IT'S SO KIDS DON'T GET EATEN.
WHAT IF A POLAR BEAR BREAKS CURFEW?
THE RANGERS COME AN' CATCH THE BEARS AN' CARRY 'EM BACK TO THE GLACIER SO THEY CAN KEEP HUNTIN' RINGED SEALS AN' WHATNOT.
THAT'S BEAUTIFUL. GOOD FOR THOSE POLAR BEARS.
IT REALLY IS SOMETHIN'.
WOW, AND SO IS THIS SHIP...

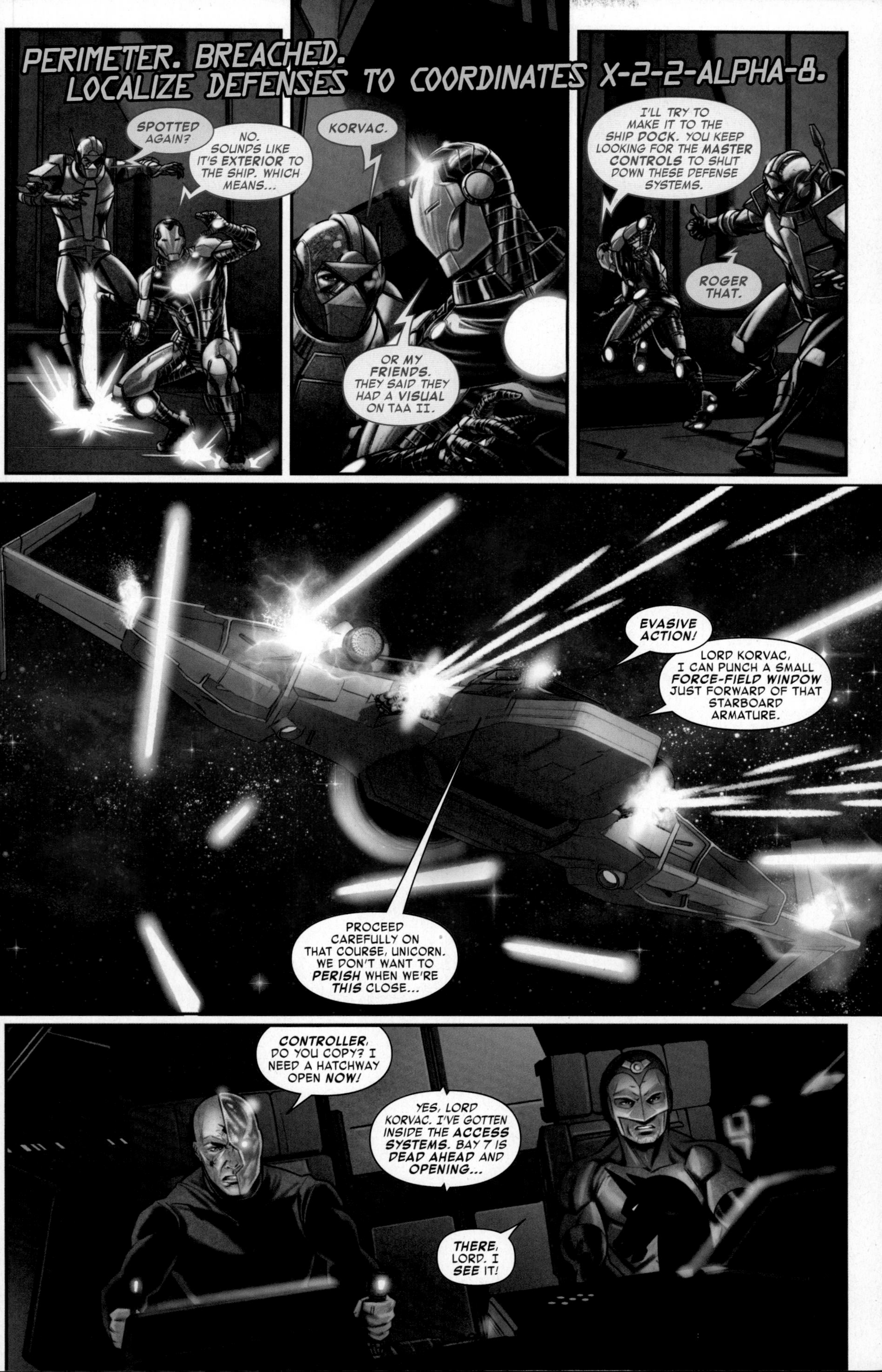

PERIMETER. BREACHED.
LOCALIZE DEFENSES TO COORDINATES X-2-2-ALPHA-8.
SPOTTED AGAIN?
NO. SOUNDS LIKE IT'S EXTERIOR TO THE SHIP. WHICH MEANS...
KORVAC.
OR MY FRIENDS. THEY SAID THEY HAD A VISUAL ON TAA II.
I'LL TRY TO MAKE IT TO THE SHIP DOCK. YOU KEEP LOOKING FOR THE MASTER CONTROLS TO SHUT DOWN THESE DEFENSE SYSTEMS.
ROGER THAT.
EVASIVE ACTION!
LORD KORVAC, I CAN PUNCH A SMALL FORCE-FIELD WINDOW JUST FORWARD OF THAT STARBOARD ARMATURE.
PROCEED CAREFULLY ON THAT COURSE, UNICORN. WE DON'T WANT TO PERISH WHEN WE'RE THIS CLOSE...
CONTROLLER, DO YOU COPY? I NEED A HATCHWAY OPEN NOW!
YES, LORD KORVAC. I'VE GOTTEN INSIDE THE ACCESS SYSTEMS. BAY 7 IS DEAD AHEAD AND OPENING...
THERE, LORD. I SEE IT!

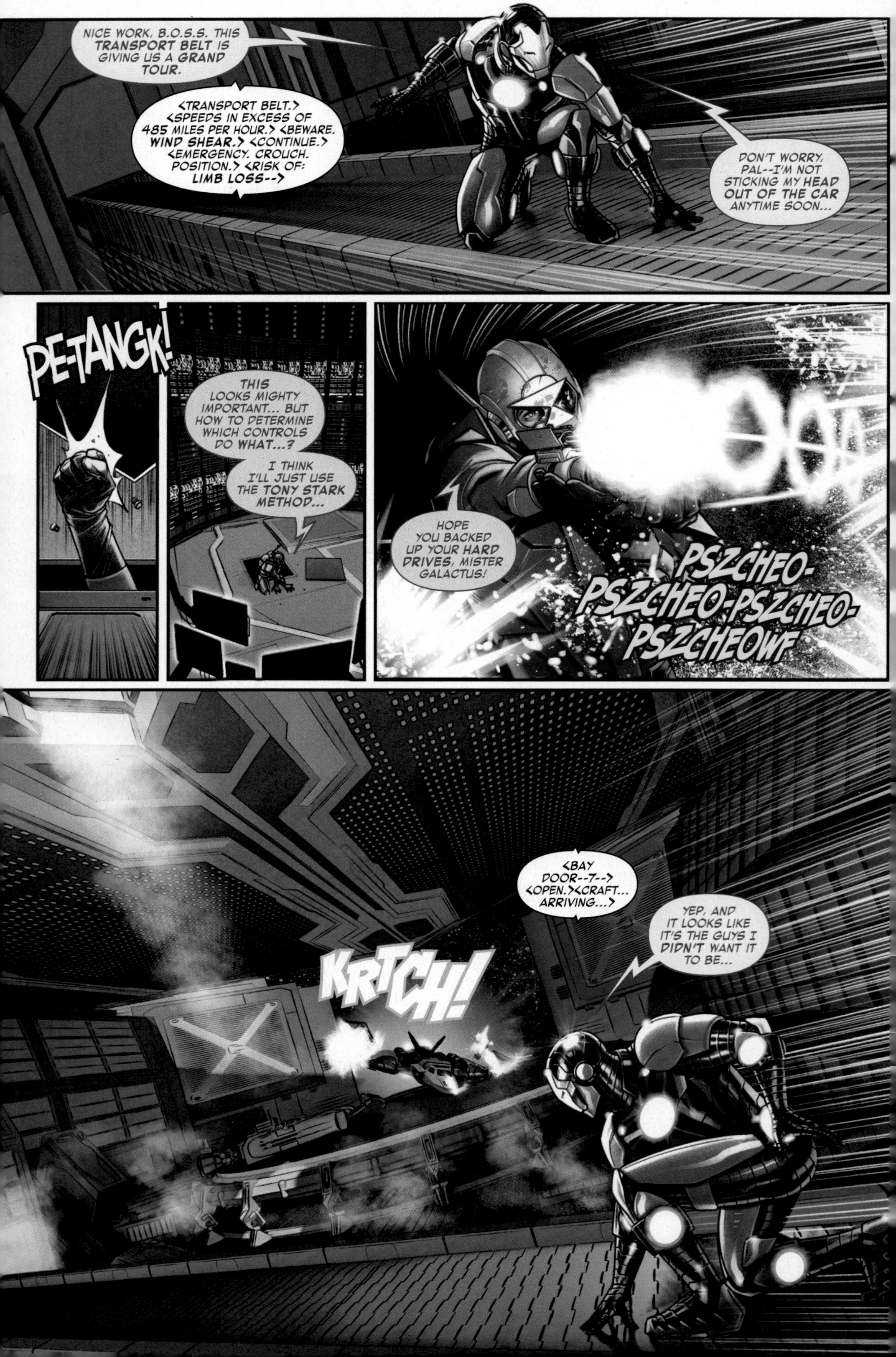

NICE WORK, B.O.S.S. THIS TRANSPORT BELT IS GIVING US A GRAND TOUR.
<TRANSPORT BELT.> <SPEEDS IN EXCESS OF 485 MILES PER HOUR.> <BEWARE. WIND SHEAR.> <CONTINUE.> <EMERGENCY. CROUCH. POSITION.> <RISK OF: LIMB LOSS-->
DON'T WORRY, PAL--I'M NOT STICKING MY HEAD OUT OF THE CAR ANYTIME SOON...
PE-TANGK!
THIS LOOKS MIGHTY IMPORTANT... BUT HOW TO DETERMINE WHICH CONTROLS DO WHAT...?
I THINK I'LL JUST USE THE TONY STARK METHOD...
HOPE YOU BACKED UP YOUR HARD DRIVES, MISTER GALACTUS!
PSZCHEO-PSZCHEO-PSZCHEO-PSZCHEOWF
<BAY DOOR--7--> <OPEN.><CRAFT... ARRIVING...>
YEP, AND IT LOOKS LIKE IT'S THE GUYS I DIDN'T WANT IT TO BE...
KRTCH!

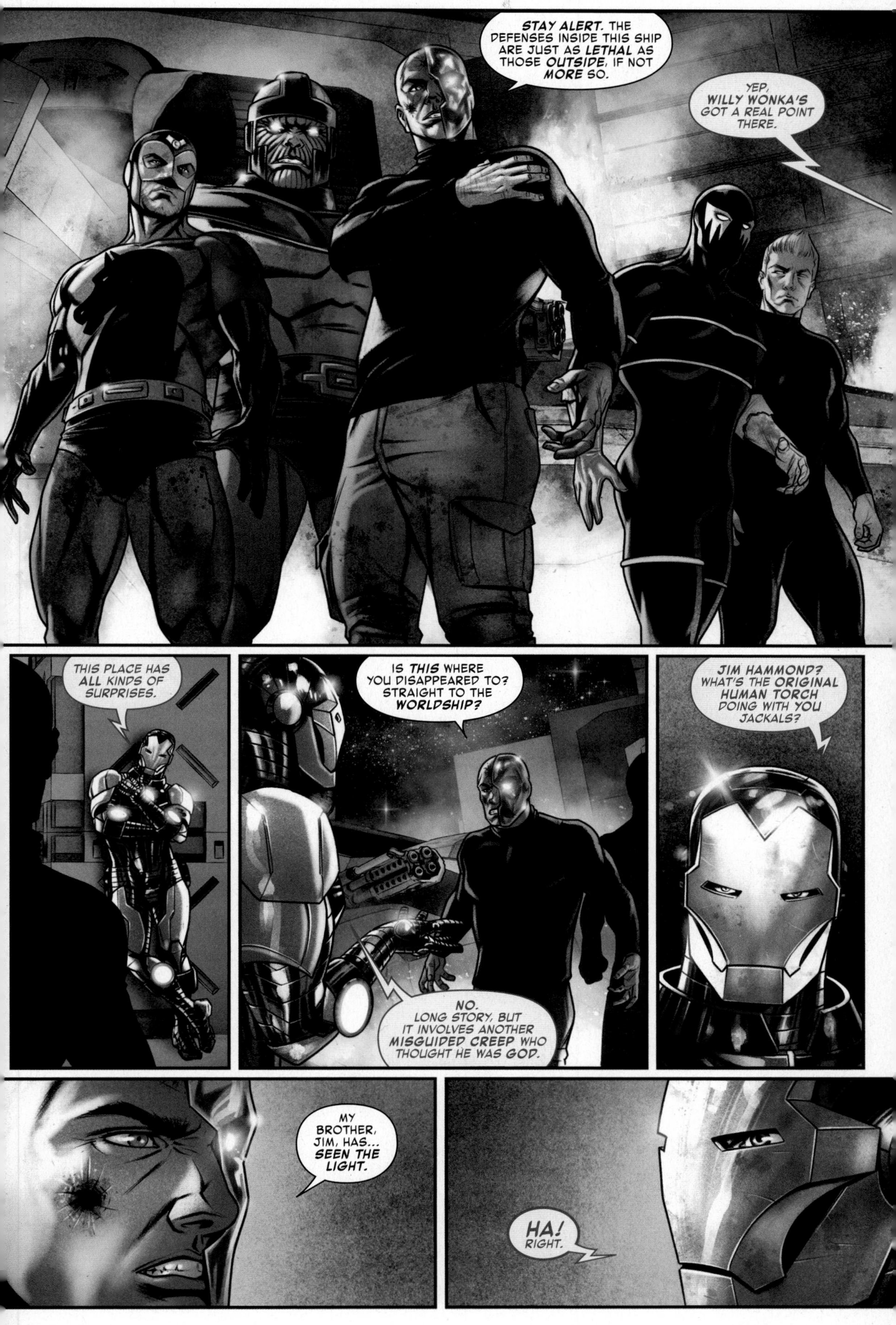

STAY ALERT. THE DEFENSES INSIDE THIS SHIP ARE JUST AS LETHAL AS THOSE OUTSIDE, IF NOT MORE SO.
YEP, WILLY WONKA'S GOT A REAL POINT THERE.
THIS PLACE HAS ALL KINDS OF SURPRISES.
IS THIS WHERE YOU DISAPPEARED TO? STRAIGHT TO THE WORLDSHIP?
NO. LONG STORY, BUT IT INVOLVES ANOTHER MISGUIDED CREEP WHO THOUGHT HE WAS GOD.
JIM HAMMOND? WHAT'S THE ORIGINAL HUMAN TORCH DOING WITH YOU JACKALS?
MY BROTHER, JIM, HAS... SEEN THE LIGHT.
HA! RIGHT.

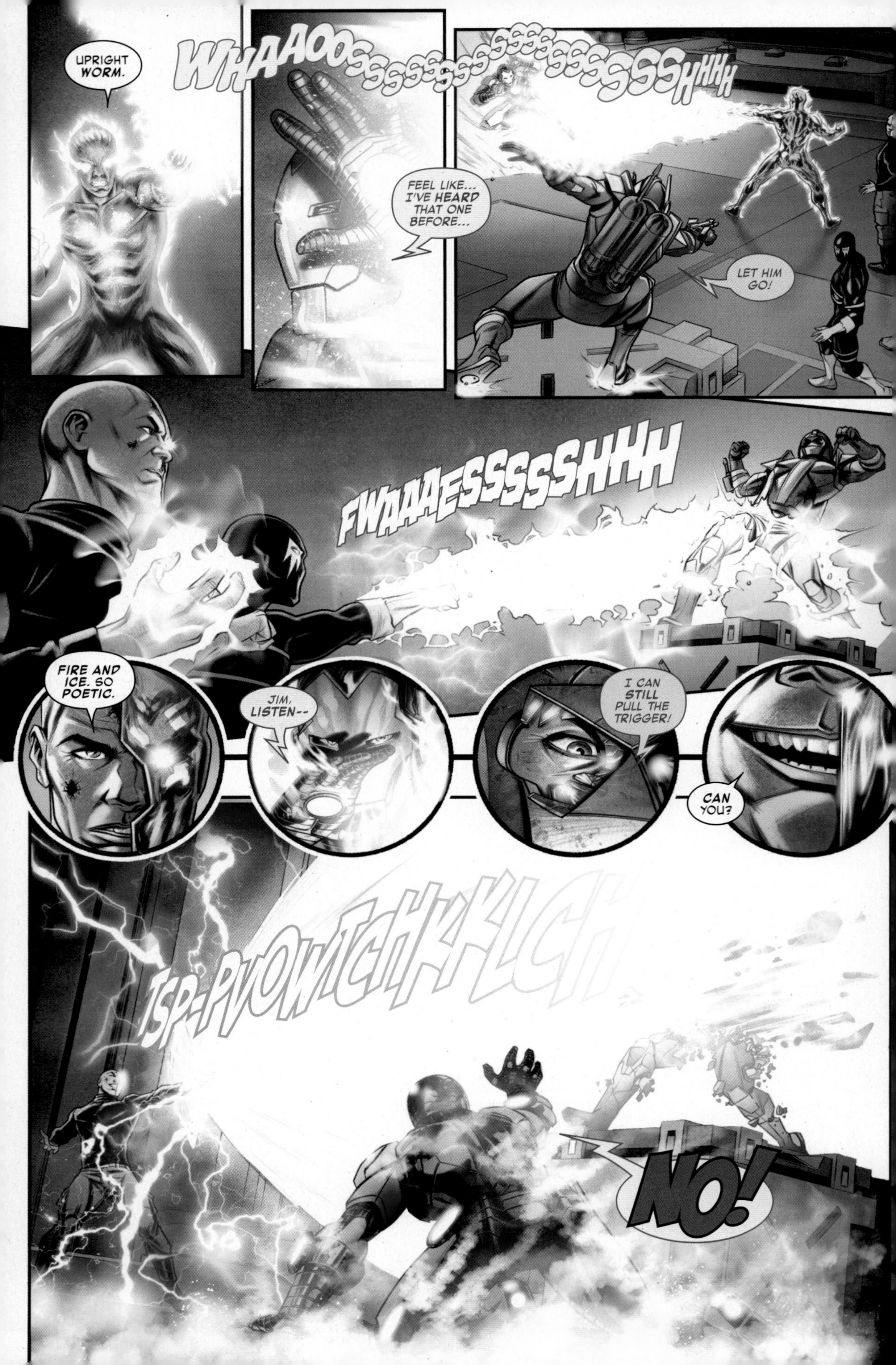
UPRIGHT WORM.
WHAAOOSSSSSSSSSSSSSSSSSSSSSHHHH
FEEL LIKE... I'VE HEARD THAT ONE BEFORE...
LET HIM GO!
FWAAAESSSSSSHHHH
FIRE AND ICE. SO POETIC.
JIM, LISTEN--
I CAN STILL PULL THE TRIGGER!
CAN YOU?
TSP-PVOWTCHKKLCH
NO!

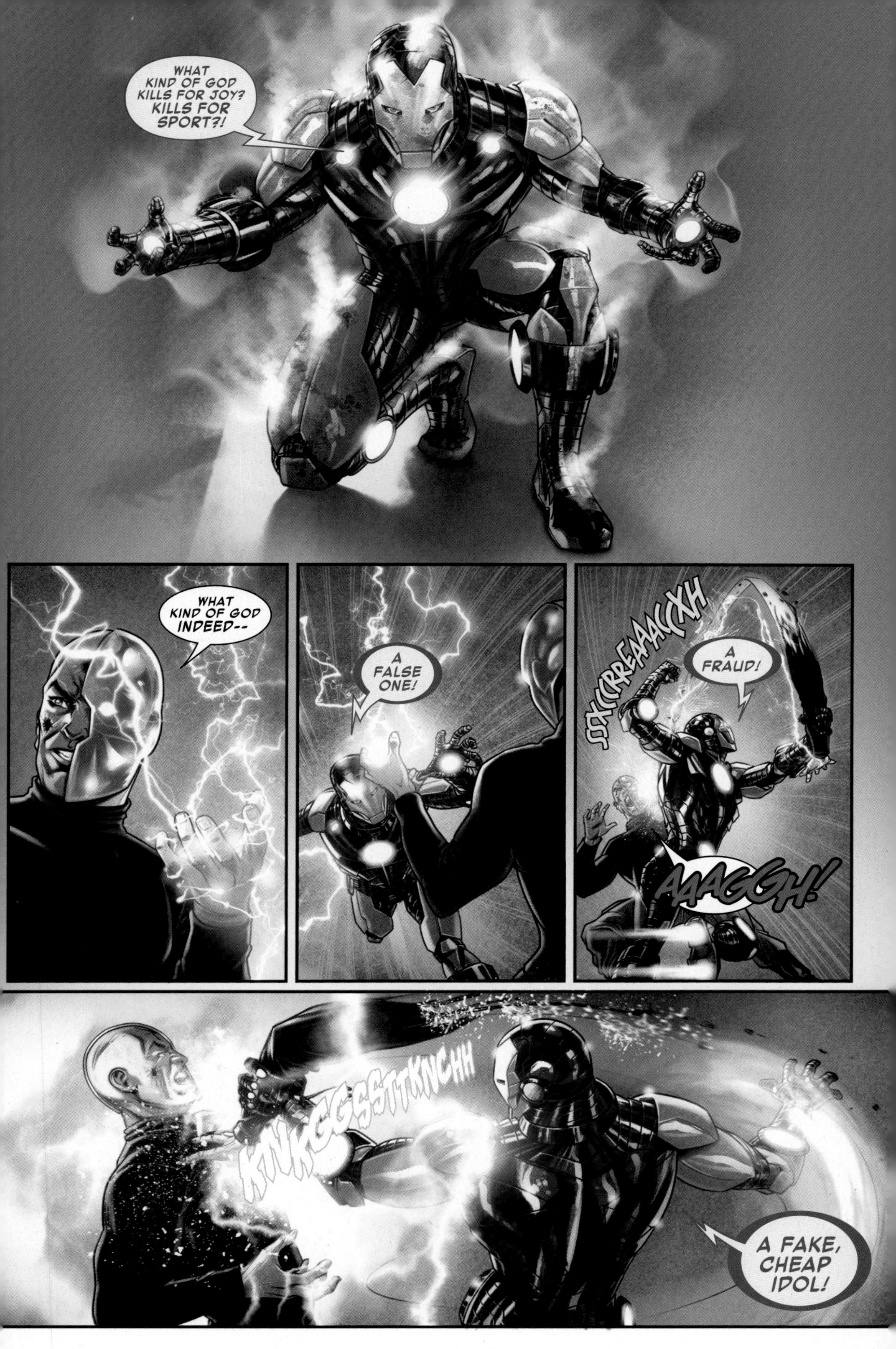
WHAT KIND OF GOD KILLS FOR JOY? KILLS FOR SPORT?!
WHAT KIND OF GOD INDEED--
A FALSE ONE!
SSKCCREEAAACCXH
A FRAUD!
AAAGGH!
KNKGGSSTTKNCHH
A FAKE, CHEAP IDOL!

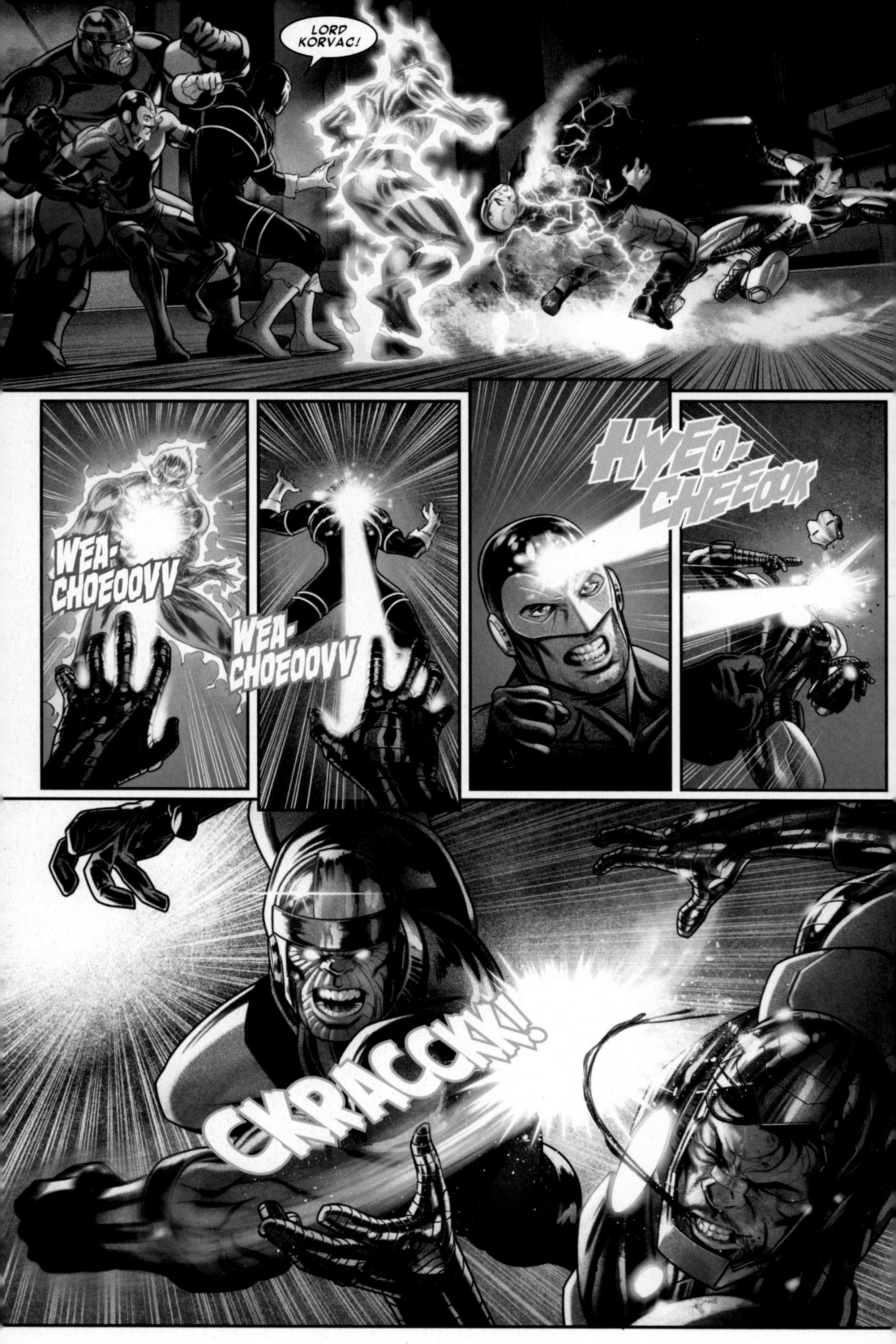
LORD KORVAC!
WEA-CHOEOOVV
WEA-CHOEOOVV
HYEO-CHEEOOK
CKRACCK!

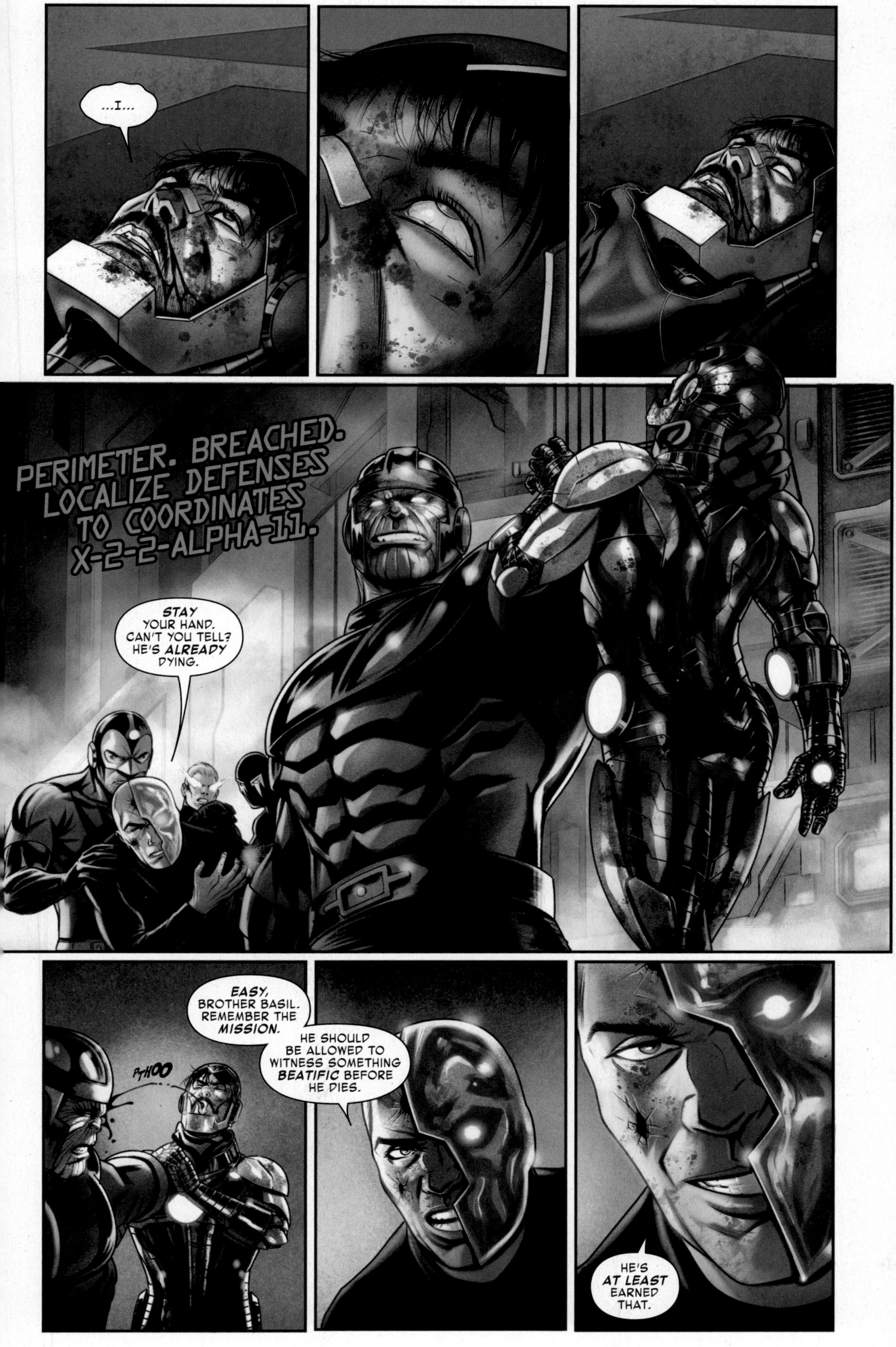

...I...
PERIMETER. BREACHED. LOCALIZE DEFENSES TO COORDINATES X-2-2-ALPHA-11.
STAY YOUR HAND. CAN'T YOU TELL? HE'S ALREADY DYING.
PTHOO
EASY, BROTHER BASIL. REMEMBER THE MISSION.
HE SHOULD BE ALLOWED TO WITNESS SOMETHING BEATIFIC BEFORE HE DIES.
HE'S AT LEAST EARNED THAT.

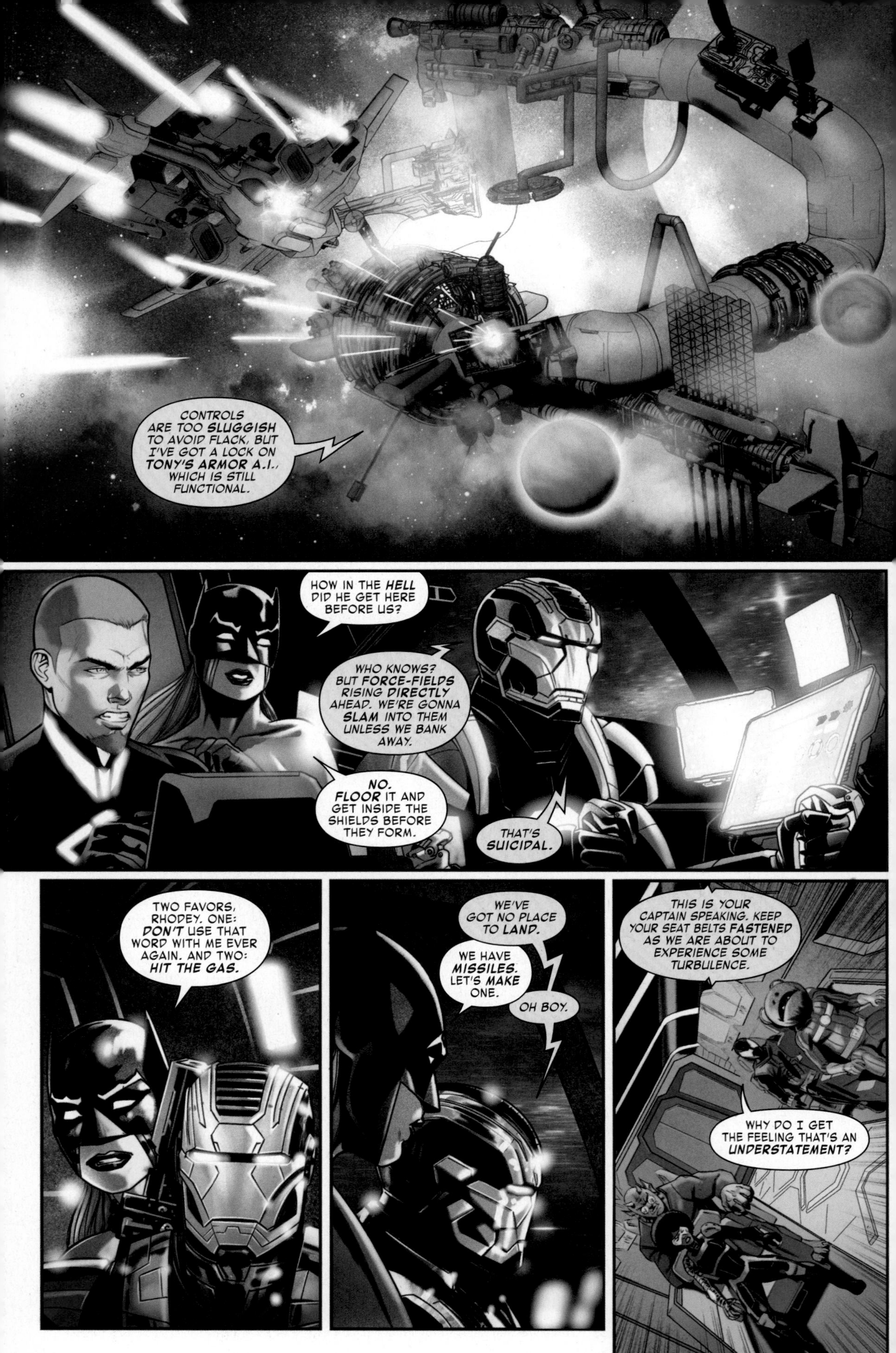
CONTROLS ARE TOO SLUGGISH TO AVOID FLACK, BUT I'VE GOT A LOCK ON TONY'S ARMOR A.I., WHICH IS STILL FUNCTIONAL.
HOW IN THE HELL DID HE GET HERE BEFORE US?
WHO KNOWS? BUT FORCE-FIELDS RISING DIRECTLY AHEAD. WE'RE GONNA SLAM INTO THEM UNLESS WE BANK AWAY.
NO. FLOOR IT AND GET INSIDE THE SHIELDS BEFORE THEY FORM.
THAT'S SUICIDAL.
TWO FAVORS, RHODEY. ONE: DON'T USE THAT WORD WITH ME EVER AGAIN. AND TWO: HIT THE GAS.
WE'VE GOT NO PLACE TO LAND.
WE HAVE MISSILES. LET'S MAKE ONE.
OH BOY.
THIS IS YOUR CAPTAIN SPEAKING. KEEP YOUR SEAT BELTS FASTENED AS WE ARE ABOUT TO EXPERIENCE SOME TURBULENCE.
WHY DO I GET THE FEELING THAT'S AN UNDERSTATEMENT?

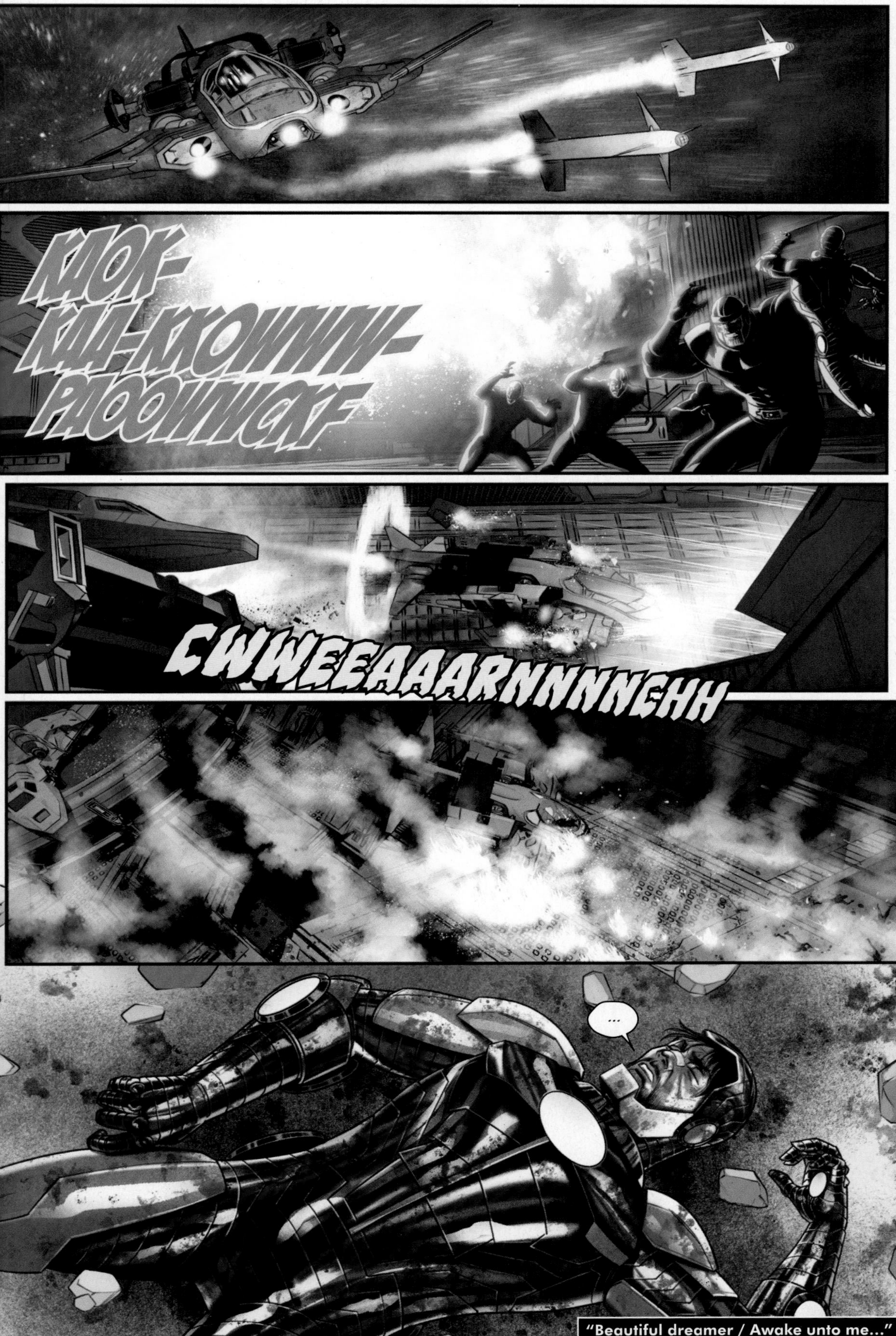
KAOK-
KAA-KKOWWW-
PAOOWWCKF
CWWEEAAARNNNNNCHH
...
"Beautiful dreamer / Awake unto me..."
--Stephen Foster, 1862

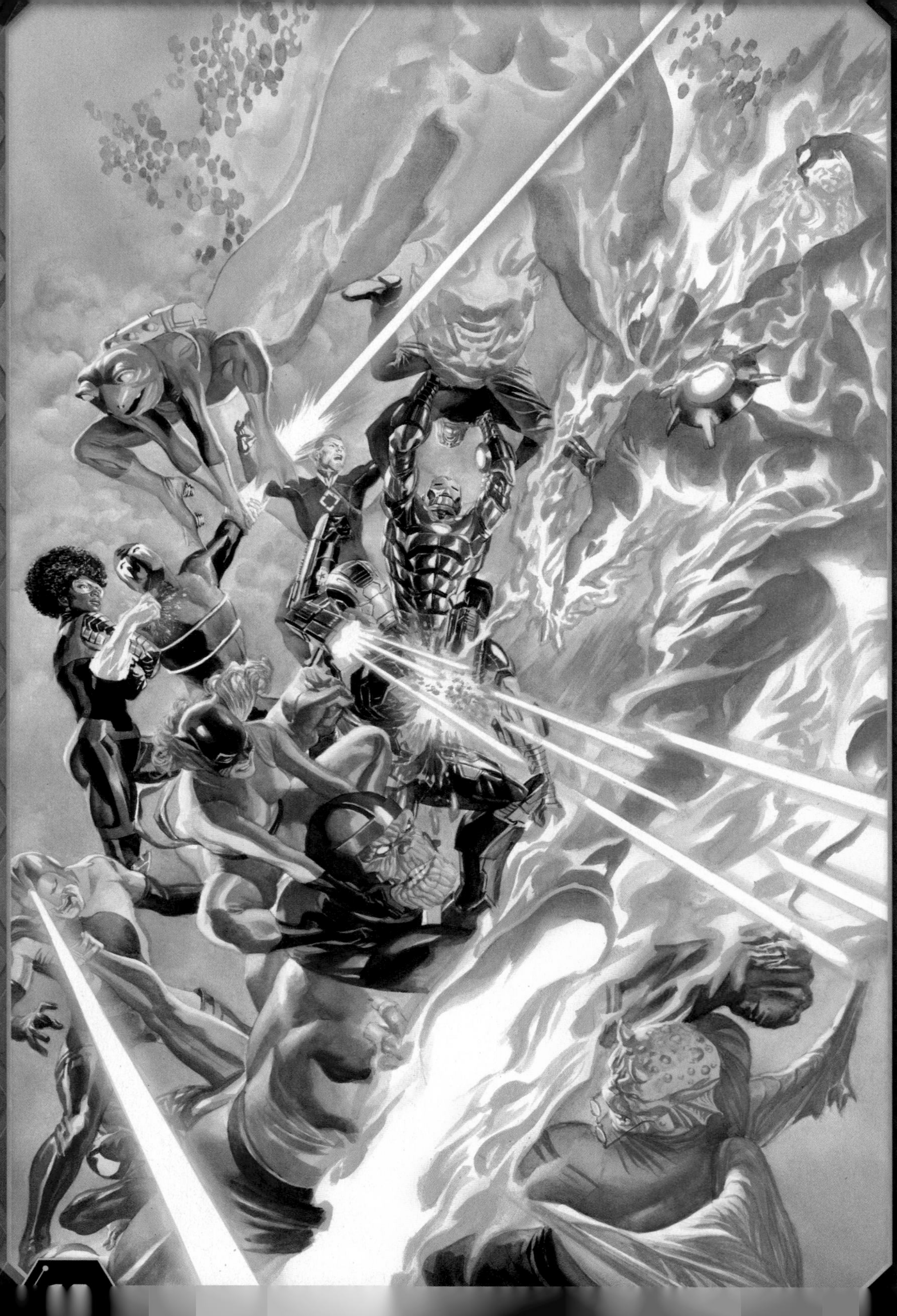

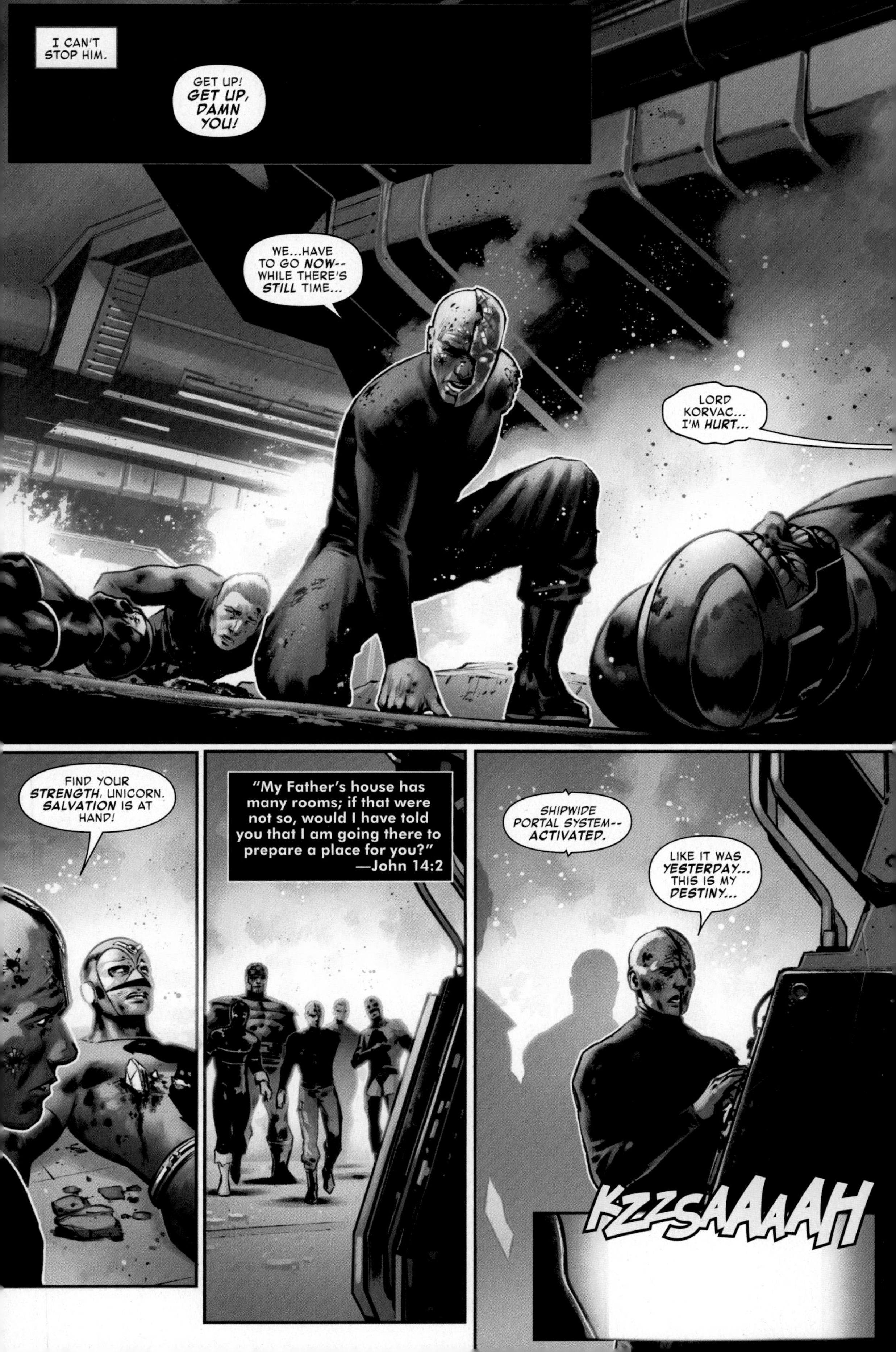
I CAN'T STOP HIM.
GET UP! GET UP, DAMN YOU!
WE...HAVE TO GO NOW--WHILE THERE'S STILL TIME...
LORD KORVAC... I'M HURT...
FIND YOUR STRENGTH, UNICORN. SALVATION IS AT HAND!
"My Father's house has many rooms; if that were not so, would I have told you that I am going there to prepare a place for you?" —John 14:2
SHIPWIDE PORTAL SYSTEM--ACTIVATED.
LIKE IT WAS YESTERDAY... THIS IS MY DESTINY...
KZZSAAAAH

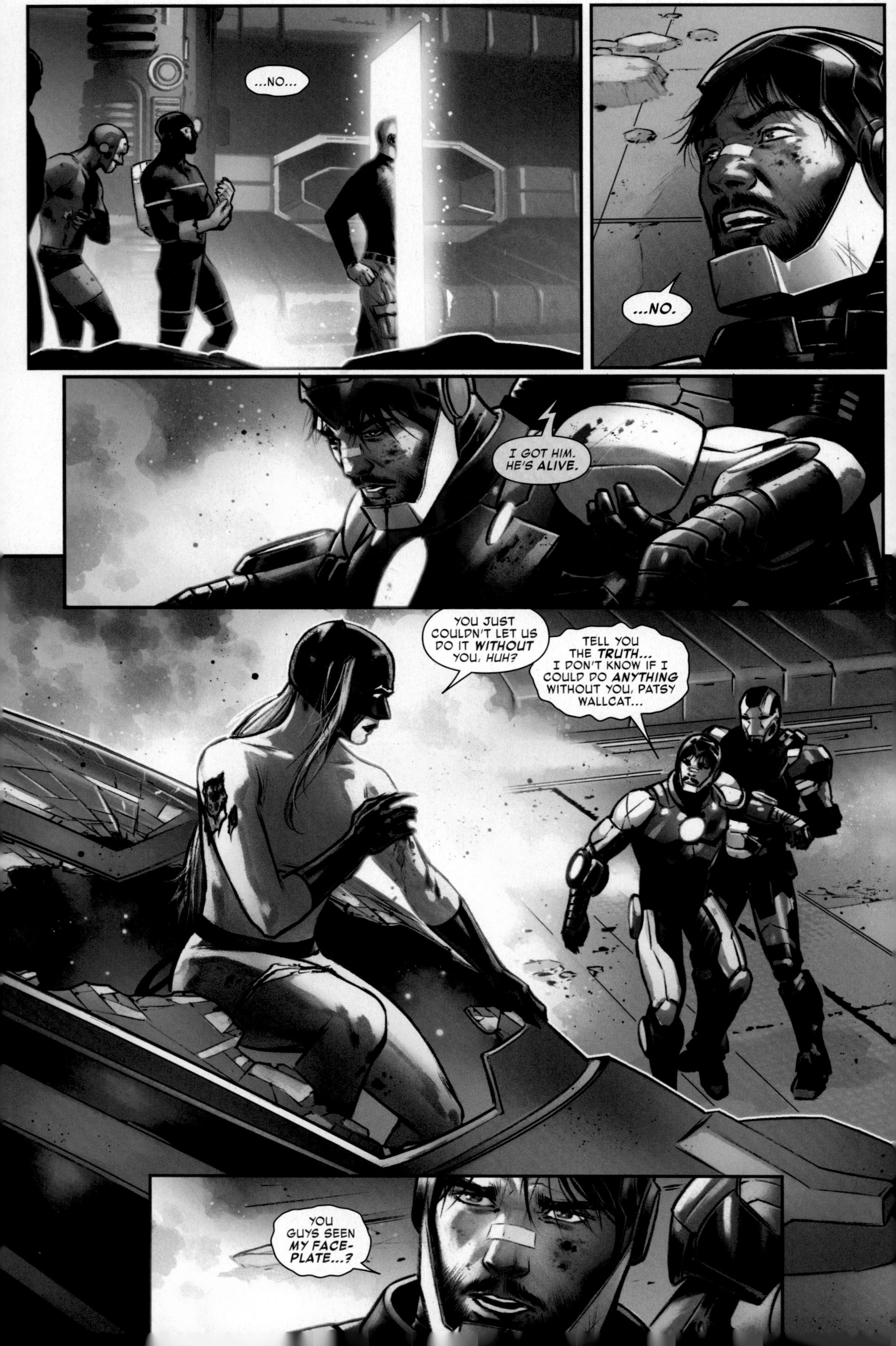
...NO...
...NO.
I GOT HIM. HE'S ALIVE.
YOU JUST COULDN'T LET US DO IT WITHOUT YOU, HUH?
TELL YOU THE TRUTH... I DON'T KNOW IF I COULD DO ANYTHING WITHOUT YOU, PATSY WALLCAT...
YOU GUYS SEEN MY FACE-PLATE...?

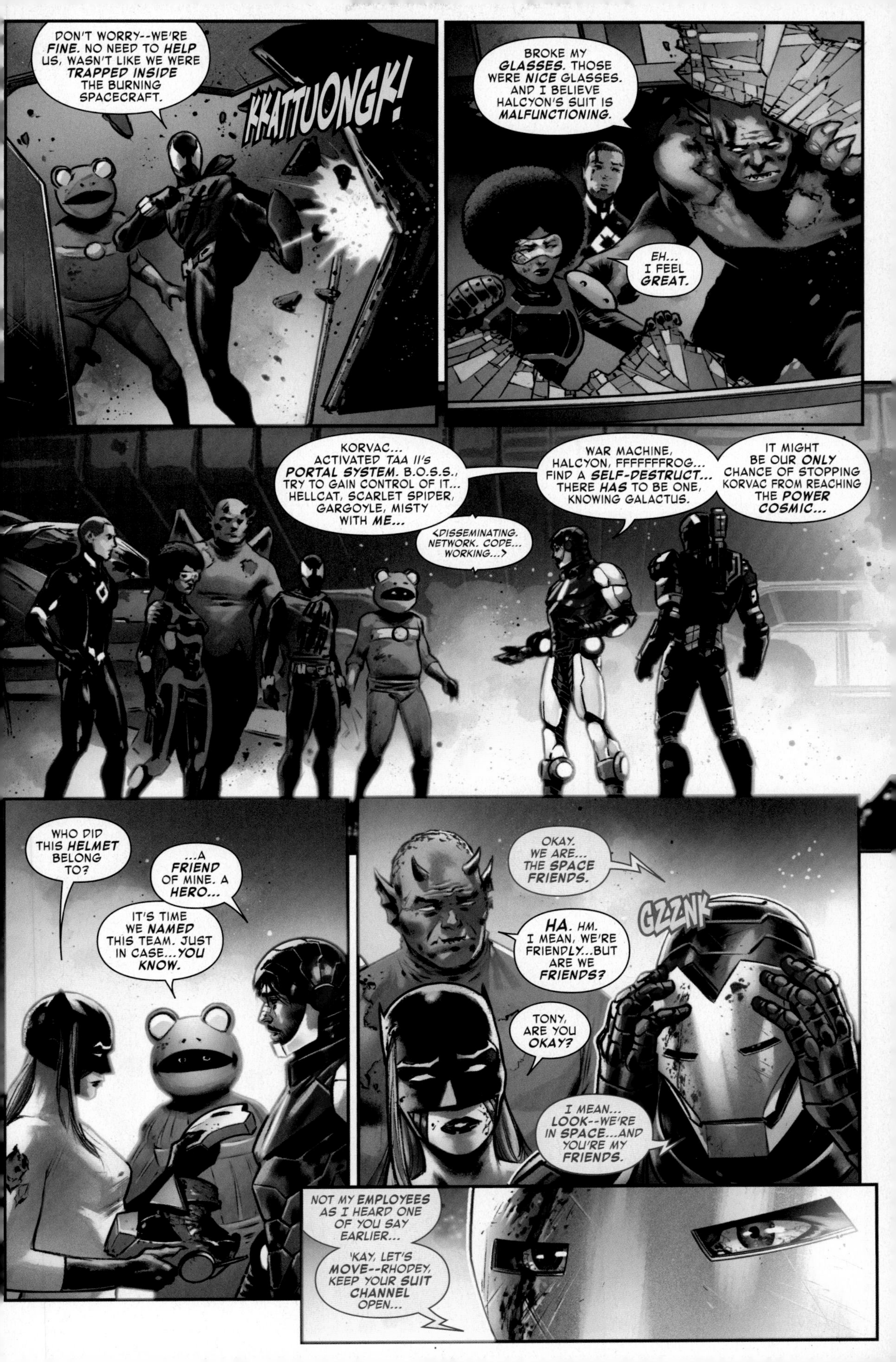

DON'T WORRY--WE'RE FINE. NO NEED TO HELP US, WASN'T LIKE WE WERE TRAPPED INSIDE THE BURNING SPACECRAFT.
KKATTUONGK!
BROKE MY GLASSES. THOSE WERE NICE GLASSES. AND I BELIEVE HALCYON'S SUIT IS MALFUNCTIONING.
EH... I FEEL GREAT.
KORVAC... ACTIVATED TAA II'S PORTAL SYSTEM. B.O.S.S., TRY TO GAIN CONTROL OF IT... HELLCAT, SCARLET SPIDER, GARGOYLE, MISTY WITH ME...
WAR MACHINE, HALCYON, FFFFFFFROG... FIND A SELF-DESTRUCT... THERE HAS TO BE ONE, KNOWING GALACTUS.
IT MIGHT BE OUR ONLY CHANCE OF STOPPING KORVAC FROM REACHING THE POWER COSMIC...
<DISSEMINATING. NETWORK. CODE... WORKING...>
WHO DID THIS HELMET BELONG TO?
...A FRIEND OF MINE. A HERO...
IT'S TIME WE NAMED THIS TEAM. JUST IN CASE...YOU KNOW.
OKAY. WE ARE... THE SPACE FRIENDS.
GZZNK
HA. HM. I MEAN, WE'RE FRIENDLY...BUT ARE WE FRIENDS?
TONY, ARE YOU OKAY?
I MEAN... LOOK--WE'RE IN SPACE...AND YOU'RE MY FRIENDS.
NOT MY EMPLOYEES AS I HEARD ONE OF YOU SAY EARLIER...
'KAY, LET'S MOVE--RHODEY, KEEP YOUR SUIT CHANNEL OPEN...

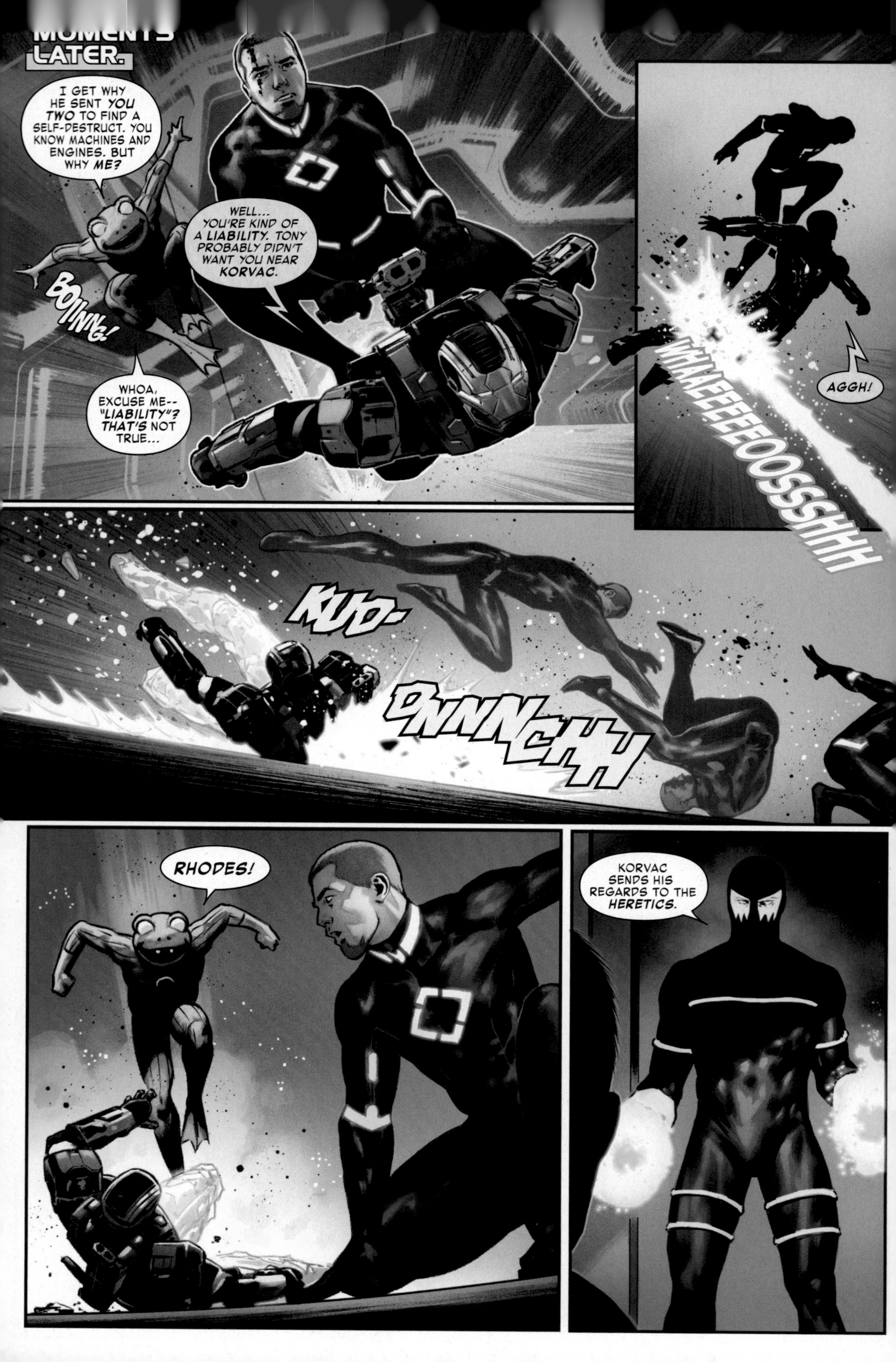
MOMENTS LATER.
I GET WHY HE SENT YOU TWO TO FIND A SELF-DESTRUCT. YOU KNOW MACHINES AND ENGINES. BUT WHY ME?
WELL... YOU'RE KIND OF A LIABILITY. TONY PROBABLY DIDN'T WANT YOU NEAR KORVAC.
BOIIING!
WHOA, EXCUSE ME-- "LIABILITY"? THAT'S NOT TRUE...
WHAEEEEOOSSHHH
AGGH!
KUD-
DNNNCHH
RHODES!
KORVAC SENDS HIS REGARDS TO THE HERETICS.

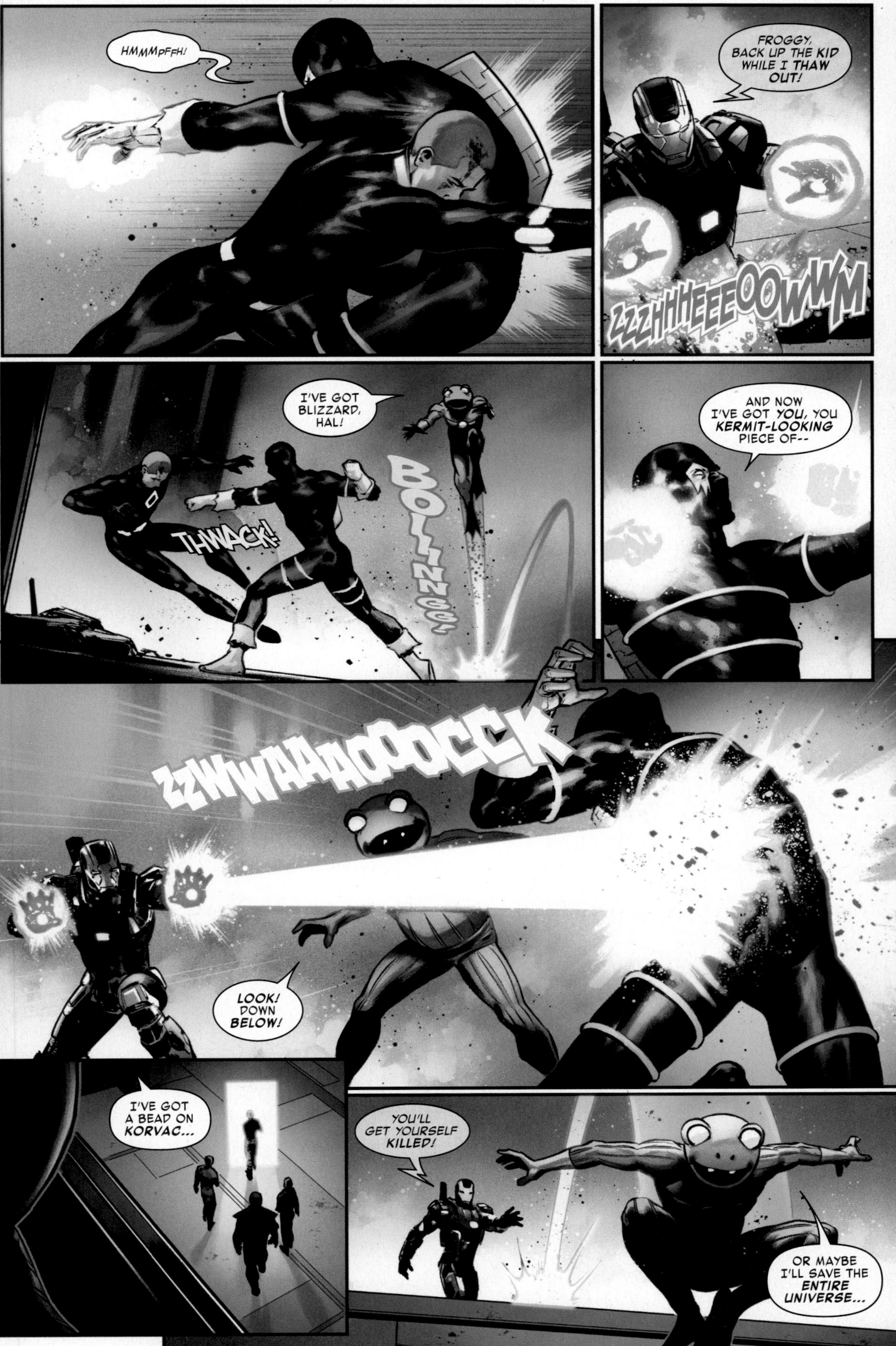
HMMMPFFH!
FROGGY, BACK UP THE KID WHILE I THAW OUT!
ZZZHHHEEEOOWWM
I'VE GOT BLIZZARD, HAL!
THWACK!
BOLLINGG!
AND NOW I'VE GOT YOU, YOU KERMIT-LOOKING PIECE OF--
ZZWWAAAOOOCCK
LOOK! DOWN BELOW!
I'VE GOT A BEAD ON KORVAC...
YOU'LL GET YOURSELF KILLED!
OR MAYBE I'LL SAVE THE ENTIRE UNIVERSE...

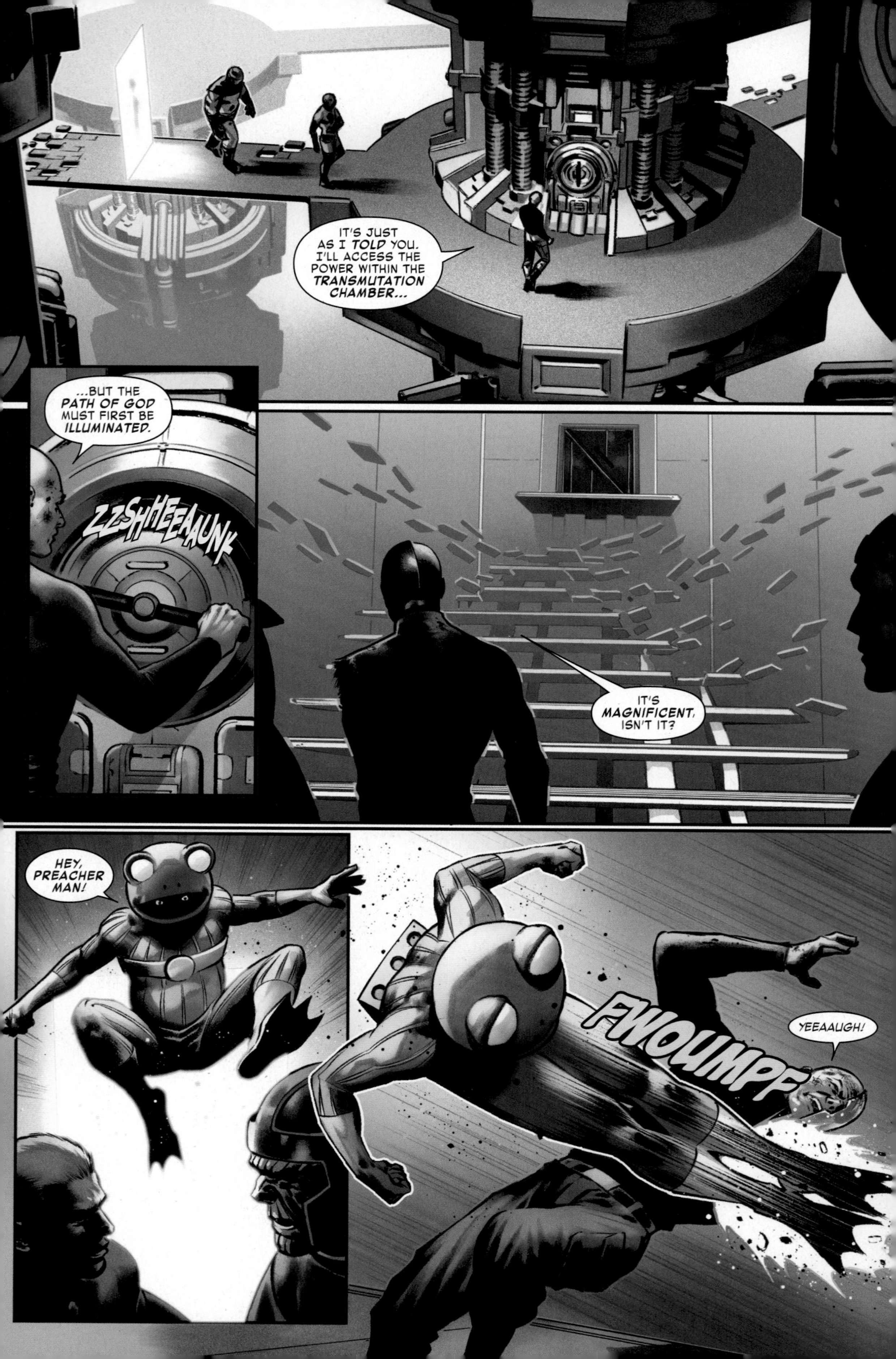
IT'S JUST AS I TOLD YOU. I'LL ACCESS THE POWER WITHIN THE TRANSMUTATION CHAMBER...
...BUT THE PATH OF GOD MUST FIRST BE ILLUMINATED.
ZZSHHEEAAUNK
IT'S MAGNIFICENT, ISN'T IT?
HEY, PREACHER MAN!
FWOUMPF
YEEAAUGH!

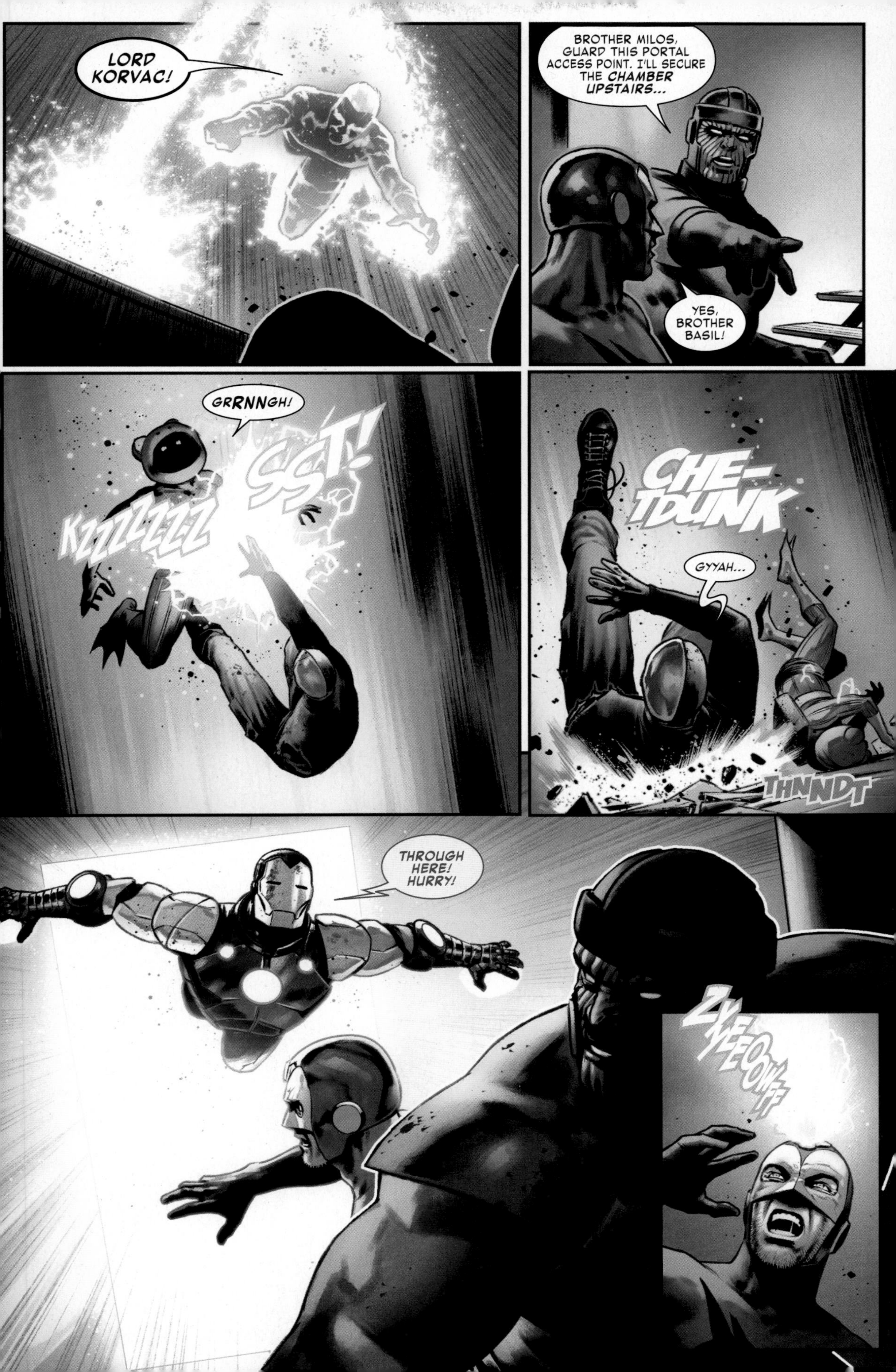
LORD KORVAC!
BROTHER MILOS, GUARD THIS PORTAL ACCESS POINT. I'LL SECURE THE CHAMBER UPSTAIRS...
YES, BROTHER BASIL!
GRRNNGH!
SST!
KZZZZZZZ
CHE-TDUNK
GYYAH...
THNNDT
THROUGH HERE! HURRY!
ZYEEOWFF

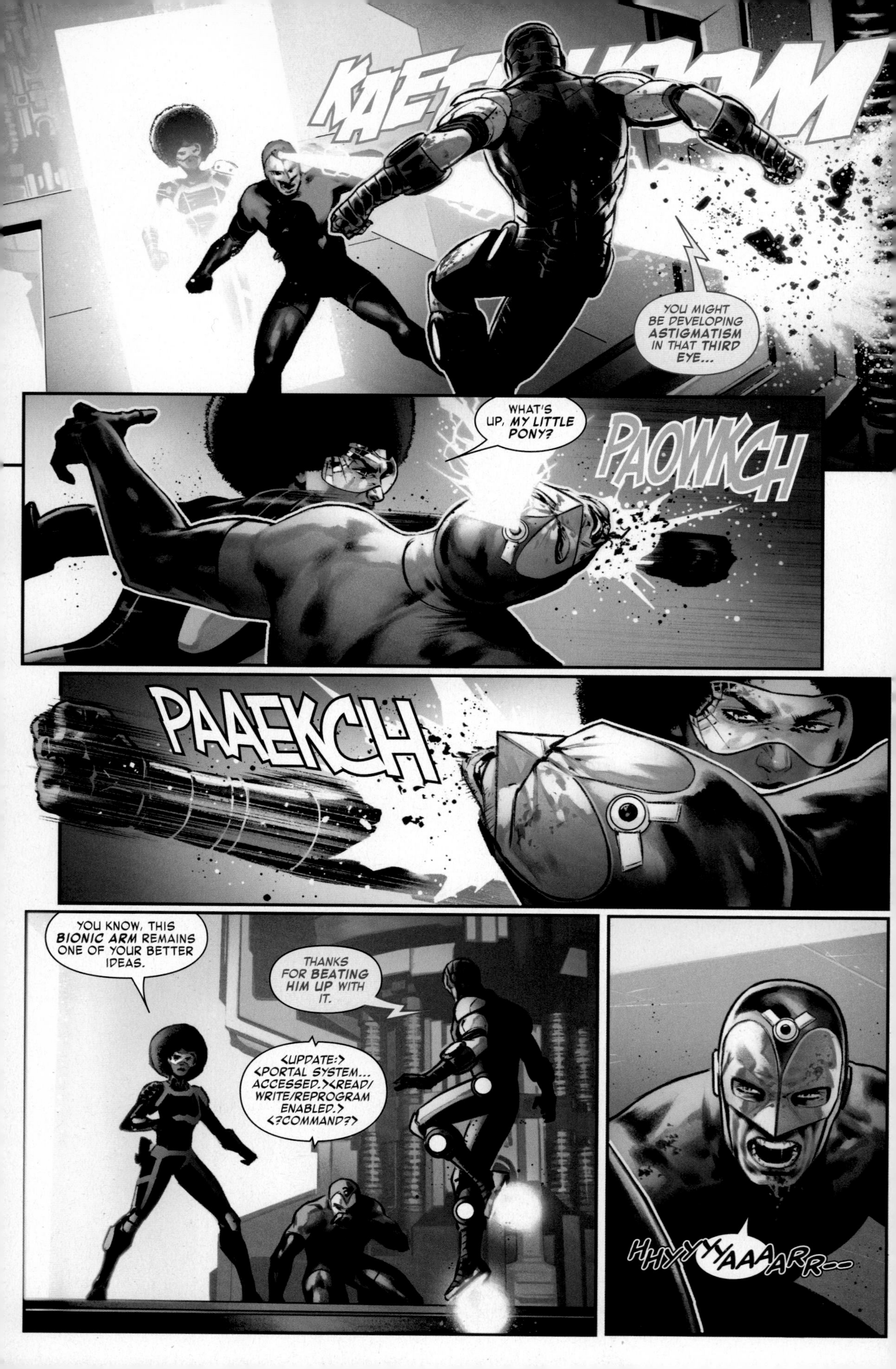
YOU MIGHT BE DEVELOPING ASTIGMATISM IN THAT THIRD EYE...
WHAT'S UP, MY LITTLE PONY?
PAOWKCH
PAAEKCH
YOU KNOW, THIS BIONIC ARM REMAINS ONE OF YOUR BETTER IDEAS.
THANKS FOR BEATING HIM UP WITH IT.
<UPDATE:> <PORTAL SYSTEM... ACCESSED.><READ/ WRITE/REPROGRAM ENABLED.> <?COMMAND?>
HHYYYYAAAARR--

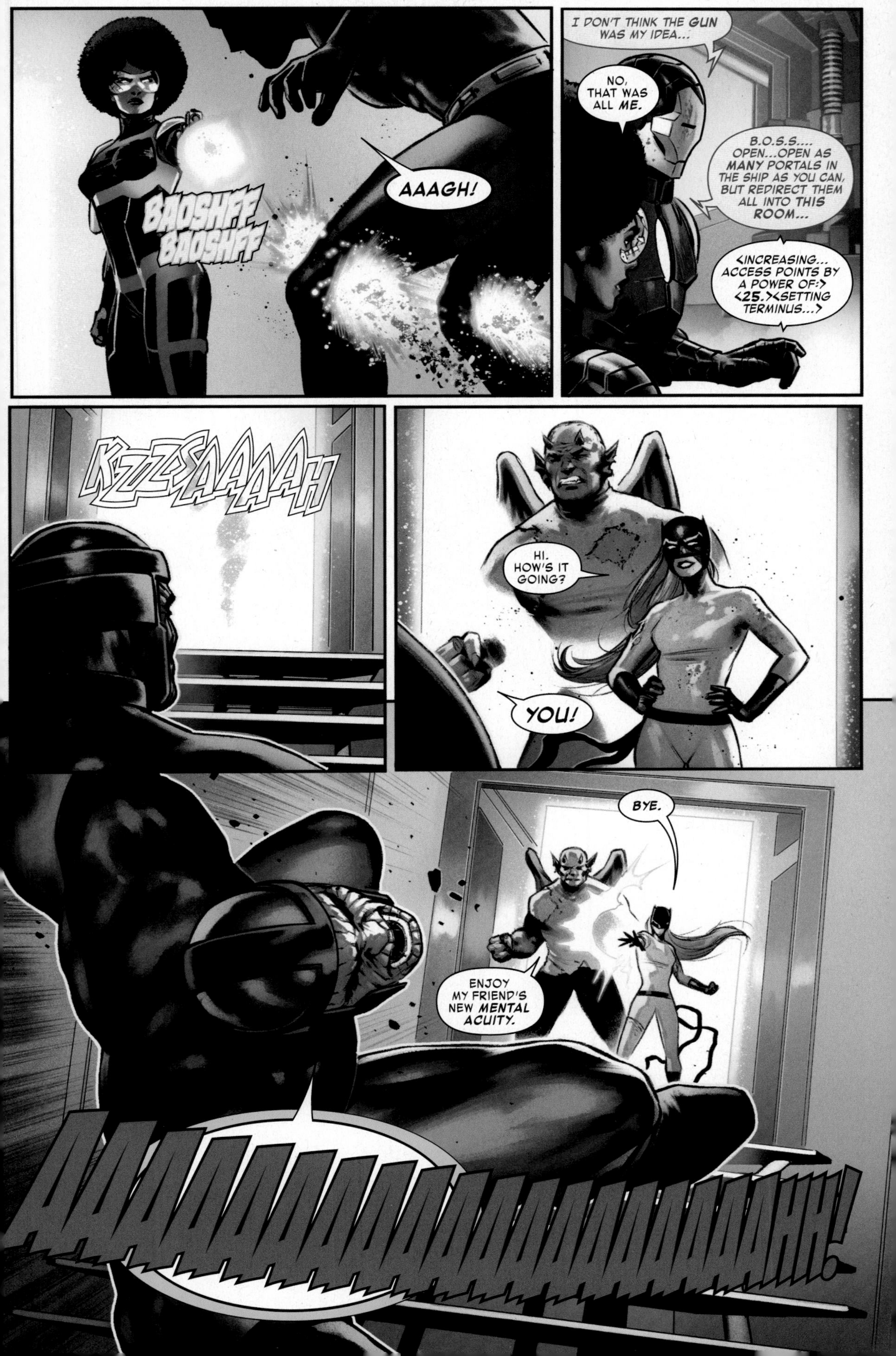
BAOSHFF
BAOSHFF
AAAGH!
I DON'T THINK THE GUN WAS MY IDEA...
NO, THAT WAS ALL ME.
B.O.S.S.... OPEN...OPEN AS MANY PORTALS IN THE SHIP AS YOU CAN, BUT REDIRECT THEM ALL INTO THIS ROOM...
<INCREASING... ACCESS POINTS BY A POWER OF:> <25.><SETTING TERMINUS...>
KZZZSAAAAAH
HI. HOW'S IT GOING?
YOU!
BYE.
ENJOY MY FRIEND'S NEW MENTAL ACUITY.
AAAAAAAAAAAAAAAAAAAAAAAAAAHH!

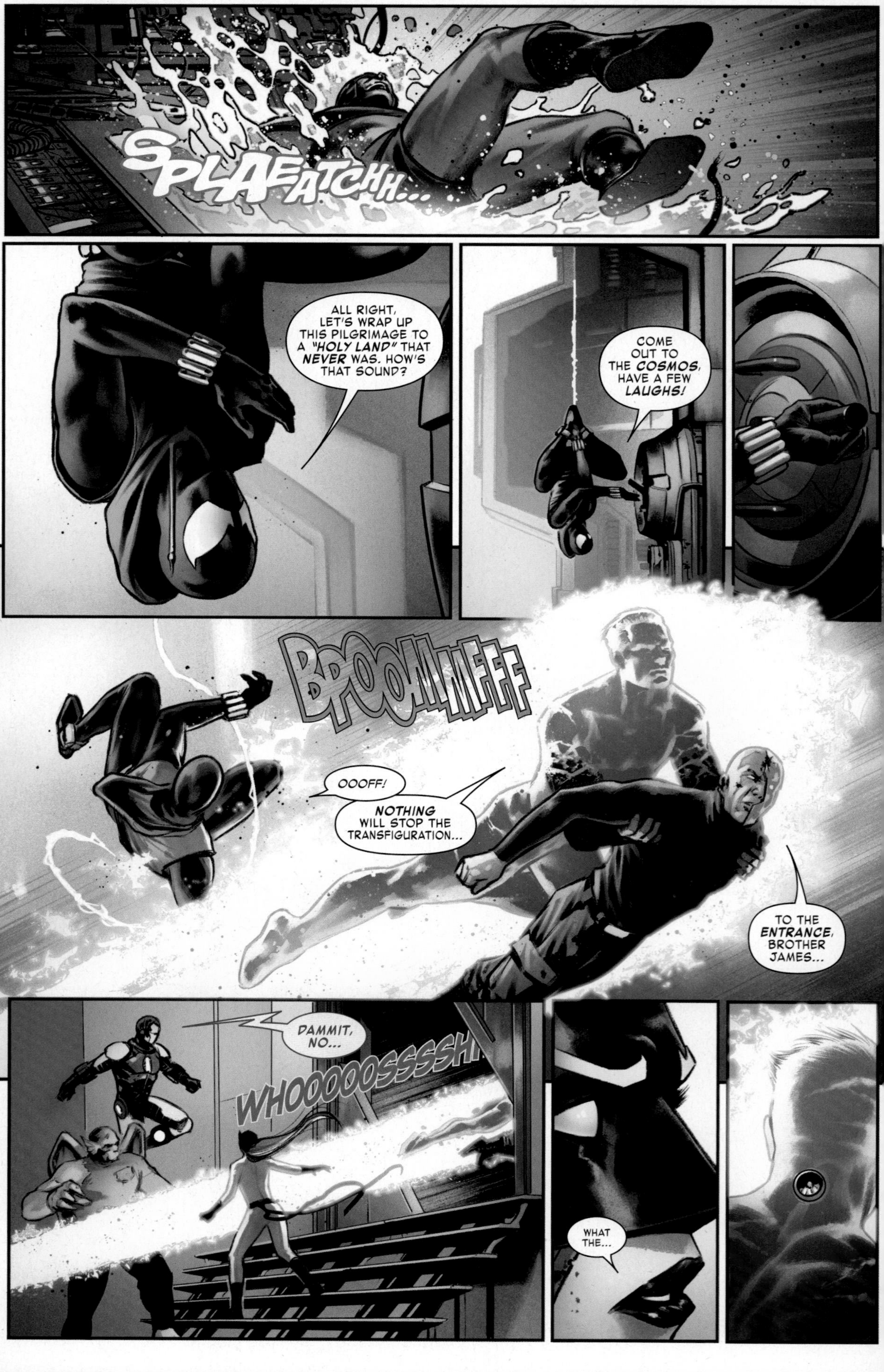
SPLAEATCHHH...
ALL RIGHT, LET'S WRAP UP THIS PILGRIMAGE TO A *"HOLY LAND"* THAT *NEVER* WAS. HOW'S THAT SOUND?
COME OUT TO THE *COSMOS*, HAVE A FEW *LAUGHS!*
BPOOMMFFF
OOOFF!
NOTHING WILL STOP THE TRANSFIGURATION...
TO THE *ENTRANCE*, BROTHER JAMES...
DAMMIT, NO...
WHOOOOOSSSSHH
WHAT THE...

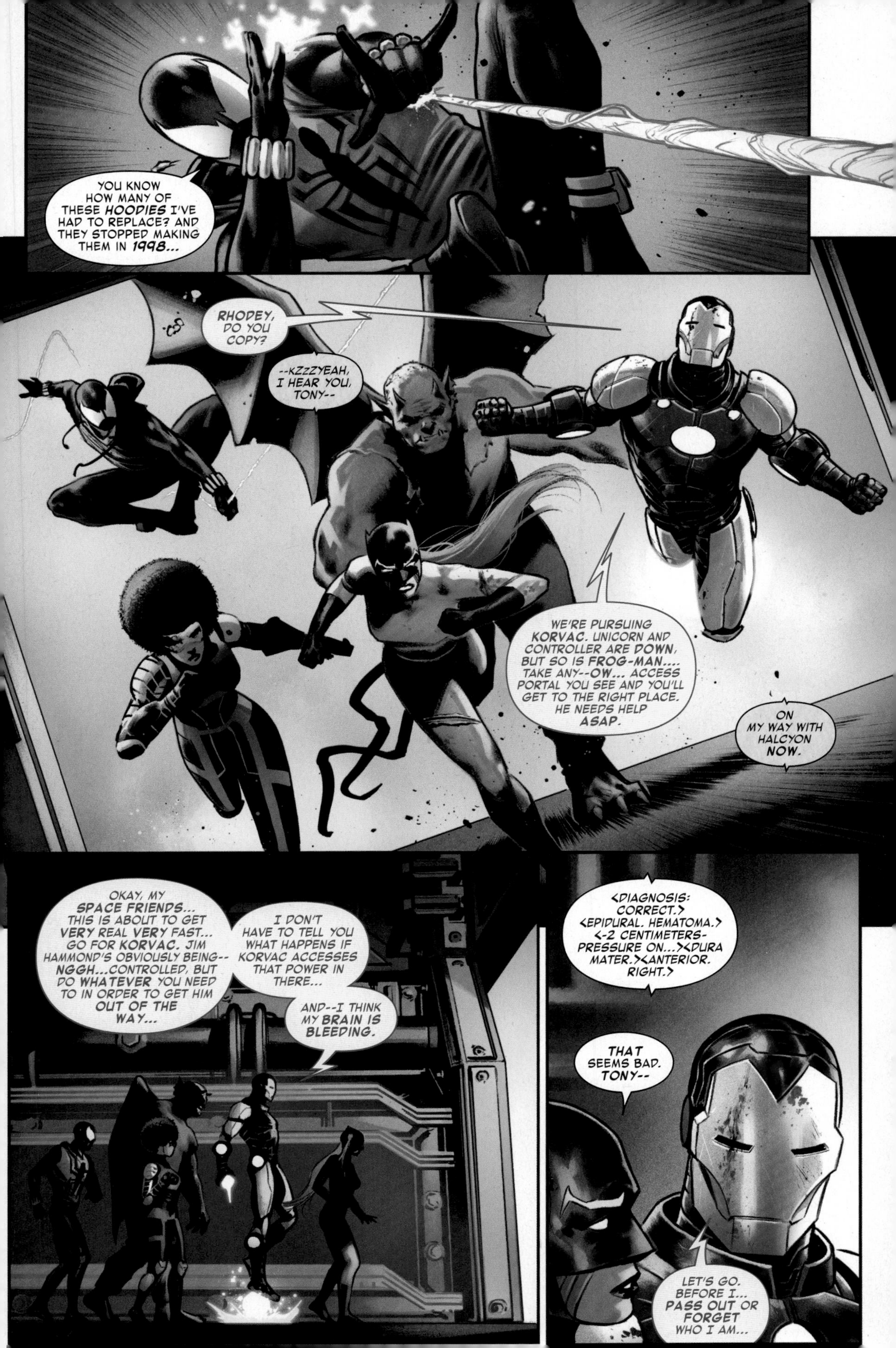
YOU KNOW HOW MANY OF THESE HOODIES I'VE HAD TO REPLACE? AND THEY STOPPED MAKING THEM IN 1998...
RHODEY, DO YOU COPY?
--KZZZYEAH, I HEAR YOU, TONY--
WE'RE PURSUING KORVAC. UNICORN AND CONTROLLER ARE DOWN, BUT SO IS FROG-MAN.... TAKE ANY--OW... ACCESS PORTAL YOU SEE AND YOU'LL GET TO THE RIGHT PLACE. HE NEEDS HELP ASAP.
ON MY WAY WITH HALCYON NOW.
OKAY, MY SPACE FRIENDS... THIS IS ABOUT TO GET VERY REAL VERY FAST... GO FOR KORVAC. JIM HAMMOND'S OBVIOUSLY BEING-- NGGH...CONTROLLED, BUT DO WHATEVER YOU NEED TO IN ORDER TO GET HIM OUT OF THE WAY...
I DON'T HAVE TO TELL YOU WHAT HAPPENS IF KORVAC ACCESSES THAT POWER IN THERE...
AND--I THINK MY BRAIN IS BLEEDING.
<DIAGNOSIS: CORRECT.> <EPIDURAL. HEMATOMA.> <-2 CENTIMETERS- PRESSURE ON...><DURA MATER.><ANTERIOR. RIGHT.>
THAT SEEMS BAD. TONY--
LET'S GO. BEFORE I... PASS OUT OR FORGET WHO I AM...

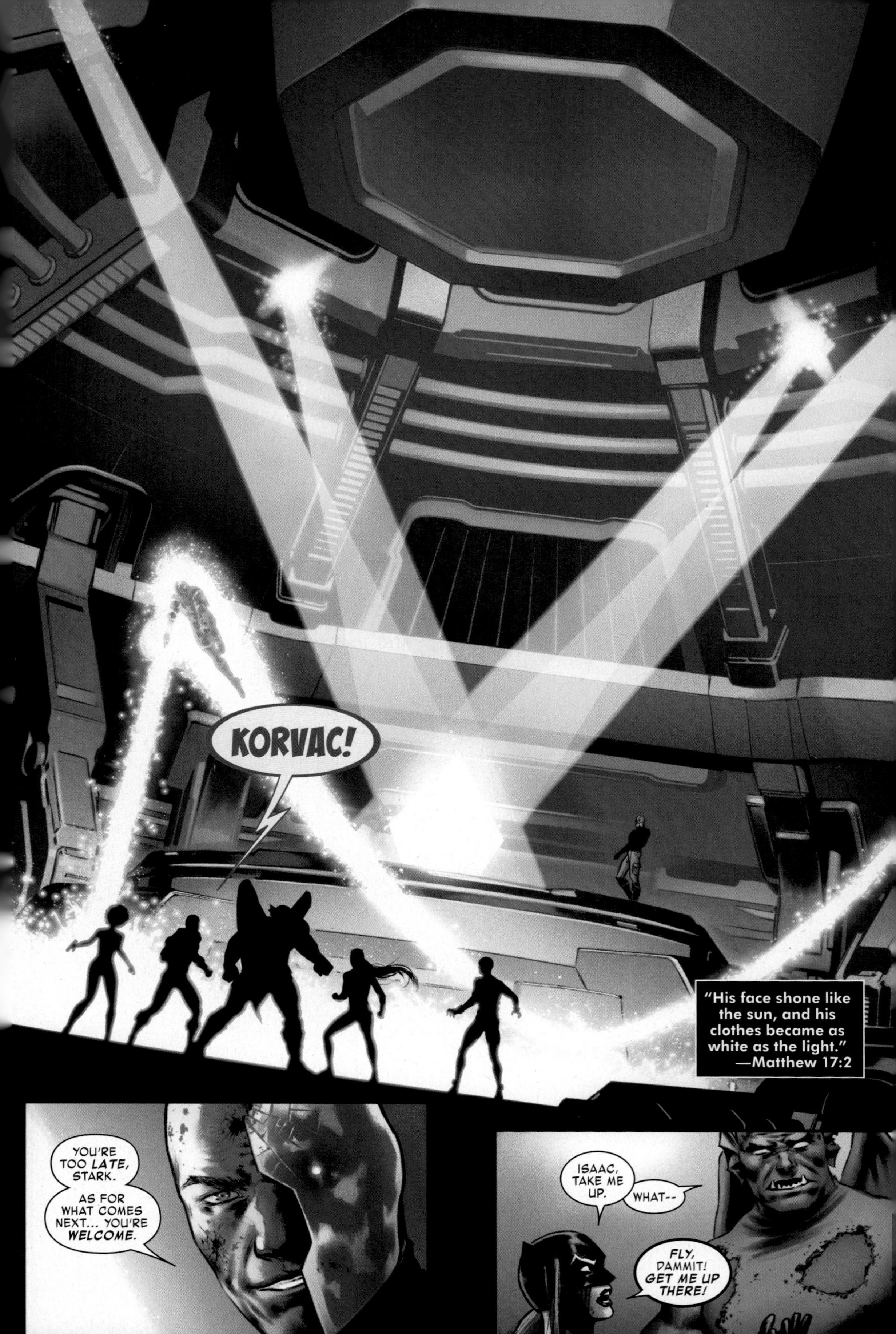
KORVAC!
"His face shone like the sun, and his clothes became as white as the light." —Matthew 17:2
YOU'RE TOO LATE, STARK.
AS FOR WHAT COMES NEXT... YOU'RE WELCOME.
ISAAC, TAKE ME UP.
WHAT--
FLY, DAMMIT! GET ME UP THERE!

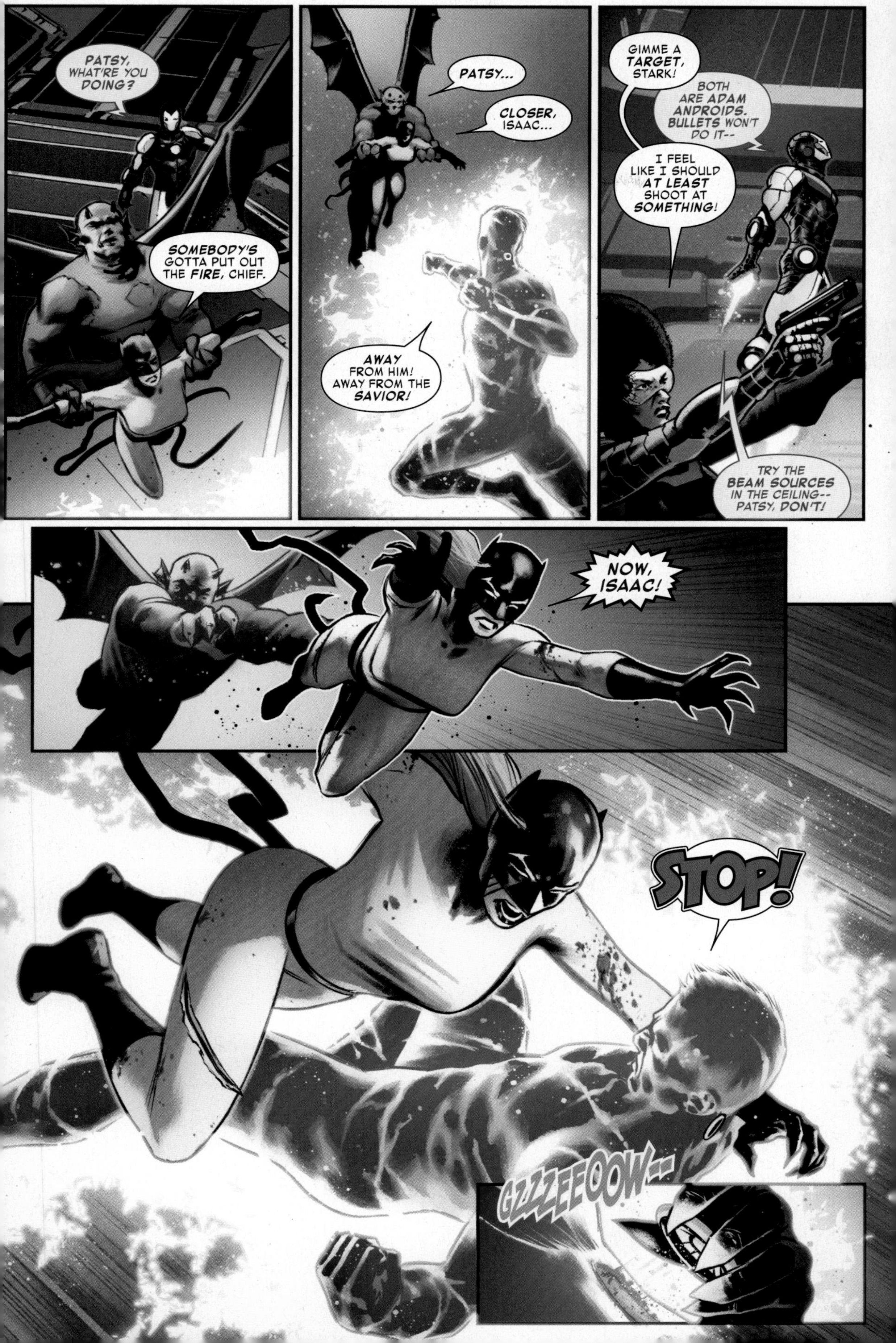
PATSY, WHAT'RE YOU DOING?
SOMEBODY'S GOTTA PUT OUT THE FIRE, CHIEF.
PATSY...
CLOSER, ISAAC...
AWAY FROM HIM! AWAY FROM THE SAVIOR!
GIMME A TARGET, STARK!
BOTH ARE ADAM ANDROIDS. BULLETS WON'T DO IT--
I FEEL LIKE I SHOULD AT LEAST SHOOT AT SOMETHING!
TRY THE BEAM SOURCES IN THE CEILING-- PATSY, DON'T!
NOW, ISAAC!
STOP!
GZZZEEOOW--

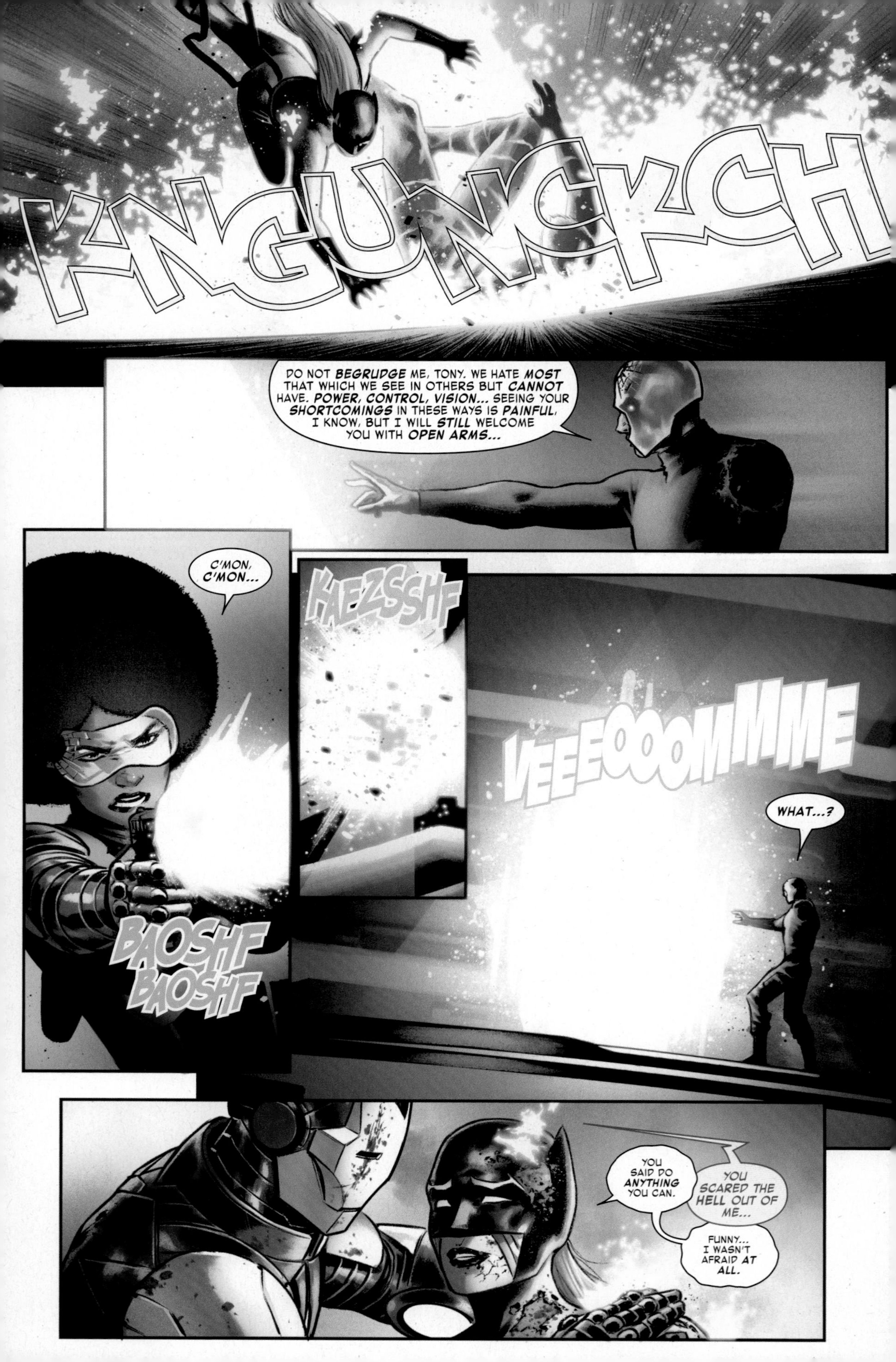

KANGUNCKCH
DO NOT BEGRUDGE ME, TONY. WE HATE MOST THAT WHICH WE SEE IN OTHERS BUT CANNOT HAVE. POWER, CONTROL, VISION... SEEING YOUR SHORTCOMINGS IN THESE WAYS IS PAINFUL, I KNOW, BUT I WILL STILL WELCOME YOU WITH OPEN ARMS...
C'MON, C'MON...
BAOSHF BAOSHF
KAEZSSHF
VEEEOOOMMME
WHAT...?
YOU SAID DO ANYTHING YOU CAN.
YOU SCARED THE HELL OUT OF ME...
FUNNY... I WASN'T AFRAID AT ALL.

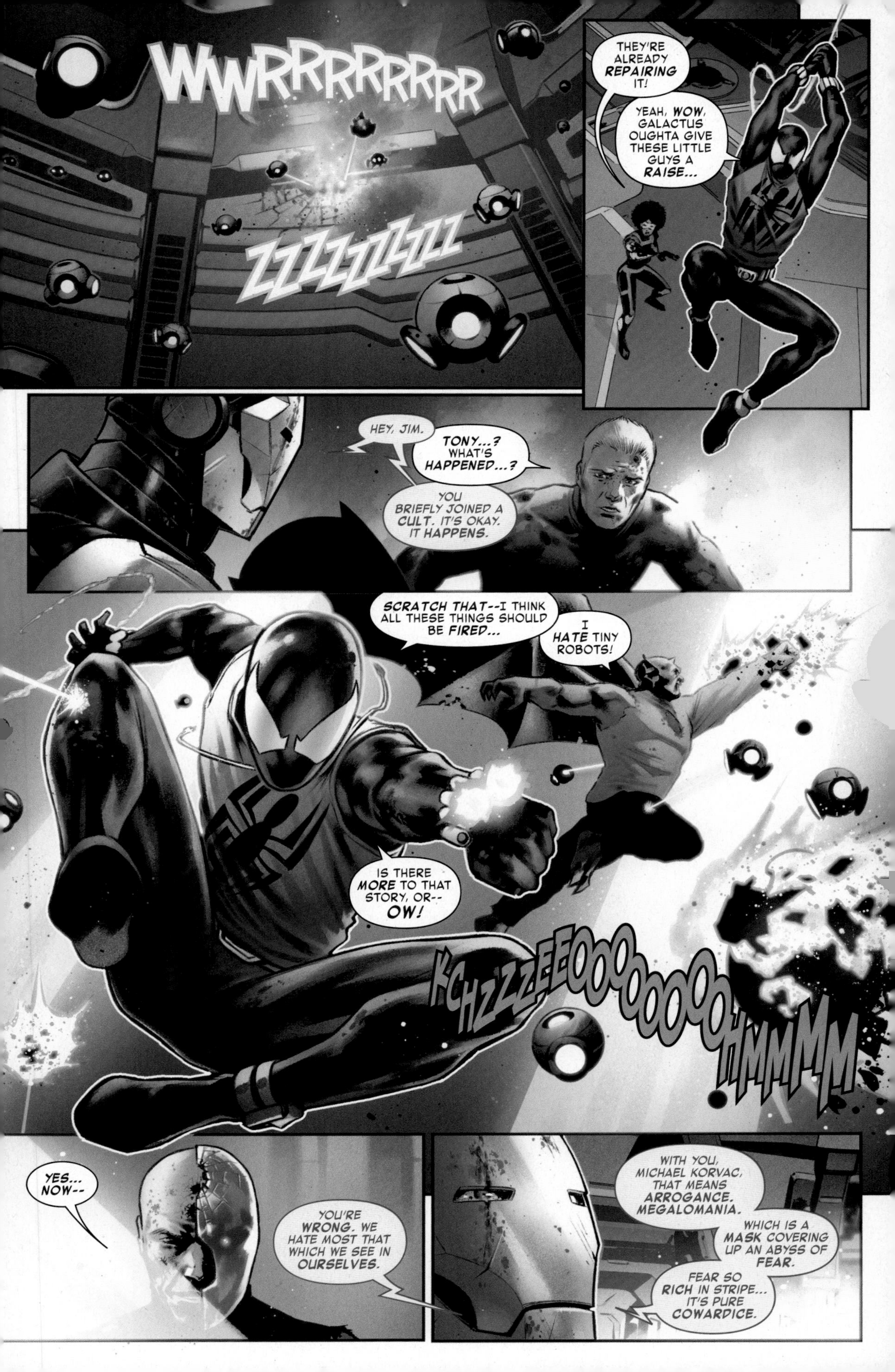
WWRRRRRRRRR
ZZZZZZZZZ
THEY'RE ALREADY REPAIRING IT!
YEAH, WOW, GALACTUS OUGHTA GIVE THESE LITTLE GUYS A RAISE...
HEY, JIM.
TONY...? WHAT'S HAPPENED...?
YOU BRIEFLY JOINED A CULT. IT'S OKAY. IT HAPPENS.
SCRATCH THAT--I THINK ALL THESE THINGS SHOULD BE FIRED...
I HATE TINY ROBOTS!
IS THERE MORE TO THAT STORY, OR-- OW!
KCHZZZEEOOOOOOOOOHMMMM
YES... NOW--
YOU'RE WRONG. WE HATE MOST THAT WHICH WE SEE IN OURSELVES.
WITH YOU, MICHAEL KORVAC, THAT MEANS ARROGANCE. MEGALOMANIA.
WHICH IS A MASK COVERING UP AN ABYSS OF FEAR.
FEAR SO RICH IN STRIPE... IT'S PURE COWARDICE.

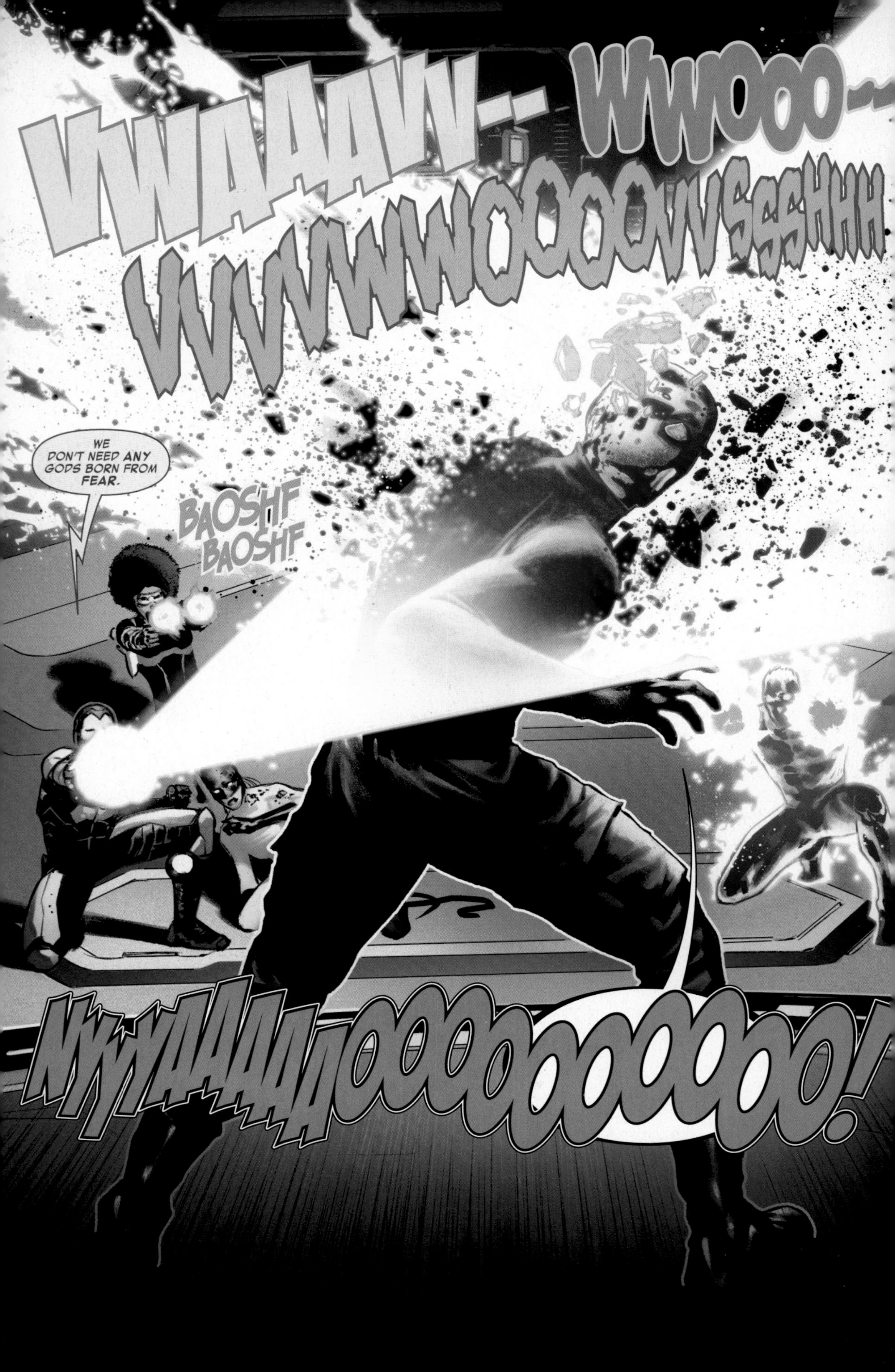
VWAAAVV--
WWOOO--
VVVVWWOOOOVVSSSHHH
WE DON'T NEED ANY GODS BORN FROM FEAR.
BAOSHF
BAOSHF
NYYAAAAOOOOOOOOOOO!

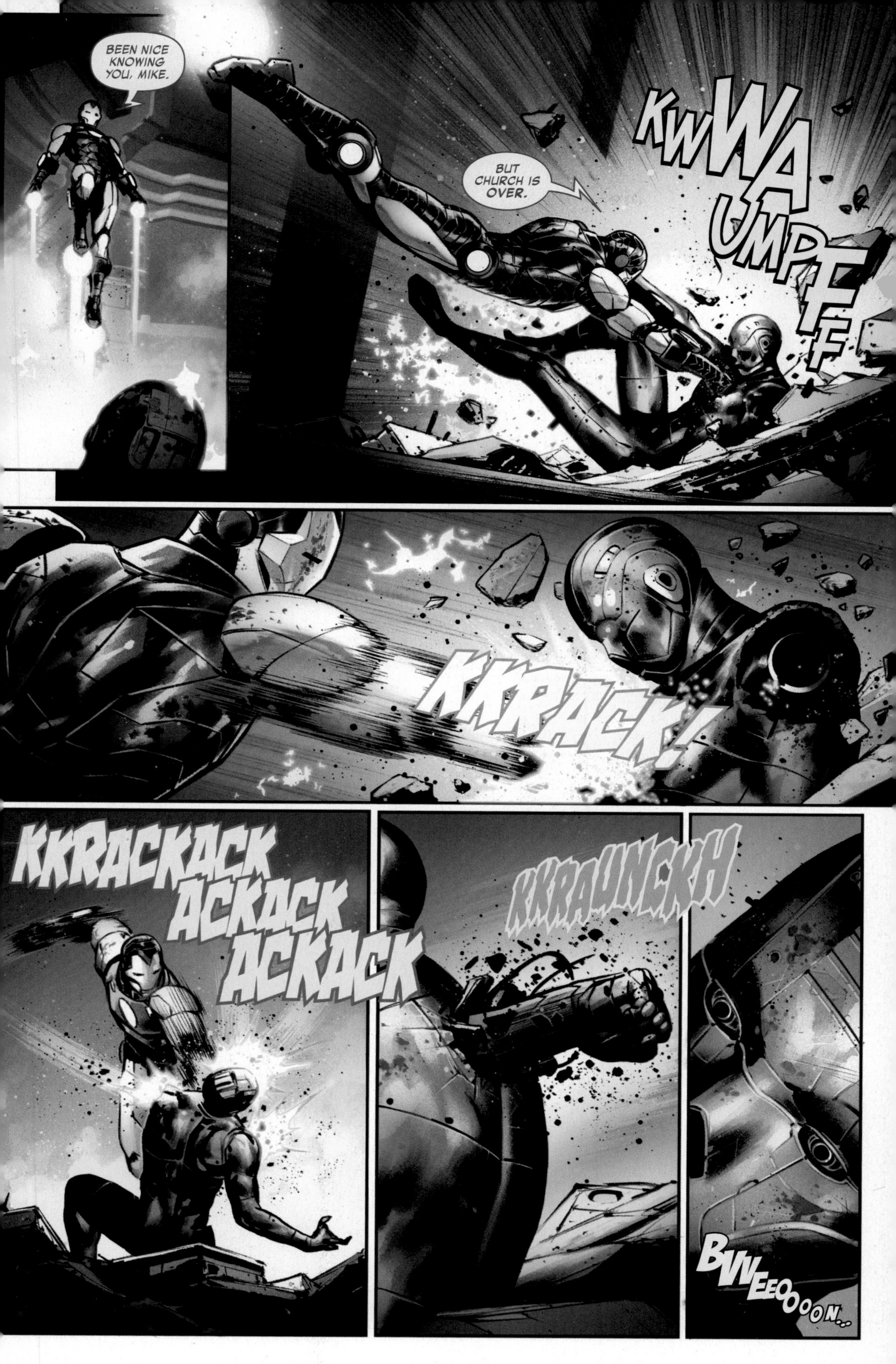
BEEN NICE KNOWING YOU, MIKE.
BUT CHURCH IS OVER.
KWWA UMPFFF
KKRACK!
KKRACKACK ACKACK ACKACK
KKRAUNCKH
BVVEEOOOOON...

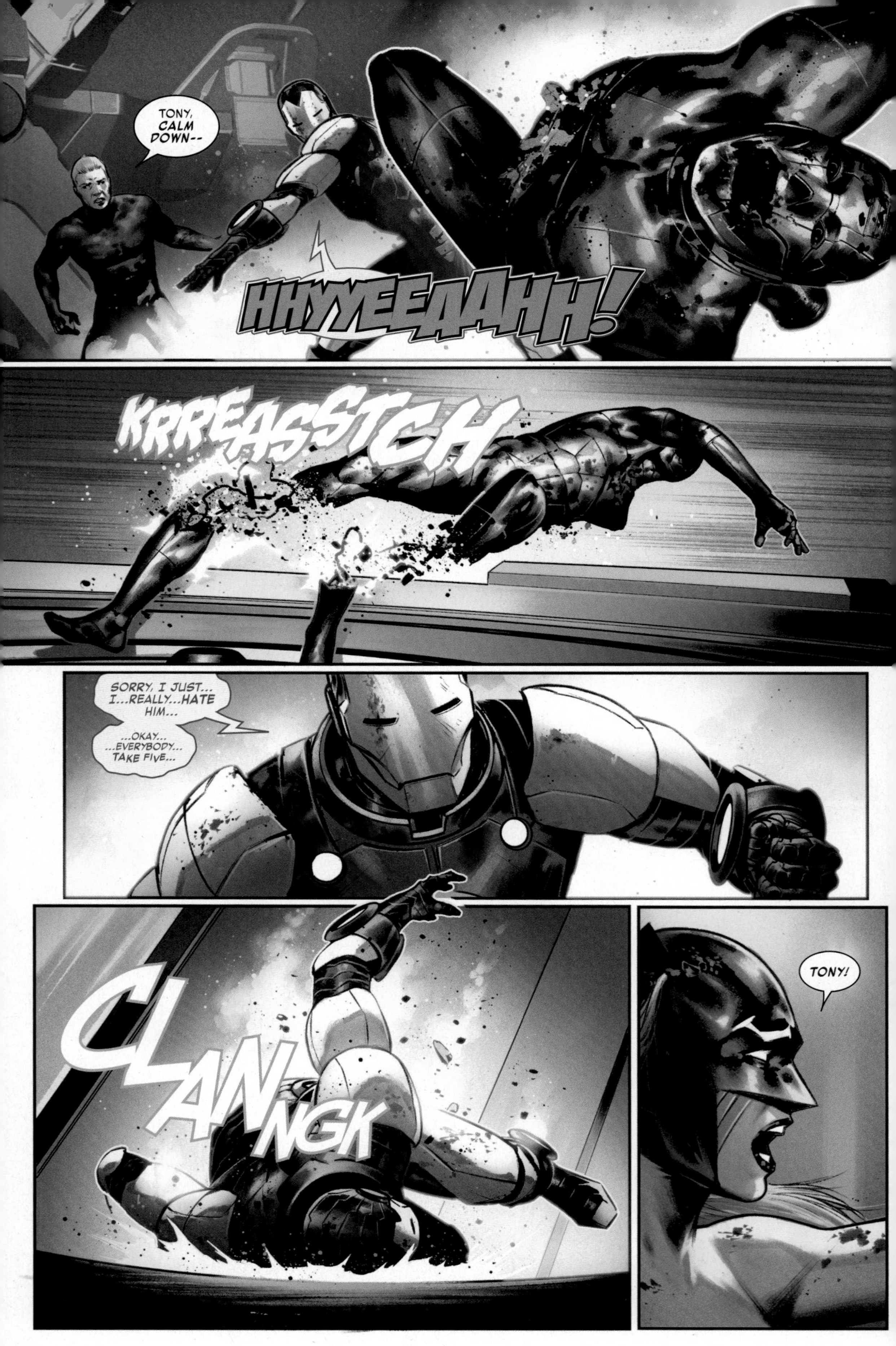
TONY, CALM DOWN--
HHYYEEAAHH!
KRREASSTCH
SORRY, I JUST... I...REALLY...HATE HIM...
...OKAY... ...EVERYBODY... TAKE FIVE...
CLANNGK
TONY!

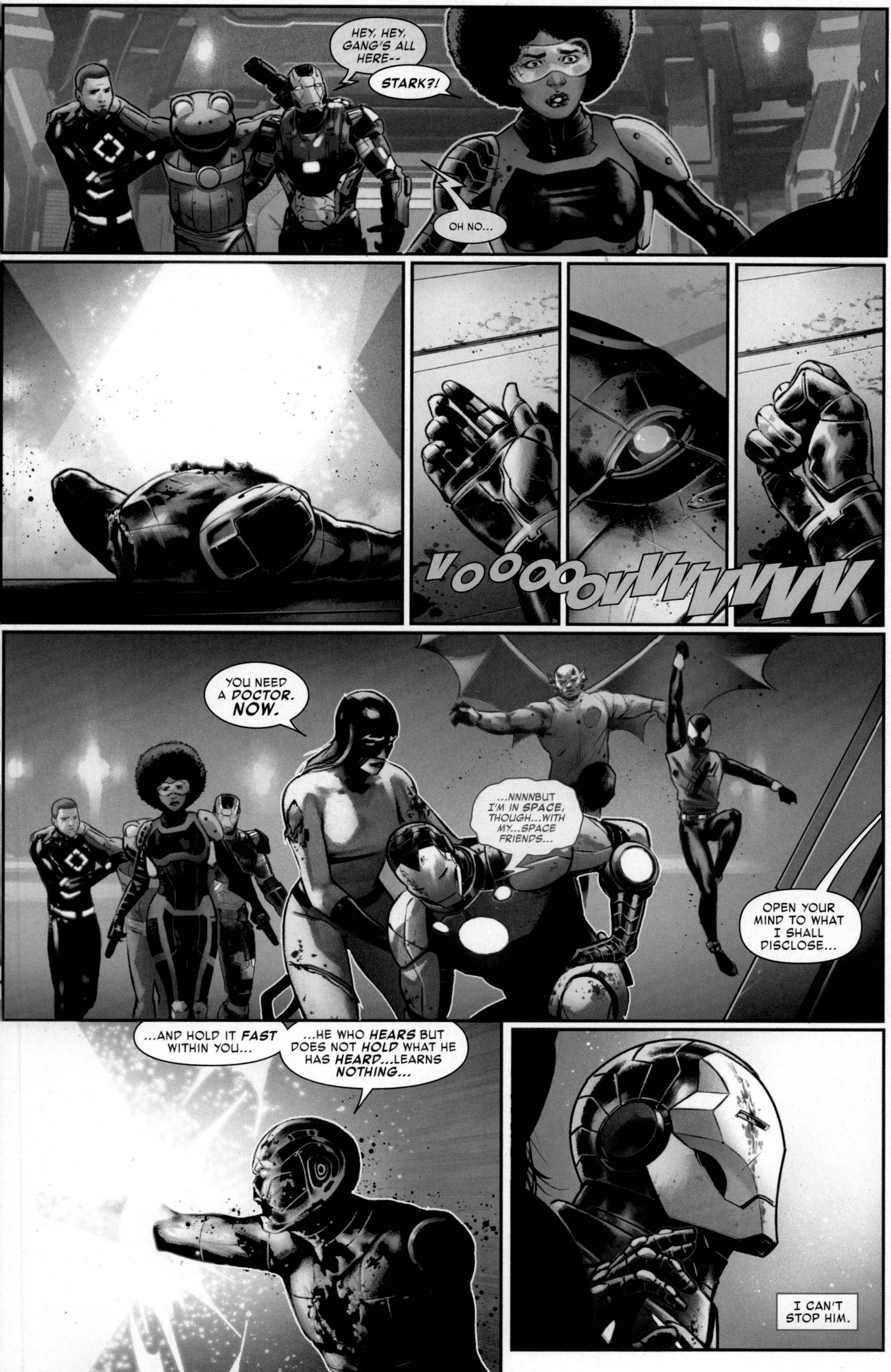
HEY, HEY, GANG'S ALL HERE--
STARK?!
OH NO...
VOOOOOOVVVVVVVV
YOU NEED A DOCTOR. NOW.
...NNNNBUT I'M IN SPACE, THOUGH...WITH MY...SPACE FRIENDS...
OPEN YOUR MIND TO WHAT I SHALL DISCLOSE...
...AND HOLD IT FAST WITHIN YOU...
...HE WHO HEARS BUT DOES NOT HOLD WHAT HE HAS HEARD...LEARNS NOTHING...
I CAN'T STOP HIM.

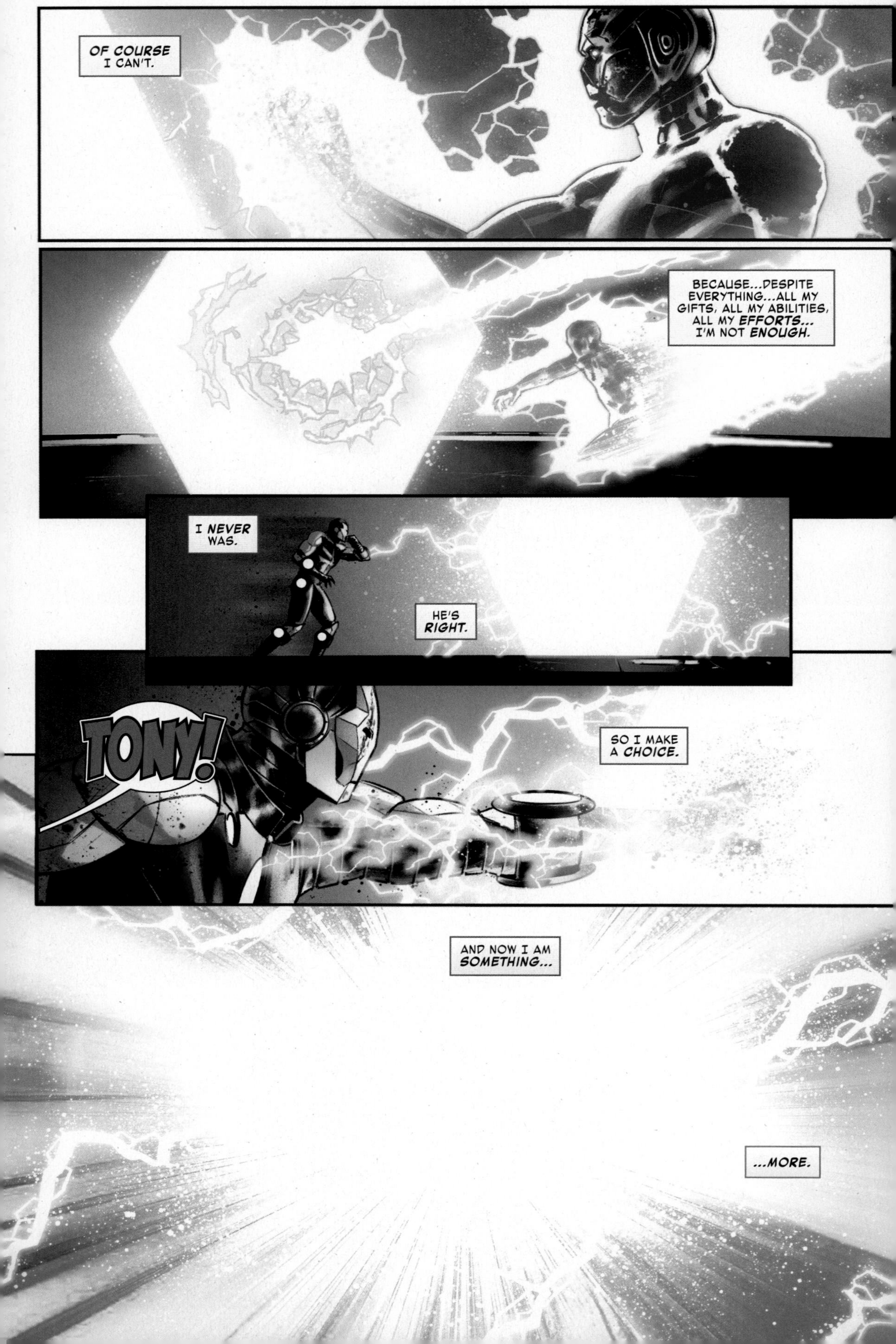
OF COURSE I CAN'T.
BECAUSE...DESPITE EVERYTHING...ALL MY GIFTS, ALL MY ABILITIES, ALL MY EFFORTS... I'M NOT ENOUGH.
I NEVER WAS.
HE'S RIGHT.
TONY!
SO I MAKE A CHOICE.
AND NOW I AM SOMETHING...
...MORE.

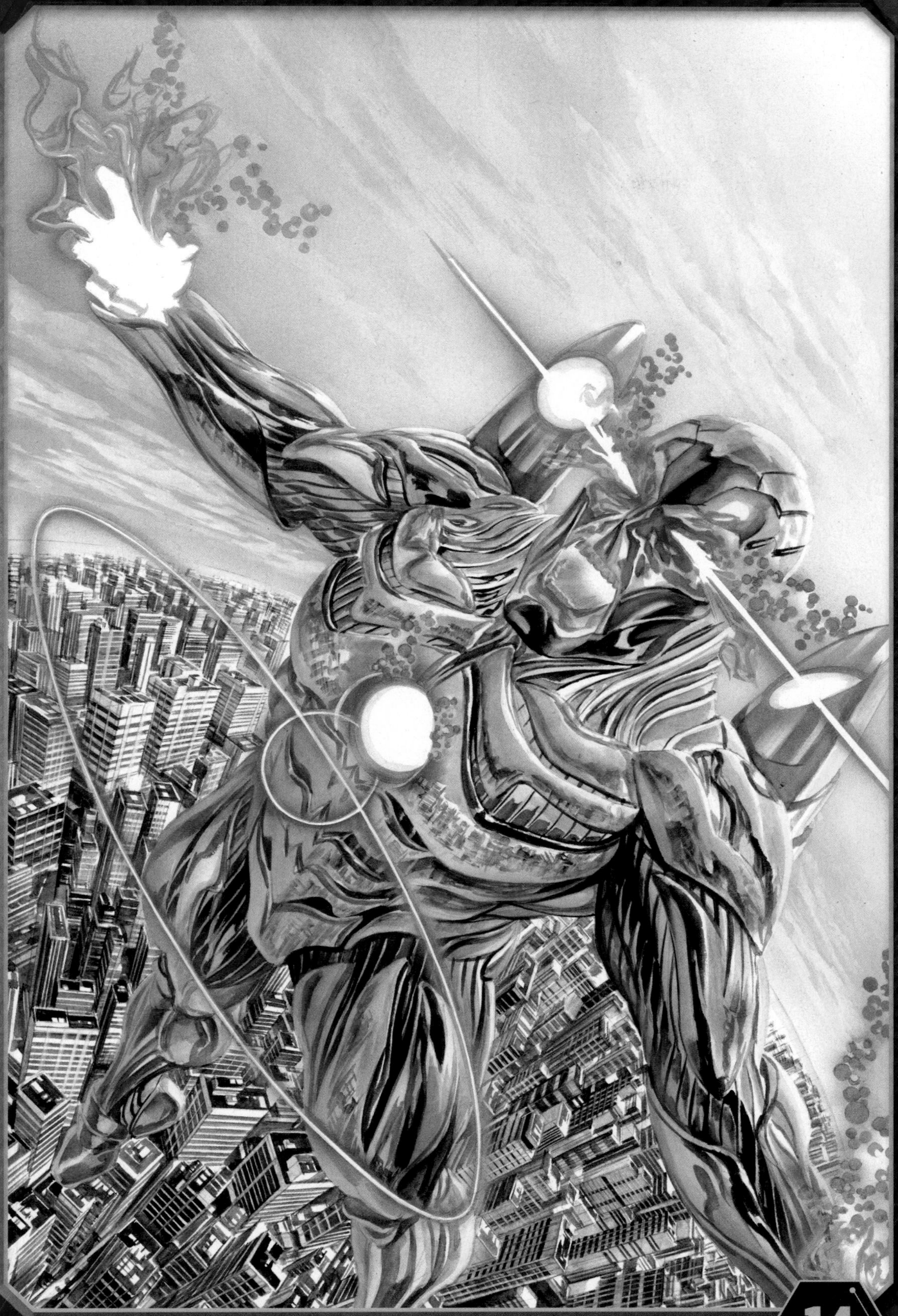

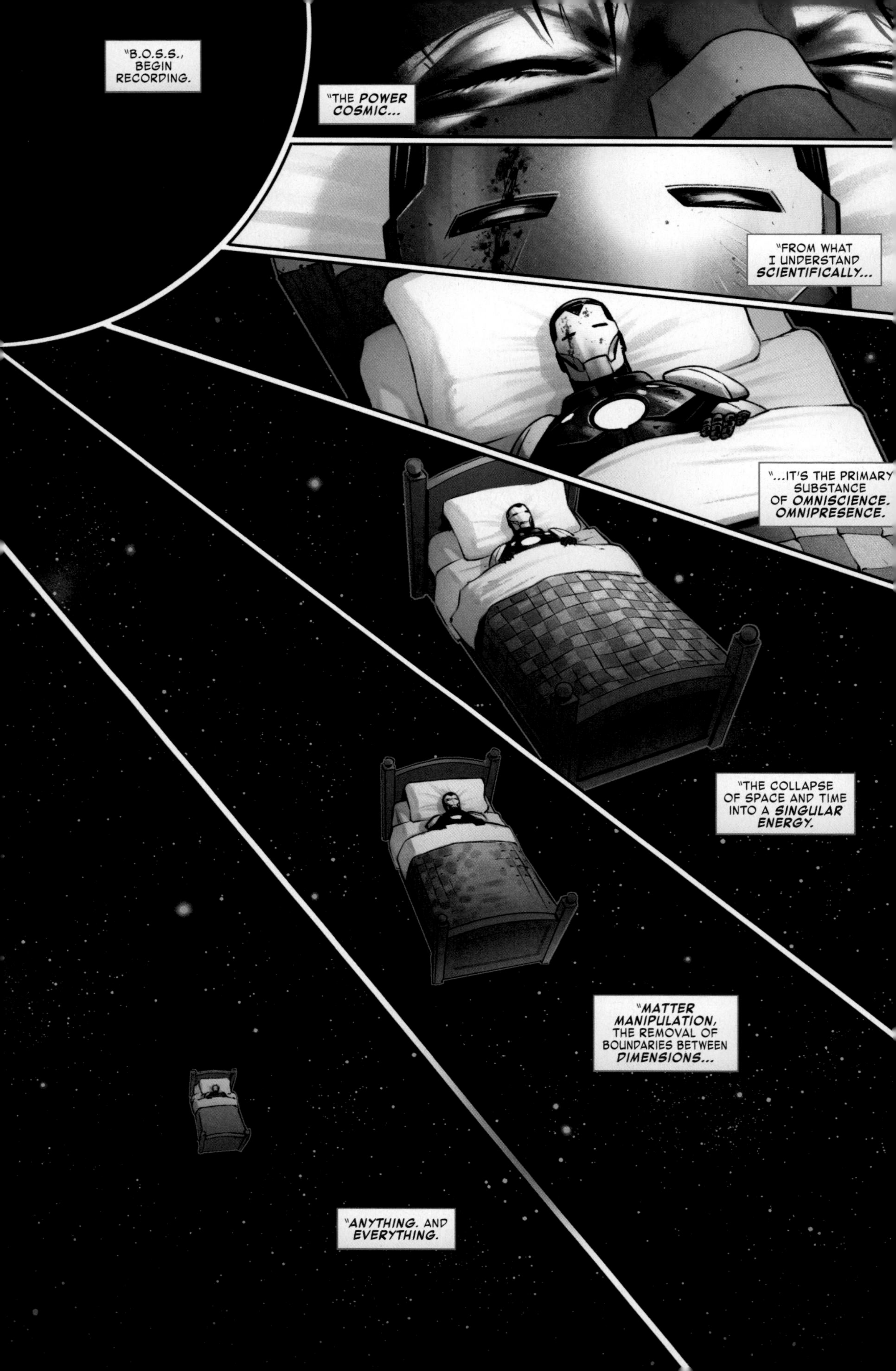
"B.O.S.S., BEGIN RECORDING.
"THE POWER COSMIC...
"FROM WHAT I UNDERSTAND SCIENTIFICALLY...
"...IT'S THE PRIMARY SUBSTANCE OF OMNISCIENCE. OMNIPRESENCE.
"THE COLLAPSE OF SPACE AND TIME INTO A SINGULAR ENERGY.
"MATTER MANIPULATION, THE REMOVAL OF BOUNDARIES BETWEEN DIMENSIONS...
"ANYTHING. AND EVERYTHING.

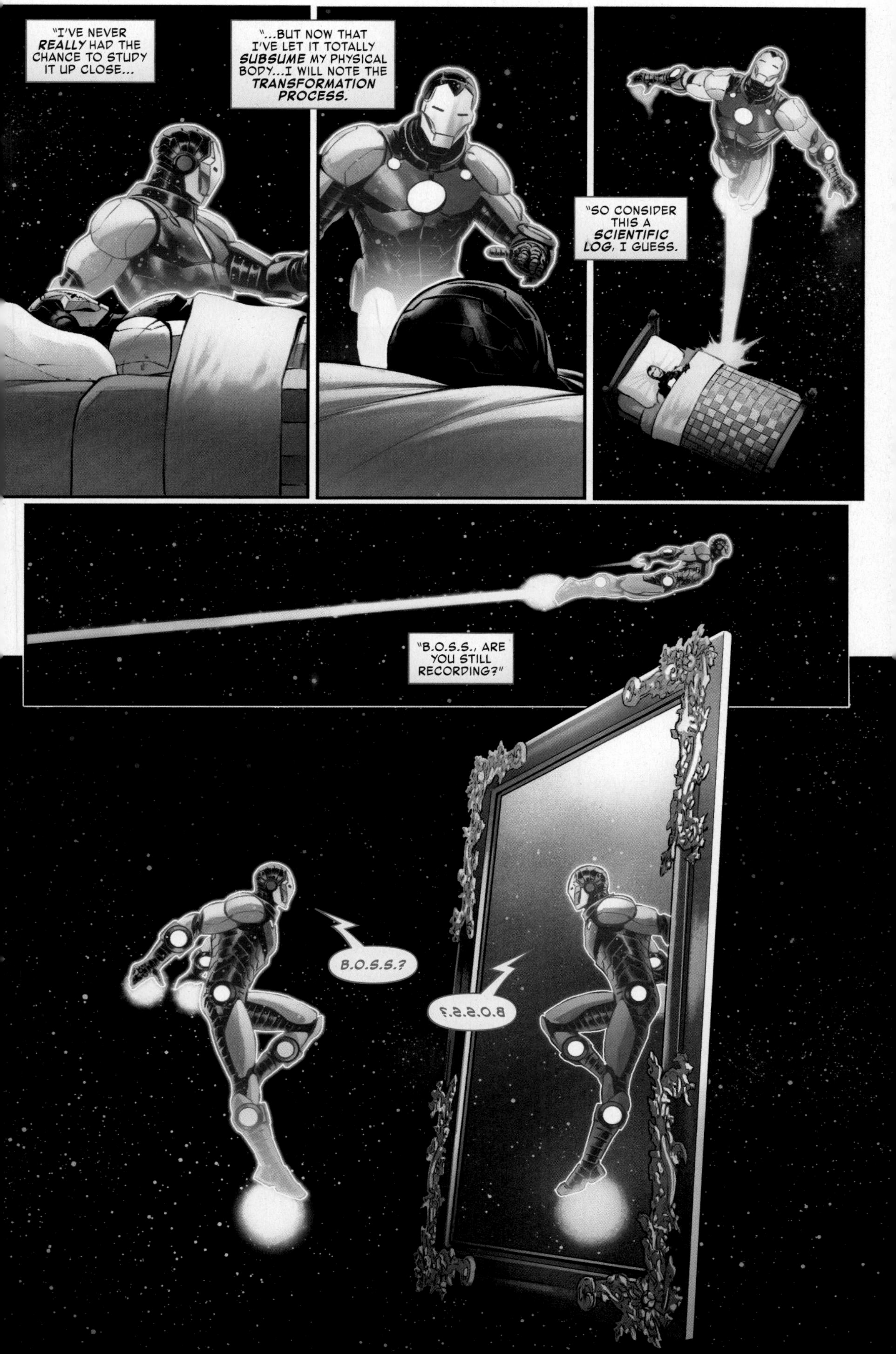
"I'VE NEVER REALLY HAD THE CHANCE TO STUDY IT UP CLOSE...
"...BUT NOW THAT I'VE LET IT TOTALLY SUBSUME MY PHYSICAL BODY...I WILL NOTE THE TRANSFORMATION PROCESS.
"SO CONSIDER THIS A SCIENTIFIC LOG, I GUESS.
"B.O.S.S., ARE YOU STILL RECORDING?"
B.O.S.S.?
B.O.S.S.?

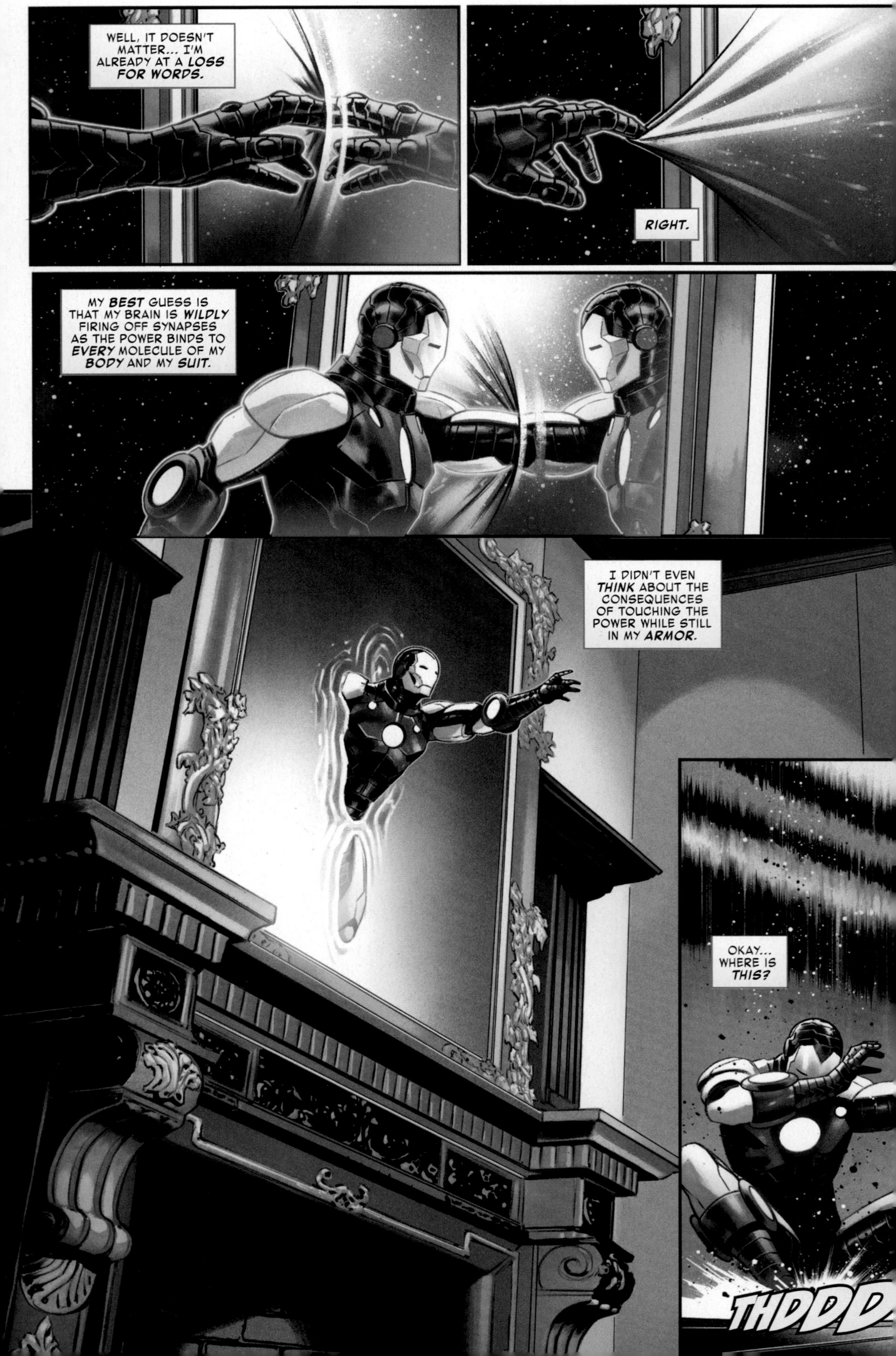
WELL, IT DOESN'T MATTER... I'M ALREADY AT A LOSS FOR WORDS.
RIGHT.
MY BEST GUESS IS THAT MY BRAIN IS WILDLY FIRING OFF SYNAPSES AS THE POWER BINDS TO EVERY MOLECULE OF MY BODY AND MY SUIT.
I DIDN'T EVEN THINK ABOUT THE CONSEQUENCES OF TOUCHING THE POWER WHILE STILL IN MY ARMOR.
OKAY... WHERE IS THIS?
THDDD

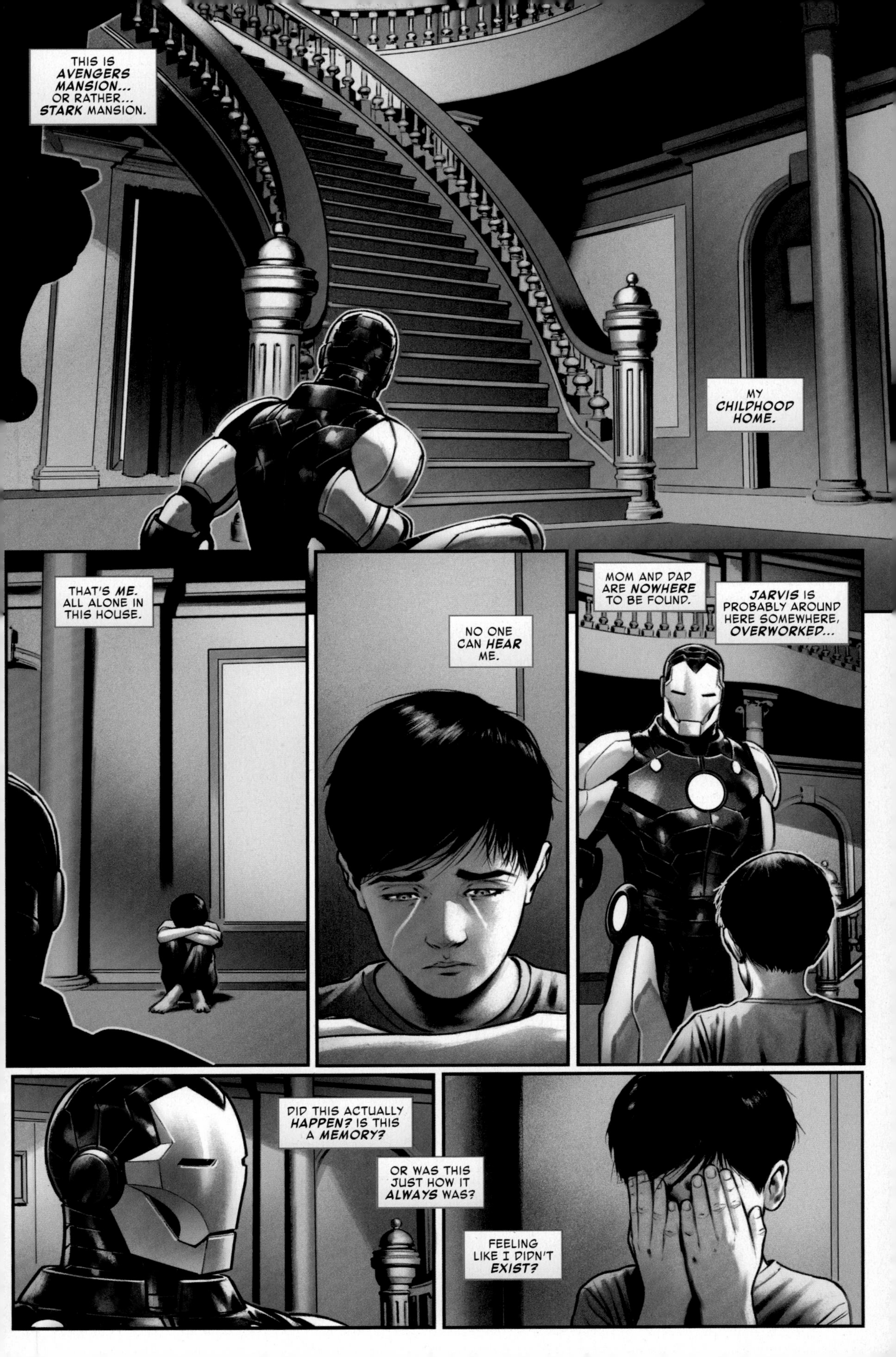
THIS IS AVENGERS MANSION... OR RATHER... STARK MANSION.
MY CHILDHOOD HOME.
THAT'S ME. ALL ALONE IN THIS HOUSE.
NO ONE CAN HEAR ME.
MOM AND DAD ARE NOWHERE TO BE FOUND.
JARVIS IS PROBABLY AROUND HERE SOMEWHERE, OVERWORKED...
DID THIS ACTUALLY HAPPEN? IS THIS A MEMORY?
OR WAS THIS JUST HOW IT ALWAYS WAS?
FEELING LIKE I DIDN'T EXIST?

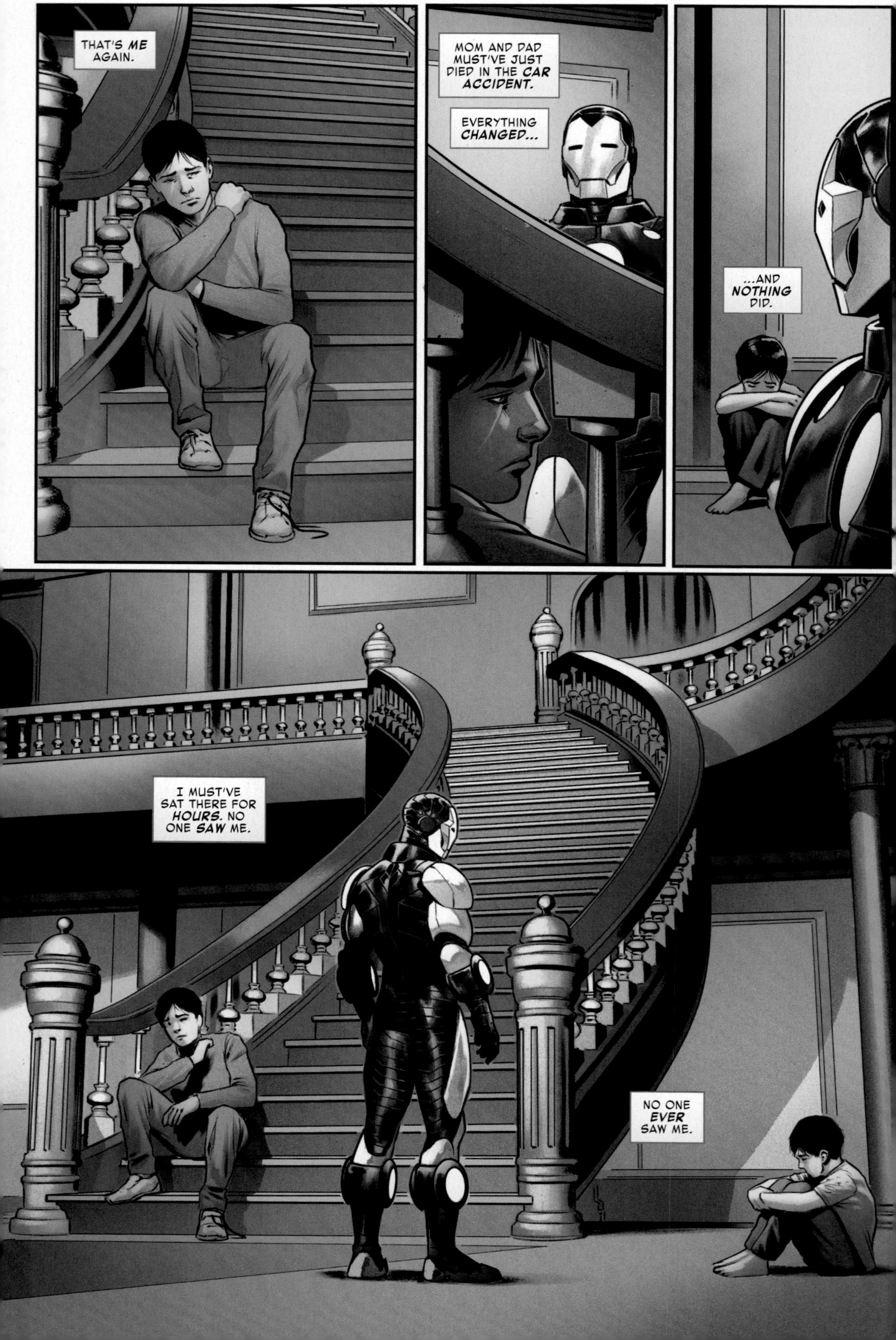
THAT'S ME AGAIN.
MOM AND DAD MUST'VE JUST DIED IN THE CAR ACCIDENT.
EVERYTHING CHANGED...
...AND NOTHING DID.
I MUST'VE SAT THERE FOR HOURS. NO ONE SAW ME.
NO ONE EVER SAW ME.

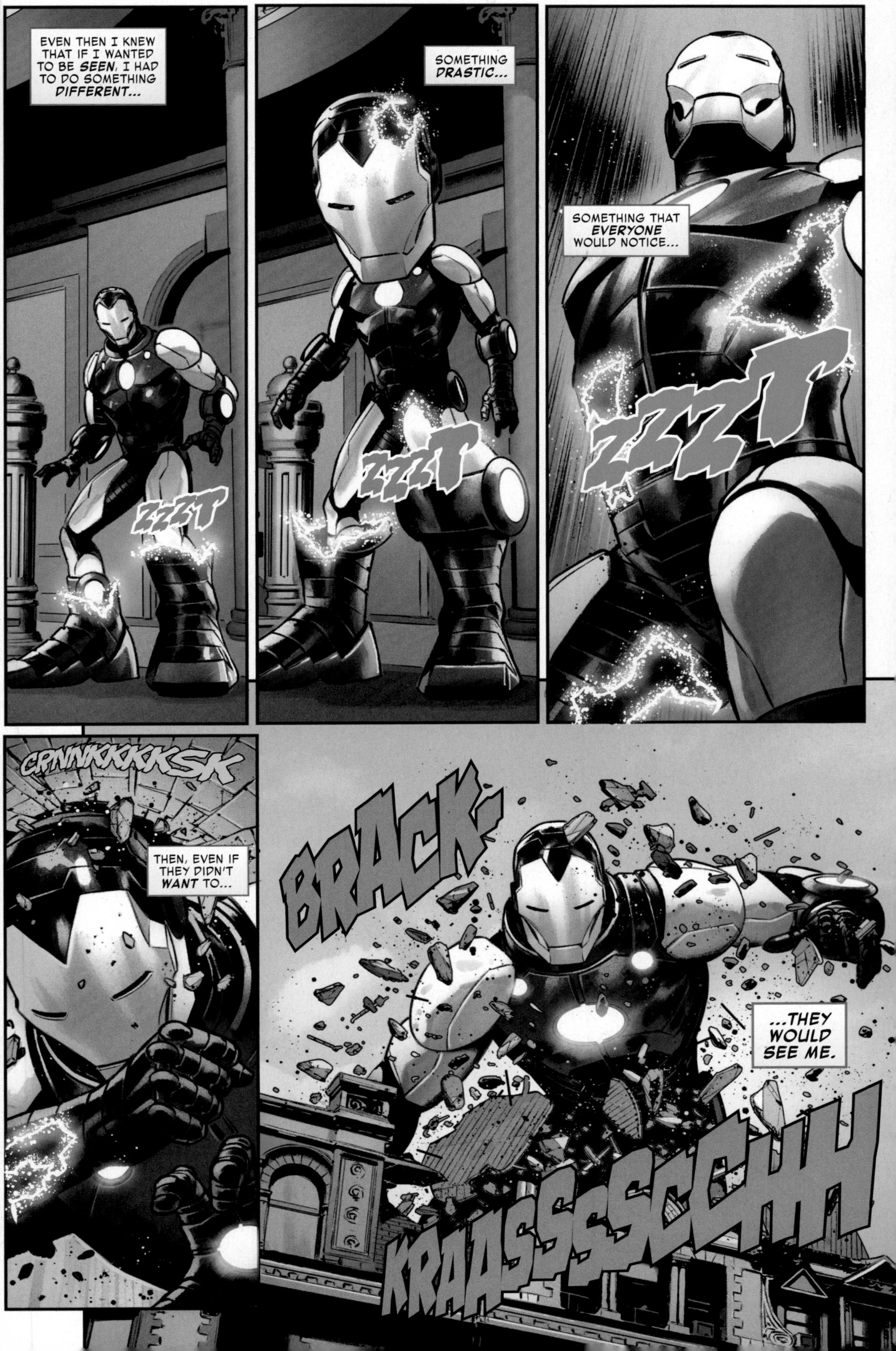
EVEN THEN I KNEW THAT IF I WANTED TO BE SEEN, I HAD TO DO SOMETHING DIFFERENT...
ZZZT
SOMETHING DRASTIC...
ZZZT
SOMETHING THAT EVERYONE WOULD NOTICE...
ZZZZT
CRNNKKKKKSK
THEN, EVEN IF THEY DIDN'T WANT TO...
BRACK-
...THEY WOULD SEE ME.
KRAASSSCCHH

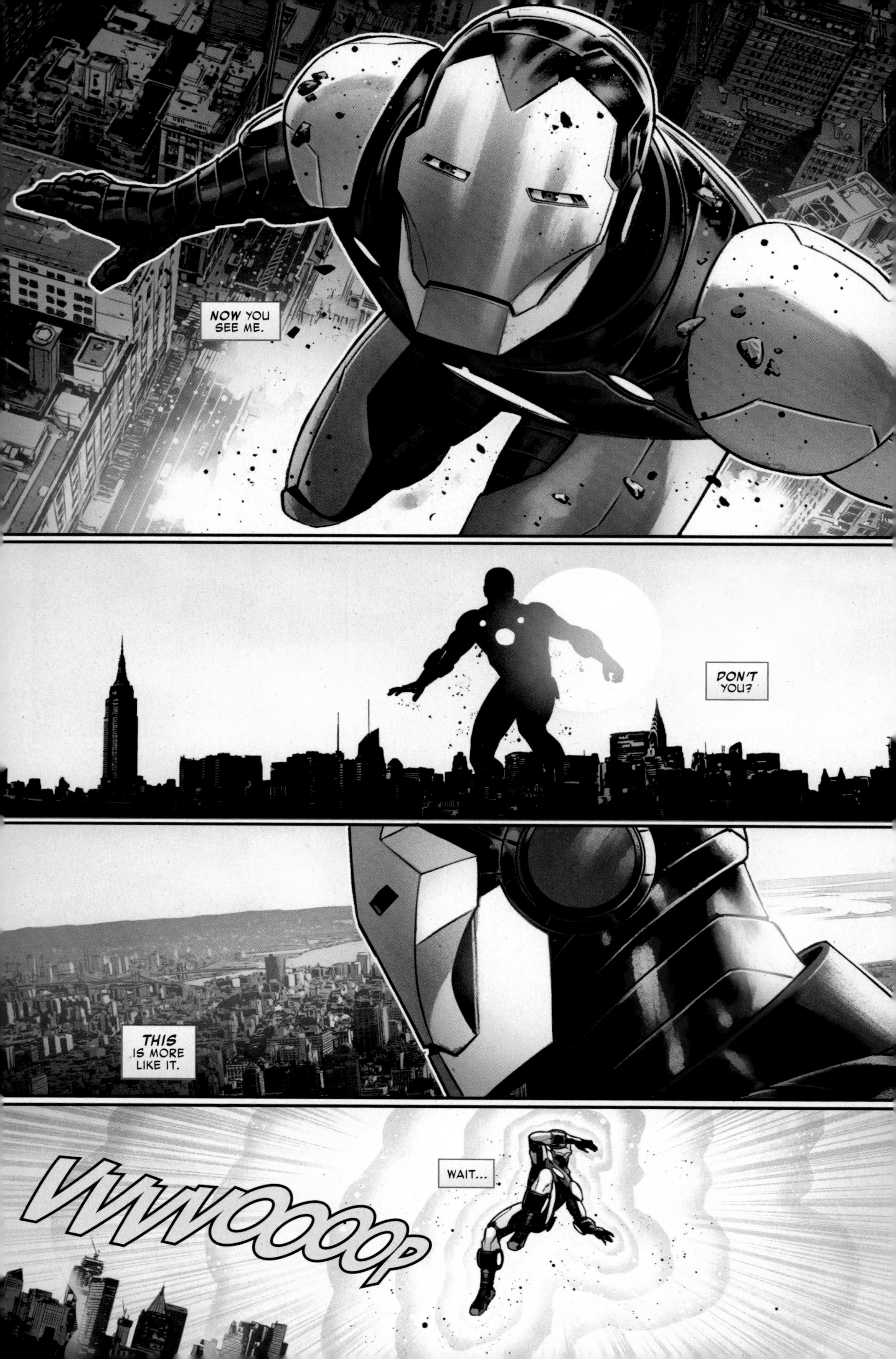
NOW YOU SEE ME.
DON'T YOU?
THIS IS MORE LIKE IT.
VVVVOOOOP
WAIT...

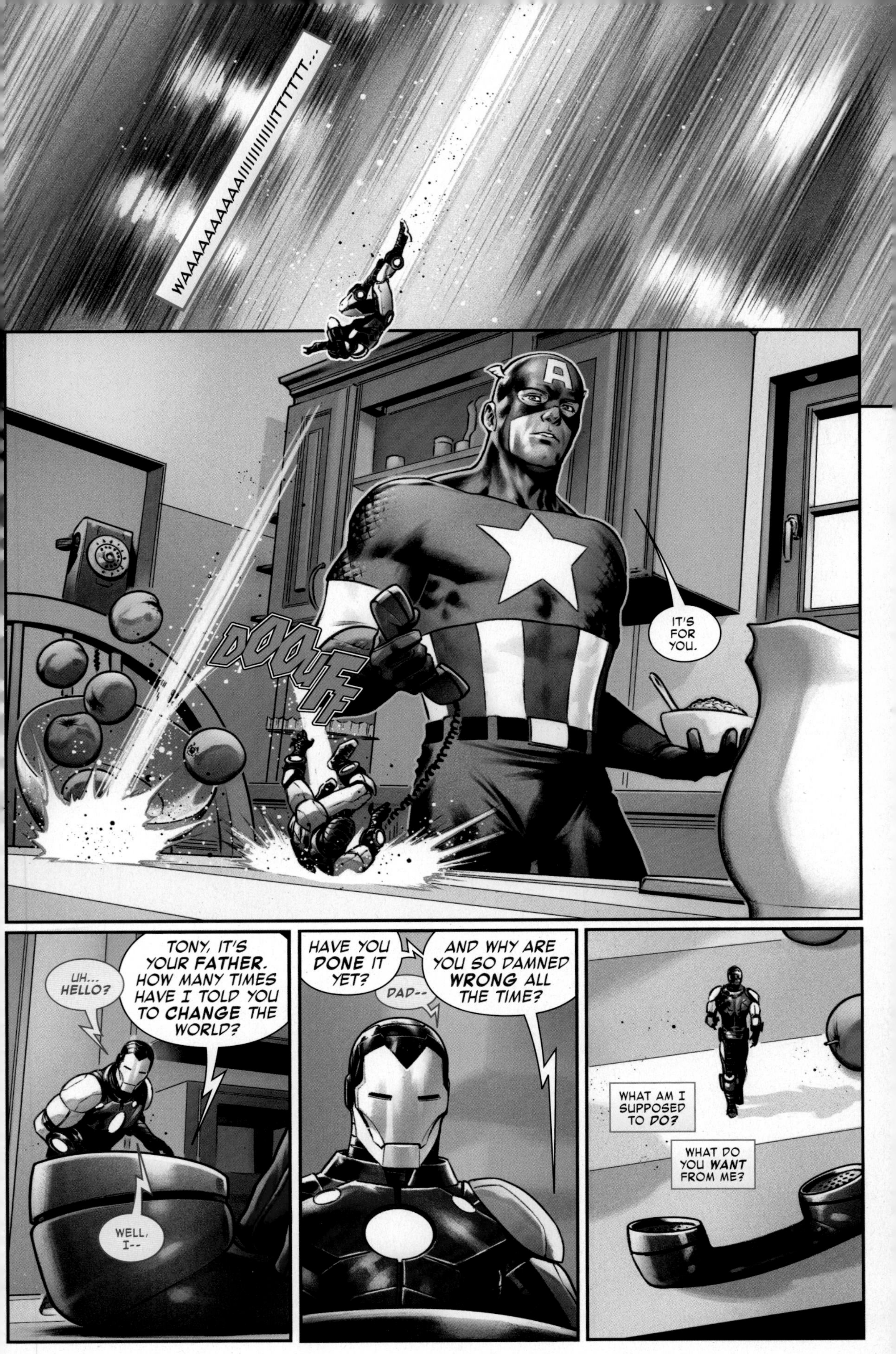
WAAAAAAAAAAIIIIIIIIIIIITTTTTT...
DOOUF
IT'S FOR YOU.
UH... HELLO?
TONY, IT'S YOUR FATHER. HOW MANY TIMES HAVE I TOLD YOU TO CHANGE THE WORLD?
WELL, I--
HAVE YOU DONE IT YET?
AND WHY ARE YOU SO DAMNED WRONG ALL THE TIME?
DAD--
WHAT AM I SUPPOSED TO DO?
WHAT DO YOU WANT FROM ME?

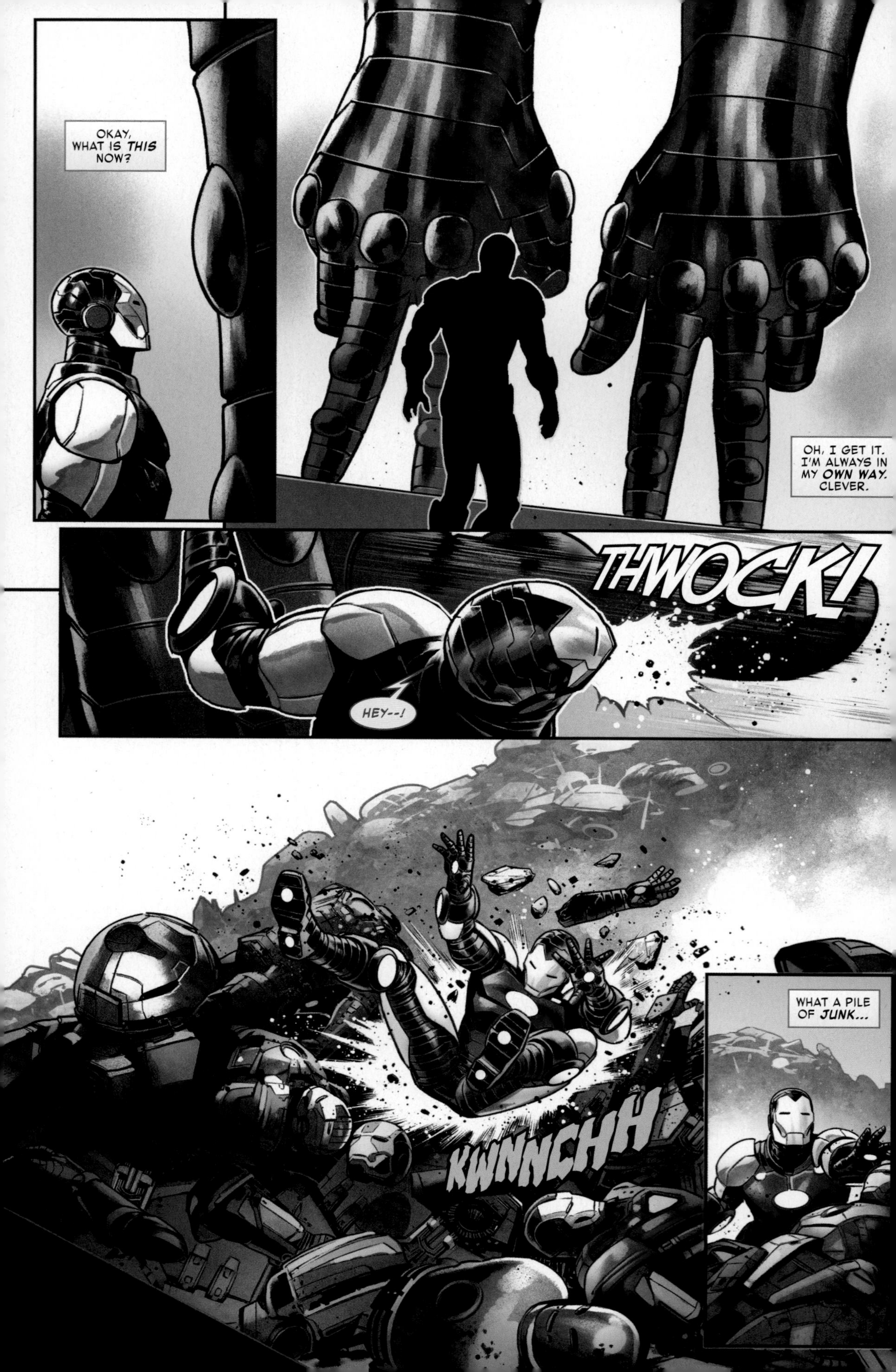
OKAY, WHAT IS THIS NOW?
OH, I GET IT. I'M ALWAYS IN MY OWN WAY. CLEVER.
THWOCK!
HEY--!
KWNNCHH
WHAT A PILE OF JUNK...

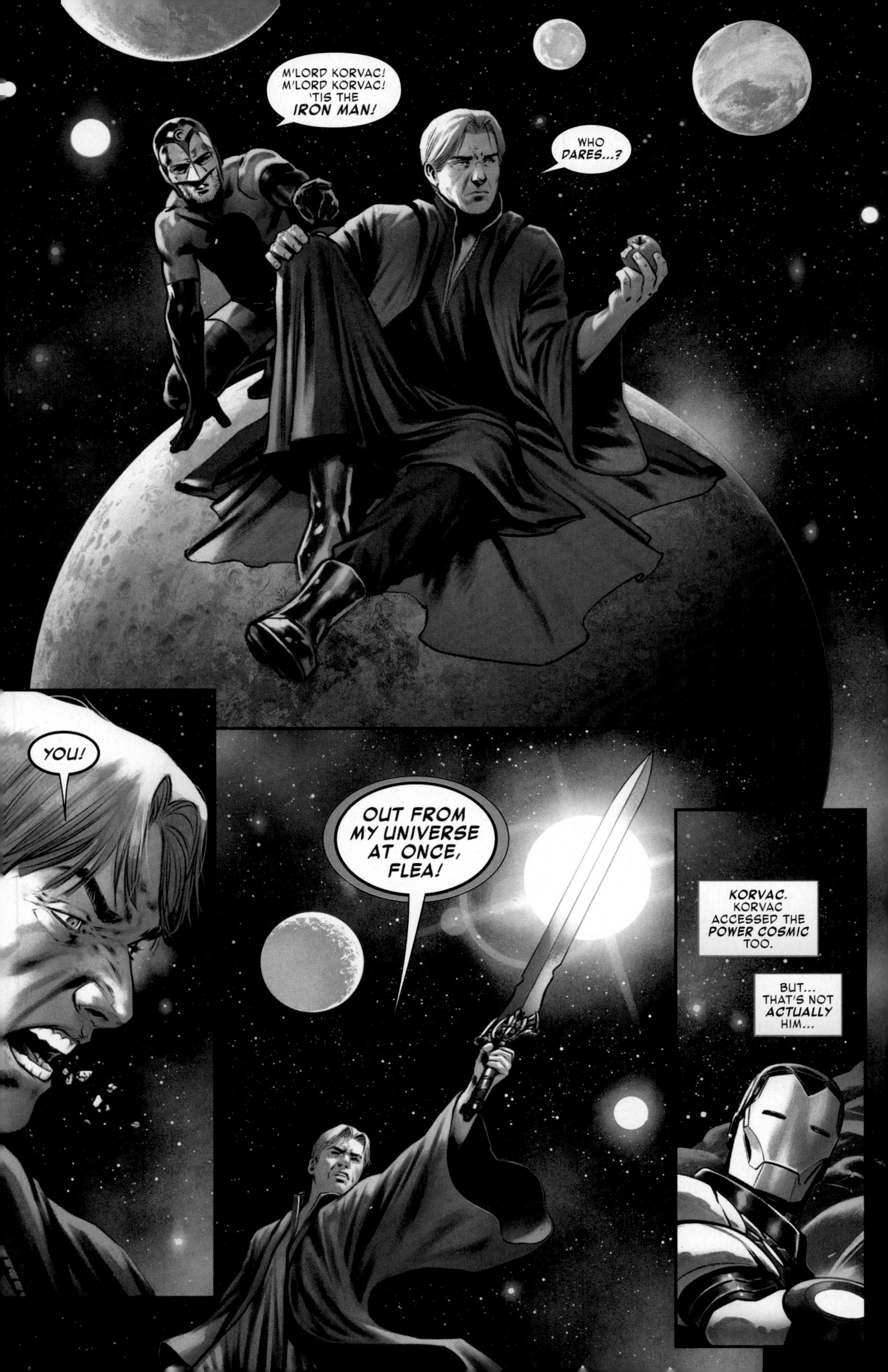
M'LORD KORVAC! M'LORD KORVAC! 'TIS THE IRON MAN!
WHO DARES...?
YOU!
OUT FROM MY UNIVERSE AT ONCE, FLEA!
KORVAC. KORVAC ACCESSED THE POWER COSMIC TOO.
BUT... THAT'S NOT ACTUALLY HIM...

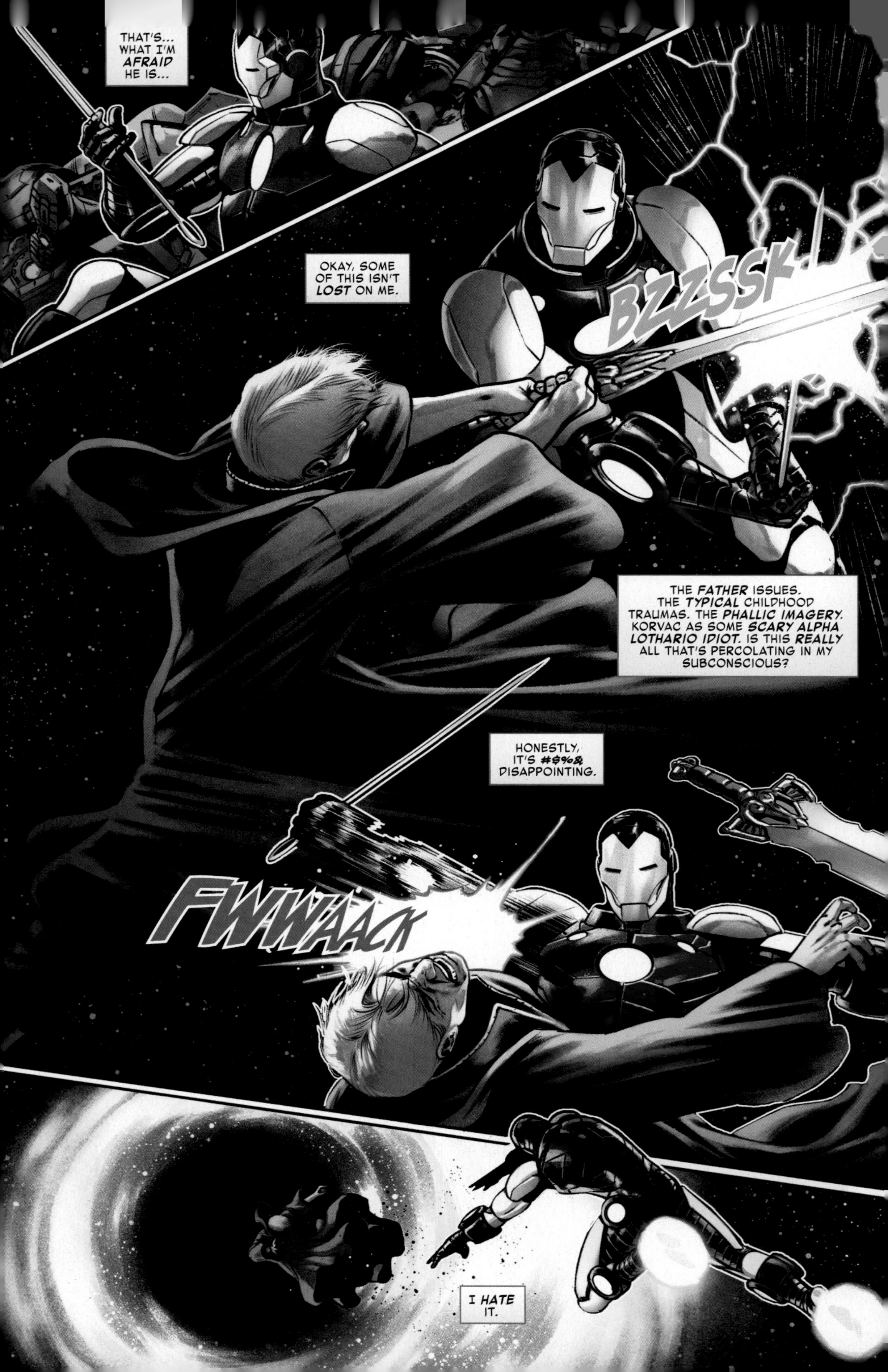
THAT'S... WHAT I'M AFRAID HE IS...
OKAY, SOME OF THIS ISN'T LOST ON ME.
BZZSSK
THE FATHER ISSUES. THE TYPICAL CHILDHOOD TRAUMAS. THE PHALLIC IMAGERY. KORVAC AS SOME SCARY ALPHA LOTHARIO IDIOT. IS THIS REALLY ALL THAT'S PERCOLATING IN MY SUBCONSCIOUS?
HONESTLY, IT'S #$%& DISAPPOINTING.
FWWAACK
I HATE IT.

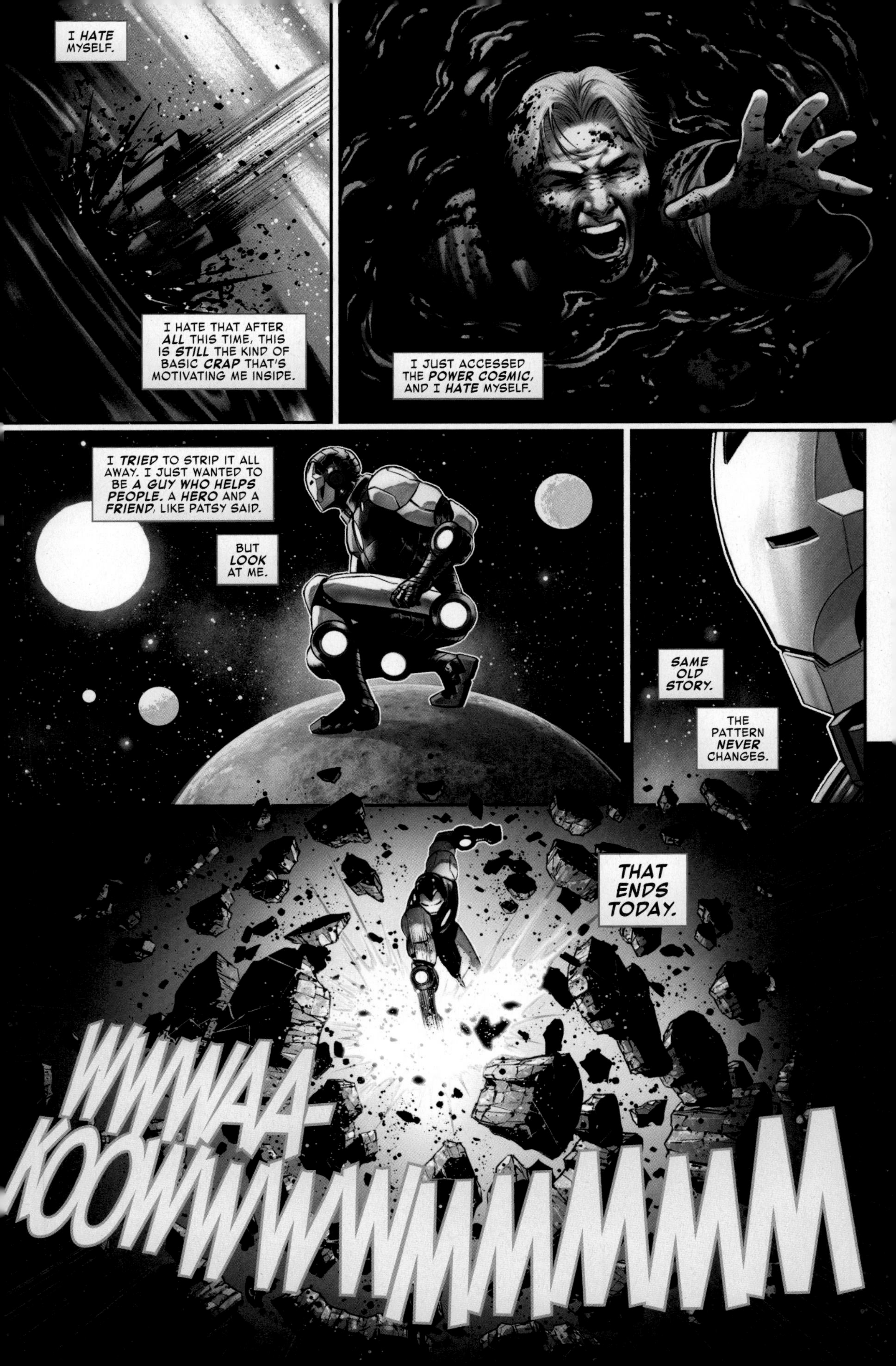
I HATE MYSELF.
I HATE THAT AFTER ALL THIS TIME, THIS IS STILL THE KIND OF BASIC CRAP THAT'S MOTIVATING ME INSIDE.
I JUST ACCESSED THE POWER COSMIC, AND I HATE MYSELF.
I TRIED TO STRIP IT ALL AWAY. I JUST WANTED TO BE A GUY WHO HELPS PEOPLE. A HERO AND A FRIEND, LIKE PATSY SAID.
BUT LOOK AT ME.
SAME OLD STORY.
THE PATTERN NEVER CHANGES.
THAT ENDS TODAY.
WWWAA-KOOMMWWMMMMMM

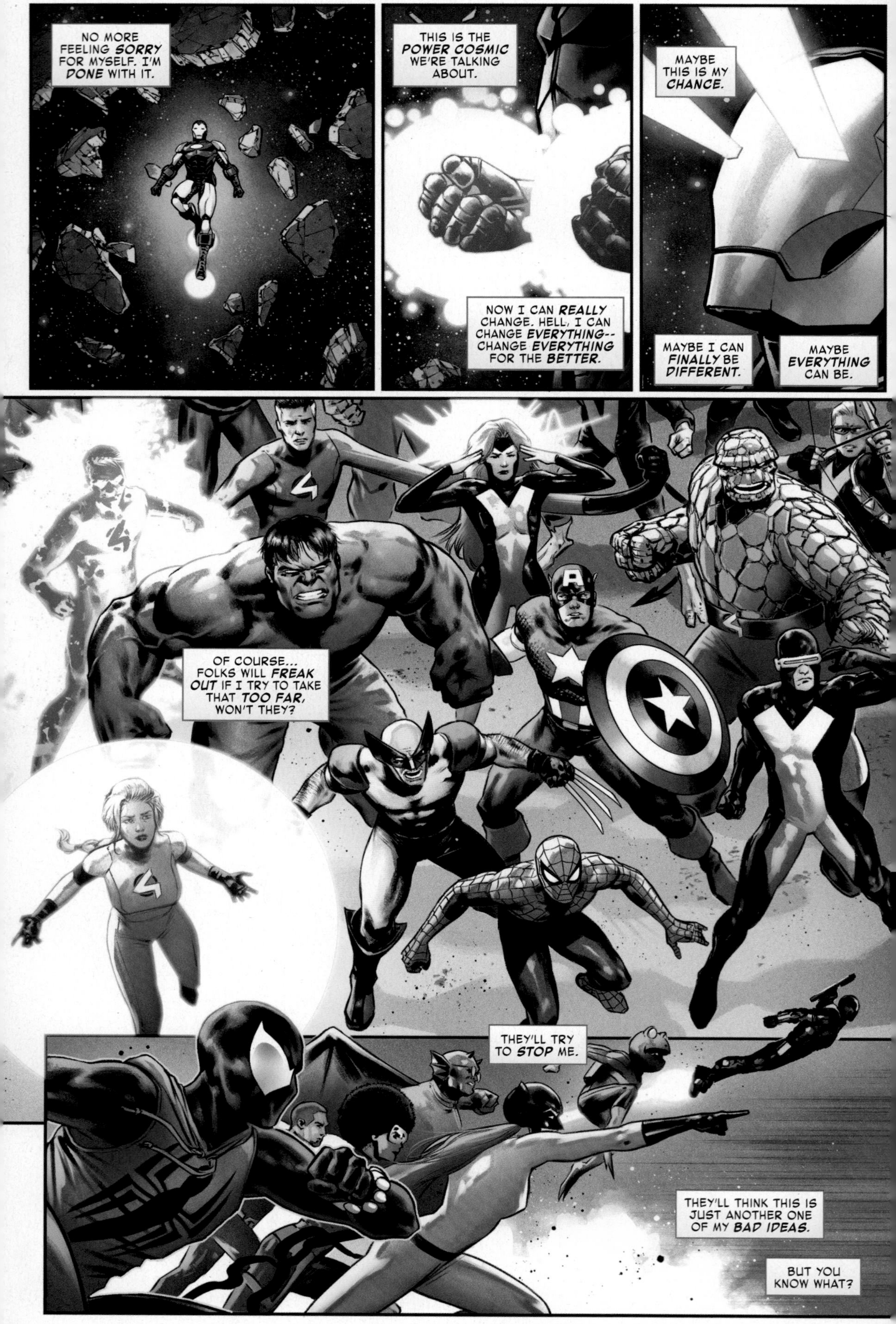
NO MORE FEELING SORRY FOR MYSELF. I'M DONE WITH IT.
THIS IS THE POWER COSMIC WE'RE TALKING ABOUT.
NOW I CAN REALLY CHANGE. HELL, I CAN CHANGE EVERYTHING-- CHANGE EVERYTHING FOR THE BETTER.
MAYBE THIS IS MY CHANCE.
MAYBE I CAN FINALLY BE DIFFERENT.
MAYBE EVERYTHING CAN BE.
OF COURSE... FOLKS WILL FREAK OUT IF I TRY TO TAKE THAT TOO FAR, WON'T THEY?
THEY'LL TRY TO STOP ME.
THEY'LL THINK THIS IS JUST ANOTHER ONE OF MY BAD IDEAS.
BUT YOU KNOW WHAT?

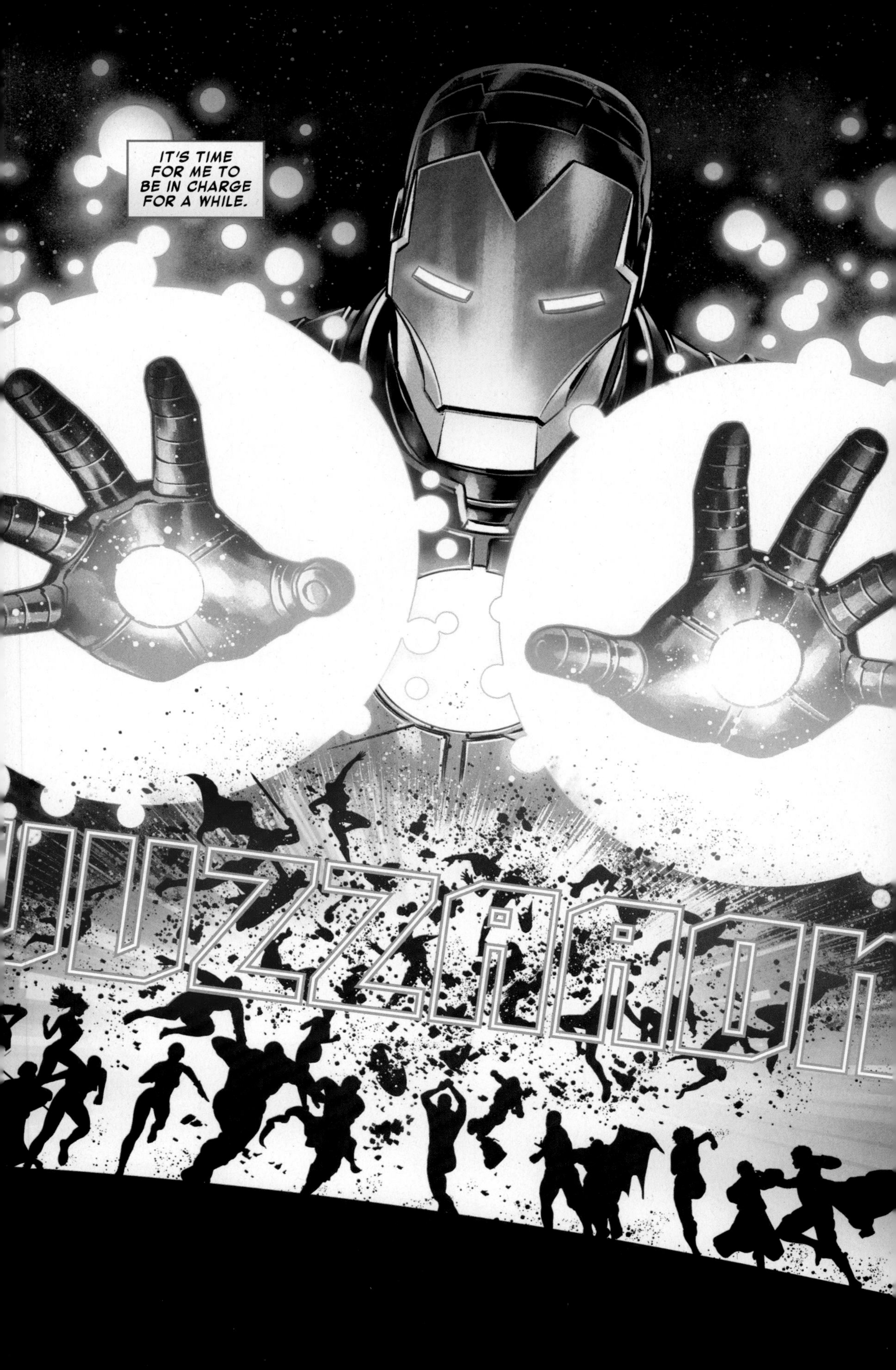
IT'S TIME FOR ME TO BE IN CHARGE FOR A WHILE.

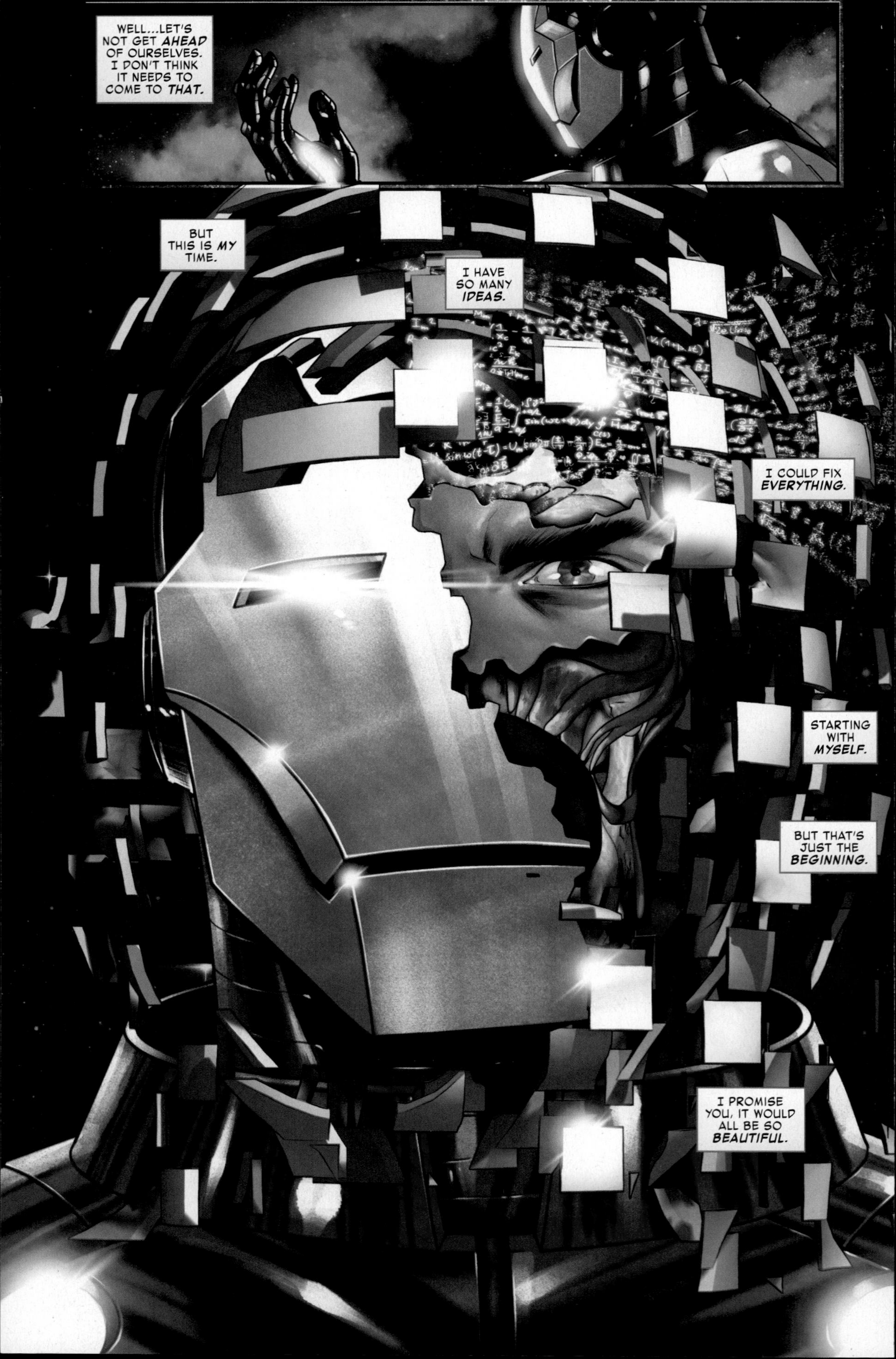
WELL...LET'S NOT GET AHEAD OF OURSELVES. I DON'T THINK IT NEEDS TO COME TO THAT.
BUT THIS IS MY TIME.
I HAVE SO MANY IDEAS.
I COULD FIX EVERYTHING.
STARTING WITH MYSELF.
BUT THAT'S JUST THE BEGINNING.
I PROMISE YOU, IT WOULD ALL BE SO BEAUTIFUL.

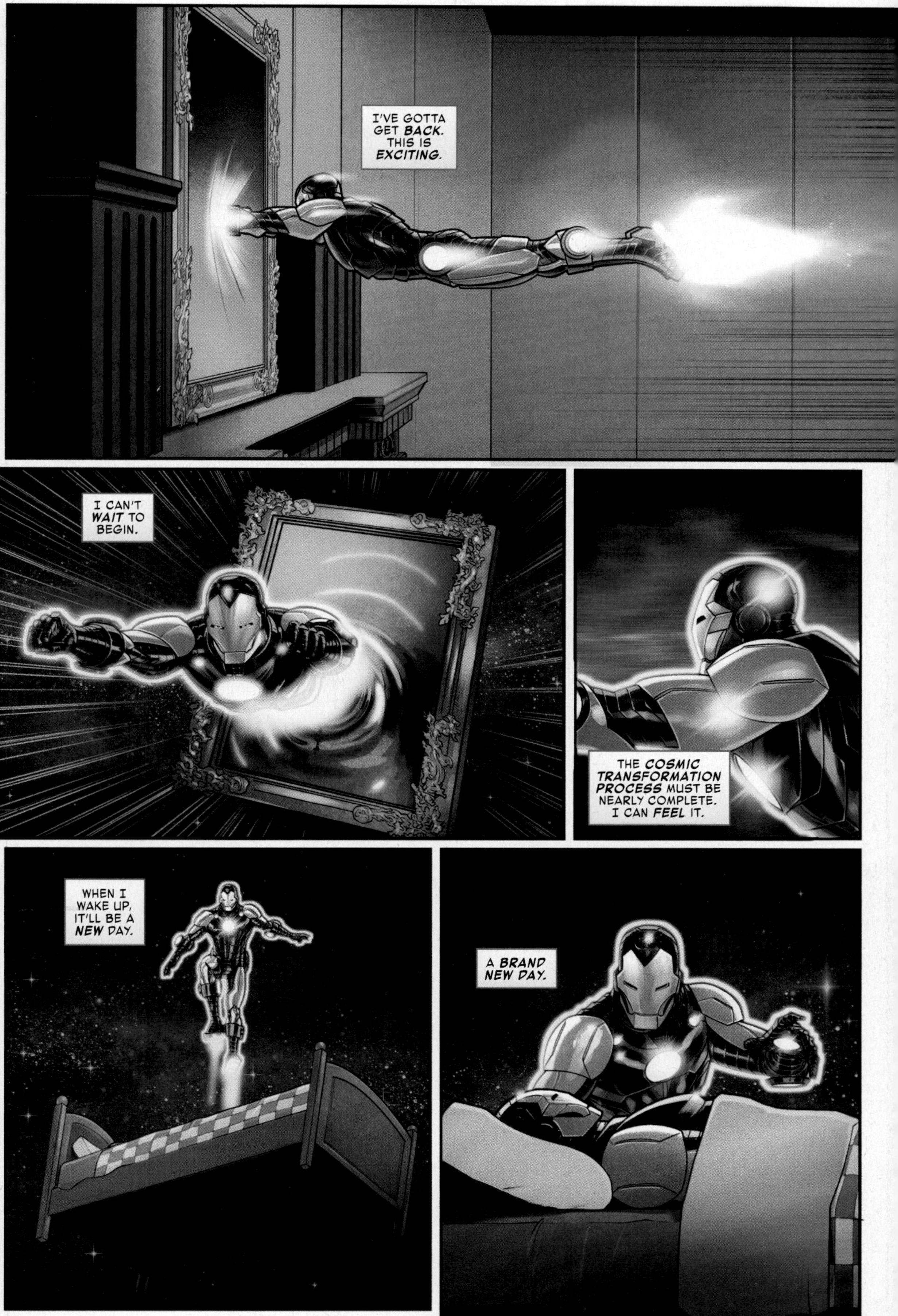
I'VE GOTTA GET BACK. THIS IS EXCITING.
I CAN'T WAIT TO BEGIN.
THE COSMIC TRANSFORMATION PROCESS MUST BE NEARLY COMPLETE. I CAN FEEL IT.
WHEN I WAKE UP, IT'LL BE A NEW DAY.
A BRAND NEW DAY.

I'LL MAKE SURE I... *REAPPEAR*--OR *RECONSTITUTE* OR WHATEVER--WITH THE OTHERS AND TELL THEM I'M *FINE*. I'M SURE THEY'RE *WORRIED* ABOUT ME.

BUT WHEN THEY *SEE* ME, THEY WON'T BE WORRIED ANYMORE.

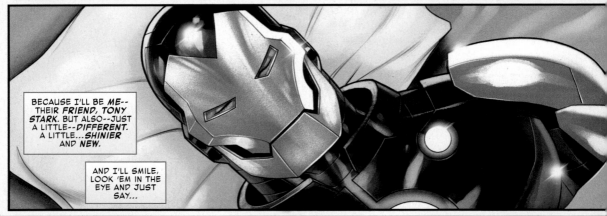

BECAUSE I'LL BE *ME*-- THEIR *FRIEND*, TONY *STARK*. BUT ALSO--JUST A LITTLE--*DIFFERENT*. A LITTLE...*SHINIER* AND *NEW*.

AND I'LL SMILE, LOOK 'EM IN THE EYE AND JUST SAY...

"...GOOD MORNING."

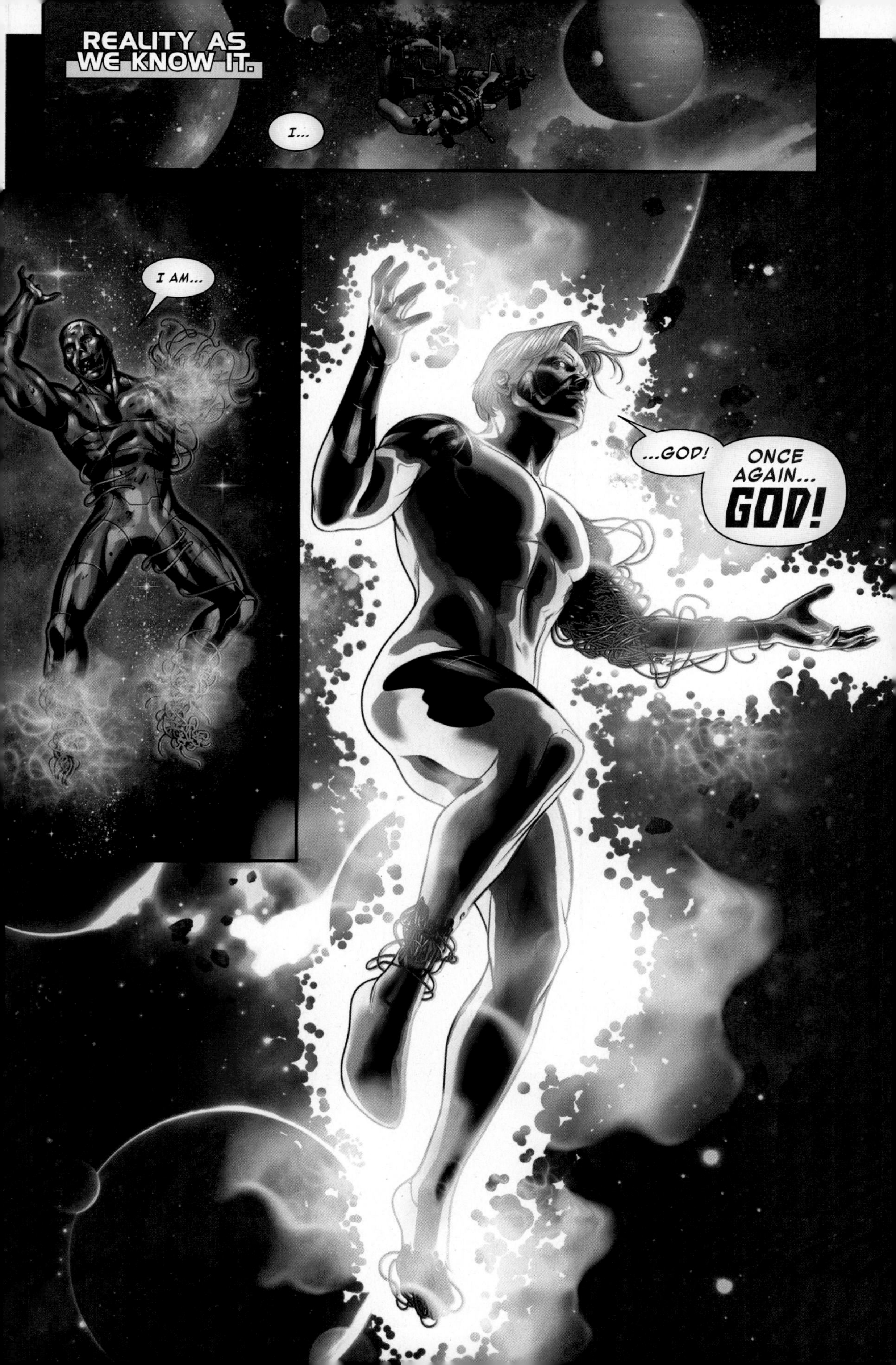
REALITY AS WE KNOW IT.
I...
I AM...
...GOD!
ONCE AGAIN... GOD!

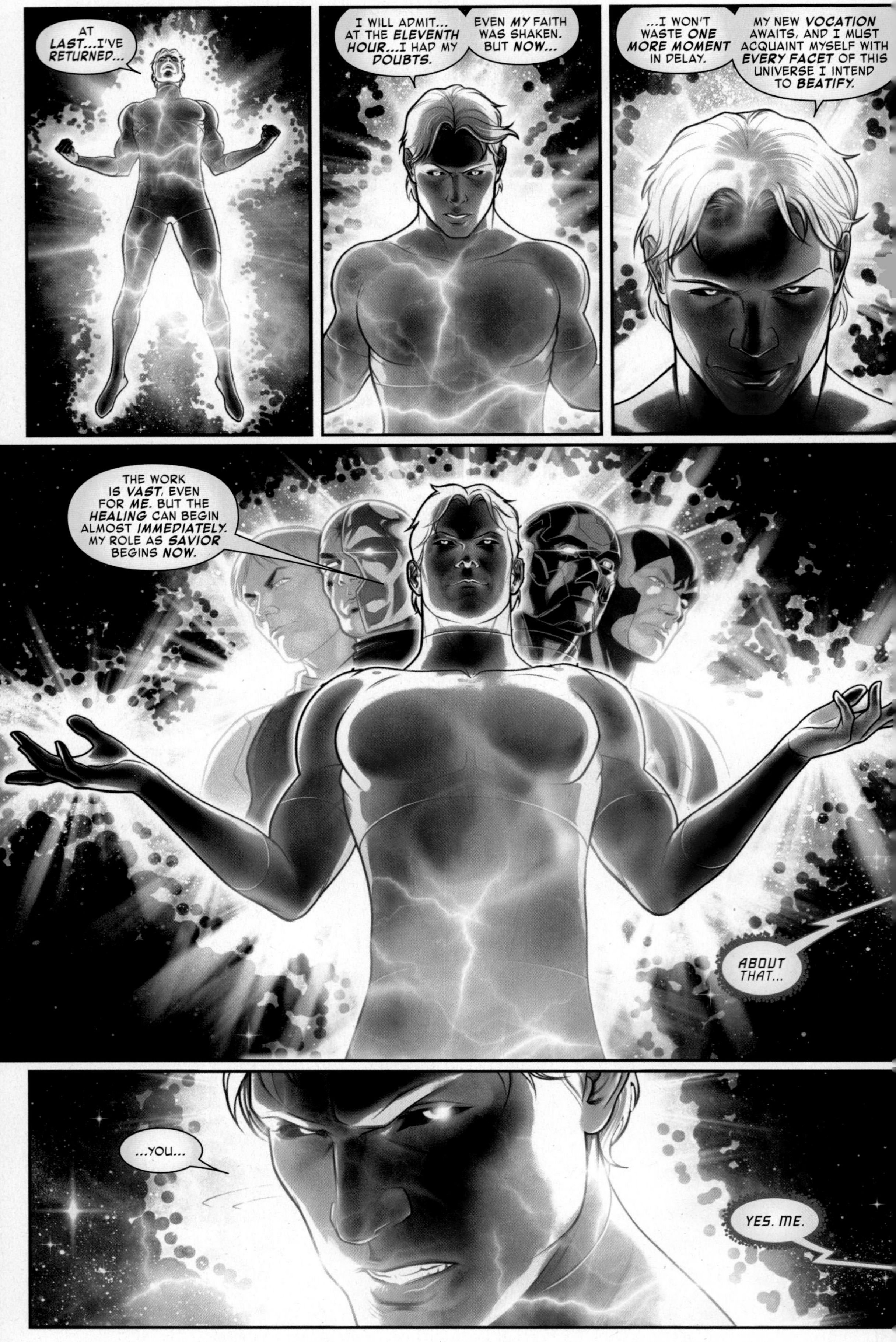
AT LAST...I'VE RETURNED...
I WILL ADMIT... AT THE ELEVENTH HOUR...I HAD MY DOUBTS.
EVEN MY FAITH WAS SHAKEN. BUT NOW...
...I WON'T WASTE ONE MORE MOMENT IN DELAY.
MY NEW VOCATION AWAITS, AND I MUST ACQUAINT MYSELF WITH EVERY FACET OF THIS UNIVERSE I INTEND TO BEATIFY.
THE WORK IS VAST, EVEN FOR ME. BUT THE HEALING CAN BEGIN ALMOST IMMEDIATELY. MY ROLE AS SAVIOR BEGINS NOW.
ABOUT THAT...
...YOU...
YES. ME.

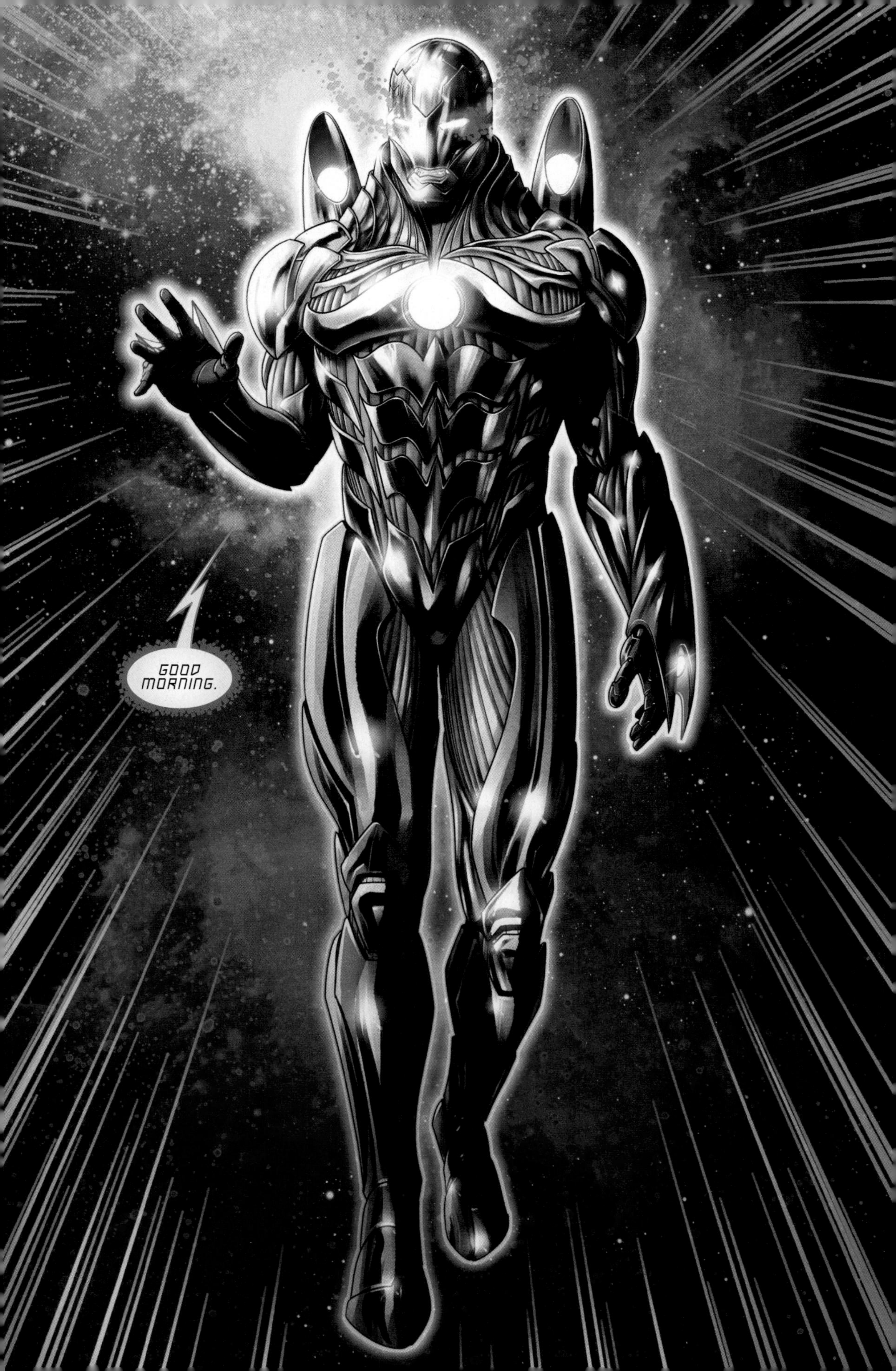
GOOD MORNING.

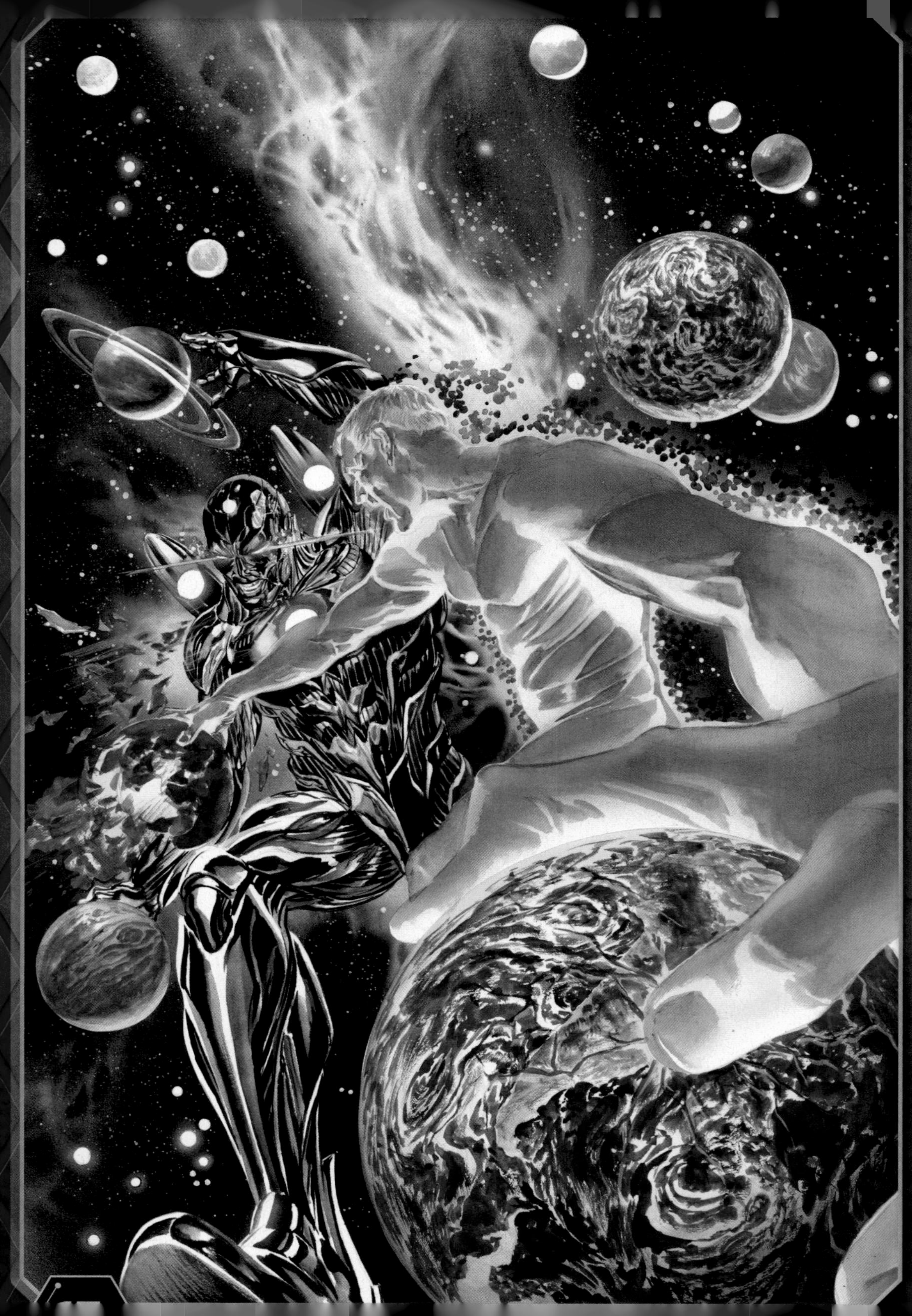

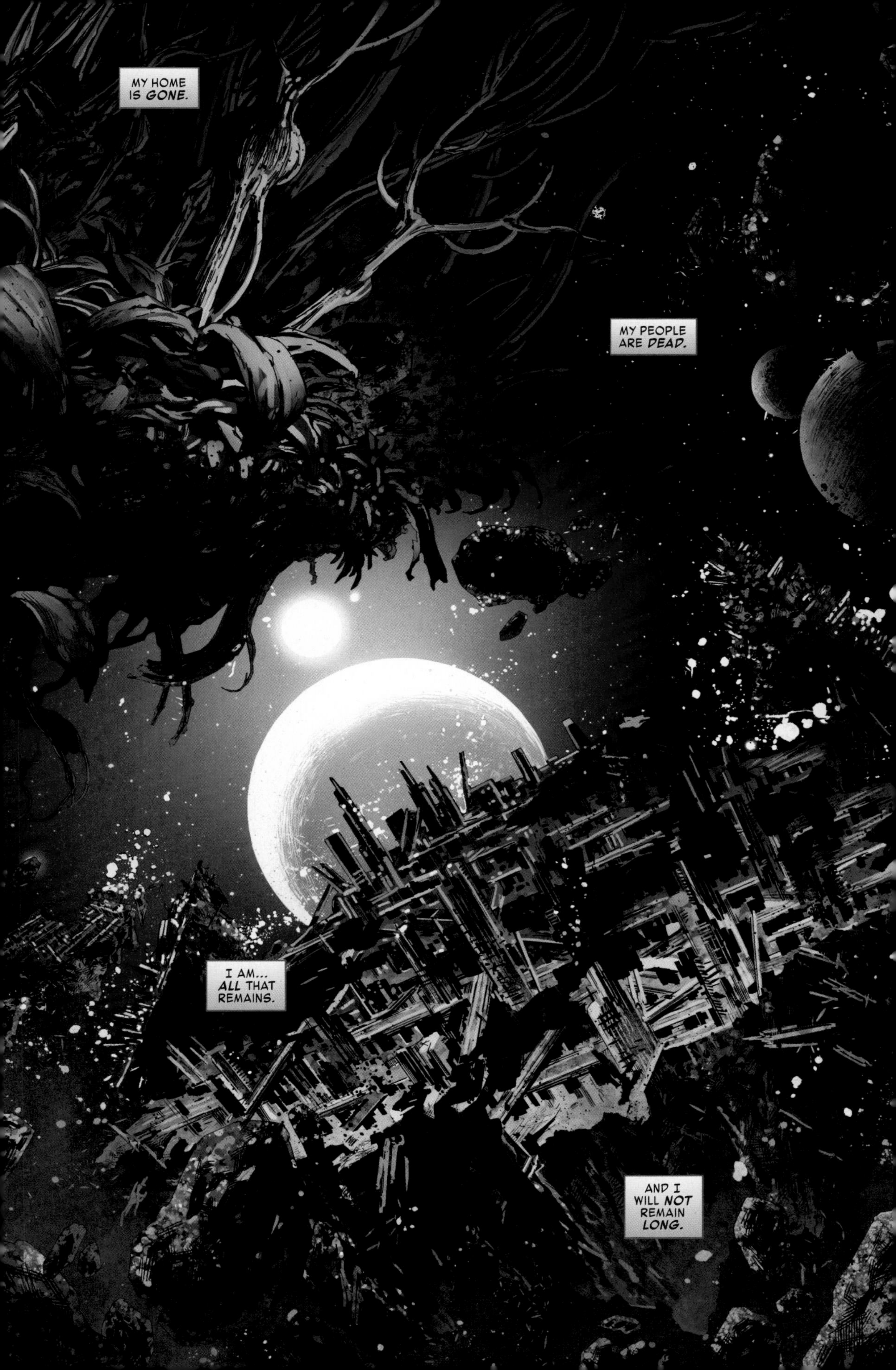
MY HOME IS GONE.
MY PEOPLE ARE DEAD.
I AM... ALL THAT REMAINS.
AND I WILL NOT REMAIN LONG.

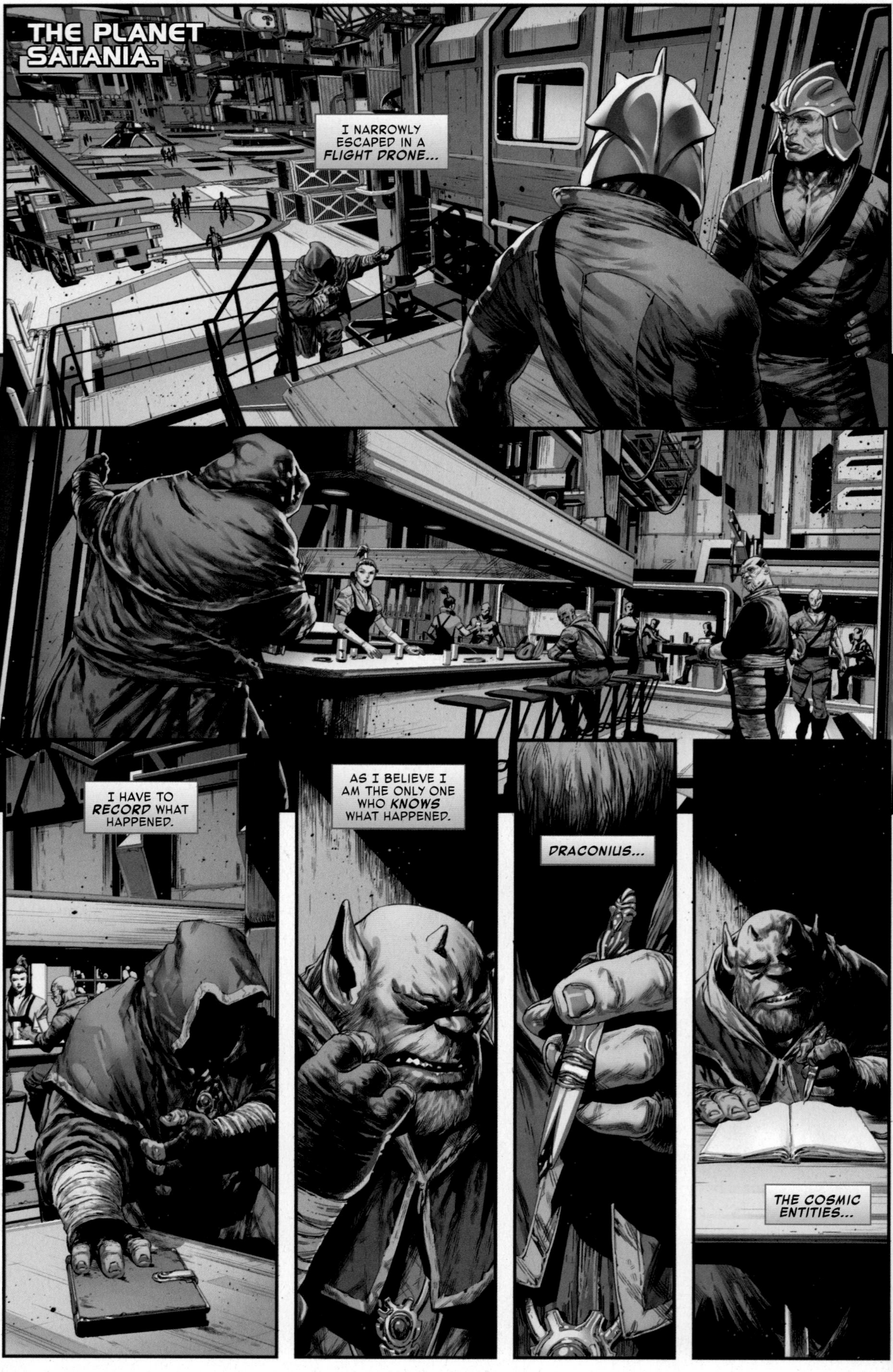
THE PLANET SATANIA.
I NARROWLY ESCAPED IN A FLIGHT DRONE...
I HAVE TO RECORD WHAT HAPPENED.
AS I BELIEVE I AM THE ONLY ONE WHO KNOWS WHAT HAPPENED.
DRACONIUS...
THE COSMIC ENTITIES...

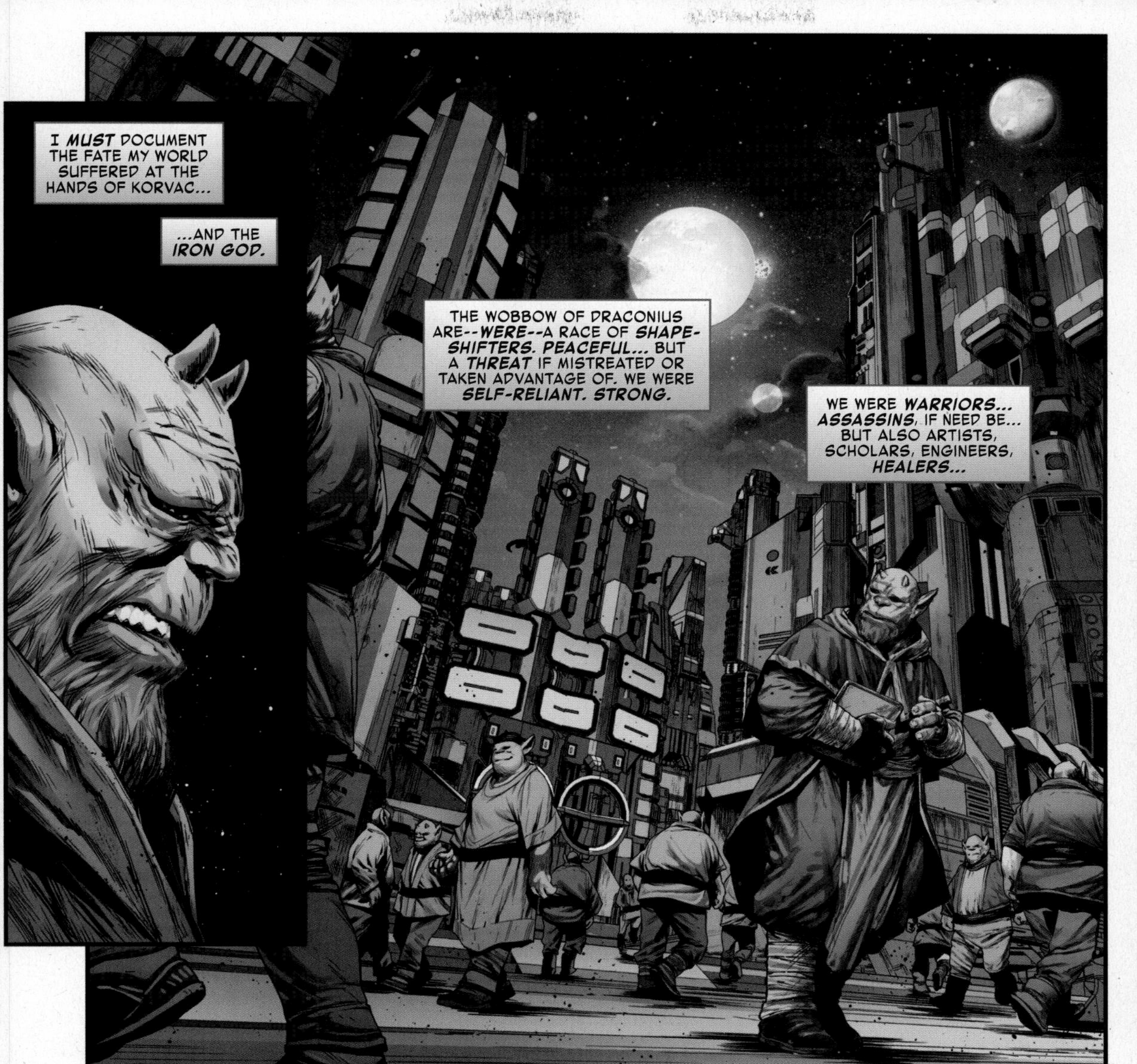
I MUST DOCUMENT THE FATE MY WORLD SUFFERED AT THE HANDS OF KORVAC...
...AND THE IRON GOD.
THE WOBBOW OF DRACONIUS ARE--WERE--A RACE OF SHAPE-SHIFTERS. PEACEFUL... BUT A THREAT IF MISTREATED OR TAKEN ADVANTAGE OF. WE WERE SELF-RELIANT. STRONG.
WE WERE WARRIORS... ASSASSINS, IF NEED BE... BUT ALSO ARTISTS, SCHOLARS, ENGINEERS, HEALERS...

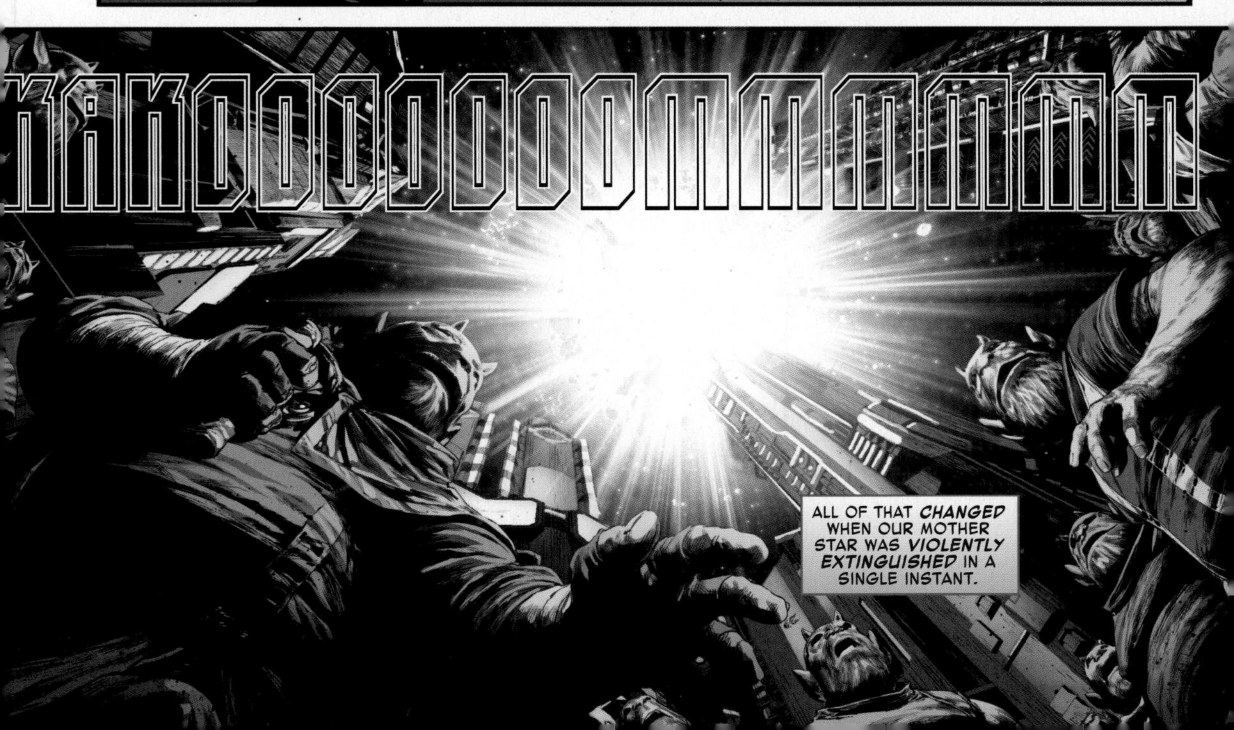
KAKOOOOOOOMMMMMM
ALL OF THAT CHANGED WHEN OUR MOTHER STAR WAS VIOLENTLY EXTINGUISHED IN A SINGLE INSTANT.

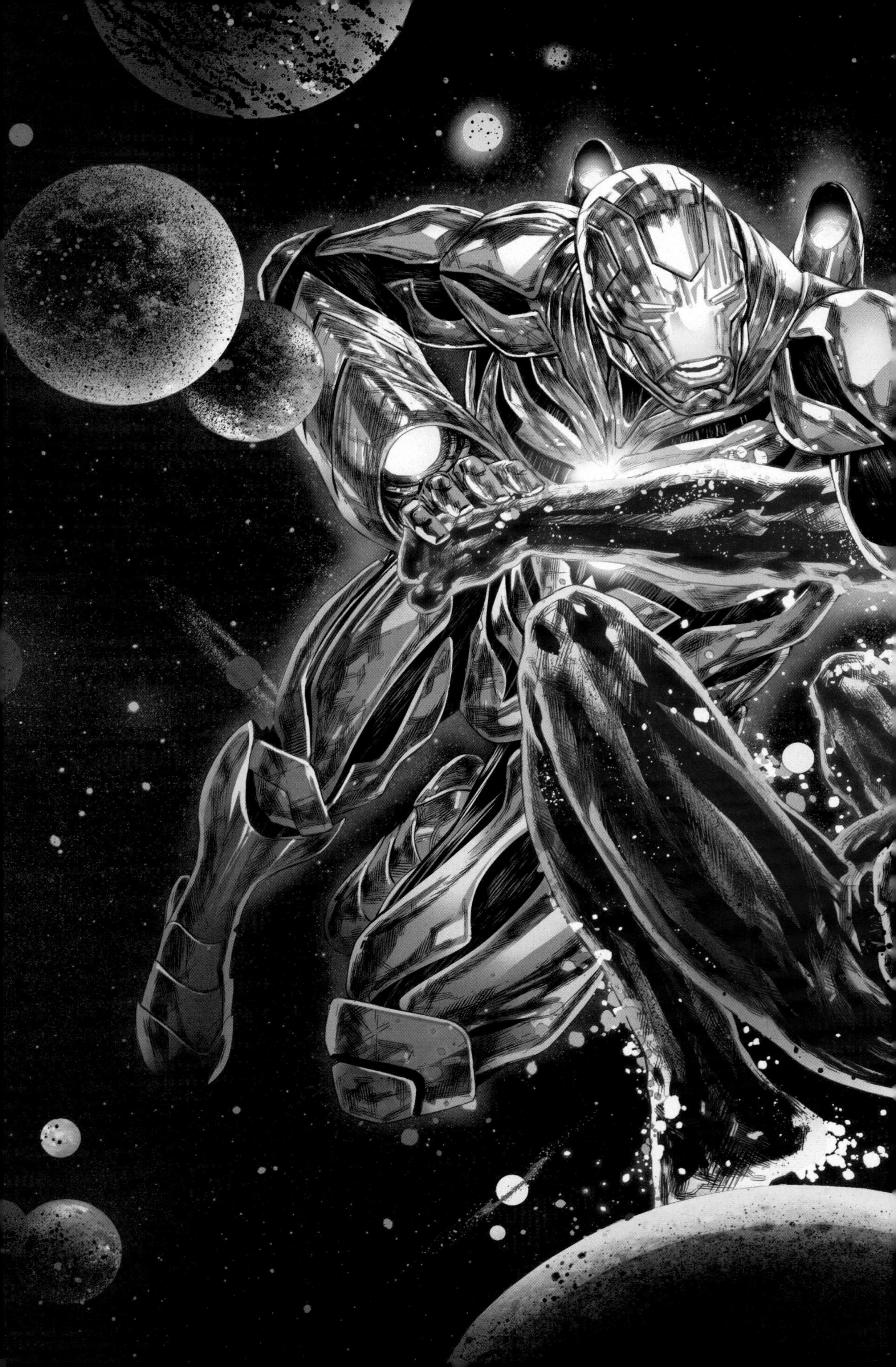

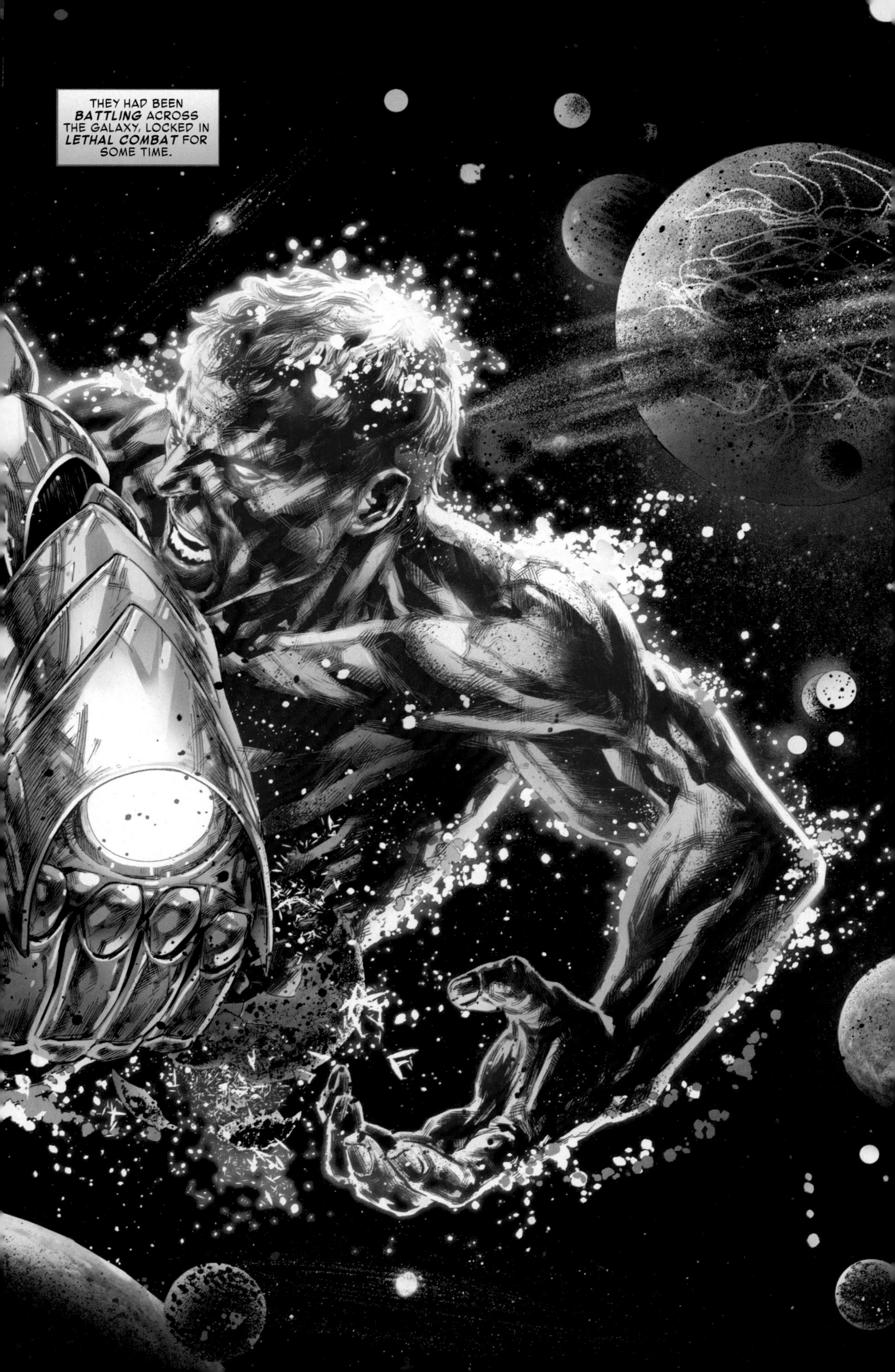
THEY HAD BEEN BATTLING ACROSS THE GALAXY, LOCKED IN LETHAL COMBAT FOR SOME TIME.

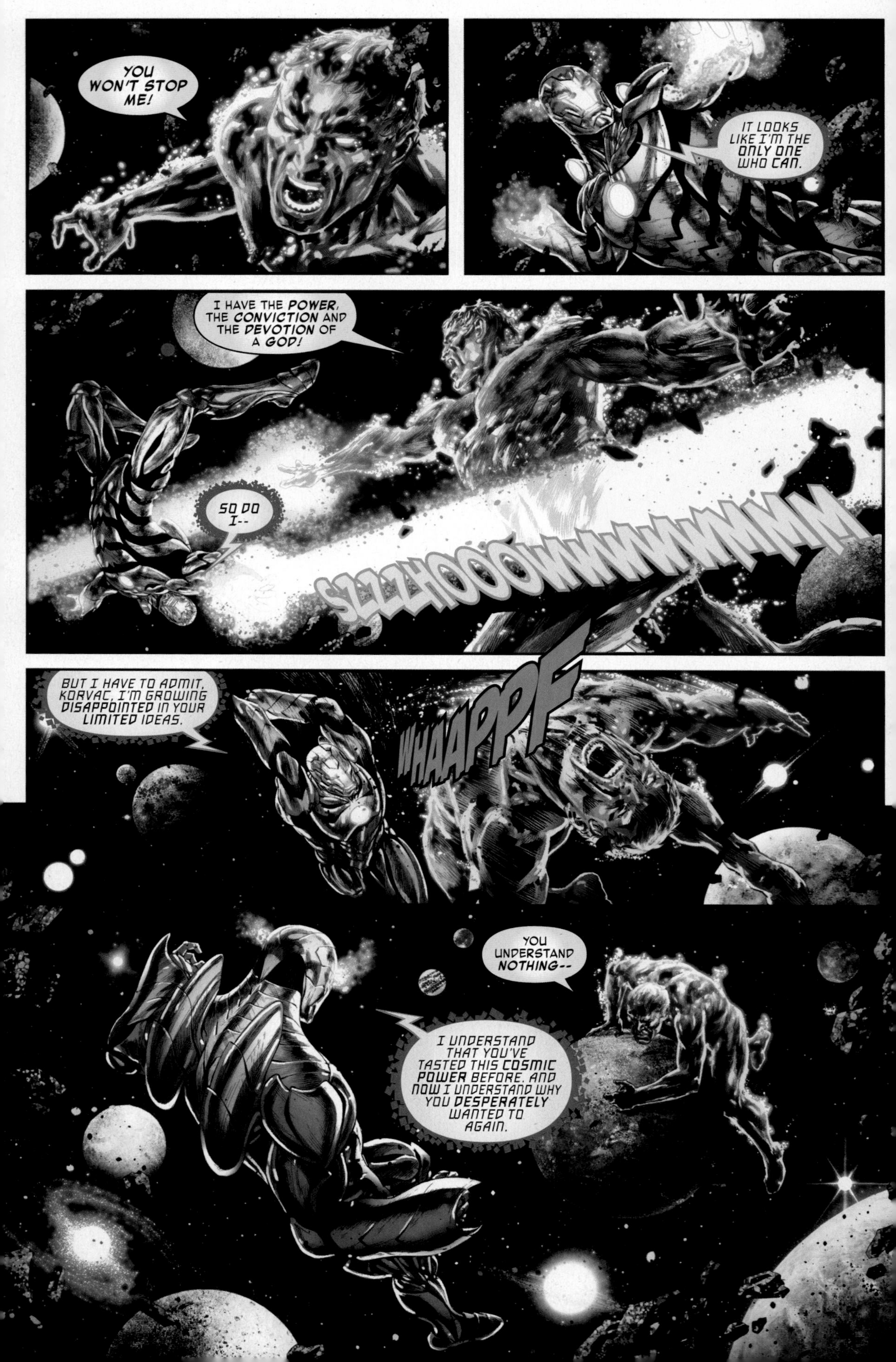
YOU WON'T STOP ME!
IT LOOKS LIKE I'M THE ONLY ONE WHO CAN.
I HAVE THE POWER, THE CONVICTION AND THE DEVOTION OF A GOD!
SO DO I--
SZZZHOOOWWWWVMMM
BUT I HAVE TO ADMIT, KORVAC, I'M GROWING DISAPPOINTED IN YOUR LIMITED IDEAS.
WHAAPPF
YOU UNDERSTAND NOTHING--
I UNDERSTAND THAT YOU'VE TASTED THIS COSMIC POWER BEFORE. AND NOW I UNDERSTAND WHY YOU DESPERATELY WANTED TO AGAIN.

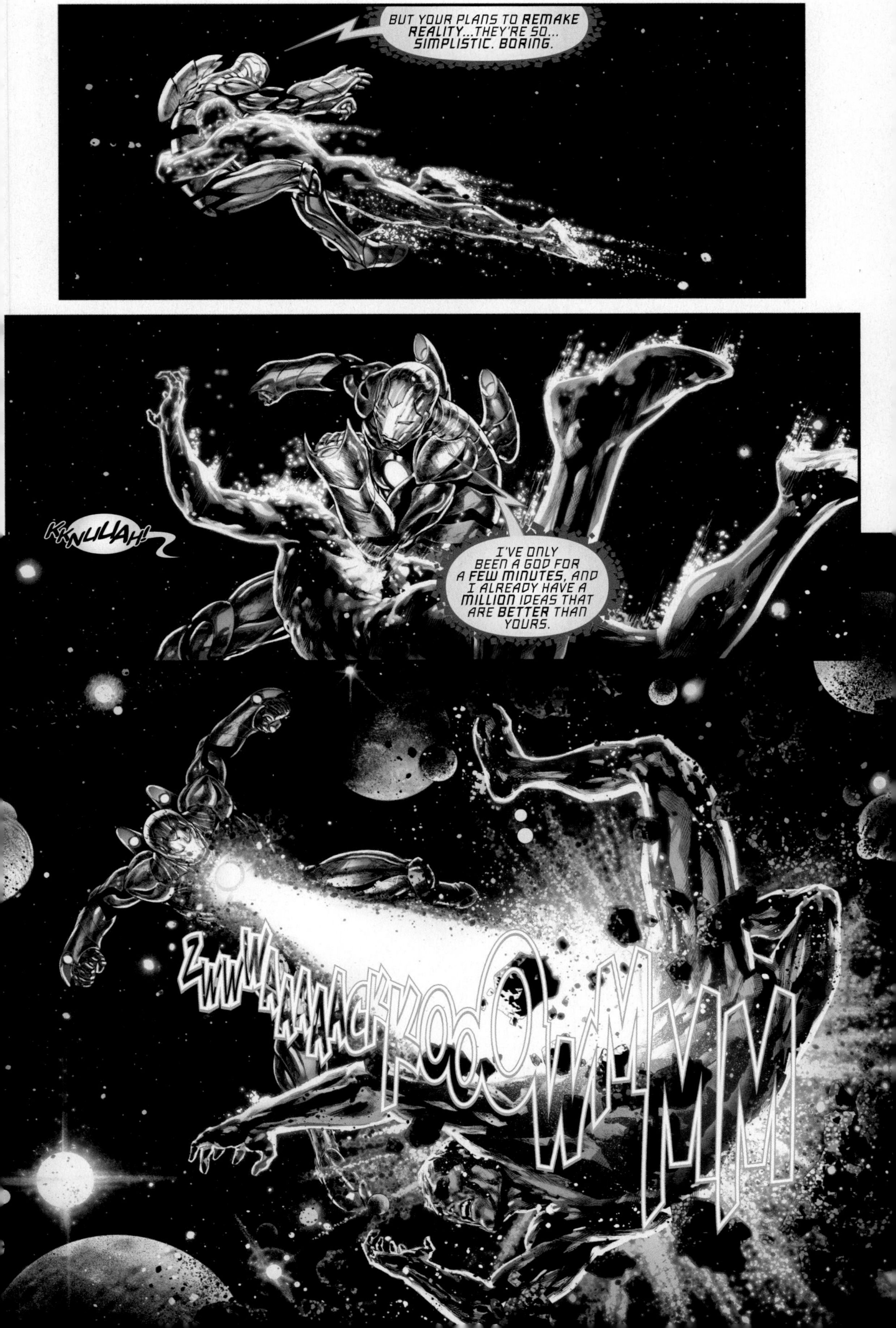
BUT YOUR PLANS TO REMAKE REALITY...THEY'RE SO... SIMPLISTIC. BORING.
KKNULLAH!
I'VE ONLY BEEN A GOD FOR A FEW MINUTES, AND I ALREADY HAVE A MILLION IDEAS THAT ARE BETTER THAN YOURS.
ZWWHAAAACKKOOOOWMMM

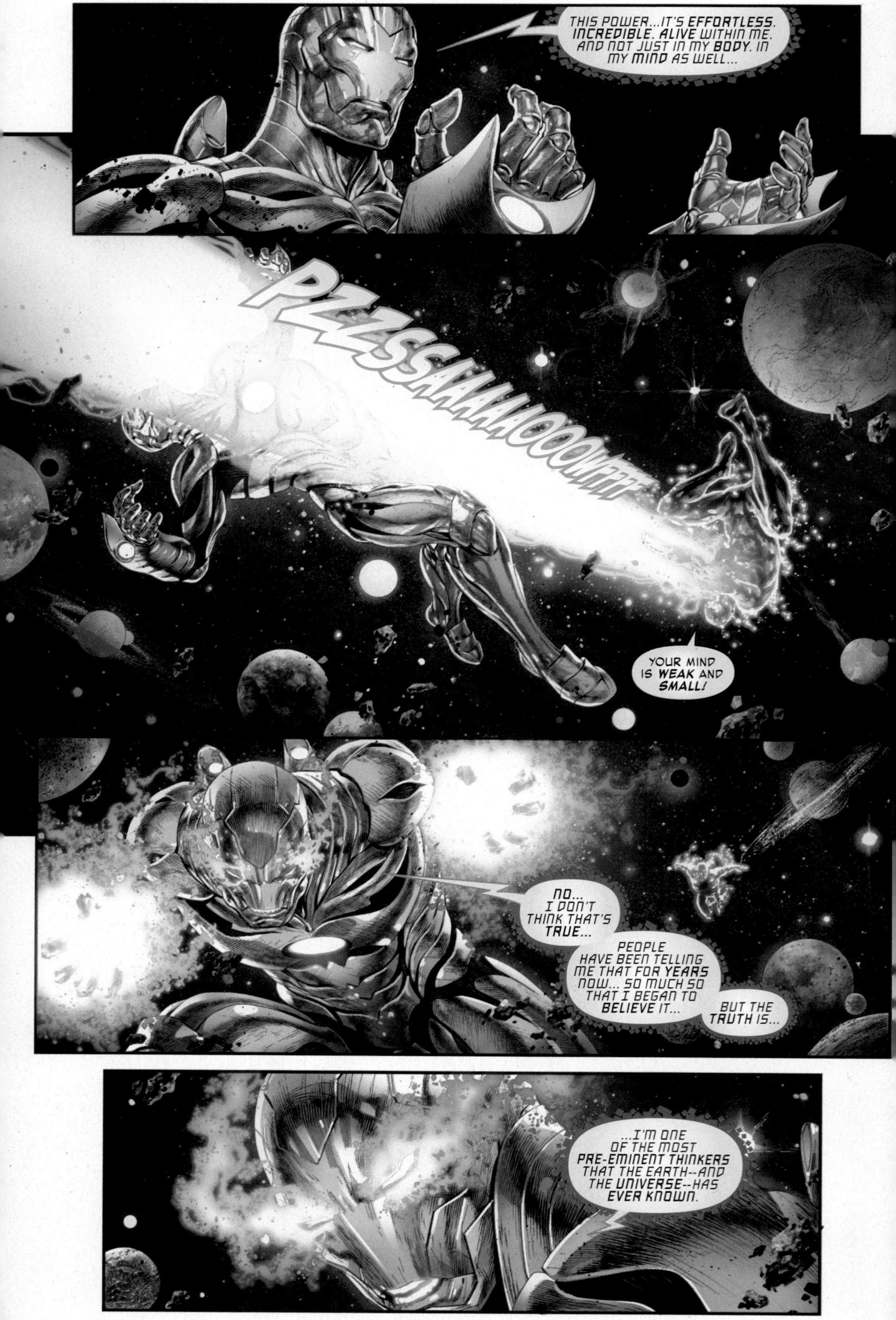
THIS POWER...IT'S EFFORTLESS. INCREDIBLE. ALIVE WITHIN ME. AND NOT JUST IN MY BODY. IN MY MIND AS WELL...
PZZSHHHOOOMMMM
YOUR MIND IS WEAK AND SMALL!
NO... I DON'T THINK THAT'S TRUE...
PEOPLE HAVE BEEN TELLING ME THAT FOR YEARS NOW... SO MUCH SO THAT I BEGAN TO BELIEVE IT...
BUT THE TRUTH IS...
...I'M ONE OF THE MOST PRE-EMINENT THINKERS THAT THE EARTH--AND THE UNIVERSE--HAS EVER KNOWN.

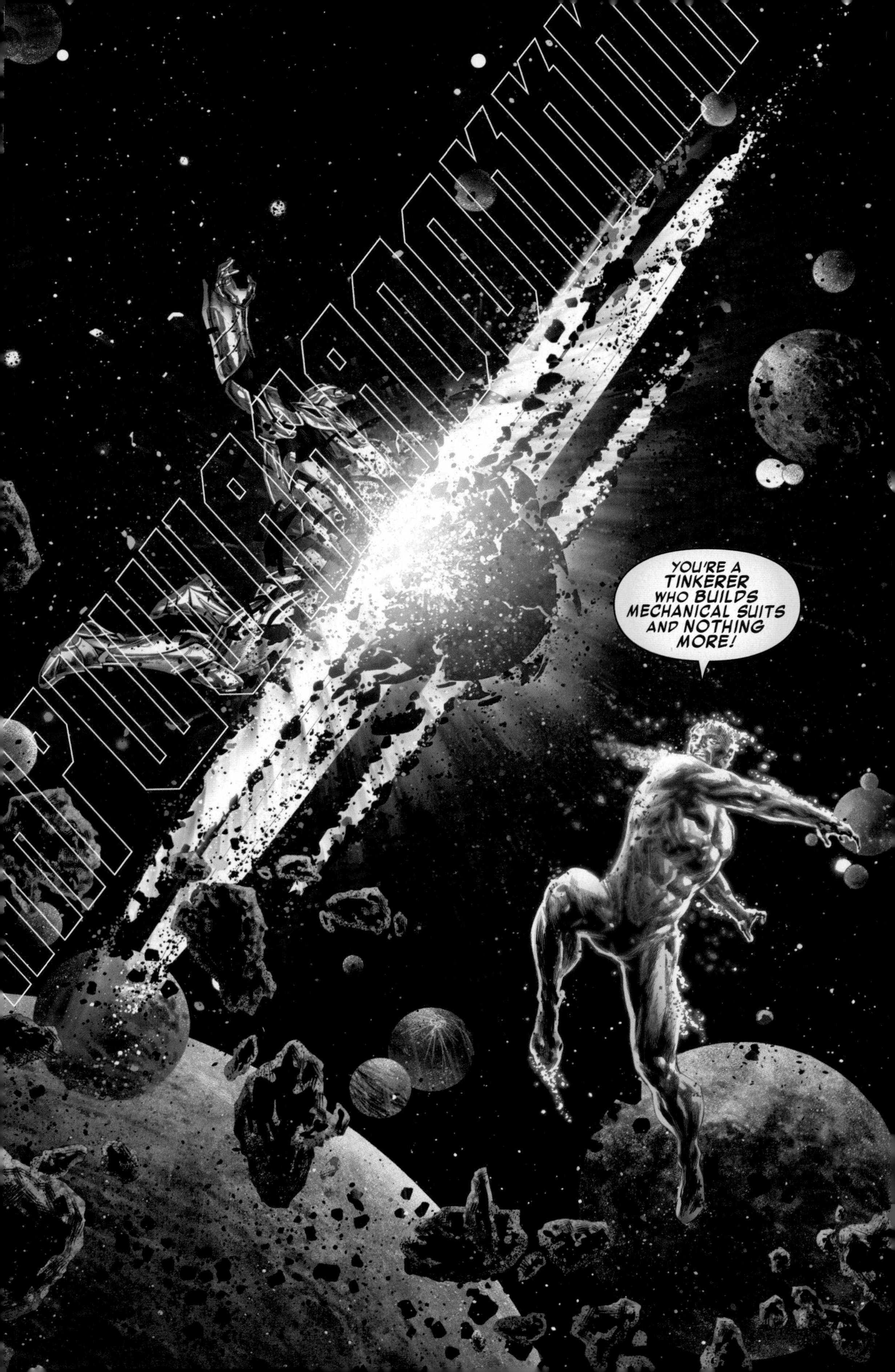
YOU'RE A TINKERER WHO BUILDS MECHANICAL SUITS AND NOTHING MORE!

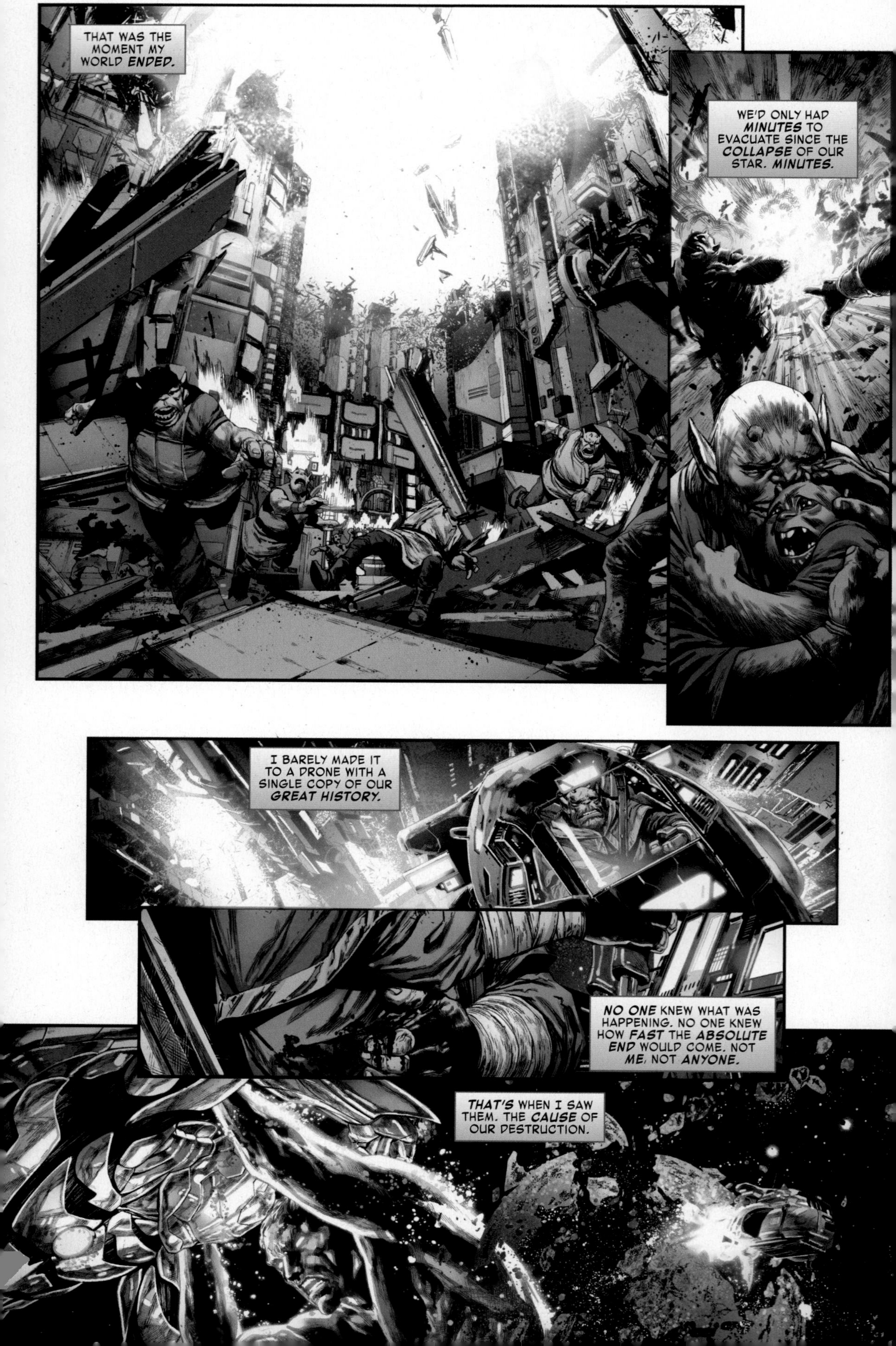
THAT WAS THE MOMENT MY WORLD ENDED.
WE'D ONLY HAD MINUTES TO EVACUATE SINCE THE COLLAPSE OF OUR STAR. MINUTES.
I BARELY MADE IT TO A DRONE WITH A SINGLE COPY OF OUR GREAT HISTORY.
NO ONE KNEW WHAT WAS HAPPENING. NO ONE KNEW HOW FAST THE ABSOLUTE END WOULD COME. NOT ME, NOT ANYONE.
THAT'S WHEN I SAW THEM. THE CAUSE OF OUR DESTRUCTION.

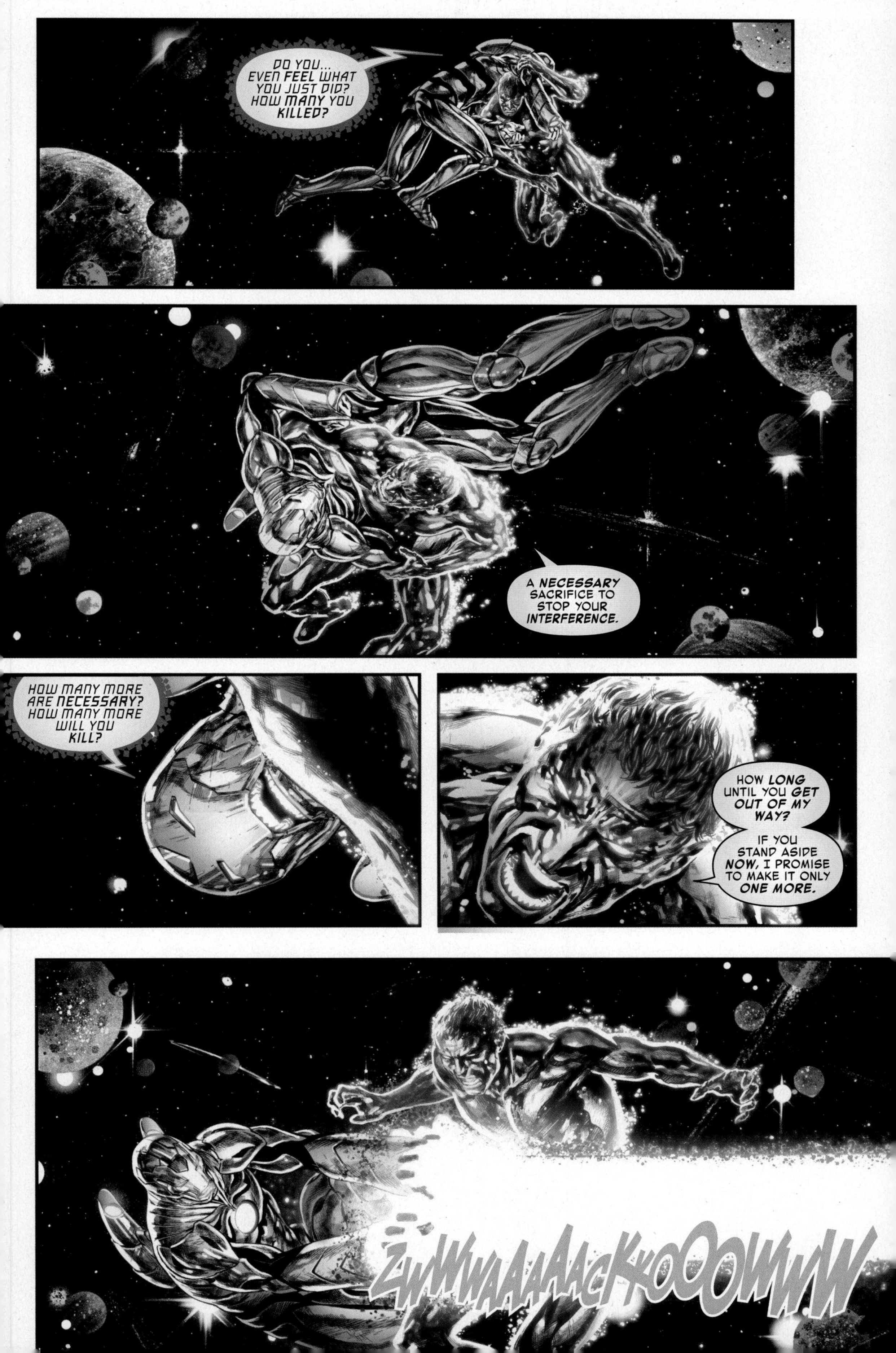
DO YOU... EVEN FEEL WHAT YOU JUST DID? HOW MANY YOU KILLED?
A NECESSARY SACRIFICE TO STOP YOUR INTERFERENCE.
HOW MANY MORE ARE NECESSARY? HOW MANY MORE WILL YOU KILL?
HOW LONG UNTIL YOU GET OUT OF MY WAY?
IF YOU STAND ASIDE NOW, I PROMISE TO MAKE IT ONLY ONE MORE.
ZWWWAAAAACKKOOOWWW

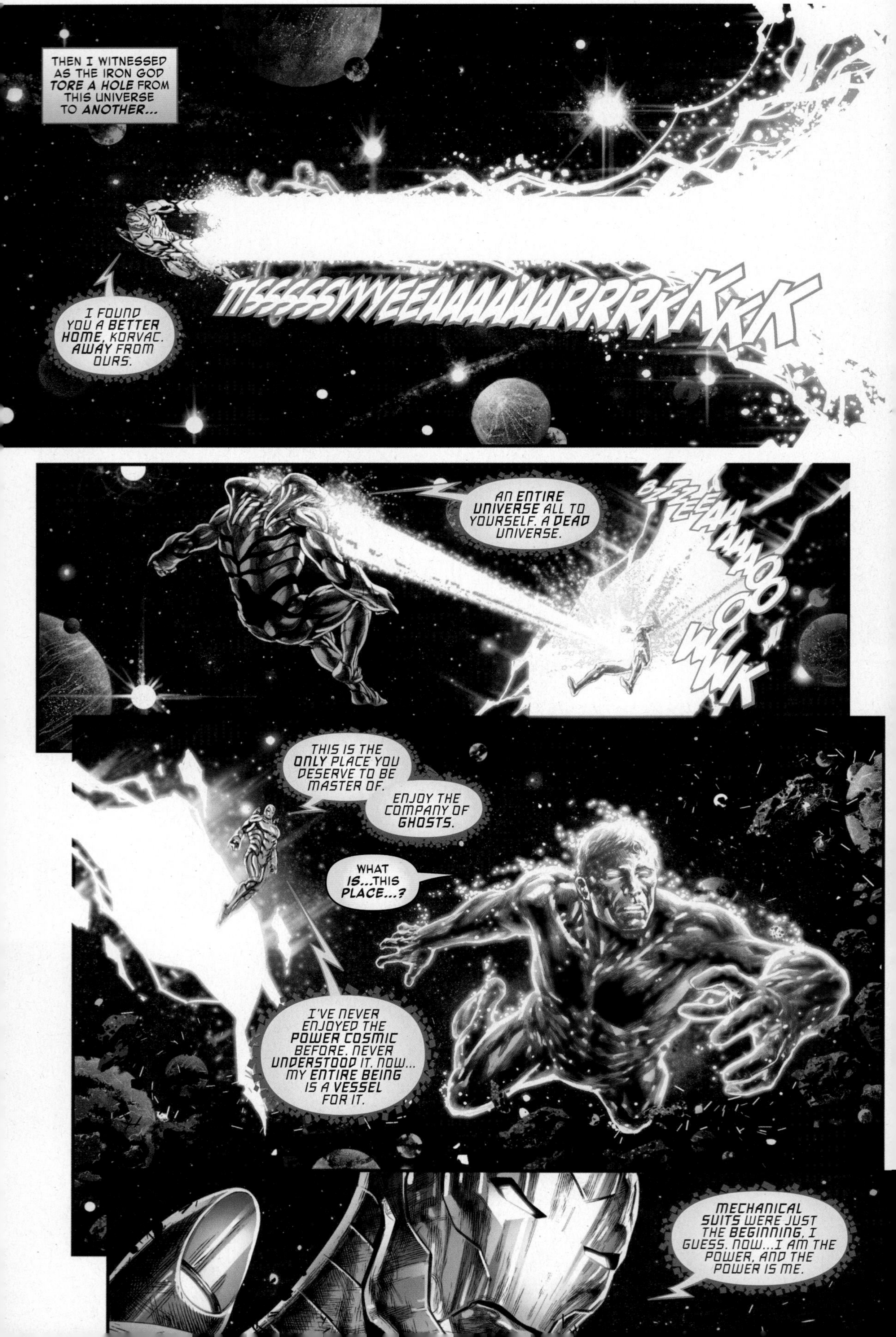

THEN I WITNESSED AS THE IRON GOD TORE A HOLE FROM THIS UNIVERSE TO ANOTHER...
I FOUND YOU A BETTER HOME, KORVAC. AWAY FROM OURS.
TTSSSSSYYYEEAAAAAAARRRRKKKK
AN ENTIRE UNIVERSE ALL TO YOURSELF. A DEAD UNIVERSE.
THIS IS THE ONLY PLACE YOU DESERVE TO BE MASTER OF.
ENJOY THE COMPANY OF GHOSTS.
WHAT IS...THIS PLACE...?
I'VE NEVER ENJOYED THE POWER COSMIC BEFORE. NEVER UNDERSTOOD IT. NOW... MY ENTIRE BEING IS A VESSEL FOR IT.
MECHANICAL SUITS WERE JUST THE BEGINNING, I GUESS. NOW...I AM THE POWER, AND THE POWER IS ME.

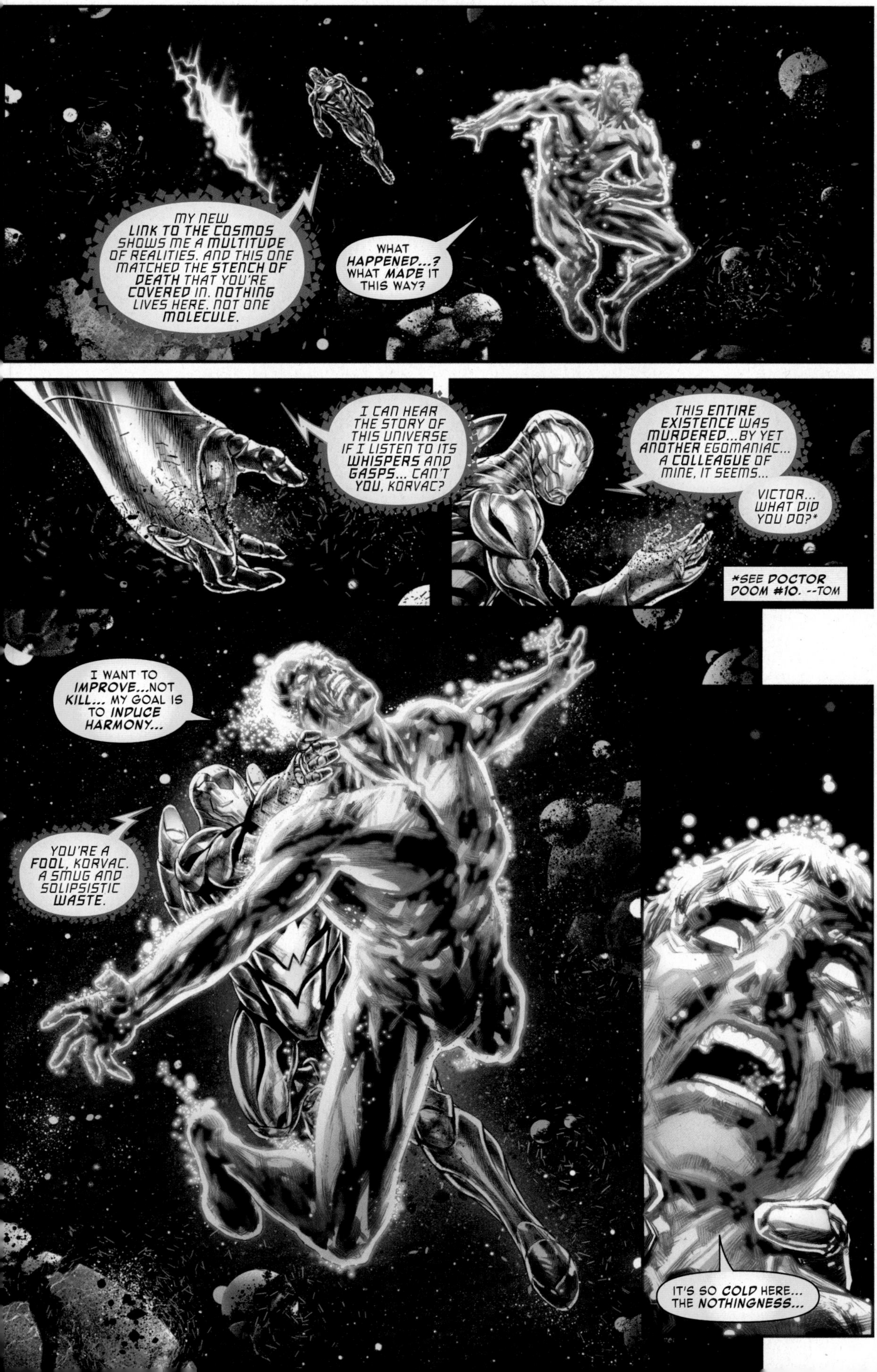
MY NEW LINK TO THE COSMOS SHOWS ME A MULTITUDE OF REALITIES. AND THIS ONE MATCHED THE STENCH OF DEATH THAT YOU'RE COVERED IN. NOTHING LIVES HERE. NOT ONE MOLECULE.
WHAT HAPPENED...? WHAT MADE IT THIS WAY?
I CAN HEAR THE STORY OF THIS UNIVERSE IF I LISTEN TO ITS WHISPERS AND GASPS... CAN'T YOU, KORVAC?
THIS ENTIRE EXISTENCE WAS MURDERED...BY YET ANOTHER EGOMANIAC... A COLLEAGUE OF MINE, IT SEEMS...
VICTOR... WHAT DID YOU DO?*
*SEE DOCTOR DOOM #10. --TOM
I WANT TO IMPROVE...NOT KILL... MY GOAL IS TO INDUCE HARMONY...
YOU'RE A FOOL, KORVAC. A SMUG AND SOLIPSISTIC WASTE.
IT'S SO COLD HERE... THE NOTHINGNESS...

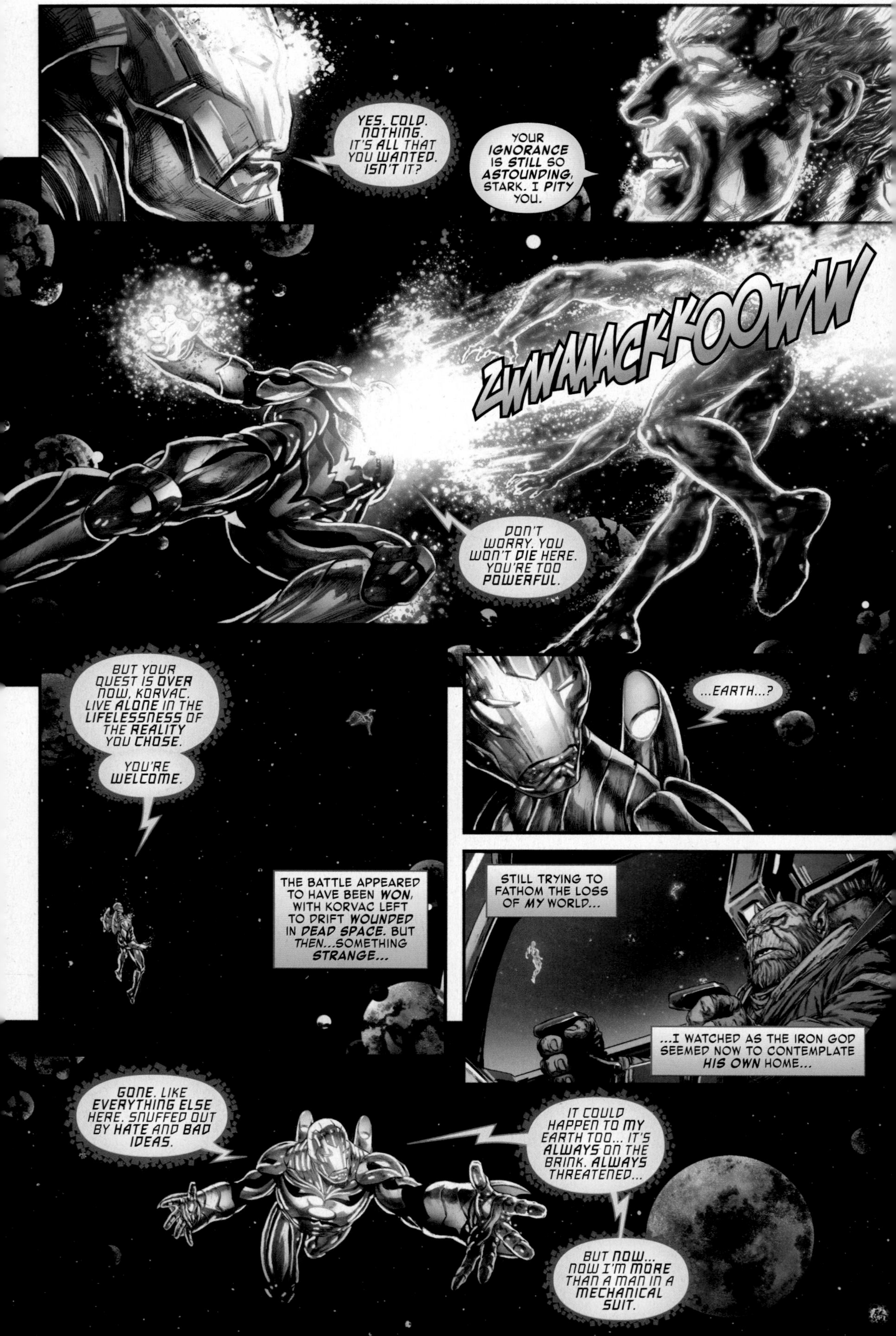
YES. COLD. NOTHING. IT'S ALL THAT YOU WANTED. ISN'T IT?
YOUR IGNORANCE IS STILL SO ASTOUNDING, STARK. I PITY YOU.
ZWAAACKKOOWW
DON'T WORRY. YOU WON'T DIE HERE. YOU'RE TOO POWERFUL.
BUT YOUR QUEST IS OVER NOW, KORVAC. LIVE ALONE IN THE LIFELESSNESS OF THE REALITY YOU CHOSE.
YOU'RE WELCOME.
...EARTH...?
THE BATTLE APPEARED TO HAVE BEEN WON, WITH KORVAC LEFT TO DRIFT WOUNDED IN DEAD SPACE. BUT THEN...SOMETHING STRANGE...
STILL TRYING TO FATHOM THE LOSS OF MY WORLD...
...I WATCHED AS THE IRON GOD SEEMED NOW TO CONTEMPLATE HIS OWN HOME...
GONE. LIKE EVERYTHING ELSE HERE. SNUFFED OUT BY HATE AND BAD IDEAS.
IT COULD HAPPEN TO MY EARTH TOO... IT'S ALWAYS ON THE BRINK. ALWAYS THREATENED...
BUT NOW... NOW I'M MORE THAN A MAN IN A MECHANICAL SUIT.

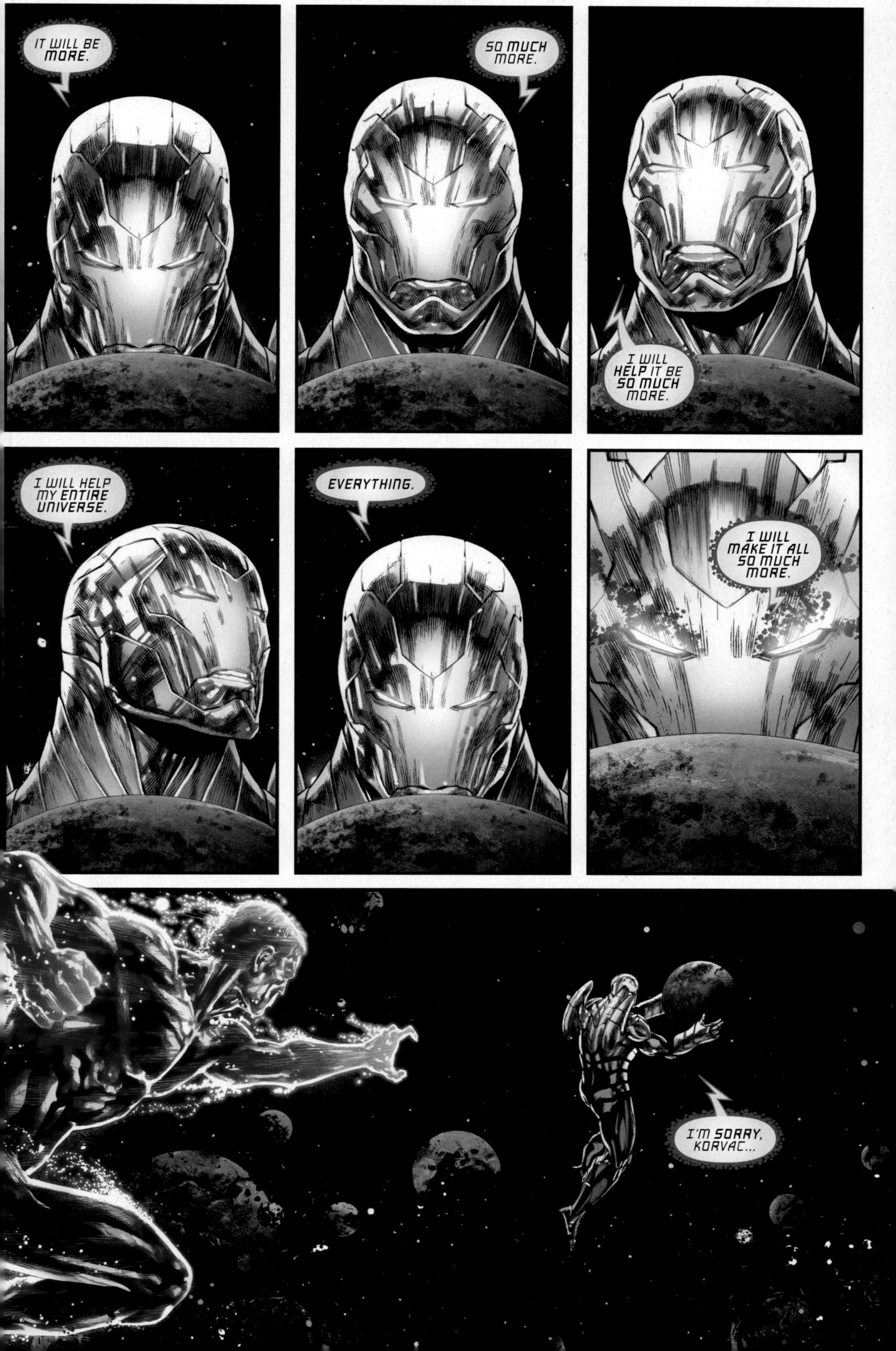
IT WILL BE MORE.
SO MUCH MORE.
I WILL HELP IT BE SO MUCH MORE.
I WILL HELP MY ENTIRE UNIVERSE.
EVERYTHING.
I WILL MAKE IT ALL SO MUCH MORE.
I'M SORRY, KORVAC...

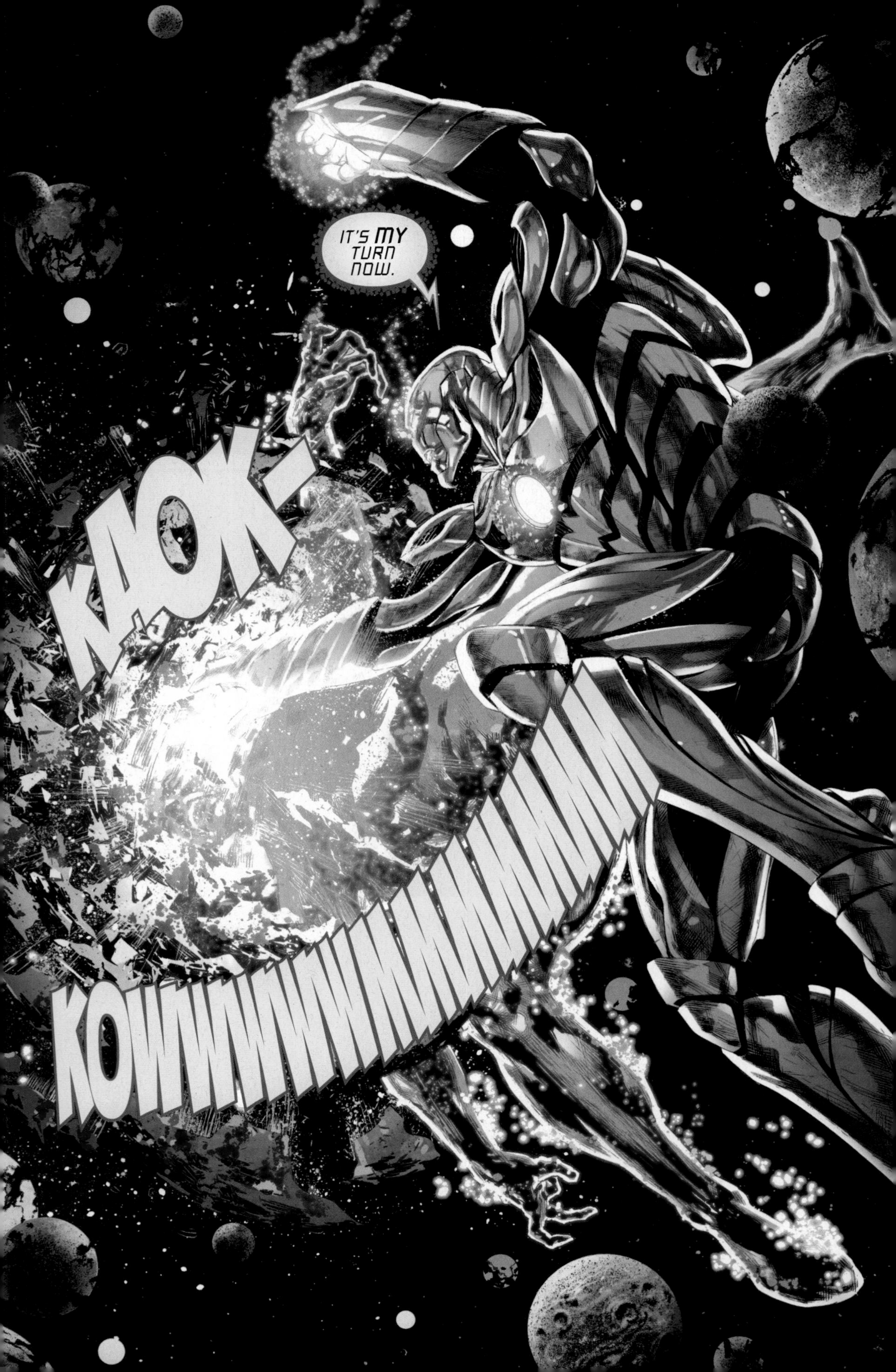

IT'S MY TURN NOW.
KAOK-
KOWWWWWWWWWWWWWWWWWWW

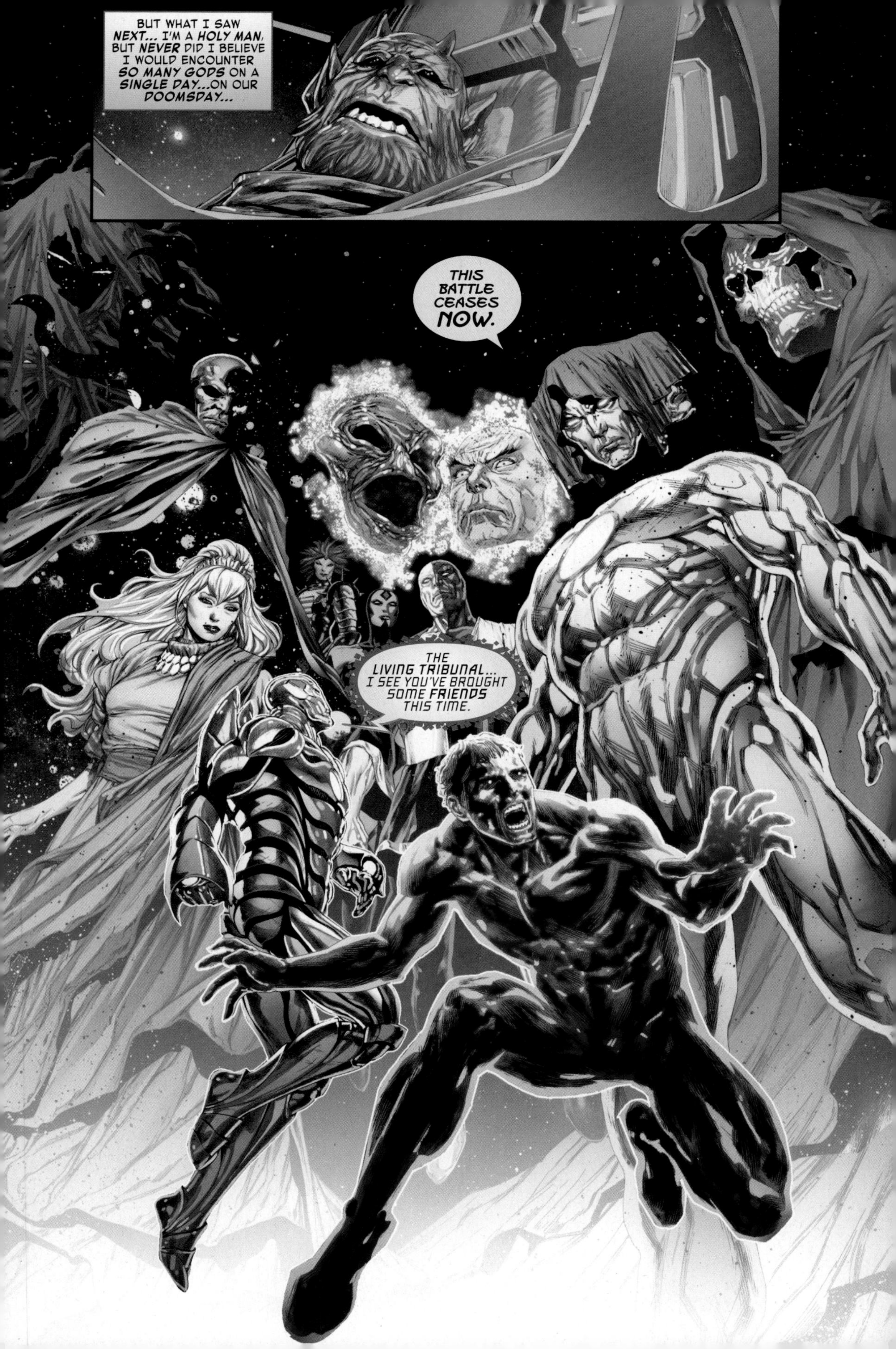
BUT WHAT I SAW NEXT... I'M A HOLY MAN, BUT NEVER DID I BELIEVE I WOULD ENCOUNTER SO MANY GODS ON A SINGLE DAY...ON OUR DOOMSDAY...
THIS BATTLE CEASES NOW.
THE LIVING TRIBUNAL... I SEE YOU'VE BROUGHT SOME FRIENDS THIS TIME.

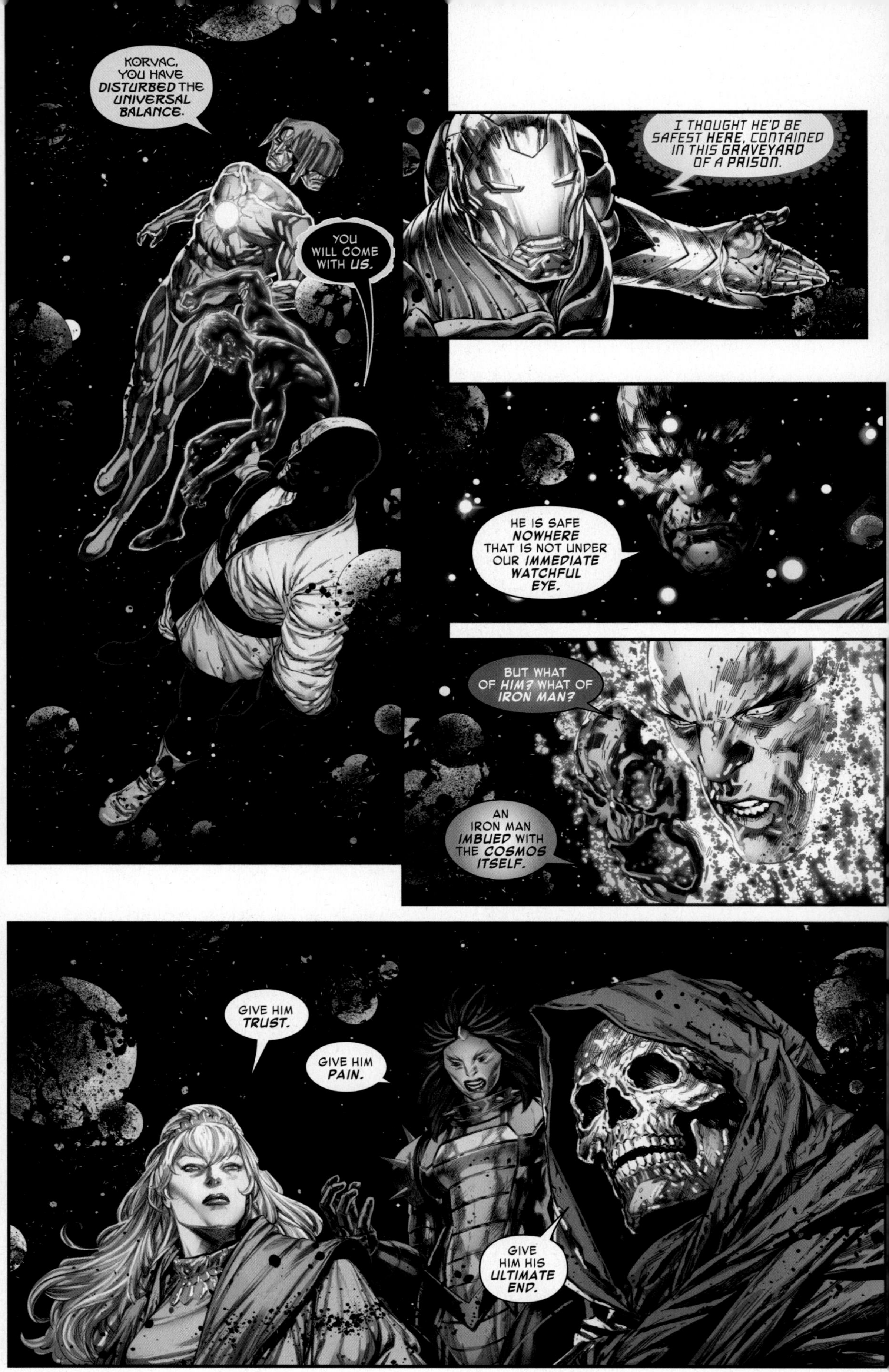
KORVAC, YOU HAVE DISTURBED THE UNIVERSAL BALANCE.
YOU WILL COME WITH US.
I THOUGHT HE'D BE SAFEST HERE, CONTAINED IN THIS GRAVEYARD OF A PRISON.
HE IS SAFE NOWHERE THAT IS NOT UNDER OUR IMMEDIATE WATCHFUL EYE.
BUT WHAT OF HIM? WHAT OF IRON MAN?
AN IRON MAN IMBUED WITH THE COSMOS ITSELF.
GIVE HIM TRUST.
GIVE HIM PAIN.
GIVE HIM HIS ULTIMATE END.

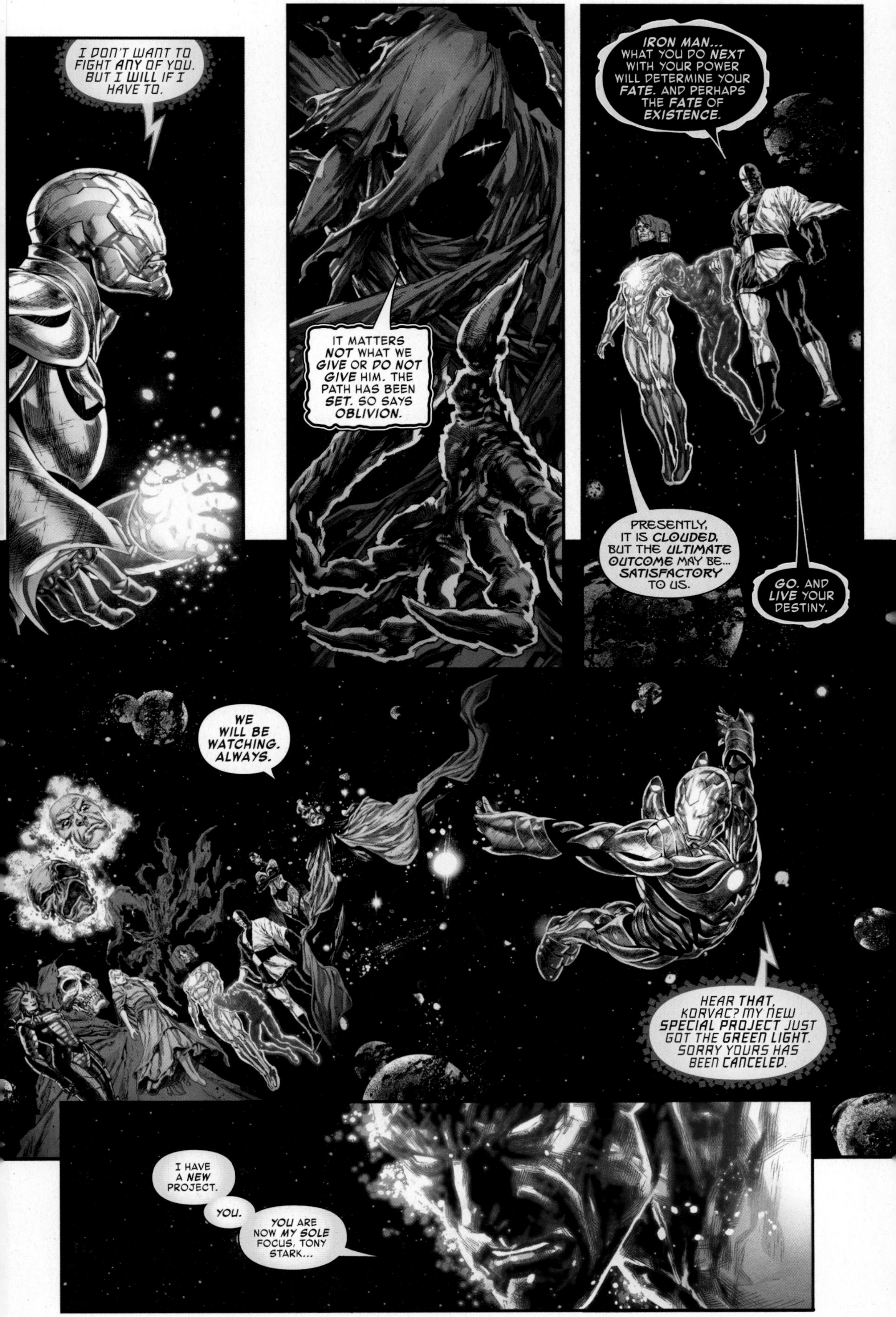

I DON'T WANT TO FIGHT ANY OF YOU. BUT I WILL IF I HAVE TO.
IT MATTERS NOT WHAT WE GIVE OR DO NOT GIVE HIM. THE PATH HAS BEEN SET. SO SAYS OBLIVION.
IRON MAN... WHAT YOU DO NEXT WITH YOUR POWER WILL DETERMINE YOUR FATE. AND PERHAPS THE FATE OF EXISTENCE.
PRESENTLY, IT IS CLOUDED, BUT THE ULTIMATE OUTCOME MAY BE... SATISFACTORY TO US.
GO. AND LIVE YOUR DESTINY.
WE WILL BE WATCHING. ALWAYS.
HEAR THAT, KORVAC? MY NEW SPECIAL PROJECT JUST GOT THE GREEN LIGHT. SORRY YOURS HAS BEEN CANCELED.
I HAVE A NEW PROJECT.
YOU.
YOU ARE NOW MY SOLE FOCUS, TONY STARK...

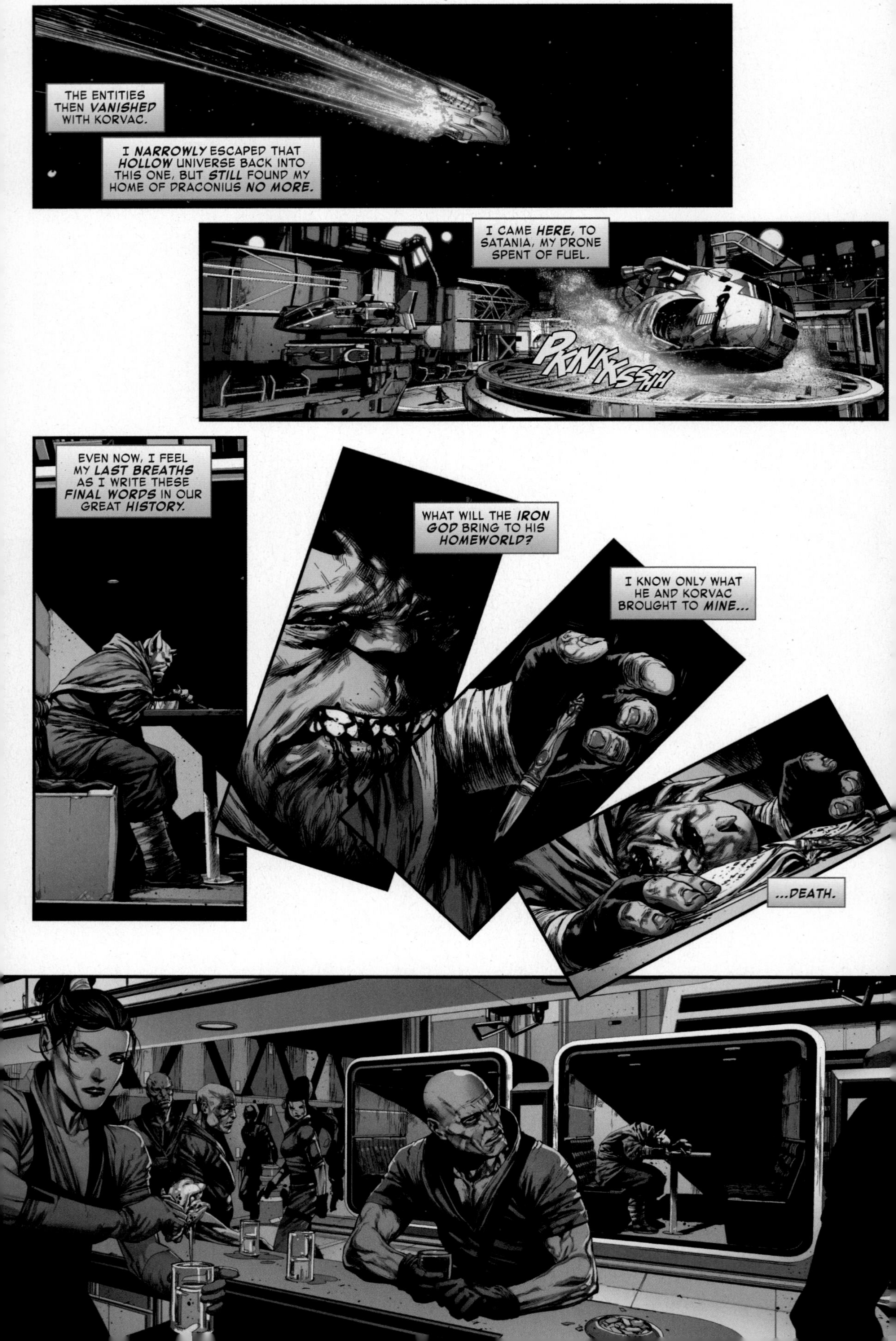
THE ENTITIES THEN VANISHED WITH KORVAC.
I NARROWLY ESCAPED THAT HOLLOW UNIVERSE BACK INTO THIS ONE, BUT STILL FOUND MY HOME OF DRACONIUS NO MORE.
I CAME HERE, TO SATANIA, MY DRONE SPENT OF FUEL.
PKNKKSSHH
EVEN NOW, I FEEL MY LAST BREATHS AS I WRITE THESE FINAL WORDS IN OUR GREAT HISTORY.
WHAT WILL THE IRON GOD BRING TO HIS HOMEWORLD?
I KNOW ONLY WHAT HE AND KORVAC BROUGHT TO MINE...
...DEATH.

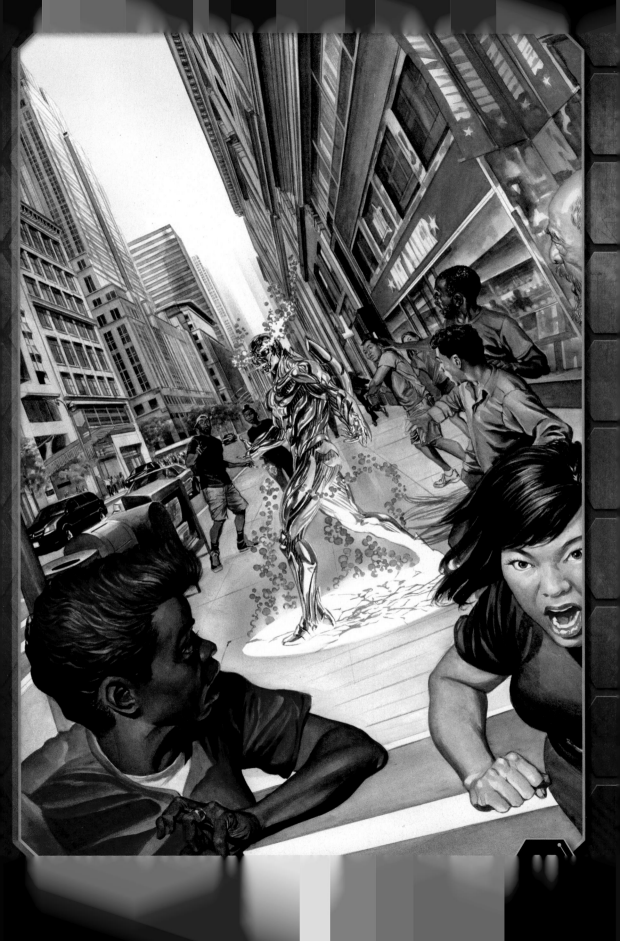

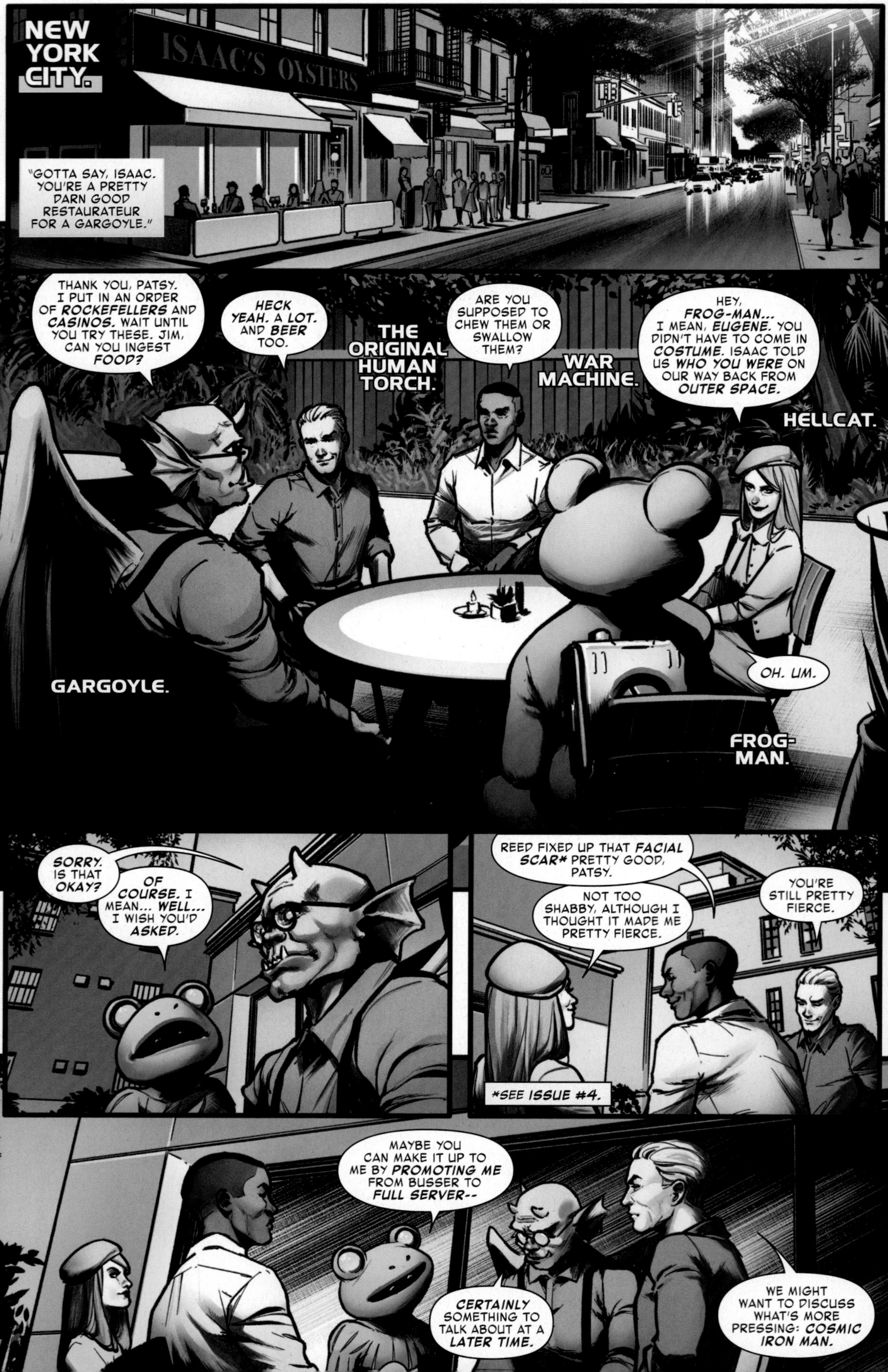
NEW YORK CITY.
ISAAC'S OYSTERS
"GOTTA SAY, ISAAC. YOU'RE A PRETTY DARN GOOD RESTAURATEUR FOR A GARGOYLE."
THANK YOU, PATSY. I PUT IN AN ORDER OF ROCKEFELLERS AND CASINOS. WAIT UNTIL YOU TRY THESE. JIM, CAN YOU INGEST FOOD?
HECK YEAH. A LOT. AND BEER TOO.
THE ORIGINAL HUMAN TORCH.
ARE YOU SUPPOSED TO CHEW THEM OR SWALLOW THEM?
WAR MACHINE.
HEY, FROG-MAN... I MEAN, EUGENE. YOU DIDN'T HAVE TO COME IN COSTUME. ISAAC TOLD US WHO YOU WERE ON OUR WAY BACK FROM OUTER SPACE.
HELLCAT.
GARGOYLE.
OH. UM.
FROG-MAN.
SORRY. IS THAT OKAY?
OF COURSE. I MEAN... WELL... I WISH YOU'D ASKED.
REED FIXED UP THAT FACIAL SCAR* PRETTY GOOD, PATSY.
NOT TOO SHABBY, ALTHOUGH I THOUGHT IT MADE ME PRETTY FIERCE.
YOU'RE STILL PRETTY FIERCE.
*SEE ISSUE #4.
MAYBE YOU CAN MAKE IT UP TO ME BY PROMOTING ME FROM BUSSER TO FULL SERVER--
CERTAINLY SOMETHING TO TALK ABOUT AT A LATER TIME.
WE MIGHT WANT TO DISCUSS WHAT'S MORE PRESSING: COSMIC IRON MAN.

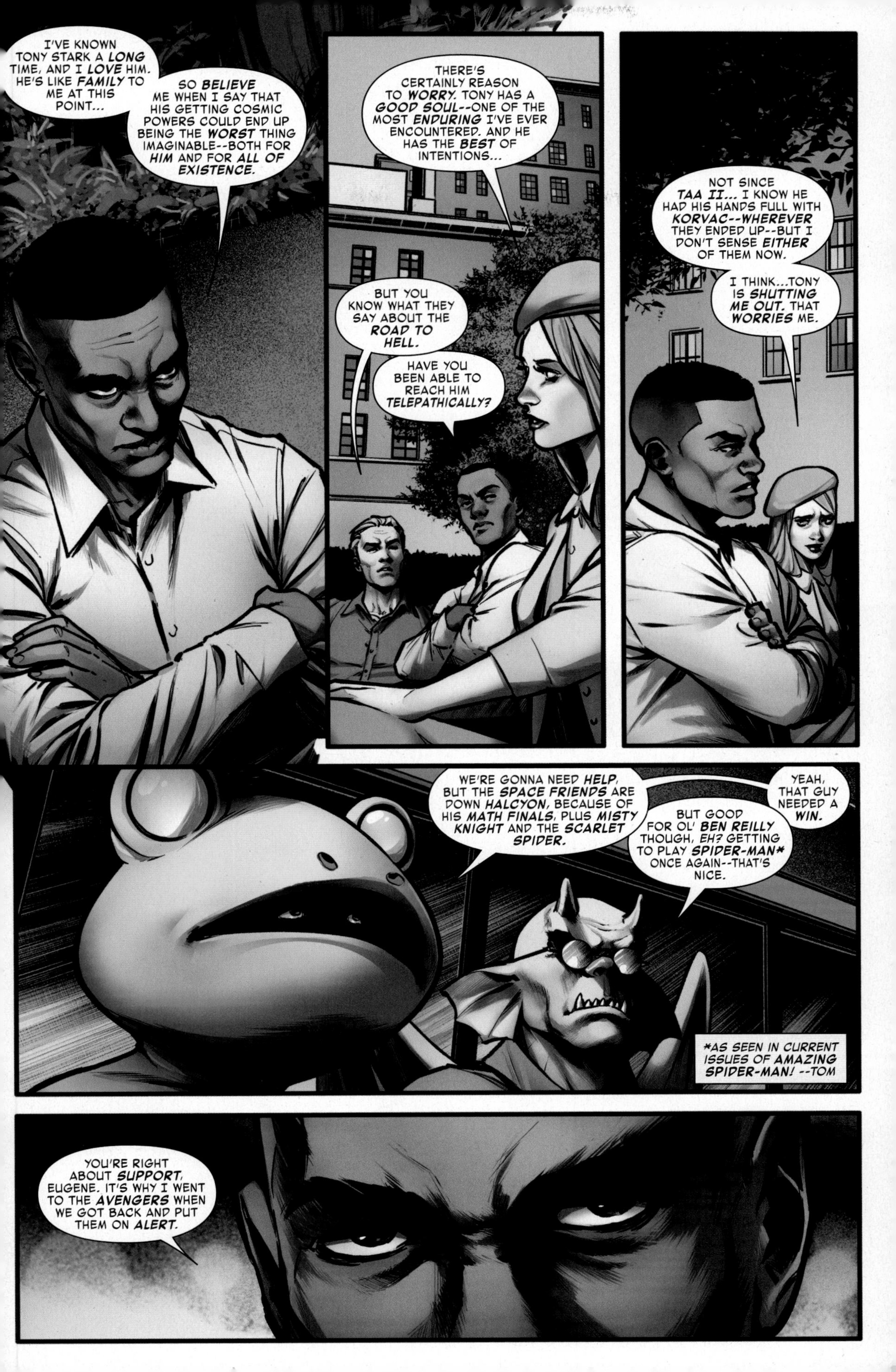

I'VE KNOWN TONY STARK A LONG TIME, AND I LOVE HIM. HE'S LIKE FAMILY TO ME AT THIS POINT...
SO BELIEVE ME WHEN I SAY THAT HIS GETTING COSMIC POWERS COULD END UP BEING THE WORST THING IMAGINABLE--BOTH FOR HIM AND FOR ALL OF EXISTENCE.
THERE'S CERTAINLY REASON TO WORRY. TONY HAS A GOOD SOUL--ONE OF THE MOST ENDURING I'VE EVER ENCOUNTERED. AND HE HAS THE BEST OF INTENTIONS...
BUT YOU KNOW WHAT THEY SAY ABOUT THE ROAD TO HELL.
HAVE YOU BEEN ABLE TO REACH HIM TELEPATHICALLY?
NOT SINCE TAA II... I KNOW HE HAD HIS HANDS FULL WITH KORVAC--WHEREVER THEY ENDED UP--BUT I DON'T SENSE EITHER OF THEM NOW.
I THINK...TONY IS SHUTTING ME OUT. THAT WORRIES ME.
WE'RE GONNA NEED HELP, BUT THE SPACE FRIENDS ARE DOWN HALCYON, BECAUSE OF HIS MATH FINALS, PLUS MISTY KNIGHT AND THE SCARLET SPIDER.
BUT GOOD FOR OL' BEN REILLY THOUGH, EH? GETTING TO PLAY SPIDER-MAN* ONCE AGAIN--THAT'S NICE.
YEAH, THAT GUY NEEDED A WIN.
*AS SEEN IN CURRENT ISSUES OF AMAZING SPIDER-MAN! --TOM
YOU'RE RIGHT ABOUT SUPPORT, EUGENE. IT'S WHY I WENT TO THE AVENGERS WHEN WE GOT BACK AND PUT THEM ON ALERT.

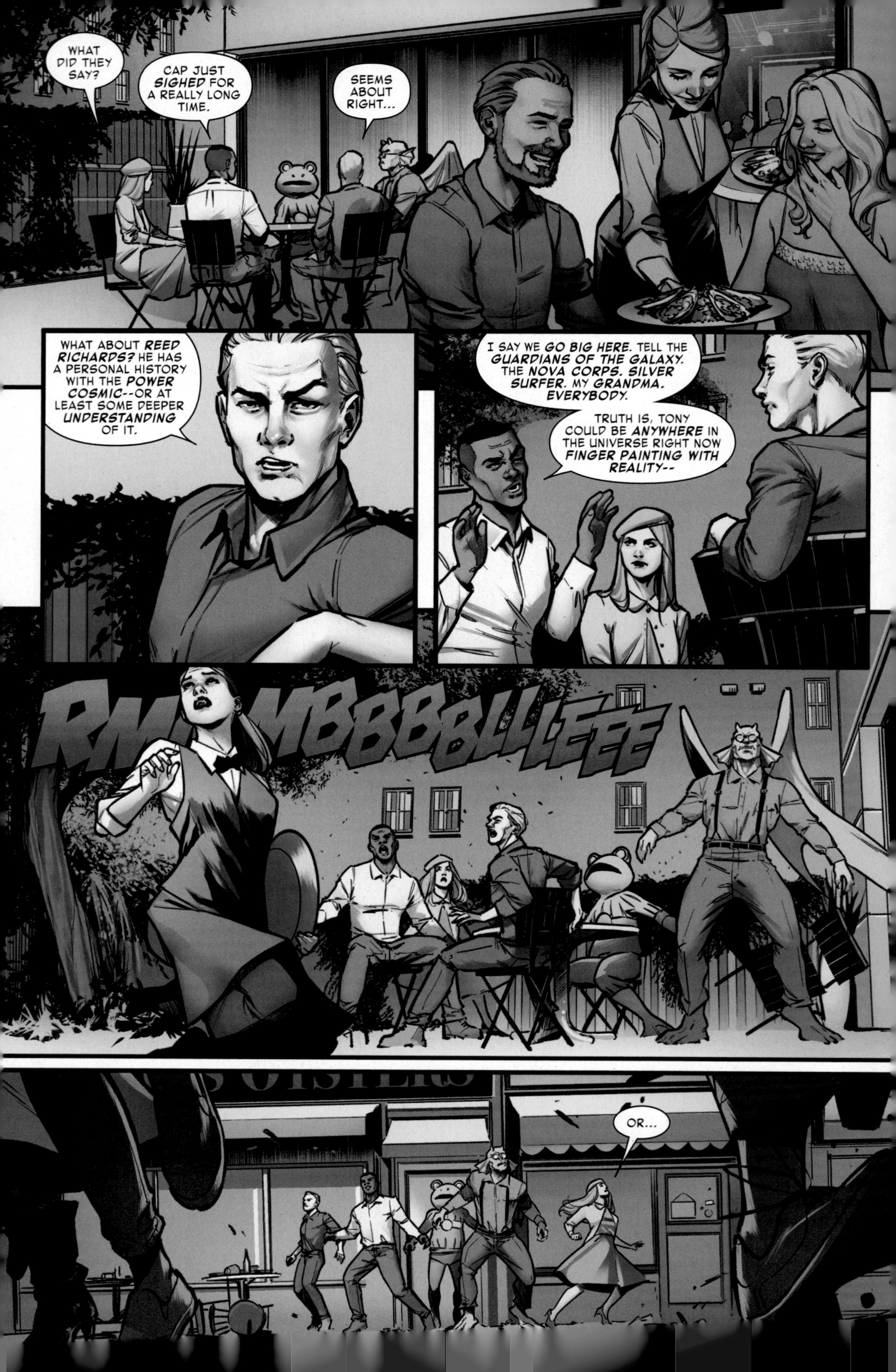
WHAT DID THEY SAY?
CAP JUST SIGHED FOR A REALLY LONG TIME.
SEEMS ABOUT RIGHT...
WHAT ABOUT REED RICHARDS? HE HAS A PERSONAL HISTORY WITH THE POWER COSMIC--OR AT LEAST SOME DEEPER UNDERSTANDING OF IT.
I SAY WE GO BIG HERE. TELL THE GUARDIANS OF THE GALAXY. THE NOVA CORPS. SILVER SURFER. MY GRANDMA. EVERYBODY.
TRUTH IS, TONY COULD BE ANYWHERE IN THE UNIVERSE RIGHT NOW FINGER PAINTING WITH REALITY--
RM MBBBBLLEEE
OR...

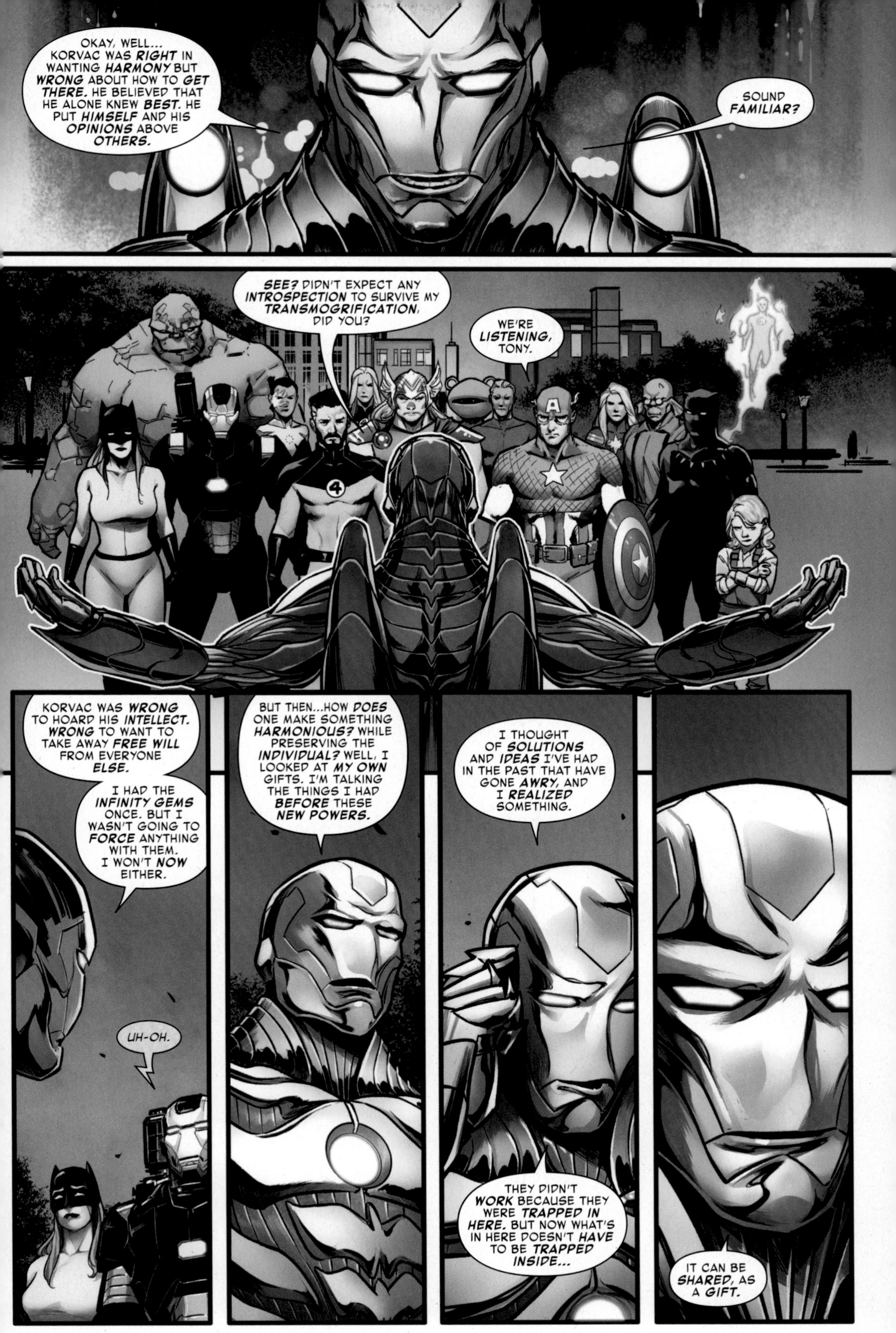
OKAY, WELL... KORVAC WAS RIGHT IN WANTING HARMONY BUT WRONG ABOUT HOW TO GET THERE. HE BELIEVED THAT HE ALONE KNEW BEST. HE PUT HIMSELF AND HIS OPINIONS ABOVE OTHERS.
SOUND FAMILIAR?
SEE? DIDN'T EXPECT ANY INTROSPECTION TO SURVIVE MY TRANSMOGRIFICATION, DID YOU?
WE'RE LISTENING, TONY.
KORVAC WAS WRONG TO HOARD HIS INTELLECT. WRONG TO WANT TO TAKE AWAY FREE WILL FROM EVERYONE ELSE.
I HAD THE INFINITY GEMS ONCE. BUT I WASN'T GOING TO FORCE ANYTHING WITH THEM. I WON'T NOW EITHER.
UH-OH.
BUT THEN...HOW DOES ONE MAKE SOMETHING HARMONIOUS? WHILE PRESERVING THE INDIVIDUAL? WELL, I LOOKED AT MY OWN GIFTS. I'M TALKING THE THINGS I HAD BEFORE THESE NEW POWERS.
I THOUGHT OF SOLUTIONS AND IDEAS I'VE HAD IN THE PAST THAT HAVE GONE AWRY, AND I REALIZED SOMETHING.
THEY DIDN'T WORK BECAUSE THEY WERE TRAPPED IN HERE. BUT NOW WHAT'S IN HERE DOESN'T HAVE TO BE TRAPPED INSIDE...
IT CAN BE SHARED, AS A GIFT.

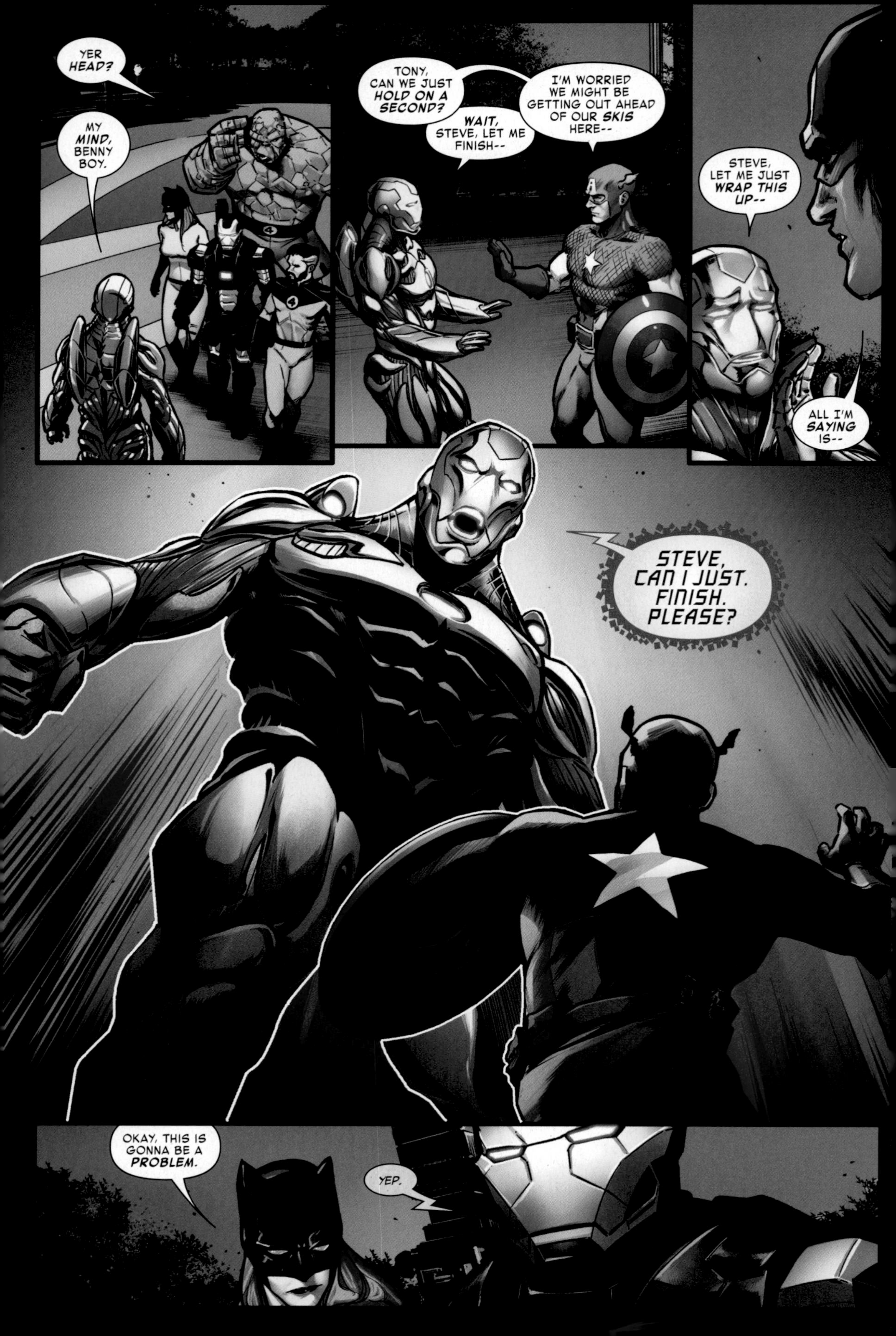
YER HEAD?
MY MIND, BENNY BOY.
TONY, CAN WE JUST HOLD ON A SECOND?
WAIT, STEVE, LET ME FINISH--
I'M WORRIED WE MIGHT BE GETTING OUT AHEAD OF OUR SKIS HERE--
STEVE, LET ME JUST WRAP THIS UP--
ALL I'M SAYING IS--
STEVE, CAN I JUST. FINISH. PLEASE?
OKAY, THIS IS GONNA BE A PROBLEM.
YEP.

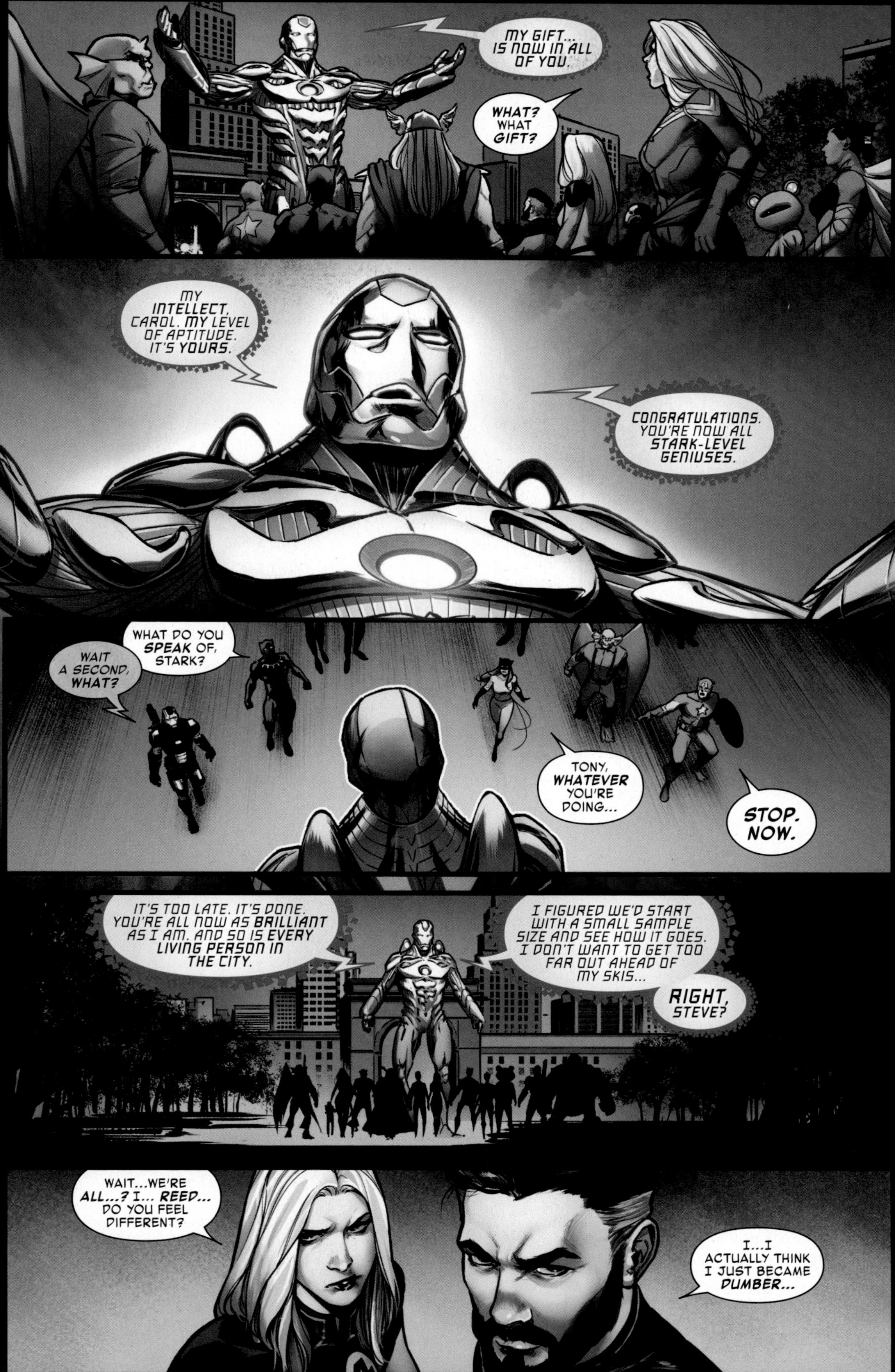
MY GIFT... IS NOW IN ALL OF YOU.
WHAT? WHAT GIFT?
MY INTELLECT, CAROL. MY LEVEL OF APTITUDE. IT'S YOURS.
CONGRATULATIONS. YOU'RE NOW ALL STARK-LEVEL GENIUSES.
WHAT DO YOU SPEAK OF, STARK?
WAIT A SECOND, WHAT?
TONY, WHATEVER YOU'RE DOING...
STOP. NOW.
IT'S TOO LATE. IT'S DONE. YOU'RE ALL NOW AS BRILLIANT AS I AM. AND SO IS EVERY LIVING PERSON IN THE CITY.
I FIGURED WE'D START WITH A SMALL SAMPLE SIZE AND SEE HOW IT GOES. I DON'T WANT TO GET TOO FAR OUT AHEAD OF MY SKIS...
RIGHT, STEVE?
WAIT...WE'RE ALL...? I... REED... DO YOU FEEL DIFFERENT?
I...I ACTUALLY THINK I JUST BECAME DUMBER...

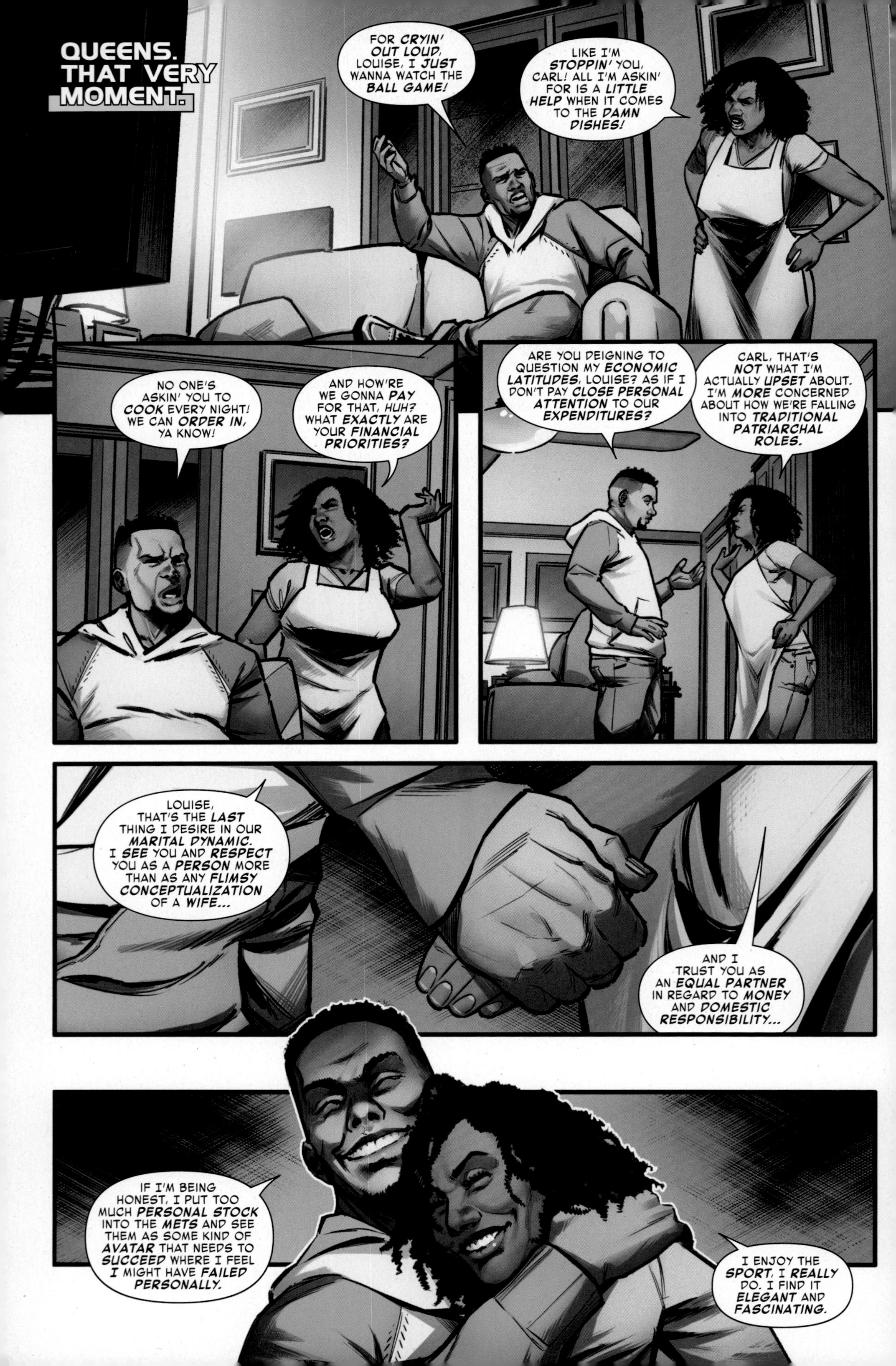
QUEENS. THAT VERY MOMENT.
FOR CRYIN' OUT LOUD, LOUISE, I JUST WANNA WATCH THE BALL GAME!
LIKE I'M STOPPIN' YOU, CARL! ALL I'M ASKIN' FOR IS A LITTLE HELP WHEN IT COMES TO THE DAMN DISHES!
NO ONE'S ASKIN' YOU TO COOK EVERY NIGHT! WE CAN ORDER IN, YA KNOW!
AND HOW'RE WE GONNA PAY FOR THAT, HUH? WHAT EXACTLY ARE YOUR FINANCIAL PRIORITIES?
ARE YOU DEIGNING TO QUESTION MY ECONOMIC LATITUDES, LOUISE? AS IF I DON'T PAY CLOSE PERSONAL ATTENTION TO OUR EXPENDITURES?
CARL, THAT'S NOT WHAT I'M ACTUALLY UPSET ABOUT. I'M MORE CONCERNED ABOUT HOW WE'RE FALLING INTO TRADITIONAL PATRIARCHAL ROLES.
LOUISE, THAT'S THE LAST THING I DESIRE IN OUR MARITAL DYNAMIC. I SEE YOU AND RESPECT YOU AS A PERSON MORE THAN AS ANY FLIMSY CONCEPTUALIZATION OF A WIFE...
AND I TRUST YOU AS AN EQUAL PARTNER IN REGARD TO MONEY AND DOMESTIC RESPONSIBILITY...
IF I'M BEING HONEST, I PUT TOO MUCH PERSONAL STOCK INTO THE METS AND SEE THEM AS SOME KIND OF AVATAR THAT NEEDS TO SUCCEED WHERE I FEEL I MIGHT HAVE FAILED PERSONALLY.
I ENJOY THE SPORT, I REALLY DO. I FIND IT ELEGANT AND FASCINATING.

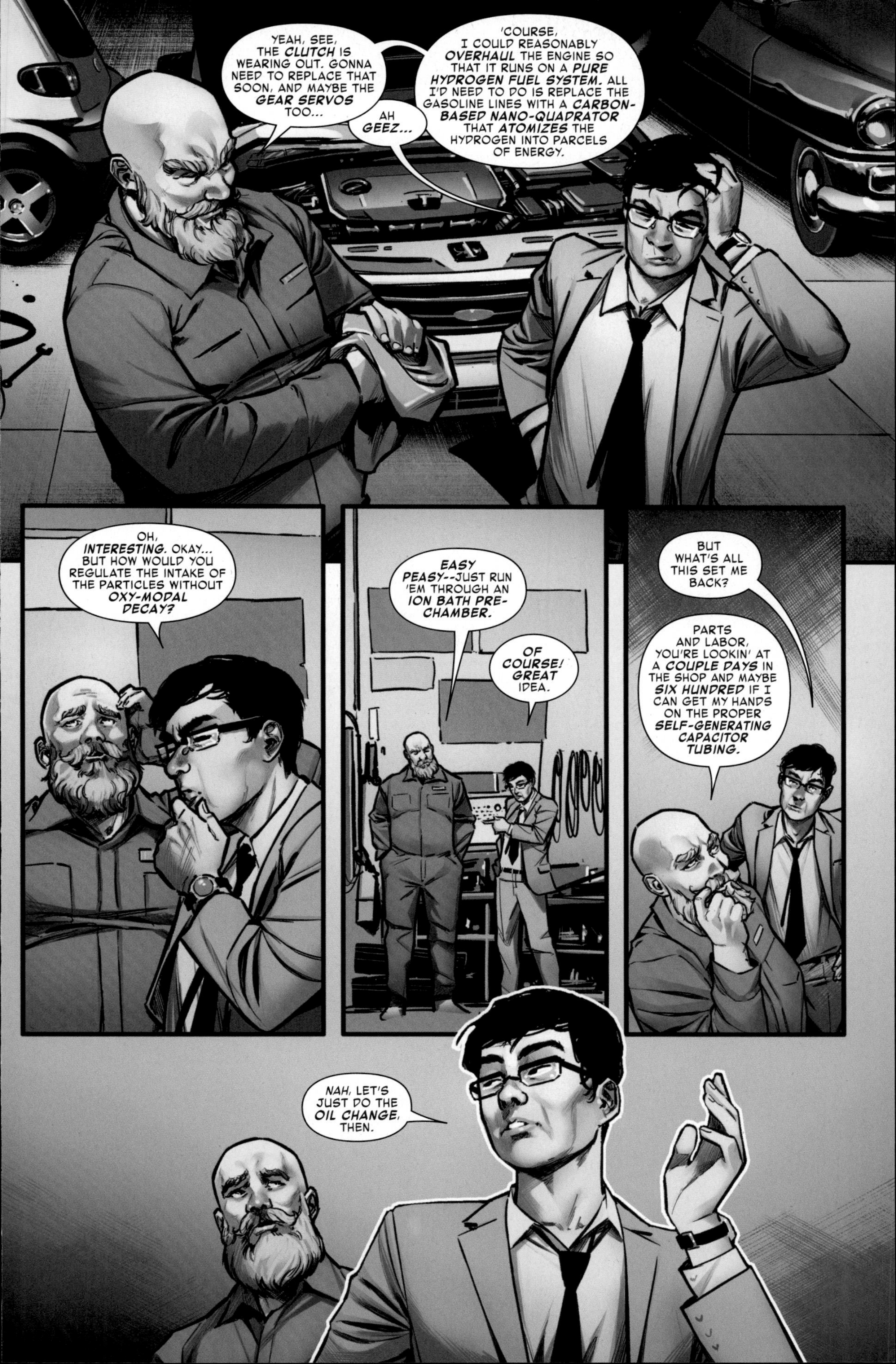
YEAH, SEE, THE CLUTCH IS WEARING OUT. GONNA NEED TO REPLACE THAT SOON, AND MAYBE THE GEAR SERVOS TOO...
AH GEEZ...
'COURSE, I COULD REASONABLY OVERHAUL THE ENGINE SO THAT IT RUNS ON A PURE HYDROGEN FUEL SYSTEM. ALL I'D NEED TO DO IS REPLACE THE GASOLINE LINES WITH A CARBON-BASED NANO-QUADRATOR THAT ATOMIZES THE HYDROGEN INTO PARCELS OF ENERGY.
OH, INTERESTING. OKAY... BUT HOW WOULD YOU REGULATE THE INTAKE OF THE PARTICLES WITHOUT OXY-MODAL DECAY?
EASY PEASY--JUST RUN 'EM THROUGH AN ION BATH PRE-CHAMBER.
OF COURSE! GREAT IDEA.
BUT WHAT'S ALL THIS SET ME BACK?
PARTS AND LABOR, YOU'RE LOOKIN' AT A COUPLE DAYS IN THE SHOP AND MAYBE SIX HUNDRED IF I CAN GET MY HANDS ON THE PROPER SELF-GENERATING CAPACITOR TUBING.
NAH, LET'S JUST DO THE OIL CHANGE, THEN.

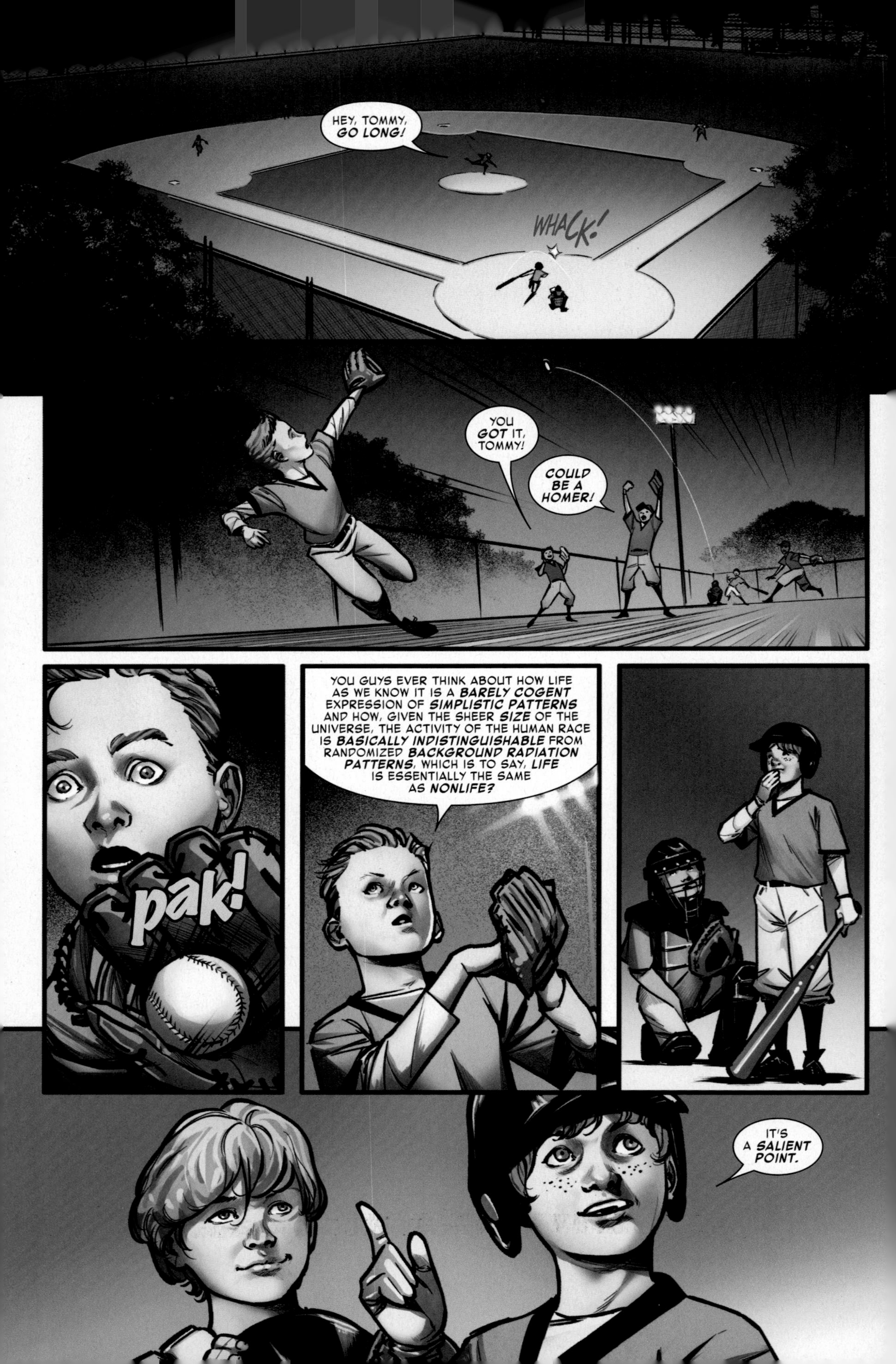
HEY, TOMMY, GO LONG!
WHACK!
YOU GOT IT, TOMMY!
COULD BE A HOMER!
pak!
YOU GUYS EVER THINK ABOUT HOW LIFE AS WE KNOW IT IS A BARELY COGENT EXPRESSION OF SIMPLISTIC PATTERNS AND HOW, GIVEN THE SHEER SIZE OF THE UNIVERSE, THE ACTIVITY OF THE HUMAN RACE IS BASICALLY INDISTINGUISHABLE FROM RANDOMIZED BACKGROUND RADIATION PATTERNS, WHICH IS TO SAY, LIFE IS ESSENTIALLY THE SAME AS NONLIFE?
IT'S A SALIENT POINT.

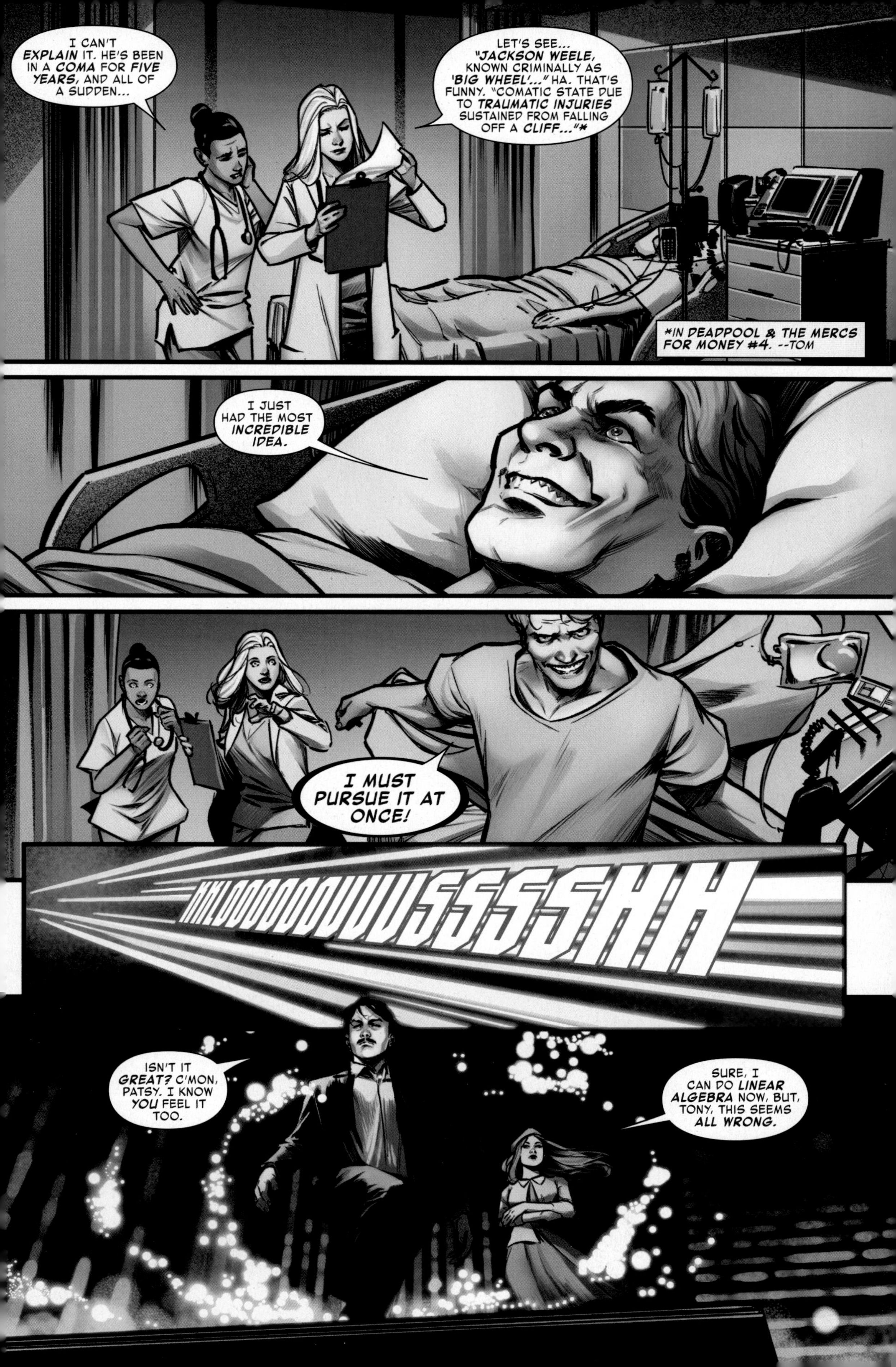
I CAN'T EXPLAIN IT. HE'S BEEN IN A COMA FOR FIVE YEARS, AND ALL OF A SUDDEN...
LET'S SEE... "JACKSON WEELE, KNOWN CRIMINALLY AS 'BIG WHEEL'..." HA. THAT'S FUNNY. "COMATIC STATE DUE TO TRAUMATIC INJURIES SUSTAINED FROM FALLING OFF A CLIFF..."*
*IN DEADPOOL & THE MERCS FOR MONEY #4. --TOM
I JUST HAD THE MOST INCREDIBLE IDEA.
I MUST PURSUE IT AT ONCE!
ISN'T IT GREAT? C'MON, PATSY. I KNOW YOU FEEL IT TOO.
SURE, I CAN DO LINEAR ALGEBRA NOW, BUT, TONY, THIS SEEMS ALL WRONG.

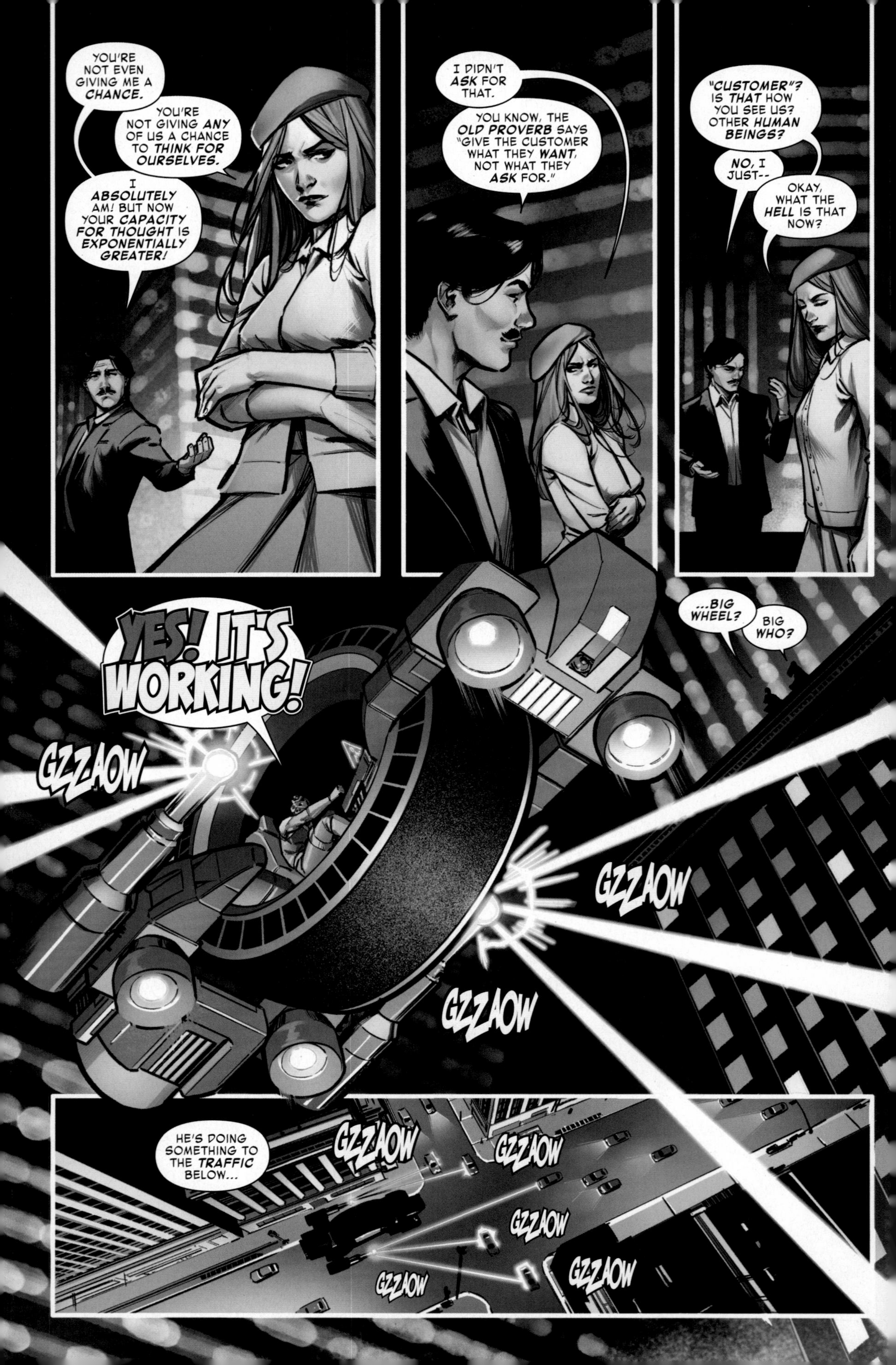
YOU'RE NOT EVEN GIVING ME A CHANCE.
YOU'RE NOT GIVING ANY OF US A CHANCE TO THINK FOR OURSELVES.
I ABSOLUTELY AM! BUT NOW YOUR CAPACITY FOR THOUGHT IS EXPONENTIALLY GREATER!
I DIDN'T ASK FOR THAT.
YOU KNOW, THE OLD PROVERB SAYS "GIVE THE CUSTOMER WHAT THEY WANT, NOT WHAT THEY ASK FOR."
"CUSTOMER"? IS THAT HOW YOU SEE US? OTHER HUMAN BEINGS?
NO, I JUST--
OKAY, WHAT THE HELL IS THAT NOW?
YES! IT'S WORKING!
GZZAOW
...BIG WHEEL?
BIG WHO?
GZZAOW
GZZAOW
HE'S DOING SOMETHING TO THE TRAFFIC BELOW...
GZZAOW
GZZAOW
GZZAOW
GZZAOW
GZZAOW

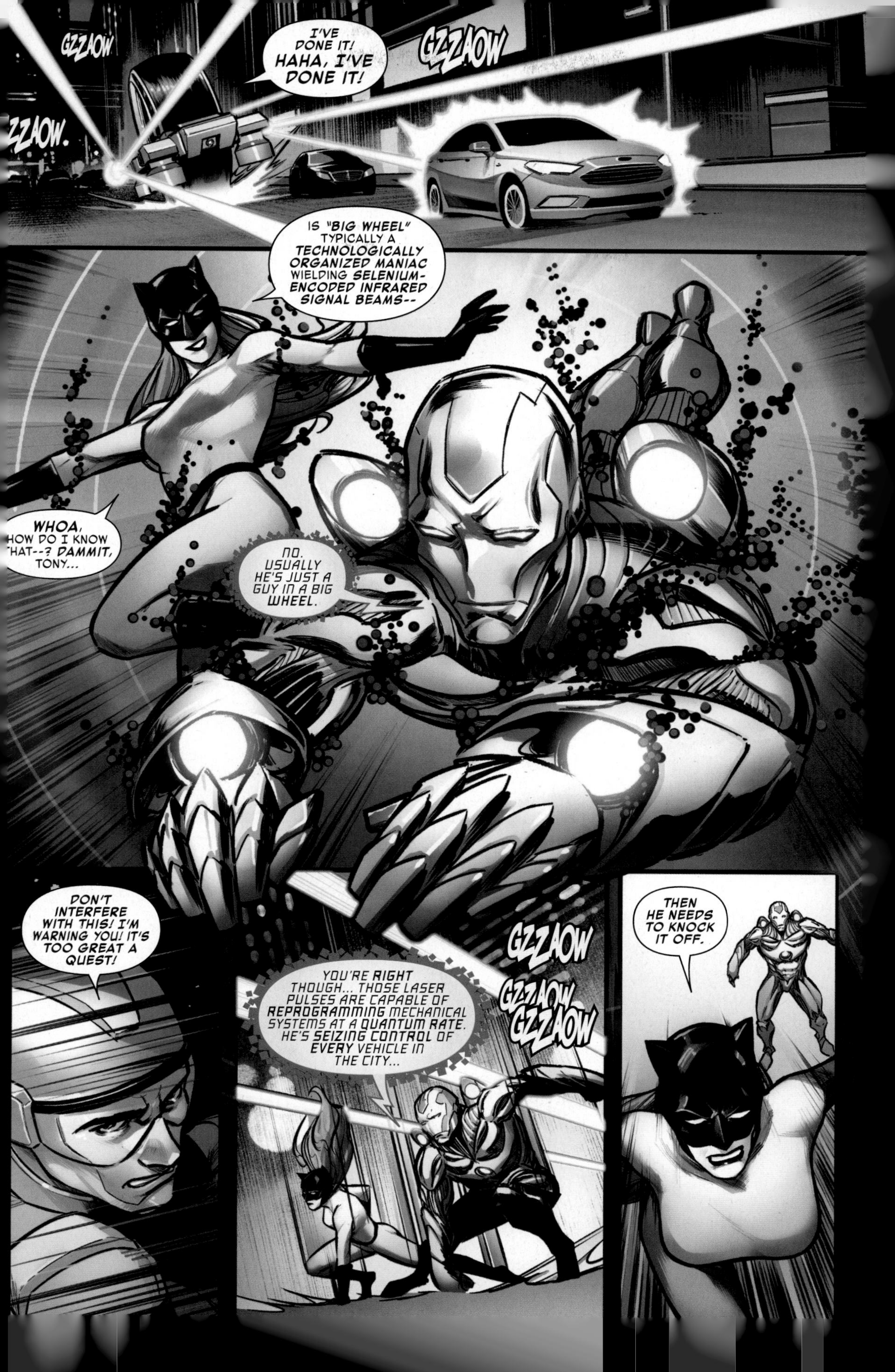
GZZAOW
I'VE DONE IT! HAHA, I'VE DONE IT!
GZZAOW
ZZAOW.
IS "BIG WHEEL" TYPICALLY A TECHNOLOGICALLY ORGANIZED MANIAC WIELDING SELENIUM-ENCODED INFRARED SIGNAL BEAMS--
WHOA, HOW DO I KNOW THAT--? DAMMIT, TONY...
NO. USUALLY HE'S JUST A GUY IN A BIG WHEEL.
DON'T INTERFERE WITH THIS! I'M WARNING YOU! IT'S TOO GREAT A QUEST!
GZZAOW
GZZAOW
GZZAOW
YOU'RE RIGHT THOUGH... THOSE LASER PULSES ARE CAPABLE OF REPROGRAMMING MECHANICAL SYSTEMS AT A QUANTUM RATE. HE'S SEIZING CONTROL OF EVERY VEHICLE IN THE CITY...
THEN HE NEEDS TO KNOCK IT OFF.

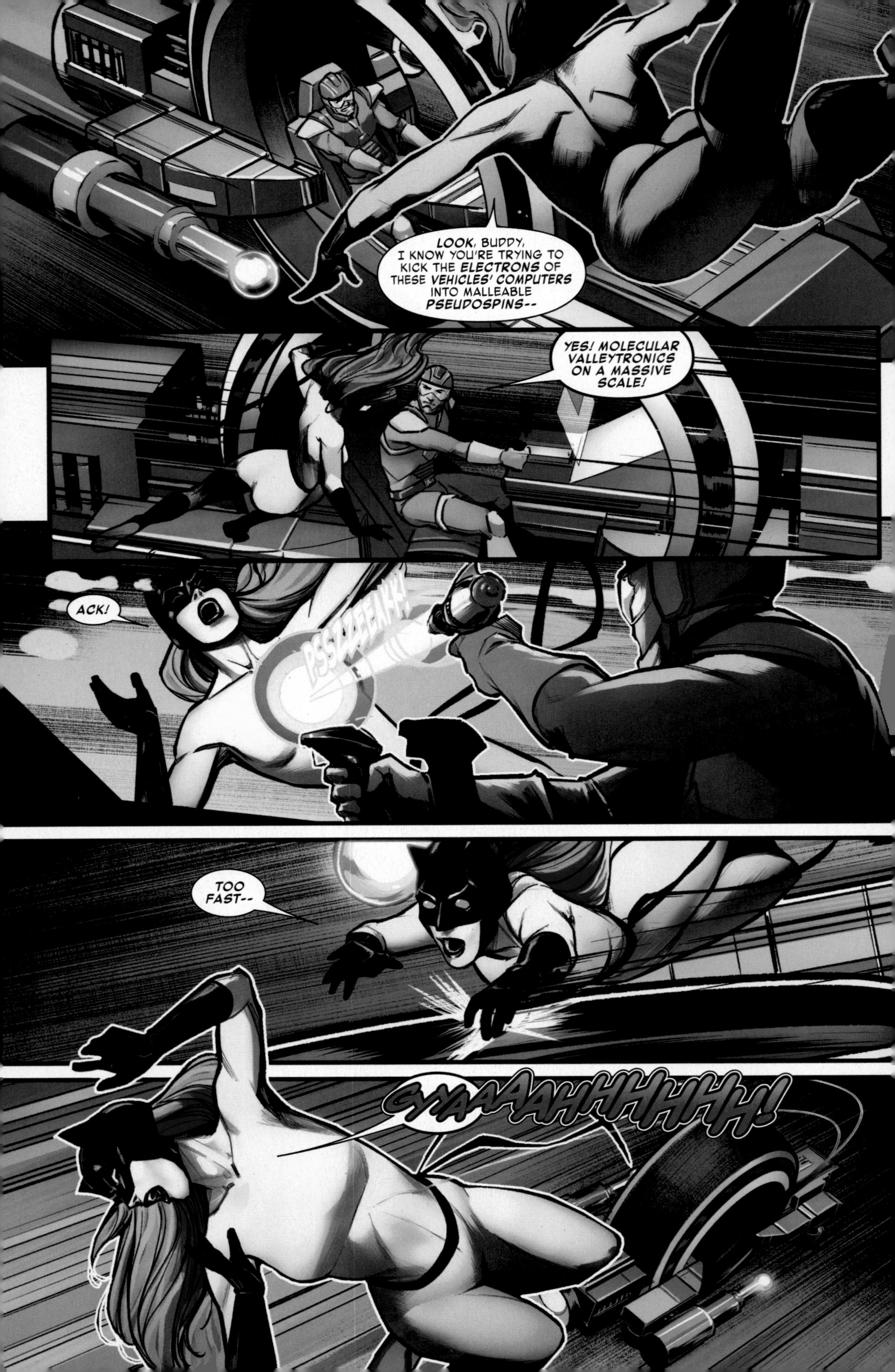
LOOK, BUDDY, I KNOW YOU'RE TRYING TO KICK THE ELECTRONS OF THESE VEHICLES' COMPUTERS INTO MALLEABLE PSEUDOSPINS--
YES! MOLECULAR VALLEYTRONICS ON A MASSIVE SCALE!
ACK!
PSSZZZEEAKK!
TOO FAST--
GYYAAAAHHHHHHH!

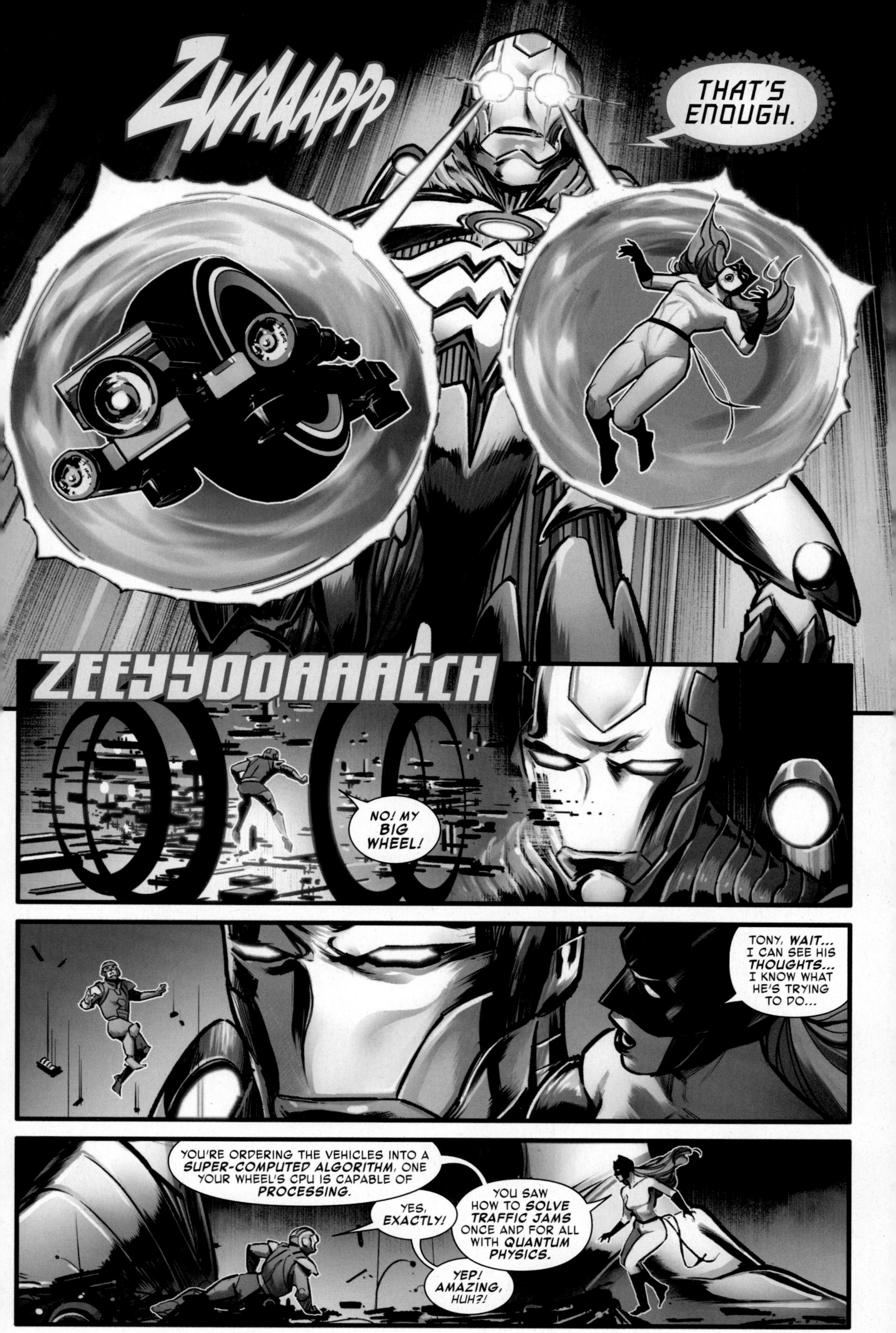
ZWAAAPPP
THAT'S ENOUGH.
ZEEYYOOAAAACCH
NO! MY BIG WHEEL!
TONY, WAIT... I CAN SEE HIS THOUGHTS... I KNOW WHAT HE'S TRYING TO DO...
YOU'RE ORDERING THE VEHICLES INTO A SUPER-COMPUTED ALGORITHM, ONE YOUR WHEEL'S CPU IS CAPABLE OF PROCESSING.
YES, EXACTLY!
YOU SAW HOW TO SOLVE TRAFFIC JAMS ONCE AND FOR ALL WITH QUANTUM PHYSICS.
YEP! AMAZING, HUH?!

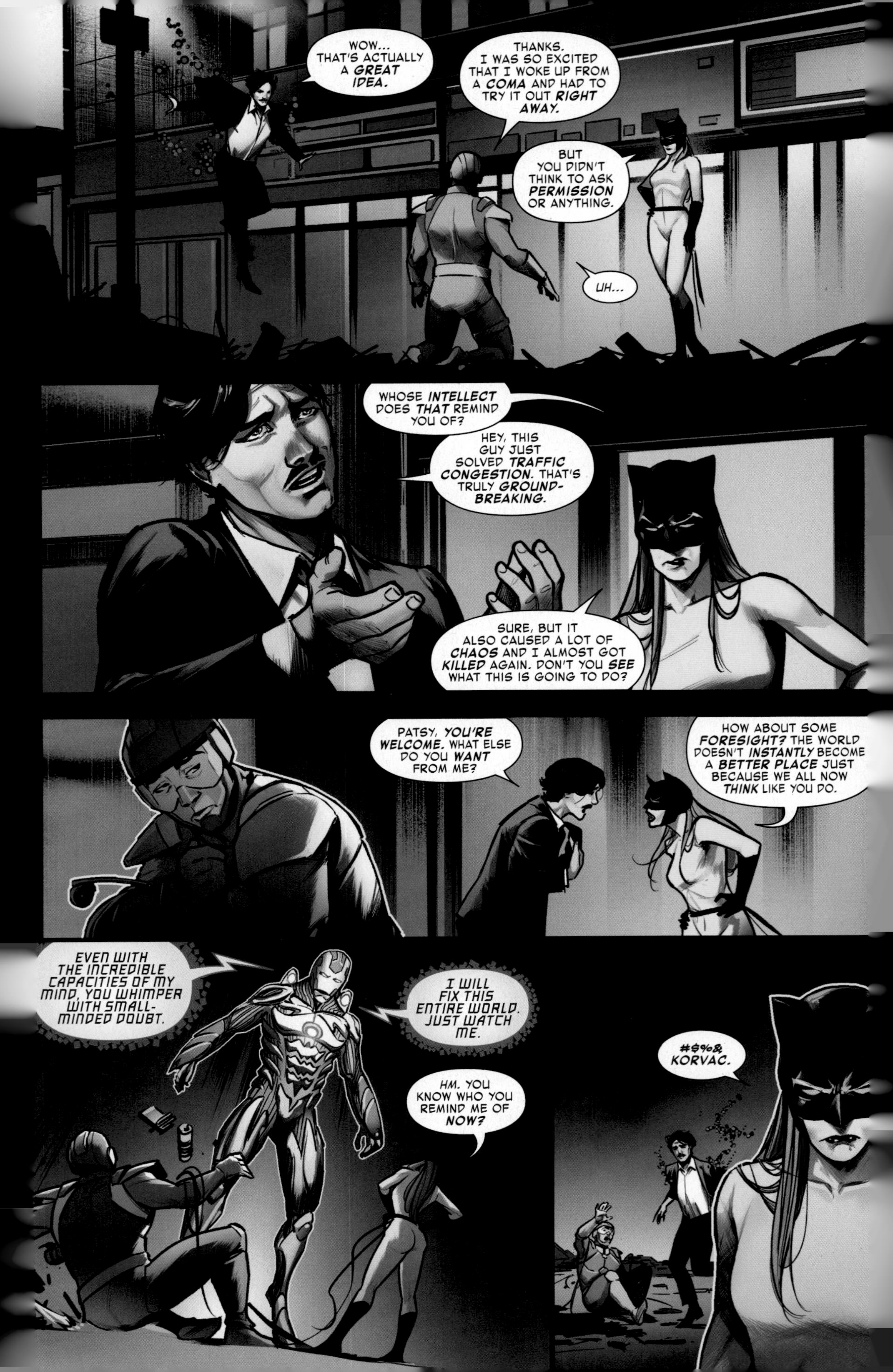
WOW... THAT'S ACTUALLY A GREAT IDEA.
THANKS. I WAS SO EXCITED THAT I WOKE UP FROM A COMA AND HAD TO TRY IT OUT RIGHT AWAY.
BUT YOU DIDN'T THINK TO ASK PERMISSION OR ANYTHING.
UH...
WHOSE INTELLECT DOES THAT REMIND YOU OF?
HEY, THIS GUY JUST SOLVED TRAFFIC CONGESTION. THAT'S TRULY GROUND-BREAKING.
SURE, BUT IT ALSO CAUSED A LOT OF CHAOS AND I ALMOST GOT KILLED AGAIN. DON'T YOU SEE WHAT THIS IS GOING TO DO?
PATSY, YOU'RE WELCOME. WHAT ELSE DO YOU WANT FROM ME?
HOW ABOUT SOME FORESIGHT? THE WORLD DOESN'T INSTANTLY BECOME A BETTER PLACE JUST BECAUSE WE ALL NOW THINK LIKE YOU DO.
EVEN WITH THE INCREDIBLE CAPACITIES OF MY MIND, YOU WHIMPER WITH SMALL-MINDED DOUBT.
I WILL FIX THIS ENTIRE WORLD. JUST WATCH ME.
HM. YOU KNOW WHO YOU REMIND ME OF NOW?
#$%& KORVAC.

"STARK--COMMONLY REFERRED TO NOW AS THE *IRON GOD*--HAS BUILT A *SPECIAL HOLDING AREA* FOR THOSE USING THEIR NEW INTELLECTUAL PROWESS TO *VIOLATE LAWS,* AS WELL AS HIS OWN DETERMINED CODE OF *MORALS* AND *ETHICS.*

"THIS COMES AS MUCH OF NEW YORK'S *LAW ENFORCEMENT* HAS RECENTLY FALLEN TO THE IRON GOD AND OTHER HEROES SINCE NEARLY THE ENTIRETY OF THE *NYPD* HAS BANDED TOGETHER TO FORM THEIR OWN *PRIVATE SPACE PROGRAM* CALLED *'BLUE MOON.'*

"BUT AFTER SEVERAL SUCCESSFUL *ESCAPES,* THE IRON GOD *REDUCED* THE IQ OF EVERY PRISONER INSIDE HIS HOLDING AREA TO *EIGHTY,* THE LOWEST END OF THE RANGE CLASSIFIED AS *'DULL NORMAL'* ON THE 1958 WECHSLER ADULT INTELLIGENCE SCALE.

"NO WORD YET ON WHAT *DUE PROCESS* WILL LOOK LIKE FOR THOSE BEING HELD WITHIN."

FIELDS of VALOR

A Novella of Yesterday by Captain Steve Roge

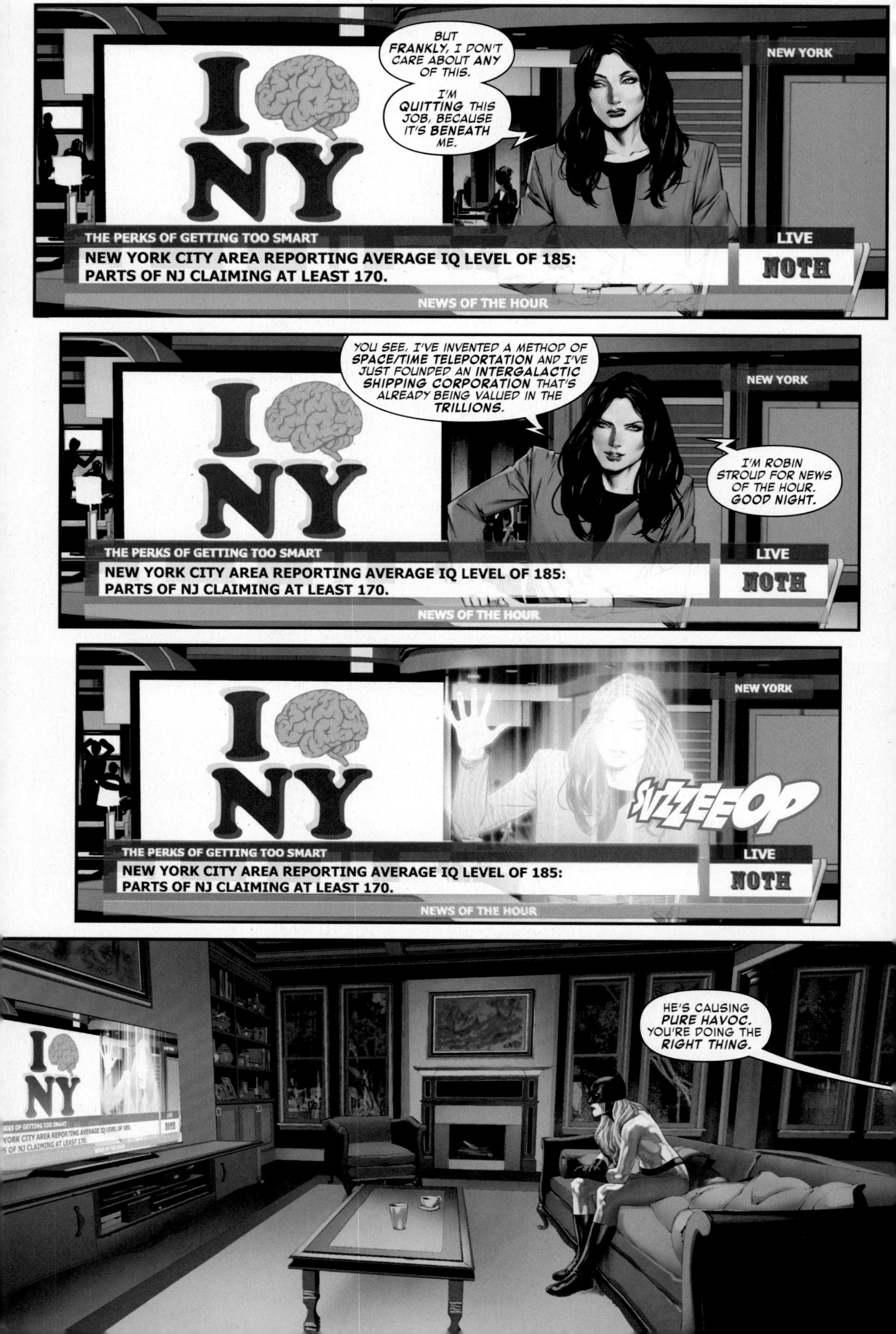

BUT FRANKLY, I DON'T CARE ABOUT ANY OF THIS.
I'M QUITTING THIS JOB, BECAUSE IT'S BENEATH ME.
NEW YORK
THE PERKS OF GETTING TOO SMART
NEW YORK CITY AREA REPORTING AVERAGE IQ LEVEL OF 185: PARTS OF NJ CLAIMING AT LEAST 170.
LIVE
NOTH
NEWS OF THE HOUR
YOU SEE, I'VE INVENTED A METHOD OF SPACE/TIME TELEPORTATION AND I'VE JUST FOUNDED AN INTERGALACTIC SHIPPING CORPORATION THAT'S ALREADY BEING VALUED IN THE TRILLIONS.
I'M ROBIN STROUD FOR NEWS OF THE HOUR. GOOD NIGHT.
SVZZEEOP
HE'S CAUSING PURE HAVOC. YOU'RE DOING THE RIGHT THING.

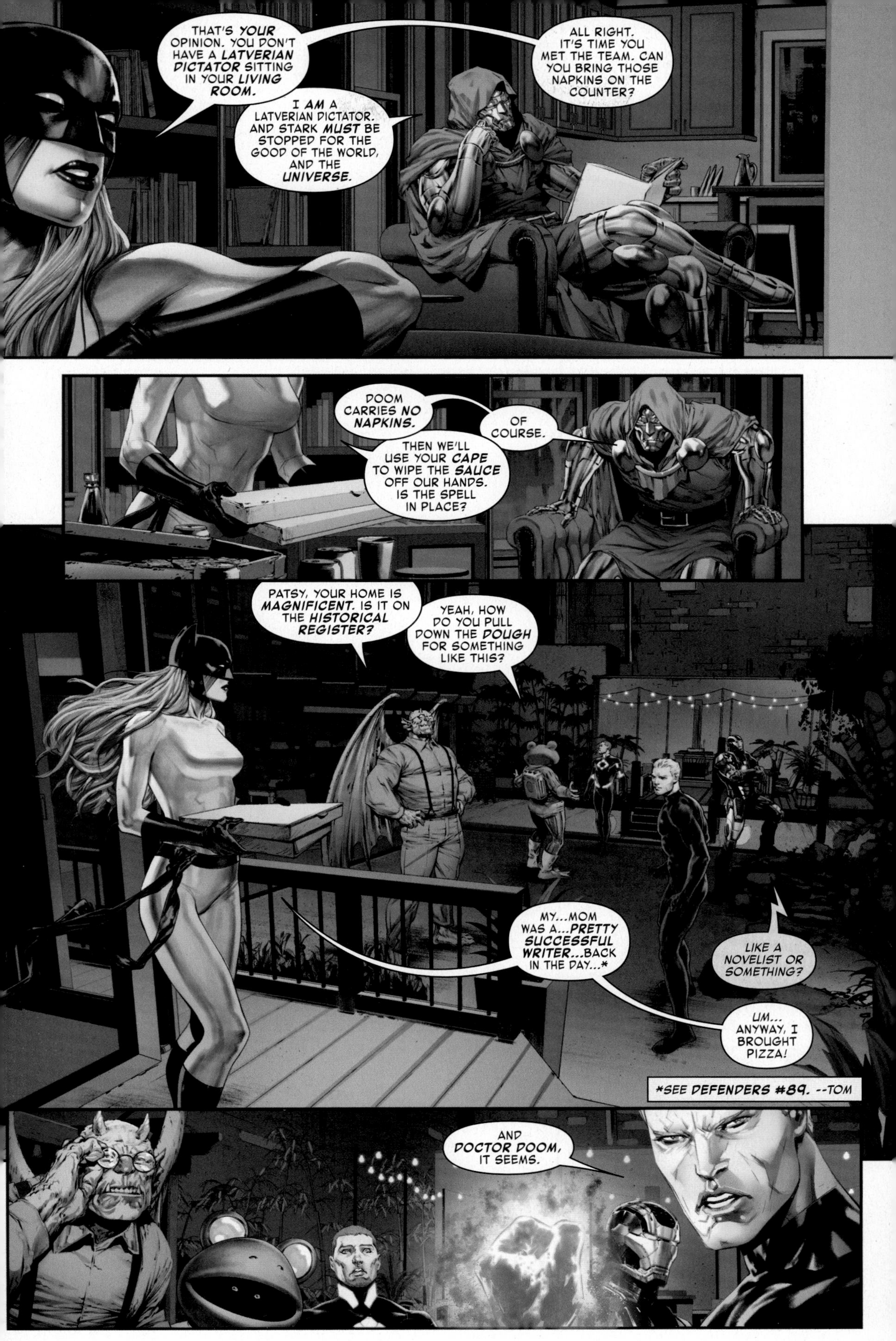
THAT'S YOUR OPINION. YOU DON'T HAVE A LATVERIAN DICTATOR SITTING IN YOUR LIVING ROOM.
I AM A LATVERIAN DICTATOR. AND STARK MUST BE STOPPED FOR THE GOOD OF THE WORLD, AND THE UNIVERSE.
ALL RIGHT. IT'S TIME YOU MET THE TEAM. CAN YOU BRING THOSE NAPKINS ON THE COUNTER?
DOOM CARRIES NO NAPKINS.
OF COURSE.
THEN WE'LL USE YOUR CAPE TO WIPE THE SAUCE OFF OUR HANDS. IS THE SPELL IN PLACE?
PATSY, YOUR HOME IS MAGNIFICENT. IS IT ON THE HISTORICAL REGISTER?
YEAH, HOW DO YOU PULL DOWN THE DOUGH FOR SOMETHING LIKE THIS?
MY...MOM WAS A...PRETTY SUCCESSFUL WRITER...BACK IN THE DAY...*
LIKE A NOVELIST OR SOMETHING?
UM... ANYWAY, I BROUGHT PIZZA!
*SEE DEFENDERS #89. --TOM
AND DOCTOR DOOM, IT SEEMS.

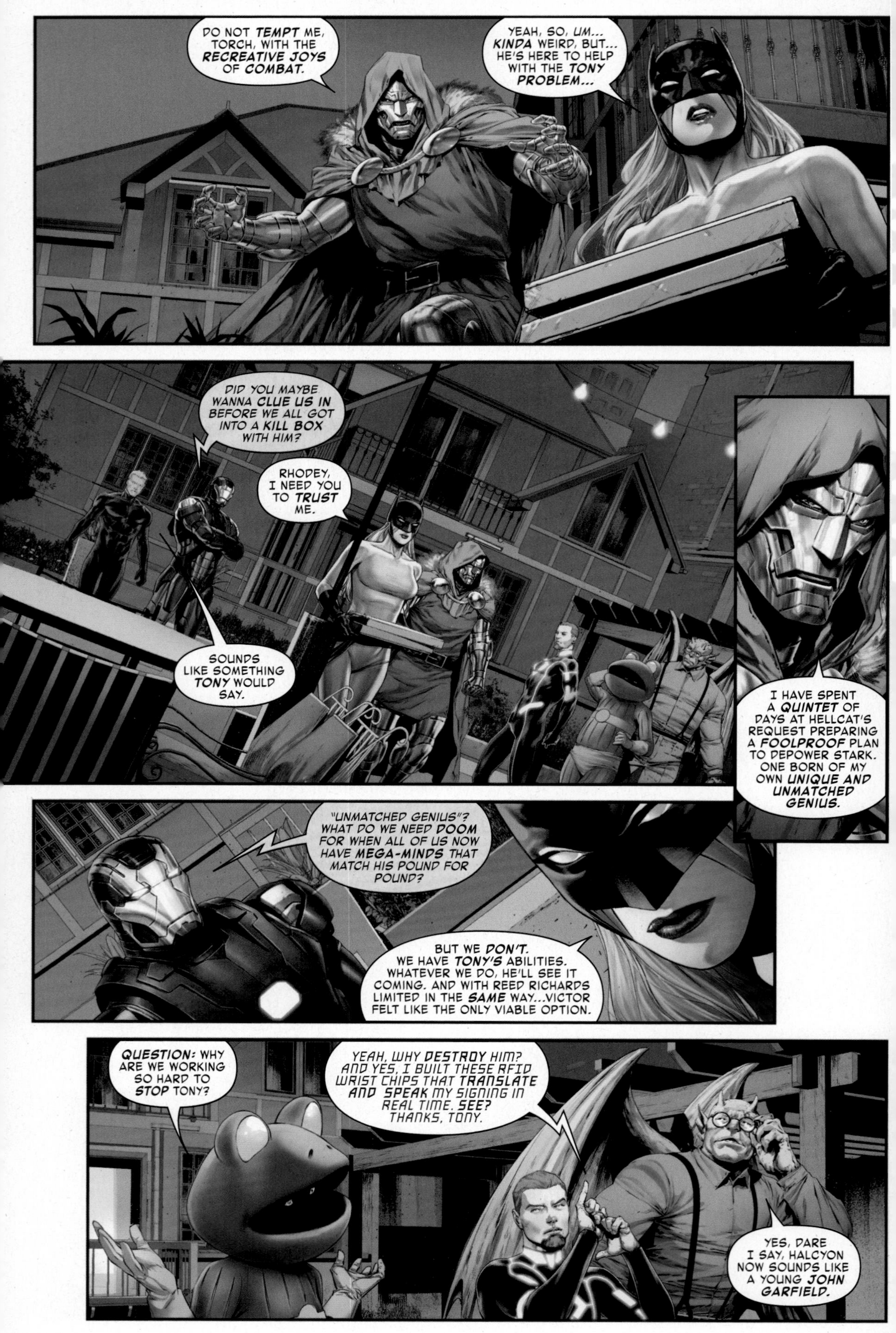
DO NOT TEMPT ME, TORCH, WITH THE RECREATIVE JOYS OF COMBAT.
YEAH, SO, UM... KINDA WEIRD, BUT... HE'S HERE TO HELP WITH THE TONY PROBLEM...
DID YOU MAYBE WANNA CLUE US IN BEFORE WE ALL GOT INTO A KILL BOX WITH HIM?
RHODEY, I NEED YOU TO TRUST ME.
SOUNDS LIKE SOMETHING TONY WOULD SAY.
I HAVE SPENT A QUINTET OF DAYS AT HELLCAT'S REQUEST PREPARING A FOOLPROOF PLAN TO DEPOWER STARK. ONE BORN OF MY OWN UNIQUE AND UNMATCHED GENIUS.
"UNMATCHED GENIUS"? WHAT DO WE NEED DOOM FOR WHEN ALL OF US NOW HAVE MEGA-MINDS THAT MATCH HIS POUND FOR POUND?
BUT WE DON'T. WE HAVE TONY'S ABILITIES. WHATEVER WE DO, HE'LL SEE IT COMING. AND WITH REED RICHARDS LIMITED IN THE SAME WAY...VICTOR FELT LIKE THE ONLY VIABLE OPTION.
QUESTION: WHY ARE WE WORKING SO HARD TO STOP TONY?
YEAH, WHY DESTROY HIM? AND YES, I BUILT THESE RFID WRIST CHIPS THAT TRANSLATE AND SPEAK MY SIGNING IN REAL TIME. SEE? THANKS, TONY.
YES, DARE I SAY, HALCYON NOW SOUNDS LIKE A YOUNG JOHN GARFIELD.

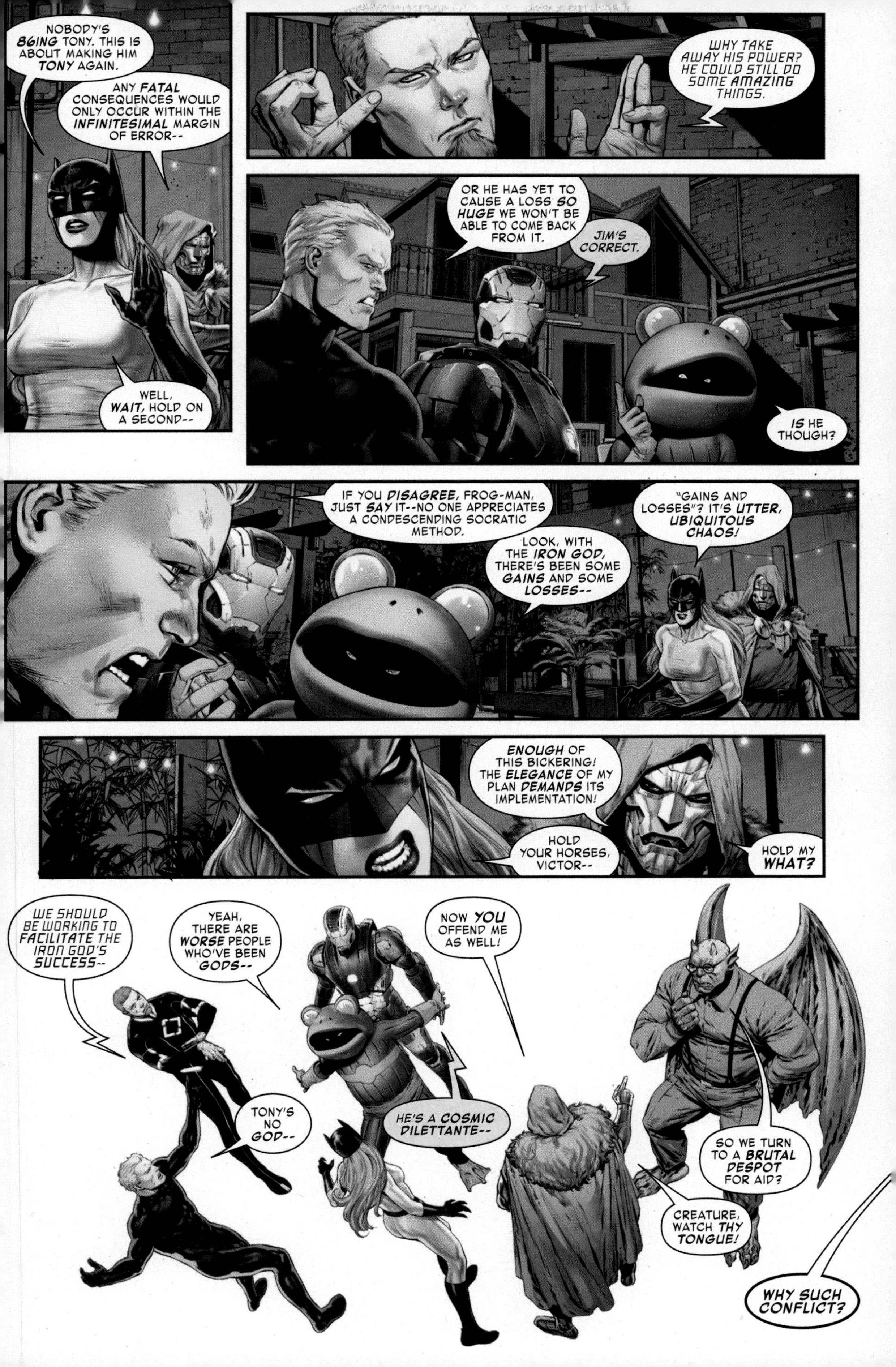
NOBODY'S 86ING TONY. THIS IS ABOUT MAKING HIM TONY AGAIN.
ANY FATAL CONSEQUENCES WOULD ONLY OCCUR WITHIN THE INFINITESIMAL MARGIN OF ERROR--
WELL, WAIT, HOLD ON A SECOND--
WHY TAKE AWAY HIS POWER? HE COULD STILL DO SOME AMAZING THINGS.
OR HE HAS YET TO CAUSE A LOSS SO HUGE WE WON'T BE ABLE TO COME BACK FROM IT.
JIM'S CORRECT.
IS HE THOUGH?
IF YOU DISAGREE, FROG-MAN, JUST SAY IT--NO ONE APPRECIATES A CONDESCENDING SOCRATIC METHOD.
LOOK, WITH THE IRON GOD, THERE'S BEEN SOME GAINS AND SOME LOSSES--
"GAINS AND LOSSES"? IT'S UTTER, UBIQUITOUS CHAOS!
ENOUGH OF THIS BICKERING! THE ELEGANCE OF MY PLAN DEMANDS ITS IMPLEMENTATION!
HOLD YOUR HORSES, VICTOR--
HOLD MY WHAT?
WE SHOULD BE WORKING TO FACILITATE THE IRON GOD'S SUCCESS--
YEAH, THERE ARE WORSE PEOPLE WHO'VE BEEN GODS--
NOW YOU OFFEND ME AS WELL!
TONY'S NO GOD--
HE'S A COSMIC DILETTANTE--
SO WE TURN TO A BRUTAL DESPOT FOR AID?
CREATURE, WATCH THY TONGUE!
WHY SUCH CONFLICT?

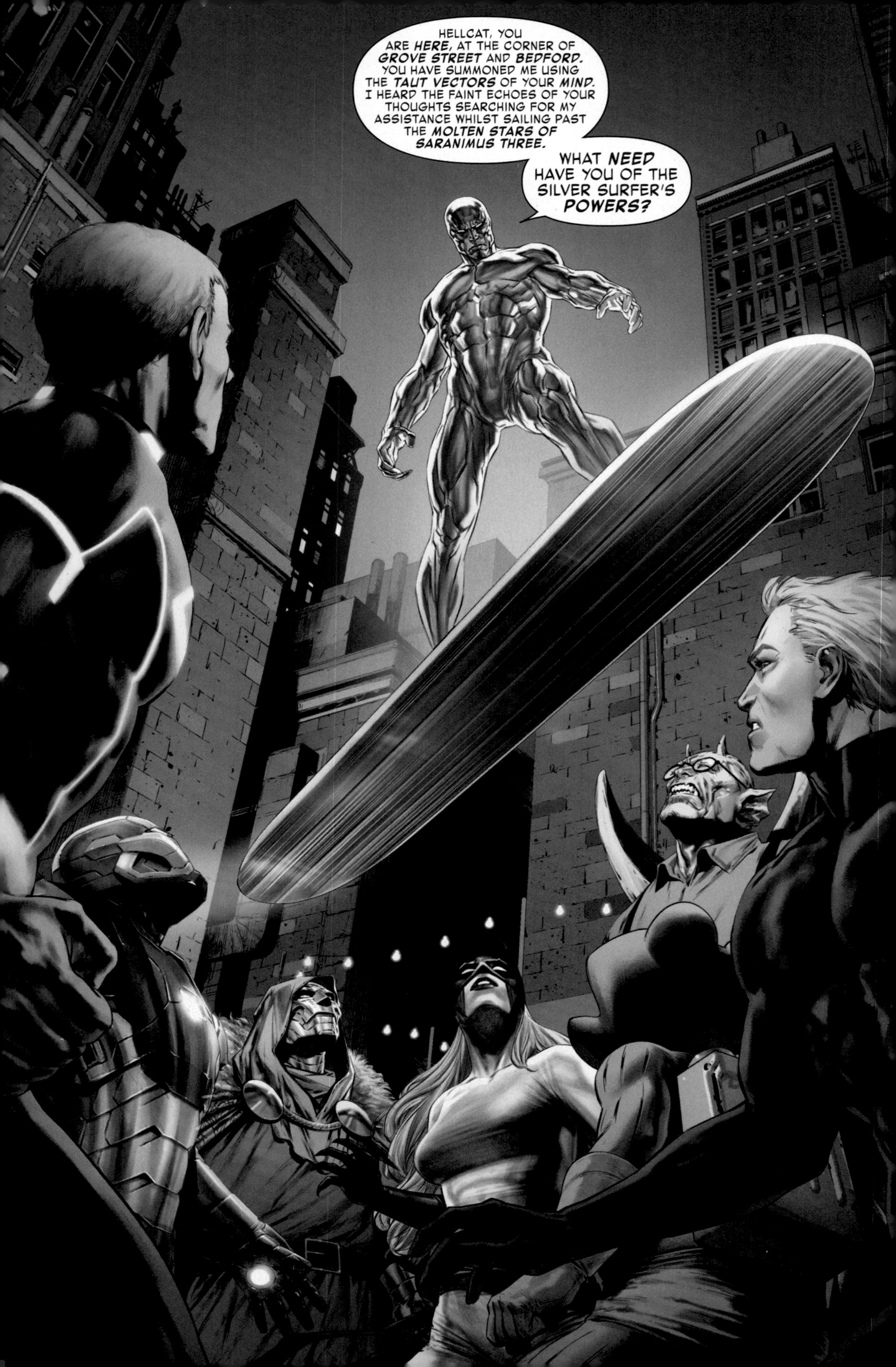
HELLCAT, YOU ARE HERE, AT THE CORNER OF GROVE STREET AND BEDFORD. YOU HAVE SUMMONED ME USING THE TAUT VECTORS OF YOUR MIND. I HEARD THE FAINT ECHOES OF YOUR THOUGHTS SEARCHING FOR MY ASSISTANCE WHILST SAILING PAST THE MOLTEN STARS OF SARANIMUS THREE.
WHAT NEED HAVE YOU OF THE SILVER SURFER'S POWERS?

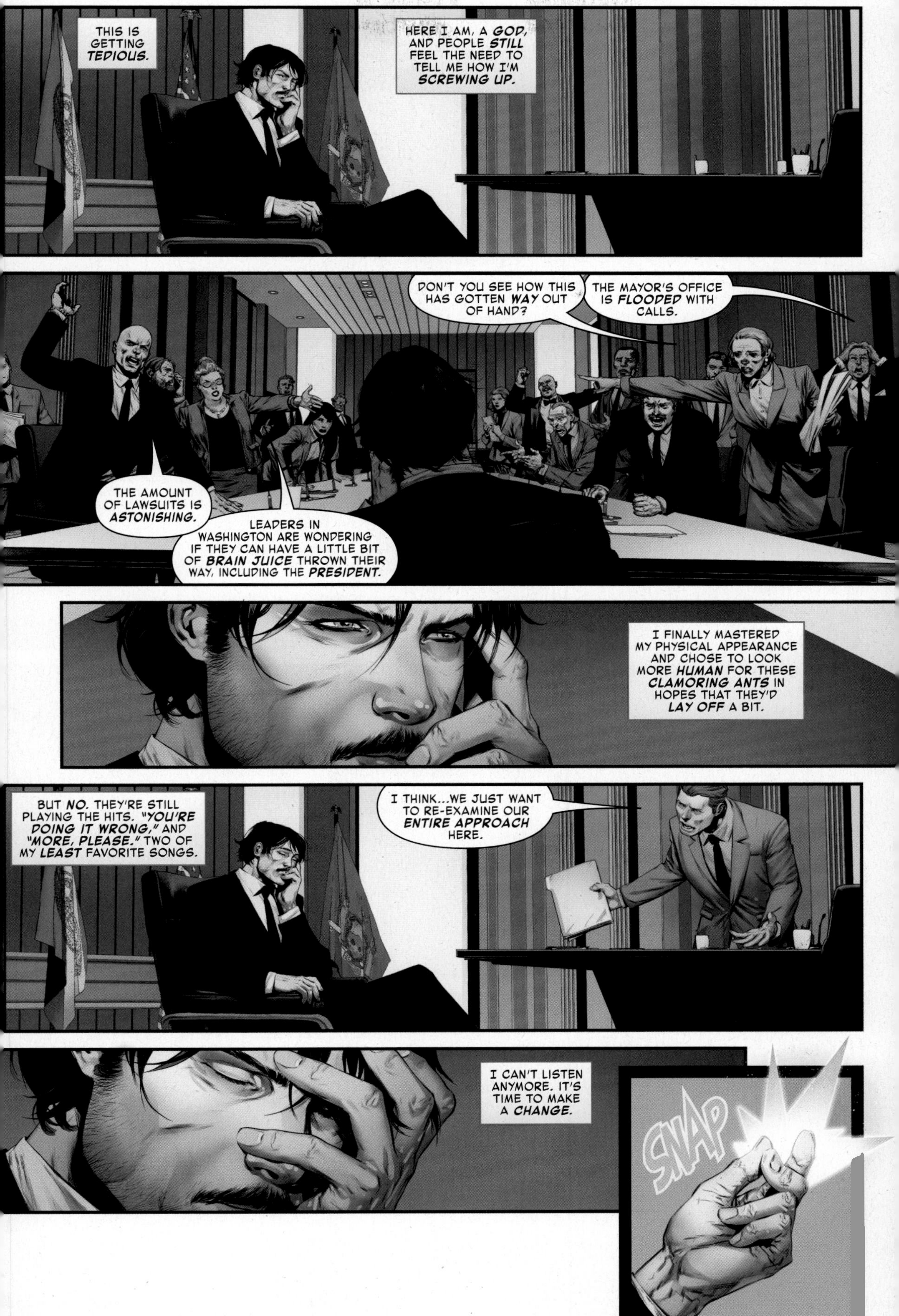
THIS IS GETTING TEDIOUS.
HERE I AM, A GOD, AND PEOPLE STILL FEEL THE NEED TO TELL ME HOW I'M SCREWING UP.
DON'T YOU SEE HOW THIS HAS GOTTEN WAY OUT OF HAND?
THE MAYOR'S OFFICE IS FLOODED WITH CALLS.
THE AMOUNT OF LAWSUITS IS ASTONISHING.
LEADERS IN WASHINGTON ARE WONDERING IF THEY CAN HAVE A LITTLE BIT OF BRAIN JUICE THROWN THEIR WAY, INCLUDING THE PRESIDENT.
I FINALLY MASTERED MY PHYSICAL APPEARANCE AND CHOSE TO LOOK MORE HUMAN FOR THESE CLAMORING ANTS IN HOPES THAT THEY'D LAY OFF A BIT.
BUT NO. THEY'RE STILL PLAYING THE HITS. "YOU'RE DOING IT WRONG," AND "MORE, PLEASE." TWO OF MY LEAST FAVORITE SONGS.
I THINK...WE JUST WANT TO RE-EXAMINE OUR ENTIRE APPROACH HERE.
I CAN'T LISTEN ANYMORE. IT'S TIME TO MAKE A CHANGE.
SNAP

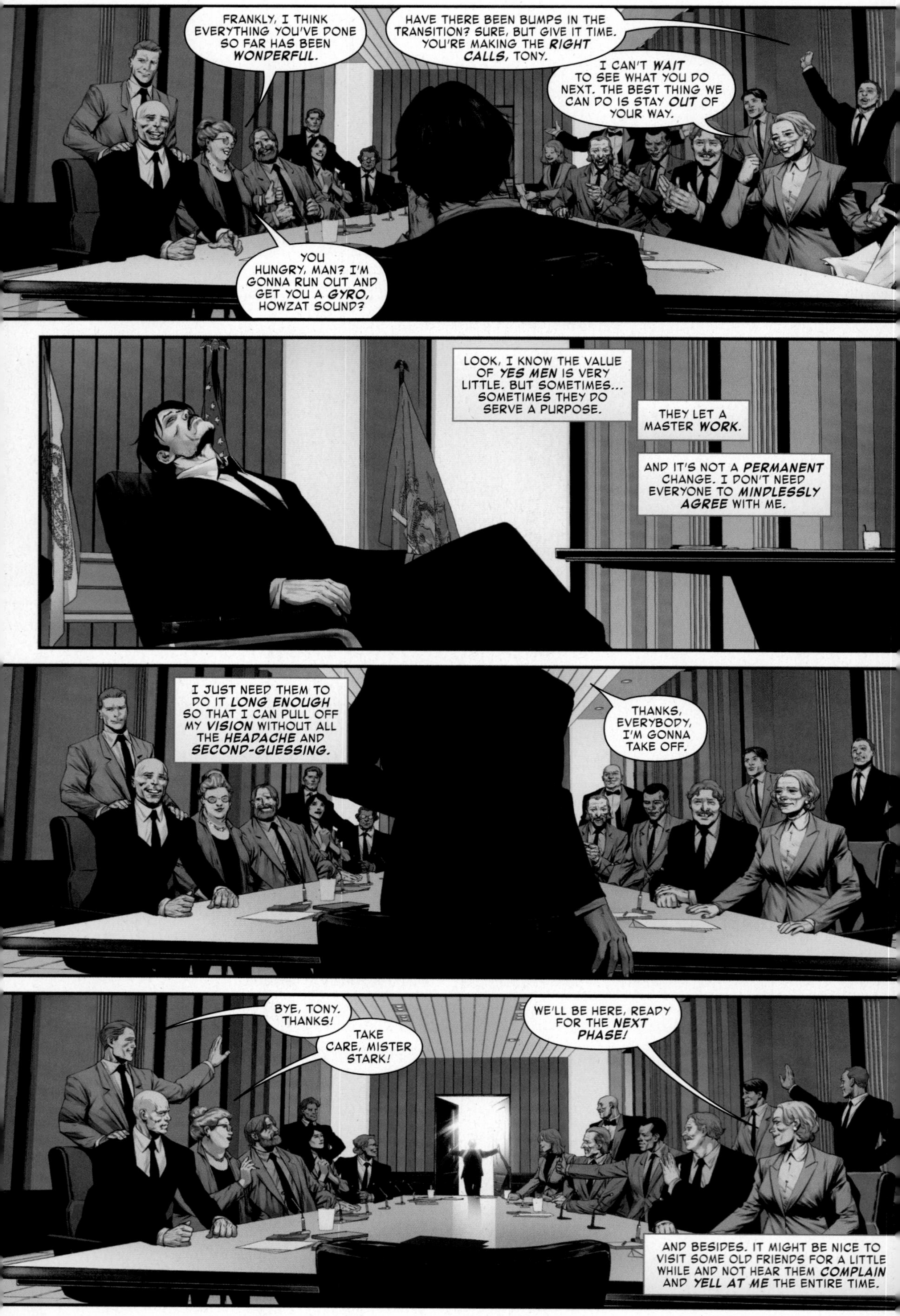
FRANKLY, I THINK EVERYTHING YOU'VE DONE SO FAR HAS BEEN WONDERFUL.
HAVE THERE BEEN BUMPS IN THE TRANSITION? SURE, BUT GIVE IT TIME. YOU'RE MAKING THE RIGHT CALLS, TONY.
I CAN'T WAIT TO SEE WHAT YOU DO NEXT. THE BEST THING WE CAN DO IS STAY OUT OF YOUR WAY.
YOU HUNGRY, MAN? I'M GONNA RUN OUT AND GET YOU A GYRO, HOWZAT SOUND?
LOOK, I KNOW THE VALUE OF YES MEN IS VERY LITTLE. BUT SOMETIMES... SOMETIMES THEY DO SERVE A PURPOSE.
THEY LET A MASTER WORK.
AND IT'S NOT A PERMANENT CHANGE. I DON'T NEED EVERYONE TO MINDLESSLY AGREE WITH ME.
I JUST NEED THEM TO DO IT LONG ENOUGH SO THAT I CAN PULL OFF MY VISION WITHOUT ALL THE HEADACHE AND SECOND-GUESSING.
THANKS, EVERYBODY, I'M GONNA TAKE OFF.
BYE, TONY. THANKS!
TAKE CARE, MISTER STARK!
WE'LL BE HERE, READY FOR THE NEXT PHASE!
AND BESIDES. IT MIGHT BE NICE TO VISIT SOME OLD FRIENDS FOR A LITTLE WHILE AND NOT HEAR THEM COMPLAIN AND YELL AT ME THE ENTIRE TIME.

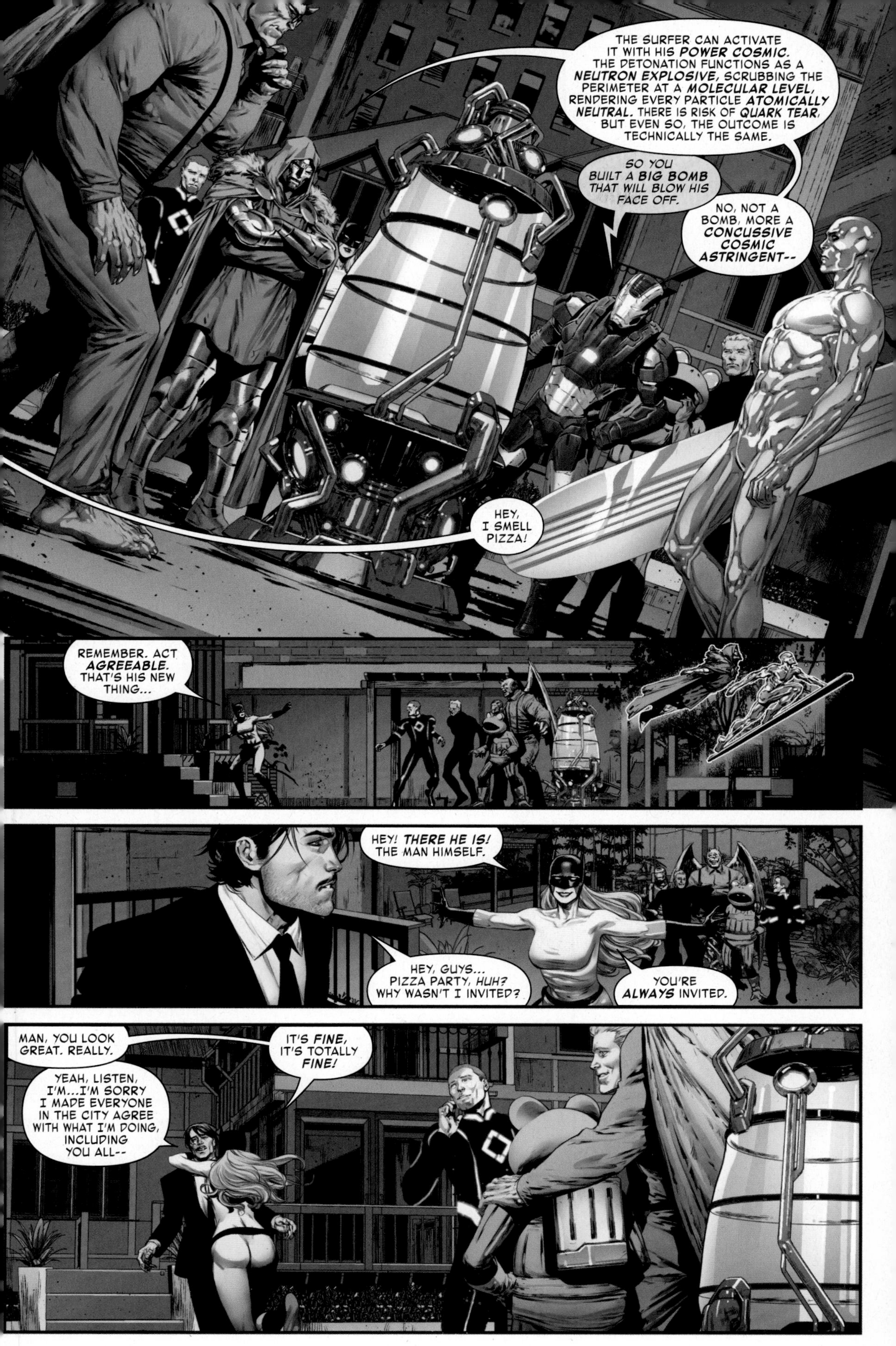
THE SURFER CAN ACTIVATE IT WITH HIS POWER COSMIC. THE DETONATION FUNCTIONS AS A NEUTRON EXPLOSIVE, SCRUBBING THE PERIMETER AT A MOLECULAR LEVEL, RENDERING EVERY PARTICLE ATOMICALLY NEUTRAL. THERE IS RISK OF QUARK TEAR, BUT EVEN SO, THE OUTCOME IS TECHNICALLY THE SAME.
SO YOU BUILT A BIG BOMB THAT WILL BLOW HIS FACE OFF.
NO, NOT A BOMB, MORE A CONCUSSIVE COSMIC ASTRINGENT--
HEY, I SMELL PIZZA!
REMEMBER. ACT AGREEABLE. THAT'S HIS NEW THING...
HEY! THERE HE IS! THE MAN HIMSELF.
HEY, GUYS... PIZZA PARTY, HUH? WHY WASN'T I INVITED?
YOU'RE ALWAYS INVITED.
MAN, YOU LOOK GREAT. REALLY.
YEAH, LISTEN, I'M...I'M SORRY I MADE EVERYONE IN THE CITY AGREE WITH WHAT I'M DOING, INCLUDING YOU ALL--
IT'S FINE, IT'S TOTALLY FINE!

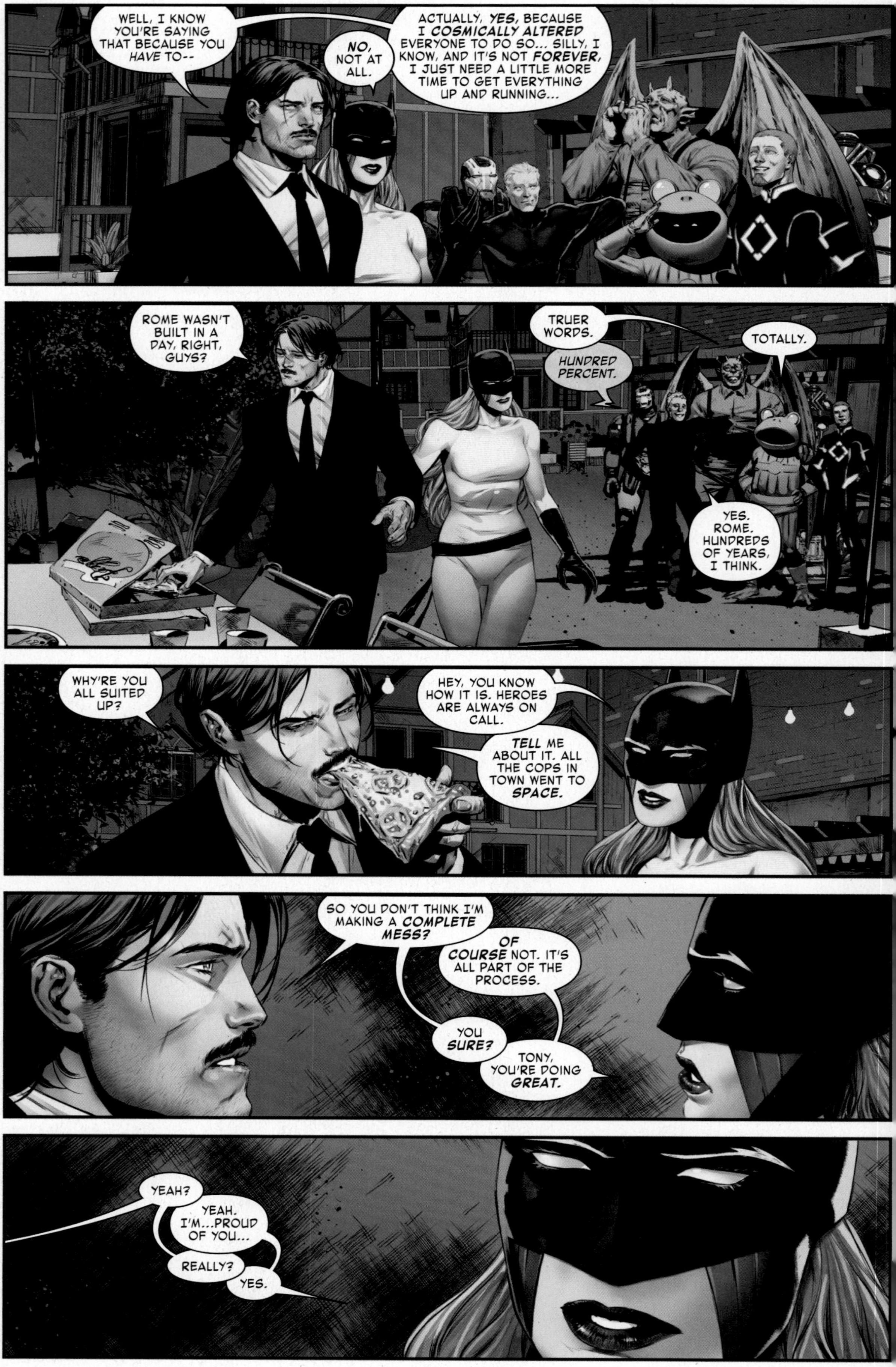

WELL, I KNOW YOU'RE SAYING THAT BECAUSE YOU HAVE TO--
NO, NOT AT ALL.
ACTUALLY, YES, BECAUSE I COSMICALLY ALTERED EVERYONE TO DO SO... SILLY, I KNOW, AND IT'S NOT FOREVER, I JUST NEED A LITTLE MORE TIME TO GET EVERYTHING UP AND RUNNING...
ROME WASN'T BUILT IN A DAY, RIGHT, GUYS?
TRUER WORDS.
HUNDRED PERCENT.
TOTALLY.
YES. ROME. HUNDREDS OF YEARS, I THINK.
WHY'RE YOU ALL SUITED UP?
HEY, YOU KNOW HOW IT IS. HEROES ARE ALWAYS ON CALL.
TELL ME ABOUT IT. ALL THE COPS IN TOWN WENT TO SPACE.
SO YOU DON'T THINK I'M MAKING A COMPLETE MESS?
OF COURSE NOT. IT'S ALL PART OF THE PROCESS.
YOU SURE?
TONY, YOU'RE DOING GREAT.
YEAH?
YEAH. I'M...PROUD OF YOU...
REALLY?
YES.

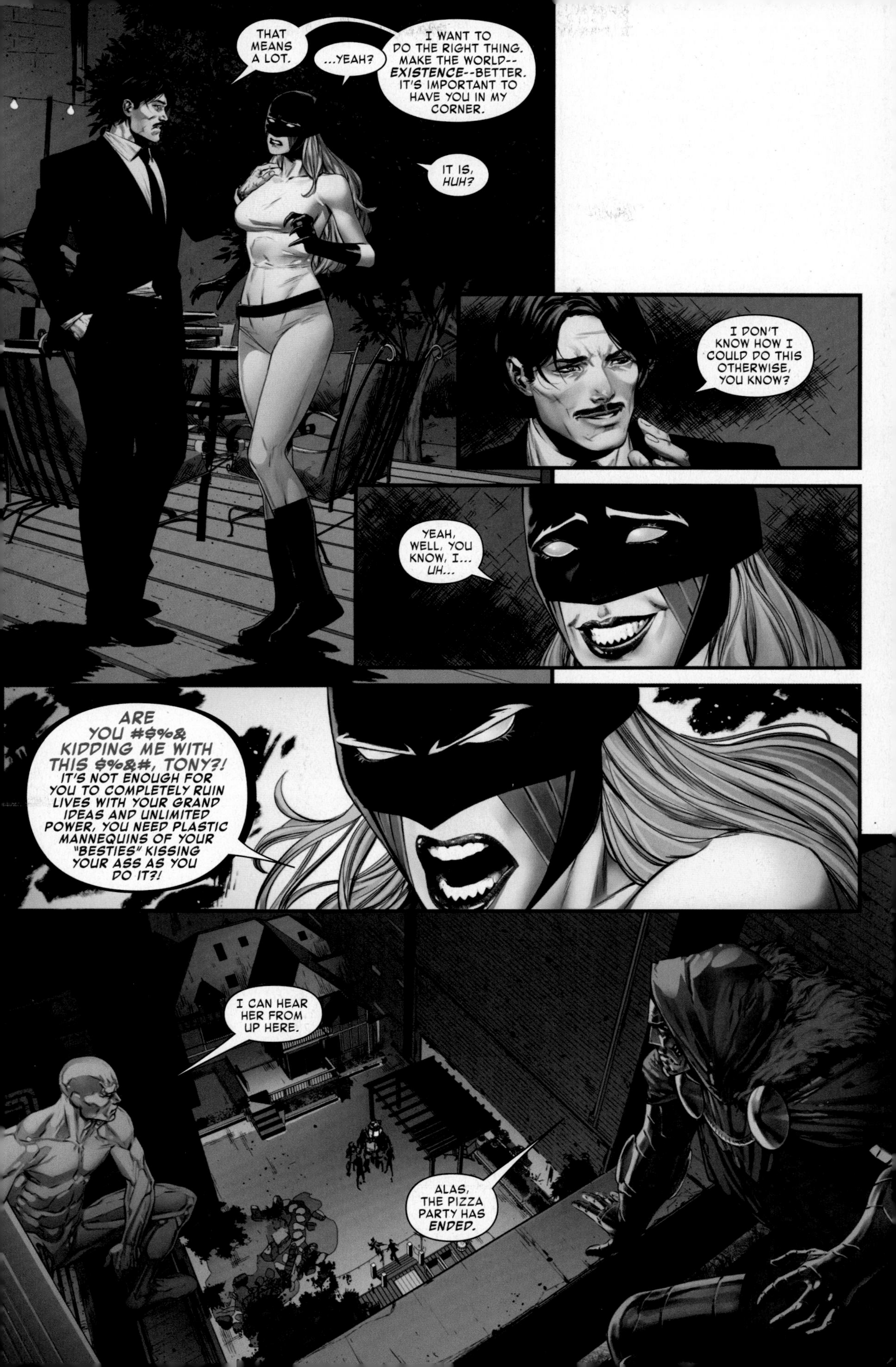

THAT MEANS A LOT.
...YEAH?
I WANT TO DO THE RIGHT THING. MAKE THE WORLD-- *EXISTENCE*--BETTER. IT'S IMPORTANT TO HAVE YOU IN MY CORNER.
IT IS, *HUH?*
I DON'T KNOW HOW I COULD DO THIS OTHERWISE, YOU KNOW?
YEAH, WELL, YOU KNOW, I... *UH...*
ARE YOU #$%& KIDDING ME WITH THIS $%&#, TONY?! IT'S NOT ENOUGH FOR YOU TO COMPLETELY RUIN LIVES WITH YOUR GRAND IDEAS AND UNLIMITED POWER, YOU NEED PLASTIC MANNEQUINS OF YOUR "BESTIES" KISSING YOUR ASS AS YOU DO IT?!
I CAN HEAR HER FROM UP HERE.
ALAS, THE PIZZA PARTY HAS *ENDED.*

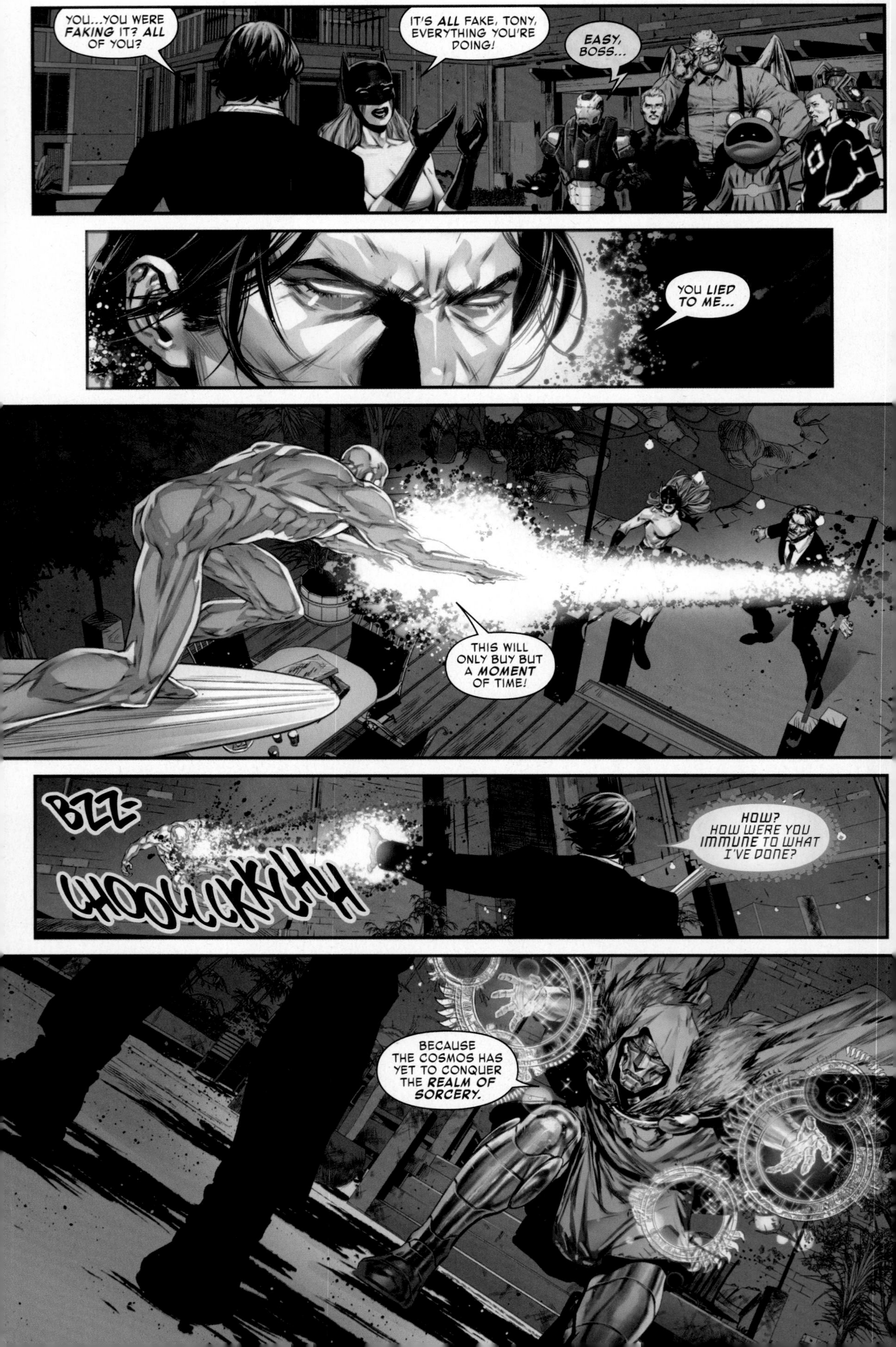

YOU...YOU WERE FAKING IT? ALL OF YOU?
IT'S ALL FAKE, TONY, EVERYTHING YOU'RE DOING!
EASY, BOSS...
YOU LIED TO ME...
THIS WILL ONLY BUY BUT A MOMENT OF TIME!
BZZ-CHOOUCKKCHHH
HOW? HOW WERE YOU IMMUNE TO WHAT I'VE DONE?
BECAUSE THE COSMOS HAS YET TO CONQUER THE REALM OF SORCERY.

OH NEAT, *DOCTOR #$%& DOOM. VERY* COOL OF YOU GUYS. SO IT WAS SOME CHEAP *PROTECTION SPELL*, THEN, *VICTOR*? A *PARLOR TRICK*?

SLANDER ME ALL YOU WANT, STARK, BUT THEN *ASK* YOURSELF, WHAT KIND OF *GOD* CAN BE MADE IMPOTENT BY A *LIVING ROOM MAGICIAN*?

OH, I SEE. YOU WANT ME *GONE*, HUH? YOU *TRUST* ME THAT LITTLE.

WE DON'T WANT YOU *GONE*, WE WANT YOU *BACK*!

WE'RE *SAVING* YOU!

WITH A *WEAPON*.

NOT SO MUCH A WEAPON AS A *CONCUSSIVE COSMIC ASTRINGENT*--

BUZZEEAACCK

SWEEOOWWFFFF

...WHO NEEDS *DOCTOR DOOM*? YOU KNOW, VICTOR, I SAW WHAT YOU DID WITH *YOUR GREAT POWER. ANNIHILATING AN ENTIRE UNIVERSE.** A *HYPOCRITE* IN ARMOR IS STILL JUST A *HYPOCRITE*.

ARRRGGGHH!

WITH FRIENDS LIKE THESE...

KVZPEEEOOOWWM

*IN IRON MAN #15. --TOM

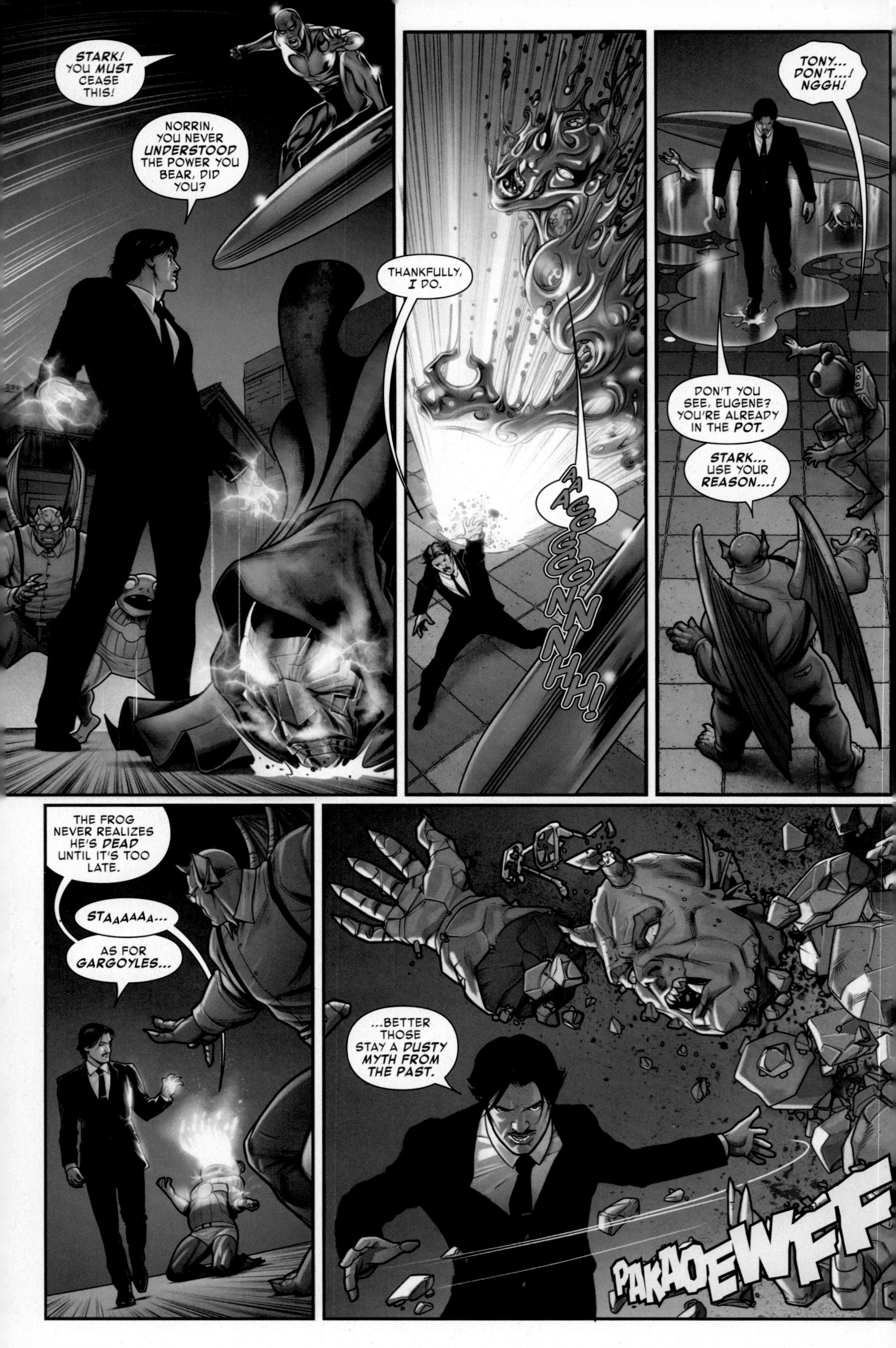
STARK! YOU MUST CEASE THIS!
NORRIN, YOU NEVER UNDERSTOOD THE POWER YOU BEAR, DID YOU?
THANKFULLY, I DO.
AAAGGGGGNNNHH!
TONY... DON'T...! NGGH!
DON'T YOU SEE, EUGENE? YOU'RE ALREADY IN THE POT.
STARK... USE YOUR REASON...!
THE FROG NEVER REALIZES HE'S DEAD UNTIL IT'S TOO LATE.
STAAAAAA...
AS FOR GARGOYLES...
...BETTER THOSE STAY A DUSTY MYTH FROM THE PAST.
PAKAOEWFF

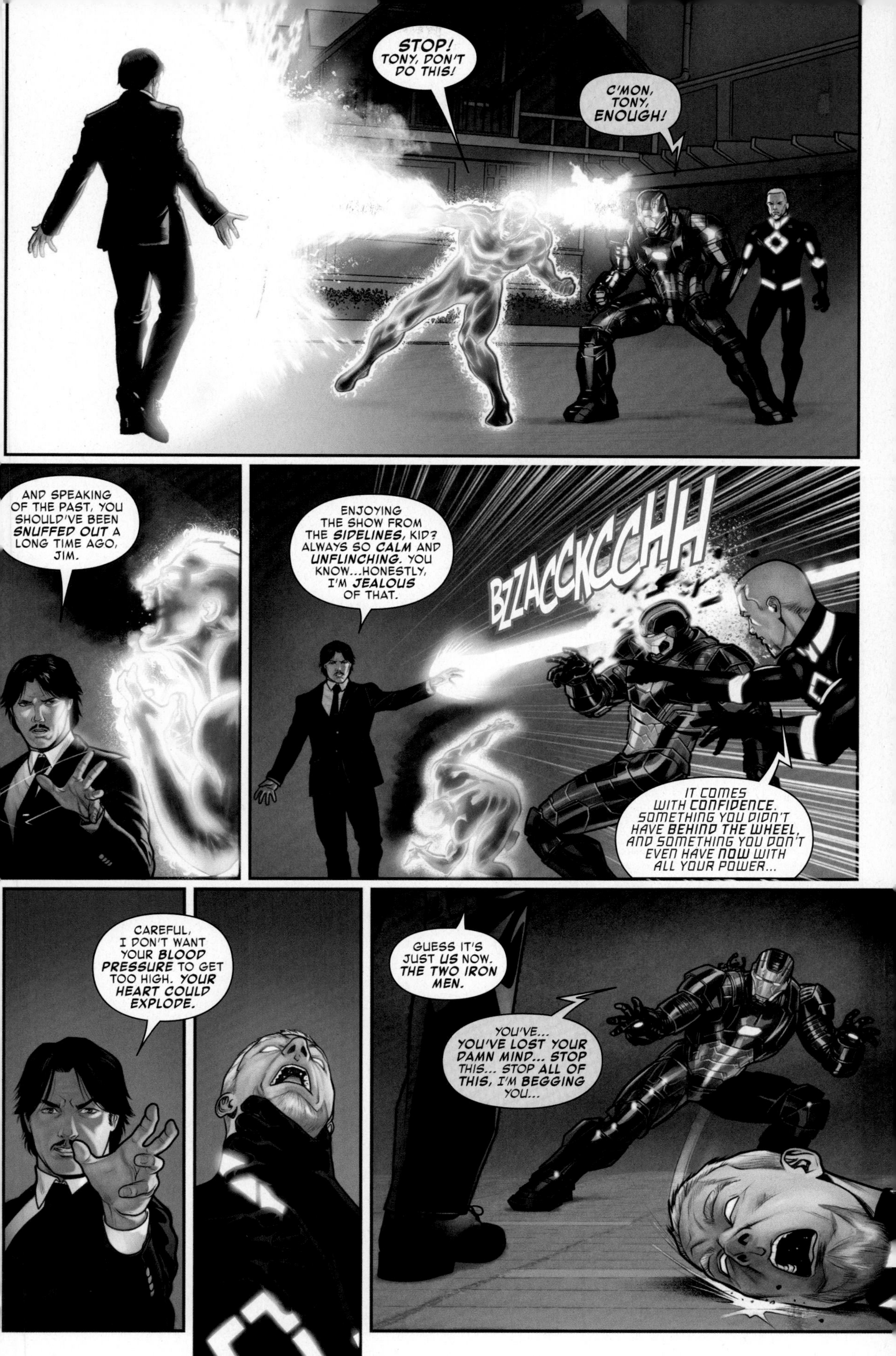
STOP! TONY, DON'T DO THIS!
C'MON, TONY, ENOUGH!
AND SPEAKING OF THE PAST, YOU SHOULD'VE BEEN SNUFFED OUT A LONG TIME AGO, JIM.
ENJOYING THE SHOW FROM THE SIDELINES, KID? ALWAYS SO CALM AND UNFLINCHING. YOU KNOW...HONESTLY, I'M JEALOUS OF THAT.
BZZACCKCCHH
IT COMES WITH CONFIDENCE. SOMETHING YOU DIDN'T HAVE BEHIND THE WHEEL, AND SOMETHING YOU DON'T EVEN HAVE NOW WITH ALL YOUR POWER...
CAREFUL, I DON'T WANT YOUR BLOOD PRESSURE TO GET TOO HIGH. YOUR HEART COULD EXPLODE.
GUESS IT'S JUST US NOW. THE TWO IRON MEN.
YOU'VE... YOU'VE LOST YOUR DAMN MIND... STOP THIS... STOP ALL OF THIS, I'M BEGGING YOU...

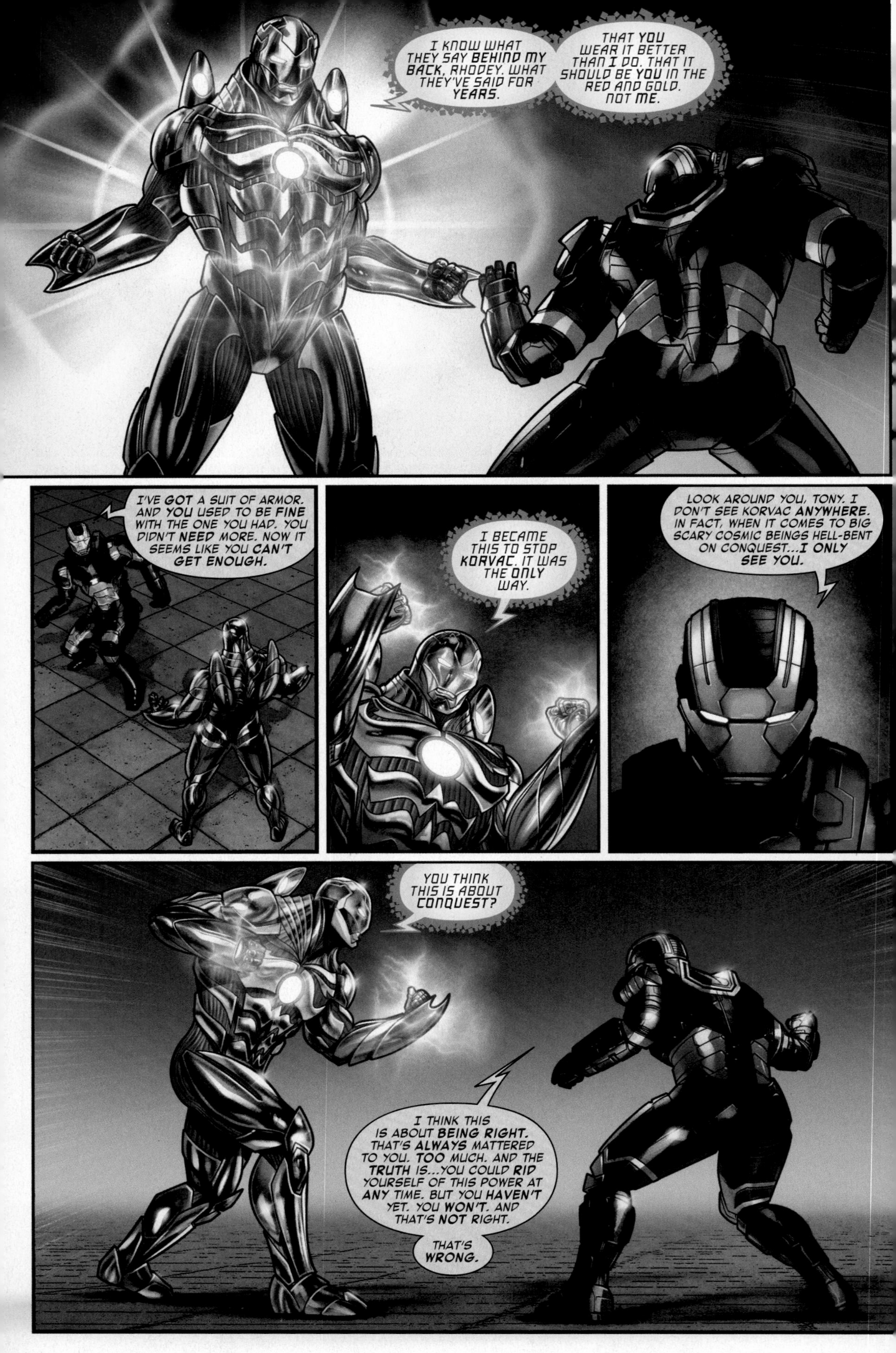
I KNOW WHAT THEY SAY BEHIND MY BACK, RHODEY. WHAT THEY'VE SAID FOR YEARS.
THAT YOU WEAR IT BETTER THAN I DO. THAT IT SHOULD BE YOU IN THE RED AND GOLD. NOT ME.
I'VE GOT A SUIT OF ARMOR. AND YOU USED TO BE FINE WITH THE ONE YOU HAD. YOU DIDN'T NEED MORE. NOW IT SEEMS LIKE YOU CAN'T GET ENOUGH.
I BECAME THIS TO STOP KORVAC. IT WAS THE ONLY WAY.
LOOK AROUND YOU, TONY. I DON'T SEE KORVAC ANYWHERE. IN FACT, WHEN IT COMES TO BIG SCARY COSMIC BEINGS HELL-BENT ON CONQUEST...I ONLY SEE YOU.
YOU THINK THIS IS ABOUT CONQUEST?
I THINK THIS IS ABOUT BEING RIGHT. THAT'S ALWAYS MATTERED TO YOU. TOO MUCH. AND THE TRUTH IS...YOU COULD RID YOURSELF OF THIS POWER AT ANY TIME. BUT YOU HAVEN'T YET. YOU WON'T. AND THAT'S NOT RIGHT.
THAT'S WRONG.

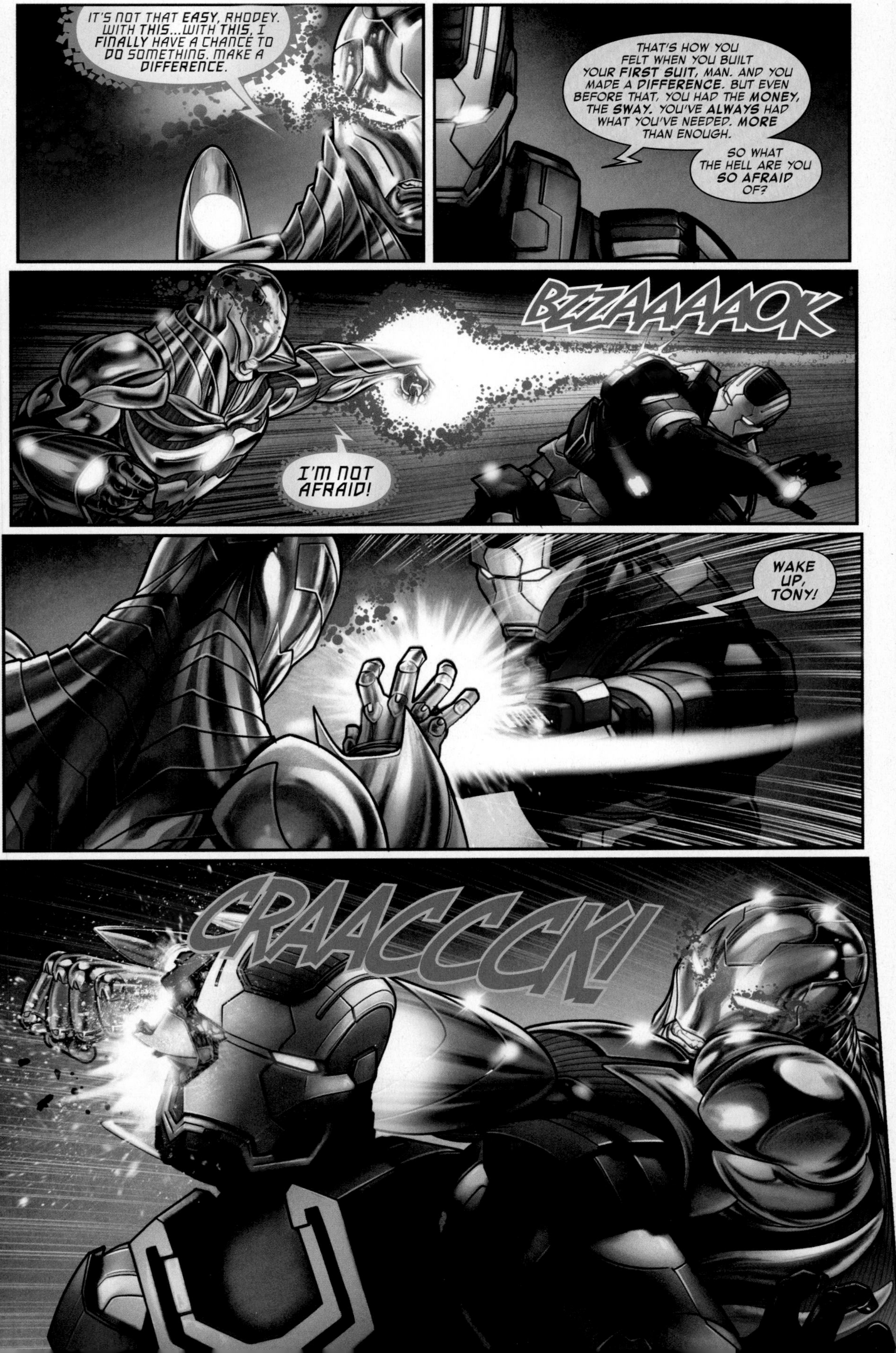
IT'S NOT THAT EASY, RHODEY. WITH THIS...WITH THIS, I FINALLY HAVE A CHANCE TO DO SOMETHING. MAKE A DIFFERENCE.
THAT'S HOW YOU FELT WHEN YOU BUILT YOUR FIRST SUIT, MAN. AND YOU MADE A DIFFERENCE. BUT EVEN BEFORE THAT, YOU HAD THE MONEY, THE SWAY. YOU'VE ALWAYS HAD WHAT YOU'VE NEEDED. MORE THAN ENOUGH.
SO WHAT THE HELL ARE YOU SO AFRAID OF?
BZZAAAAAOK
I'M NOT AFRAID!
WAKE UP, TONY!
CRAACCCK!

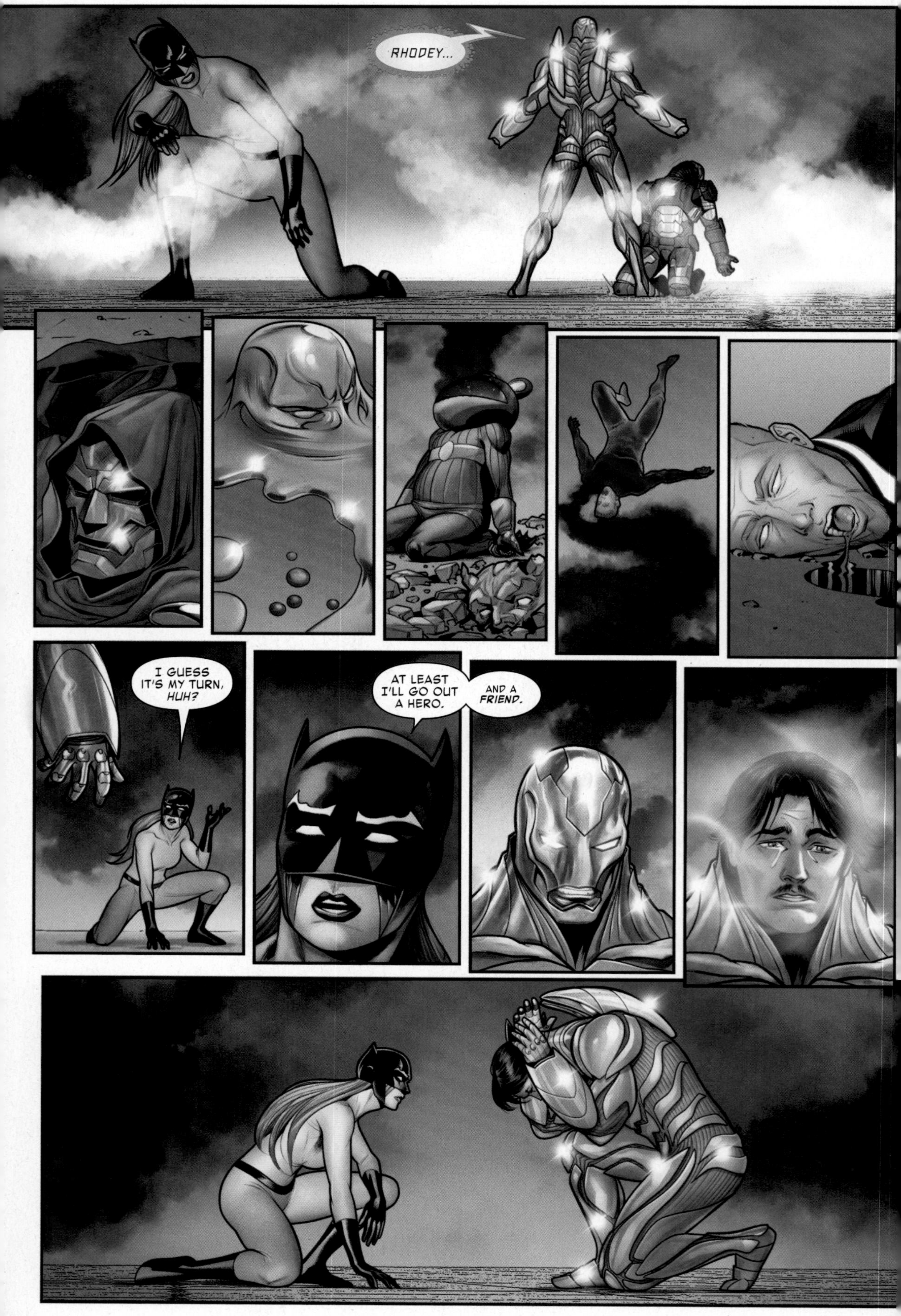
RHODEY...
I GUESS IT'S MY TURN, HUH?
AT LEAST I'LL GO OUT A HERO.
AND A FRIEND.

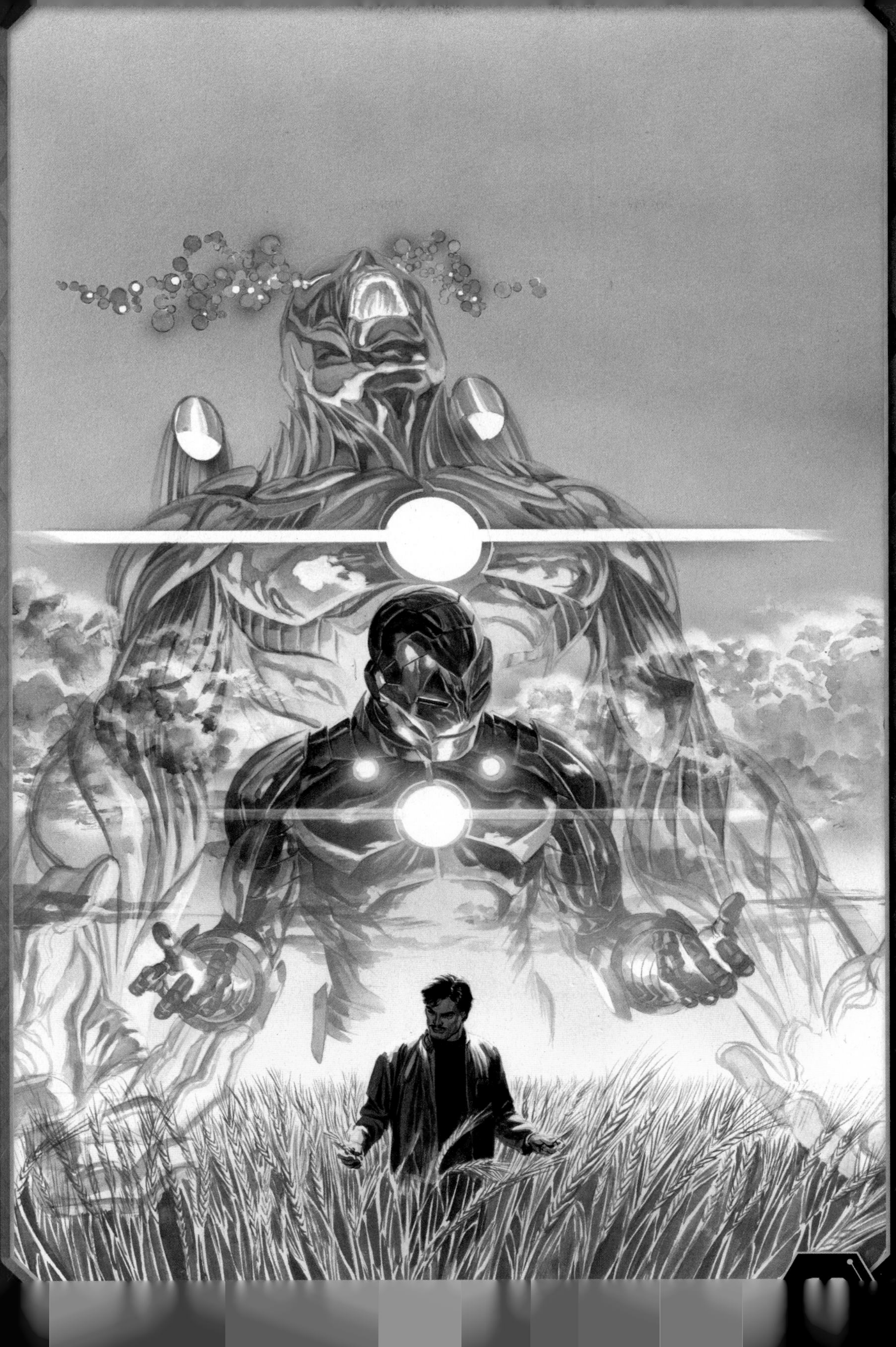

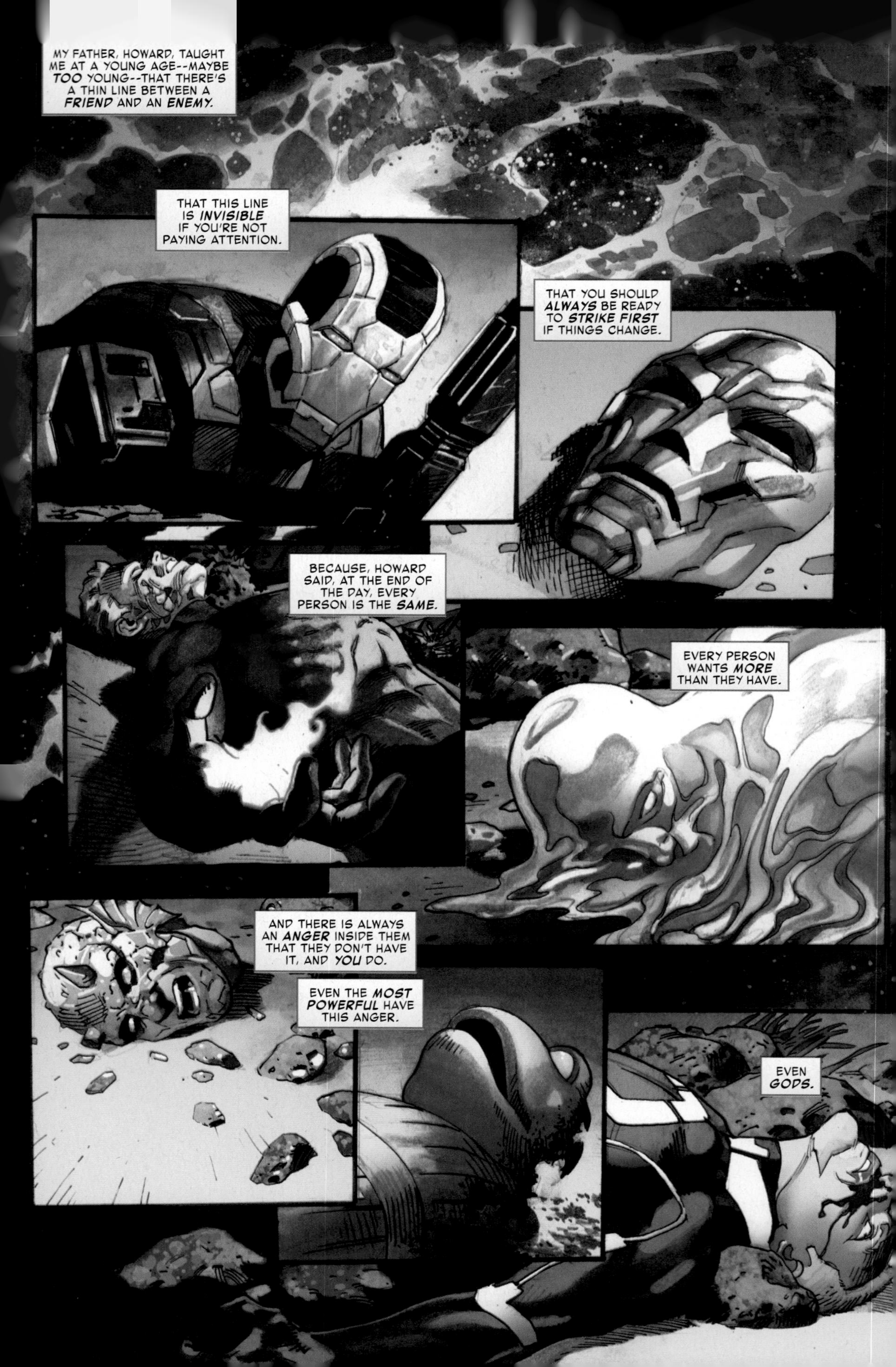
MY FATHER, HOWARD, TAUGHT ME AT A YOUNG AGE--MAYBE TOO YOUNG--THAT THERE'S A THIN LINE BETWEEN A FRIEND AND AN ENEMY.
THAT THIS LINE IS INVISIBLE IF YOU'RE NOT PAYING ATTENTION.
THAT YOU SHOULD ALWAYS BE READY TO STRIKE FIRST IF THINGS CHANGE.
BECAUSE, HOWARD SAID, AT THE END OF THE DAY, EVERY PERSON IS THE SAME.
EVERY PERSON WANTS MORE THAN THEY HAVE.
AND THERE IS ALWAYS AN ANGER INSIDE THEM THAT THEY DON'T HAVE IT, AND YOU DO.
EVEN THE MOST POWERFUL HAVE THIS ANGER.
EVEN GODS.

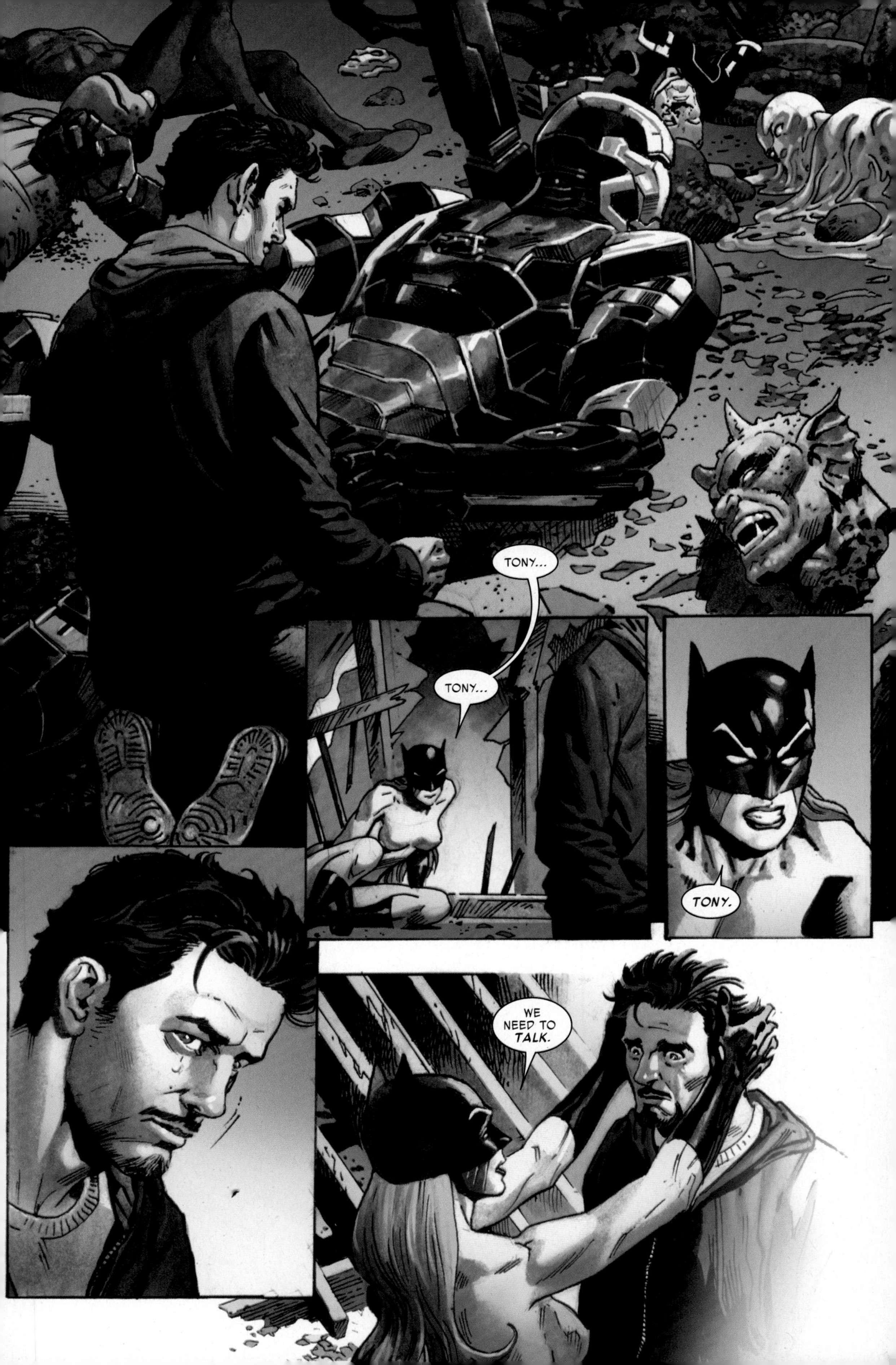
TONY...
TONY...
TONY.
WE NEED TO TALK.

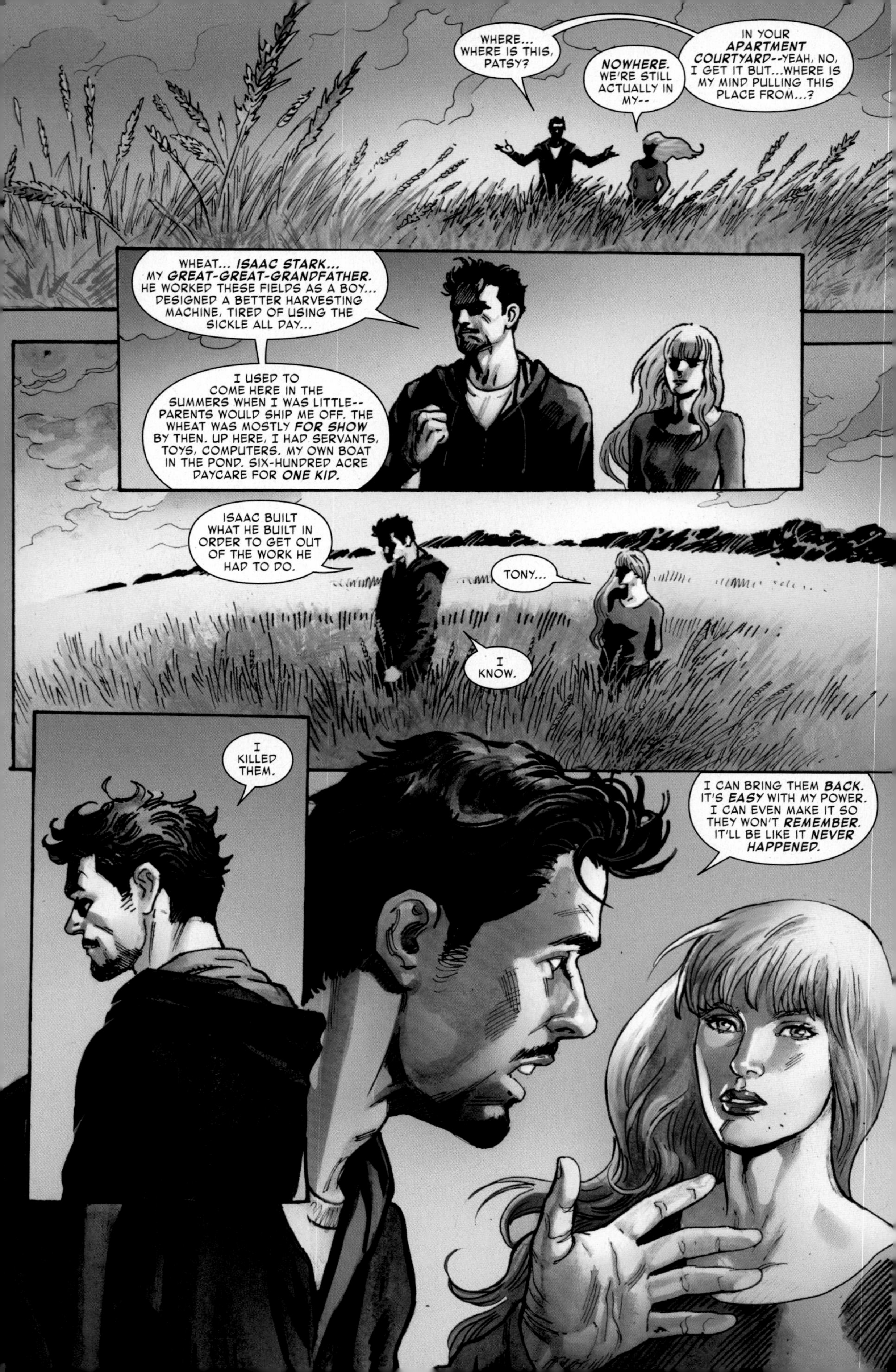

WHERE... WHERE IS THIS, PATSY?
NOWHERE. WE'RE STILL ACTUALLY IN MY--
IN YOUR APARTMENT COURTYARD--YEAH, NO, I GET IT BUT...WHERE IS MY MIND PULLING THIS PLACE FROM...?
WHEAT... ISAAC STARK... MY GREAT-GREAT-GRANDFATHER. HE WORKED THESE FIELDS AS A BOY... DESIGNED A BETTER HARVESTING MACHINE, TIRED OF USING THE SICKLE ALL DAY...
I USED TO COME HERE IN THE SUMMERS WHEN I WAS LITTLE-- PARENTS WOULD SHIP ME OFF. THE WHEAT WAS MOSTLY FOR SHOW BY THEN. UP HERE, I HAD SERVANTS, TOYS, COMPUTERS. MY OWN BOAT IN THE POND. SIX-HUNDRED ACRE DAYCARE FOR ONE KID.
ISAAC BUILT WHAT HE BUILT IN ORDER TO GET OUT OF THE WORK HE HAD TO DO.
TONY...
I KNOW.
I KILLED THEM.
I CAN BRING THEM BACK. IT'S EASY WITH MY POWER. I CAN EVEN MAKE IT SO THEY WON'T REMEMBER. IT'LL BE LIKE IT NEVER HAPPENED.

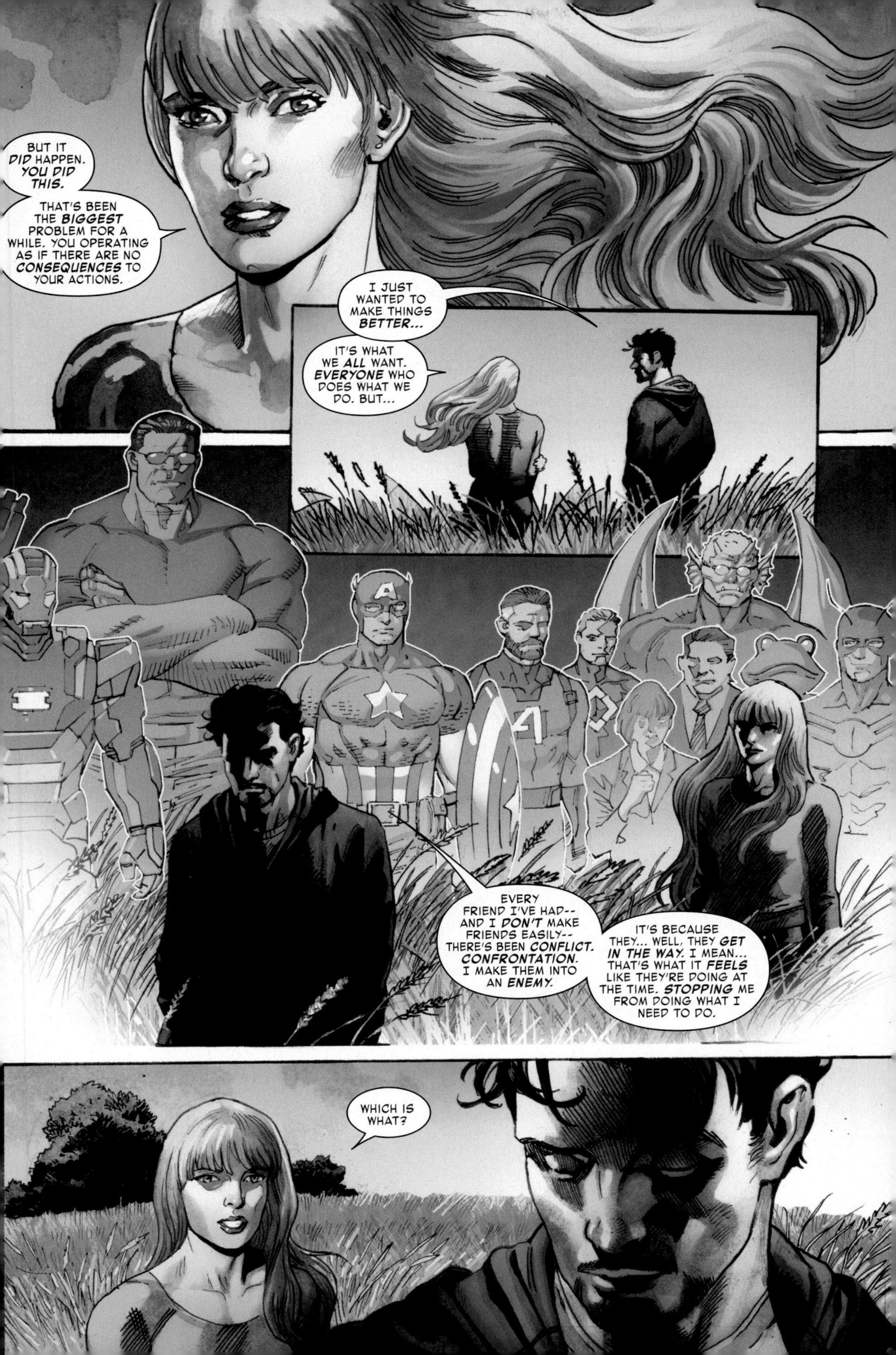

BUT IT DID HAPPEN. YOU DID THIS.
THAT'S BEEN THE BIGGEST PROBLEM FOR A WHILE. YOU OPERATING AS IF THERE ARE NO CONSEQUENCES TO YOUR ACTIONS.
I JUST WANTED TO MAKE THINGS BETTER...
IT'S WHAT WE ALL WANT. EVERYONE WHO DOES WHAT WE DO. BUT...
EVERY FRIEND I'VE HAD-- AND I DON'T MAKE FRIENDS EASILY-- THERE'S BEEN CONFLICT. CONFRONTATION. I MAKE THEM INTO AN ENEMY.
IT'S BECAUSE THEY... WELL, THEY GET IN THE WAY. I MEAN... THAT'S WHAT IT FEELS LIKE THEY'RE DOING AT THE TIME. STOPPING ME FROM DOING WHAT I NEED TO DO.
WHICH IS WHAT?

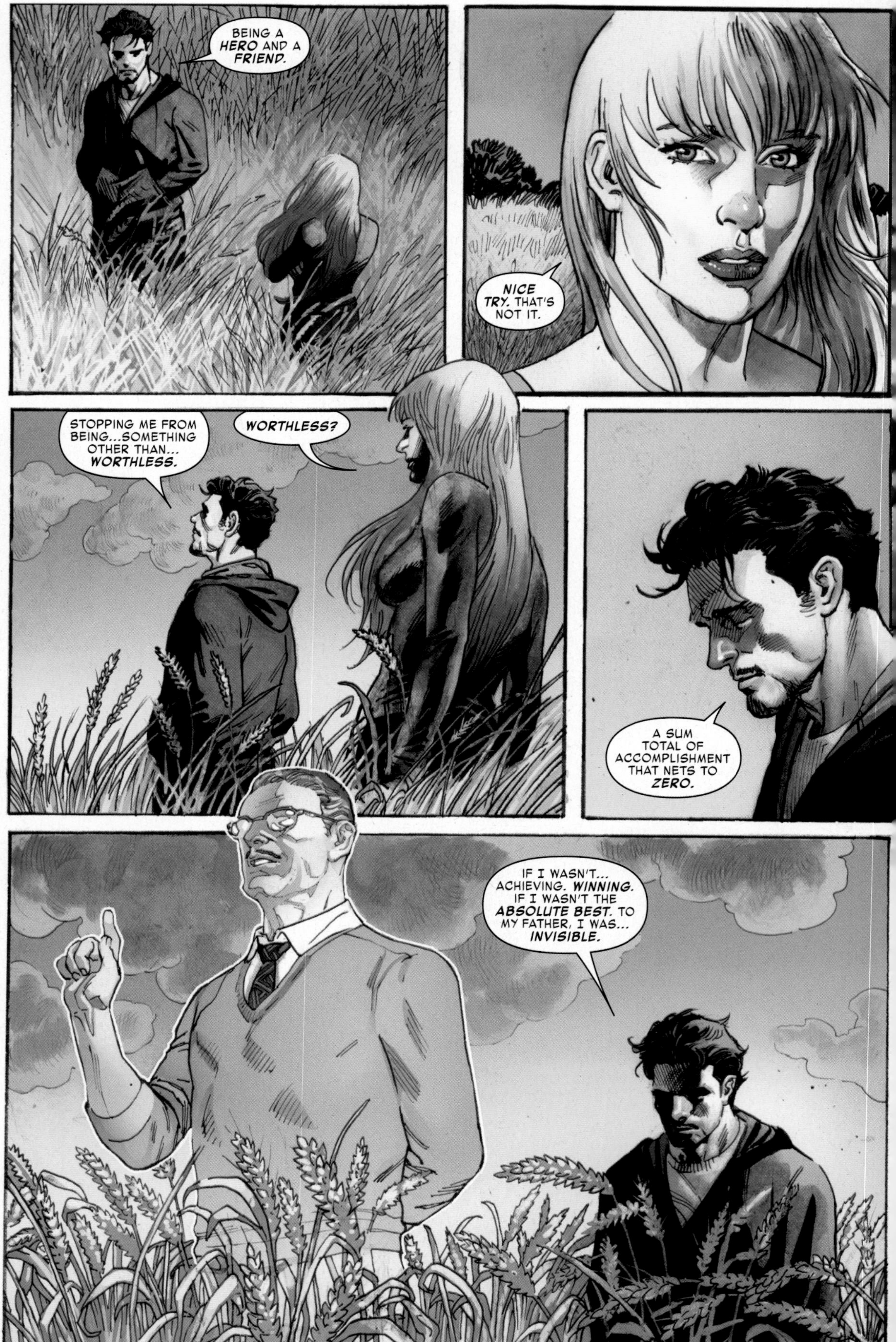
BEING A HERO AND A FRIEND.
NICE TRY. THAT'S NOT IT.
STOPPING ME FROM BEING...SOMETHING OTHER THAN... WORTHLESS.
WORTHLESS?
A SUM TOTAL OF ACCOMPLISHMENT THAT NETS TO ZERO.
IF I WASN'T... ACHIEVING. WINNING. IF I WASN'T THE ABSOLUTE BEST. TO MY FATHER, I WAS... INVISIBLE.

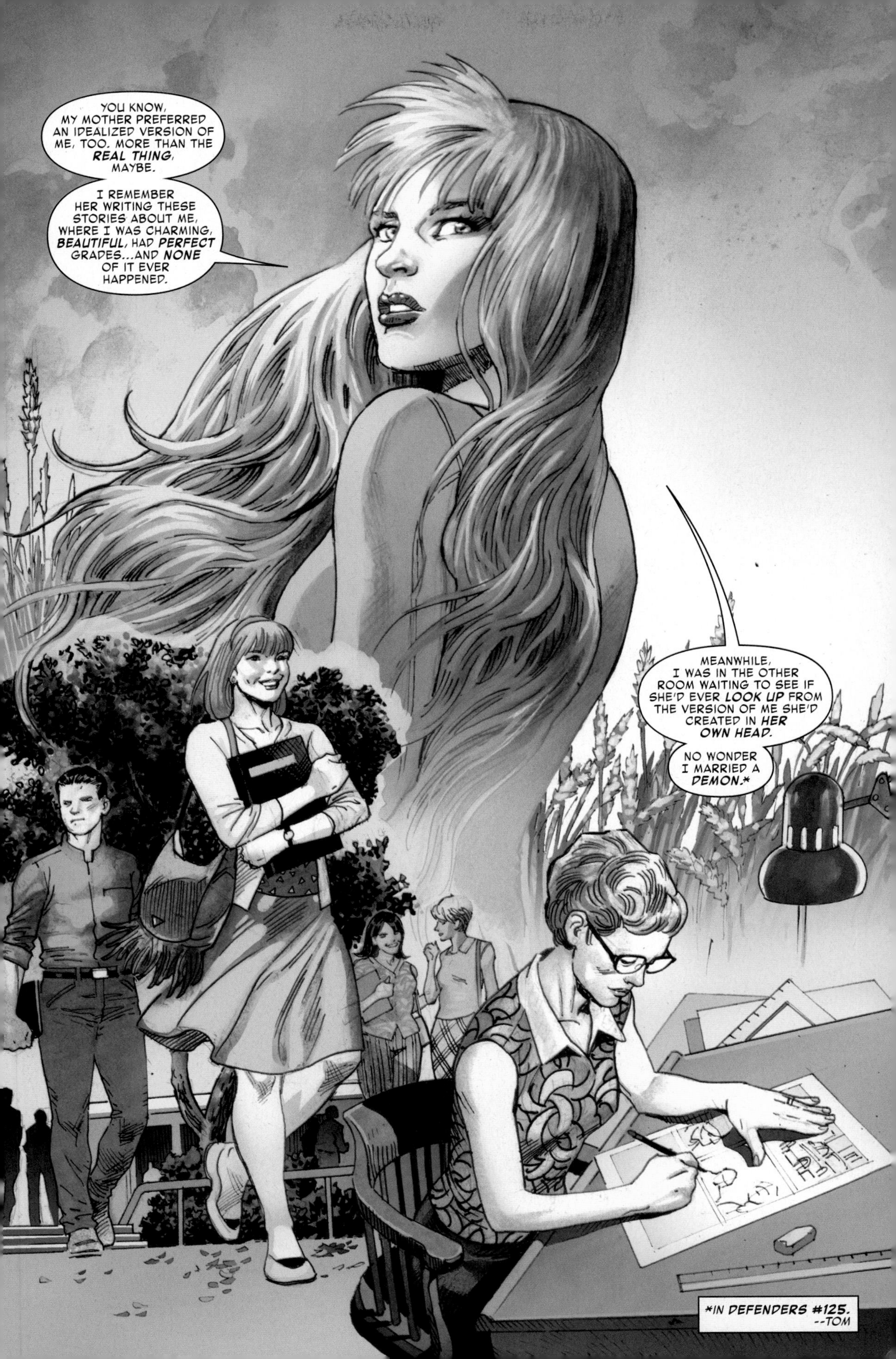
YOU KNOW, MY MOTHER PREFERRED AN IDEALIZED VERSION OF ME, TOO. MORE THAN THE REAL THING, MAYBE.
I REMEMBER HER WRITING THESE STORIES ABOUT ME, WHERE I WAS CHARMING, BEAUTIFUL, HAD PERFECT GRADES...AND NONE OF IT EVER HAPPENED.
MEANWHILE, I WAS IN THE OTHER ROOM WAITING TO SEE IF SHE'D EVER LOOK UP FROM THE VERSION OF ME SHE'D CREATED IN HER OWN HEAD.
NO WONDER I MARRIED A DEMON.*
*IN DEFENDERS #125. --TOM

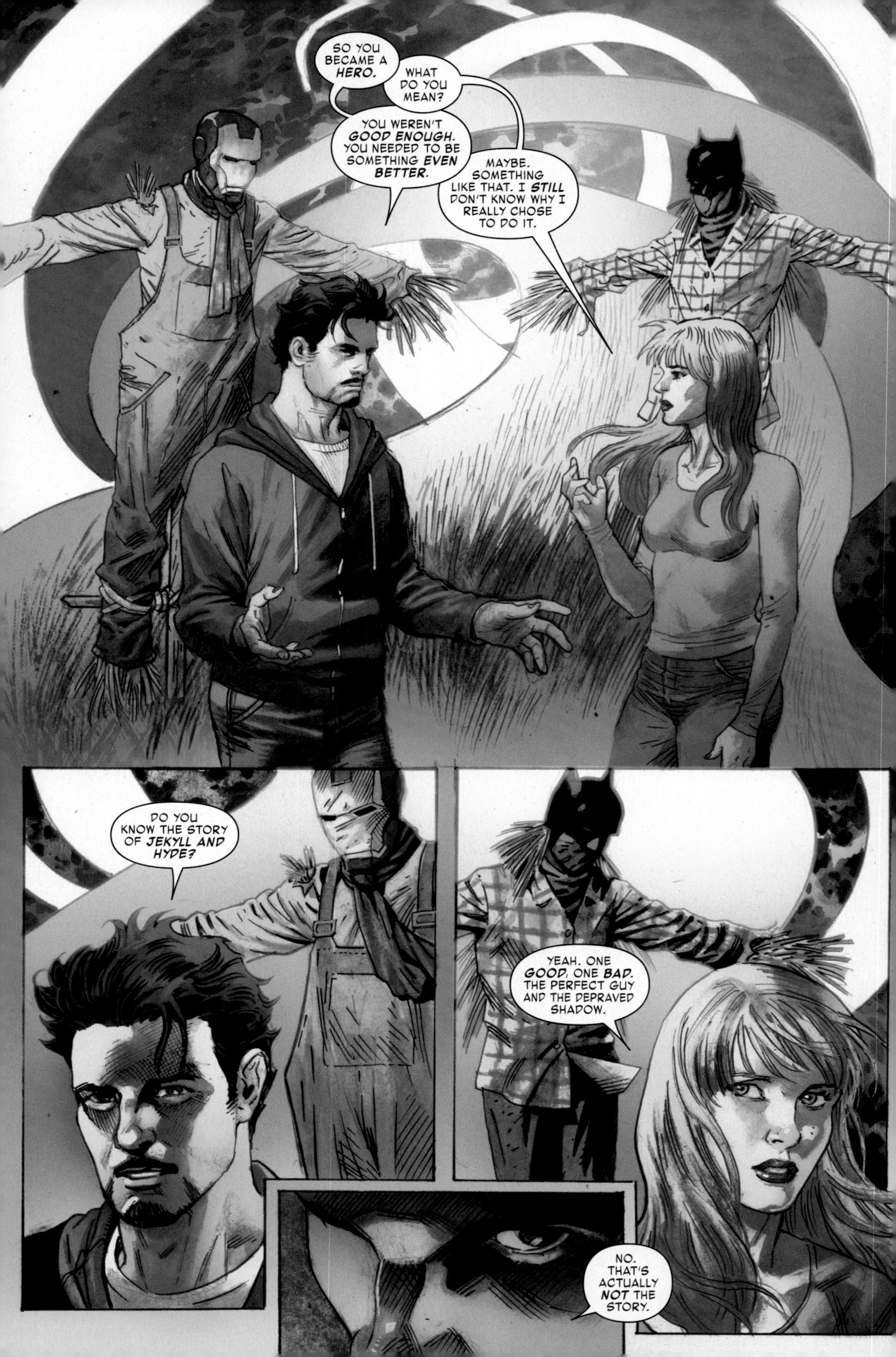
SO YOU BECAME A HERO.
WHAT DO YOU MEAN?
YOU WEREN'T GOOD ENOUGH. YOU NEEDED TO BE SOMETHING EVEN BETTER.
MAYBE. SOMETHING LIKE THAT. I STILL DON'T KNOW WHY I REALLY CHOSE TO DO IT.
DO YOU KNOW THE STORY OF JEKYLL AND HYDE?
YEAH. ONE GOOD, ONE BAD. THE PERFECT GUY AND THE DEPRAVED SHADOW.
NO. THAT'S ACTUALLY NOT THE STORY.

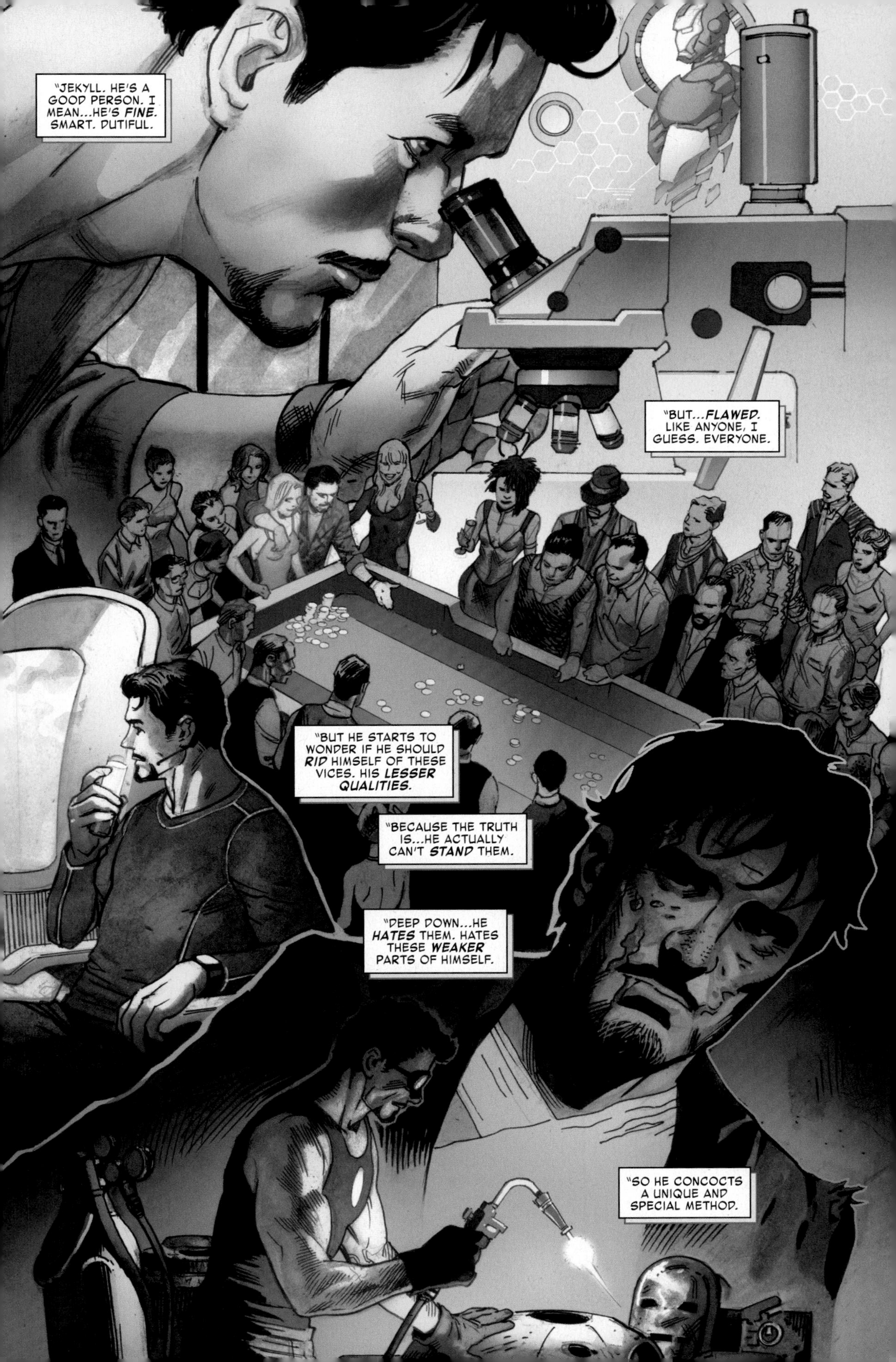

"JEKYLL. HE'S A GOOD PERSON. I MEAN...HE'S *FINE.* SMART. DUTIFUL.
"BUT...*FLAWED.* LIKE ANYONE, I GUESS. EVERYONE.
"BUT HE STARTS TO WONDER IF HE SHOULD *RID* HIMSELF OF THESE VICES. HIS *LESSER QUALITIES.*
"BECAUSE THE TRUTH IS...HE ACTUALLY CAN'T *STAND* THEM.
"DEEP DOWN...HE *HATES* THEM. HATES THESE *WEAKER* PARTS OF HIMSELF.
"SO HE CONCOCTS A UNIQUE AND SPECIAL METHOD.

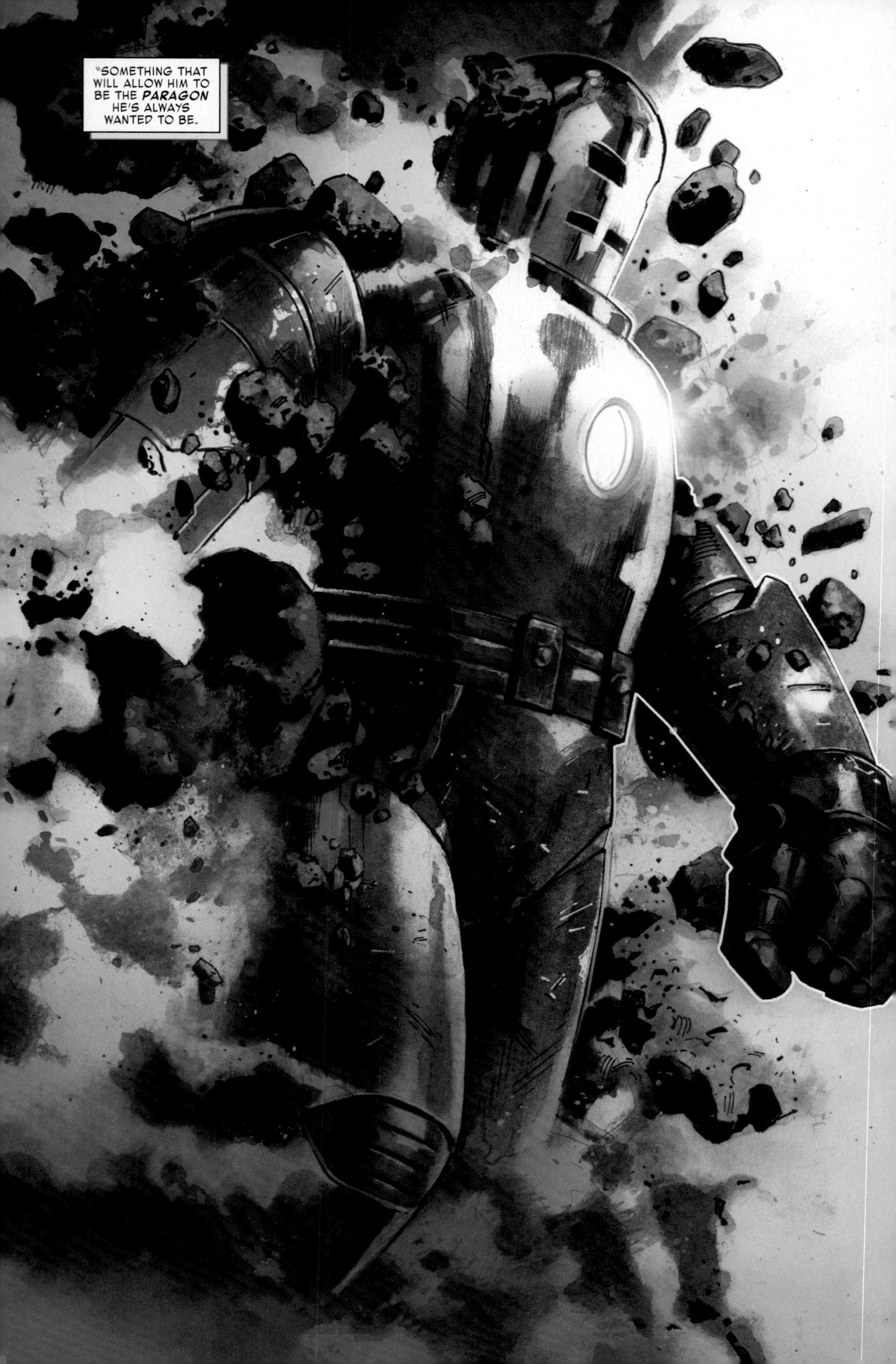
"SOMETHING THAT WILL ALLOW HIM TO BE THE *PARAGON* HE'S ALWAYS WANTED TO BE.

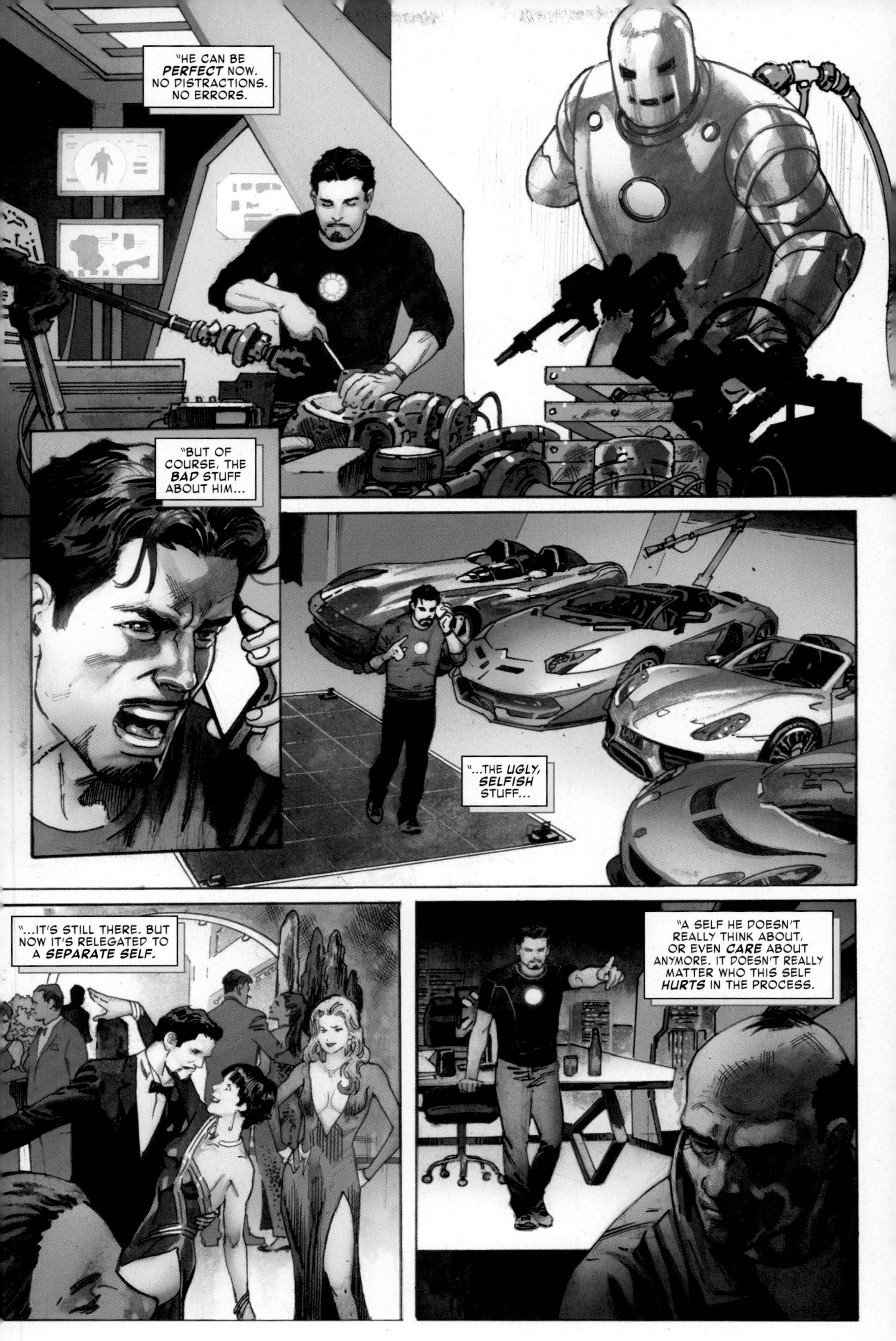
"HE CAN BE PERFECT NOW. NO DISTRACTIONS. NO ERRORS.
"BUT OF COURSE, THE BAD STUFF ABOUT HIM...
"...THE UGLY, SELFISH STUFF...
"...IT'S STILL THERE. BUT NOW IT'S RELEGATED TO A SEPARATE SELF.
"A SELF HE DOESN'T REALLY THINK ABOUT, OR EVEN CARE ABOUT ANYMORE. IT DOESN'T REALLY MATTER WHO THIS SELF HURTS IN THE PROCESS.

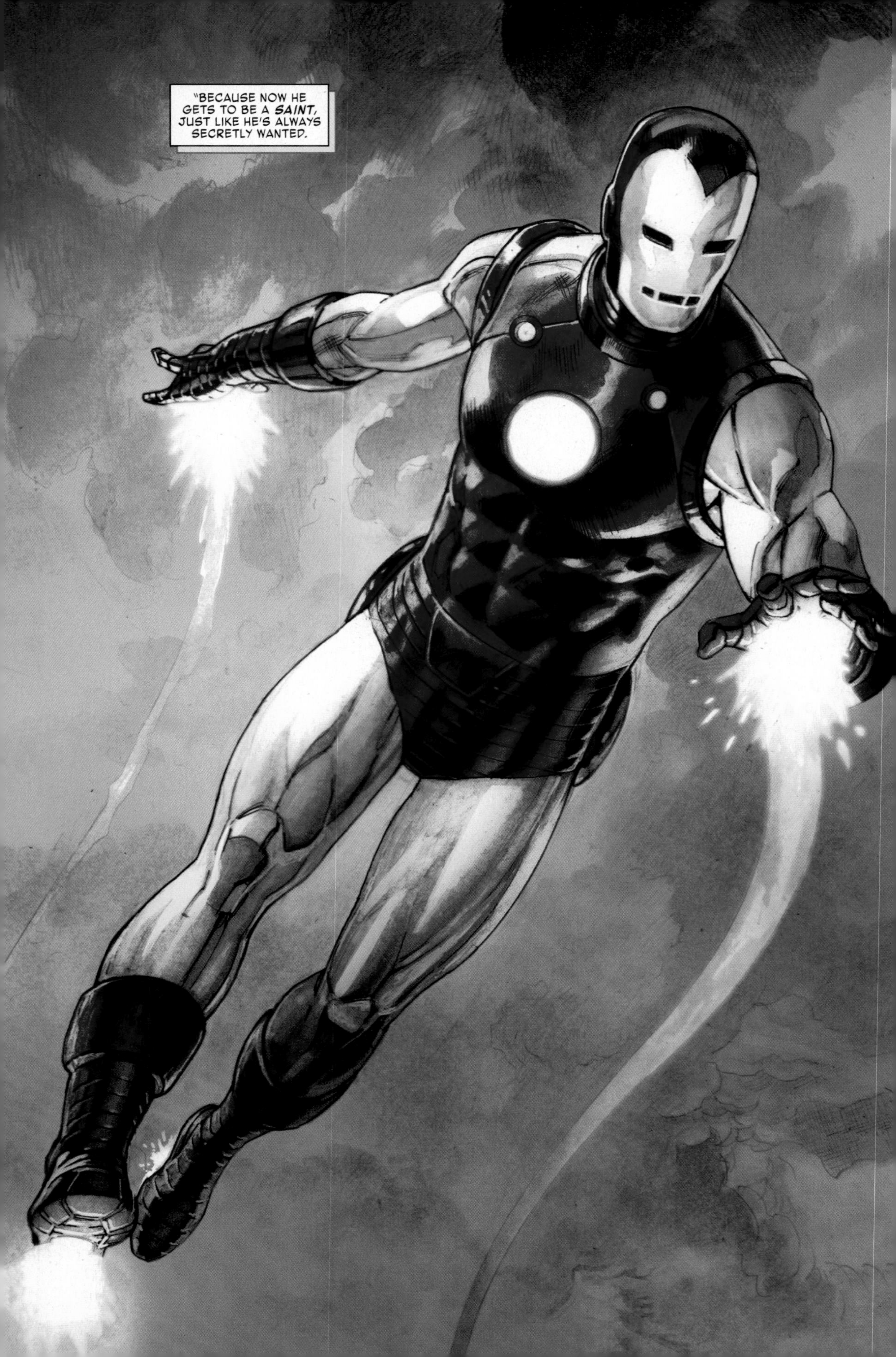
"BECAUSE NOW HE GETS TO BE A SAINT, JUST LIKE HE'S ALWAYS SECRETLY WANTED.

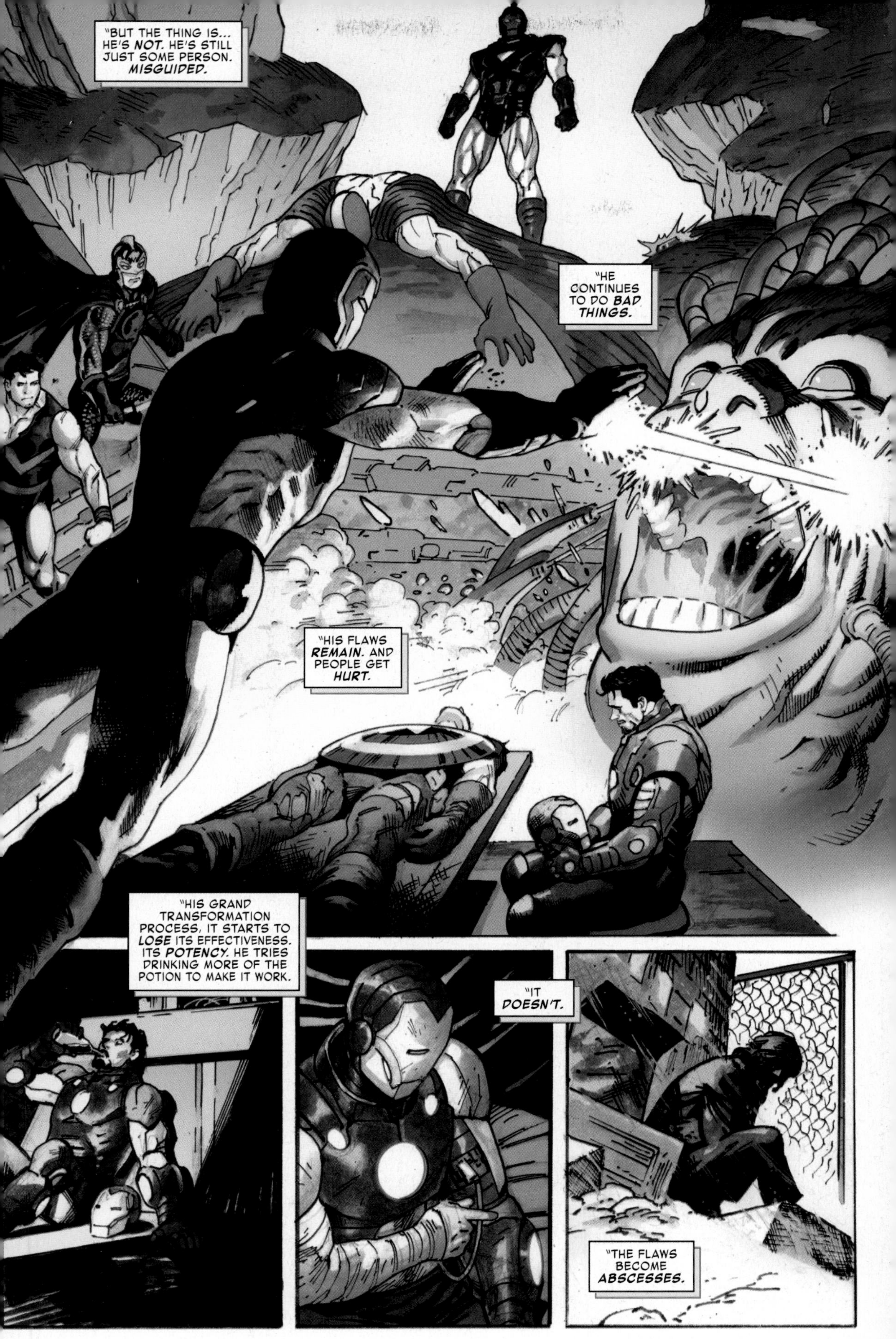
"BUT THE THING IS... HE'S NOT. HE'S STILL JUST SOME PERSON. MISGUIDED.
"HE CONTINUES TO DO BAD THINGS.
"HIS FLAWS REMAIN. AND PEOPLE GET HURT.
"HIS GRAND TRANSFORMATION PROCESS, IT STARTS TO LOSE ITS EFFECTIVENESS. ITS POTENCY. HE TRIES DRINKING MORE OF THE POTION TO MAKE IT WORK.
"IT DOESN'T.
"THE FLAWS BECOME ABSCESSES.

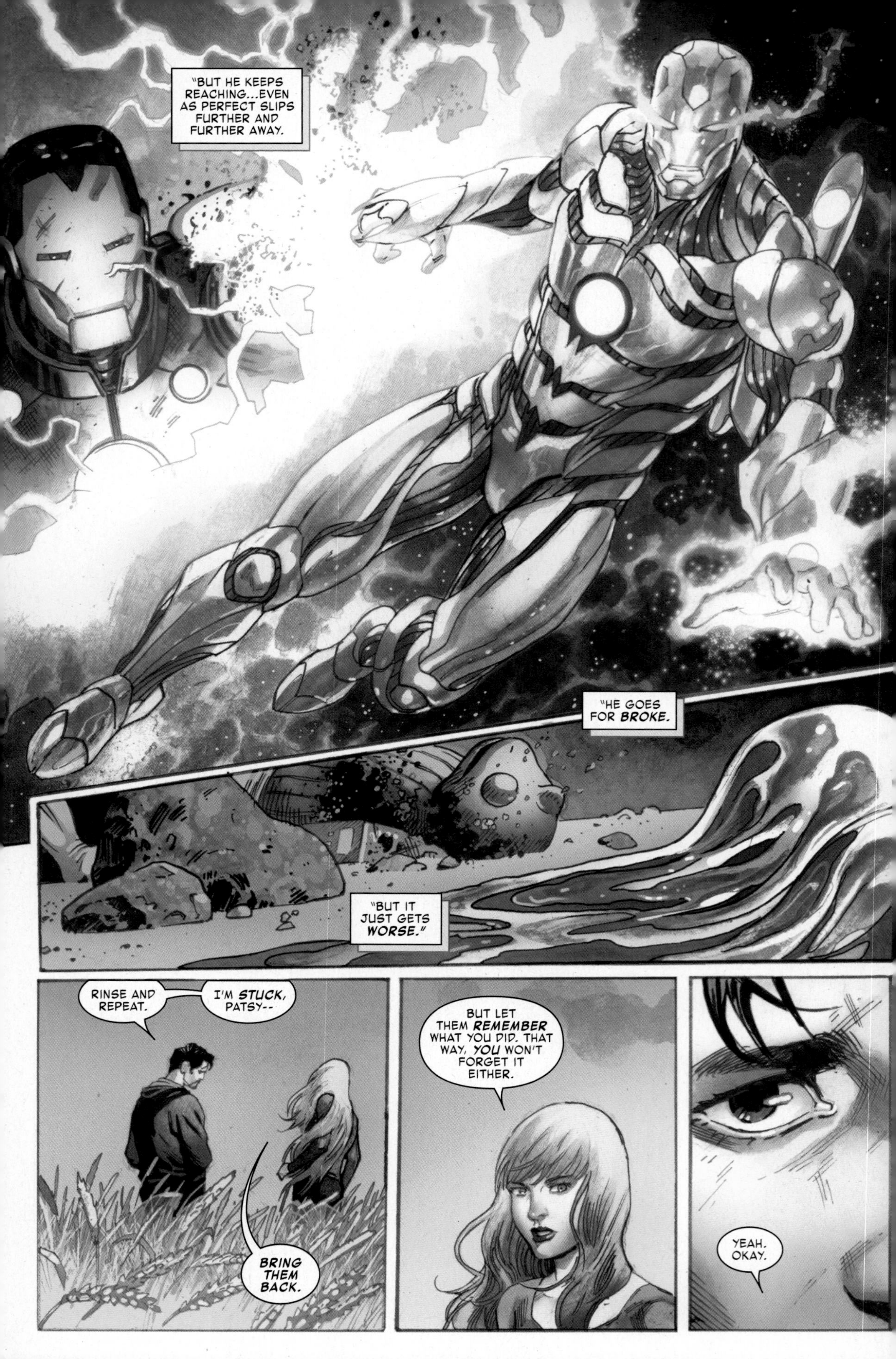
"BUT HE KEEPS REACHING...EVEN AS PERFECT SLIPS FURTHER AND FURTHER AWAY.
"HE GOES FOR BROKE.
"BUT IT JUST GETS WORSE."
RINSE AND REPEAT.
I'M STUCK, PATSY--
BRING THEM BACK.
BUT LET THEM REMEMBER WHAT YOU DID. THAT WAY, YOU WON'T FORGET IT EITHER.
YEAH. OKAY.

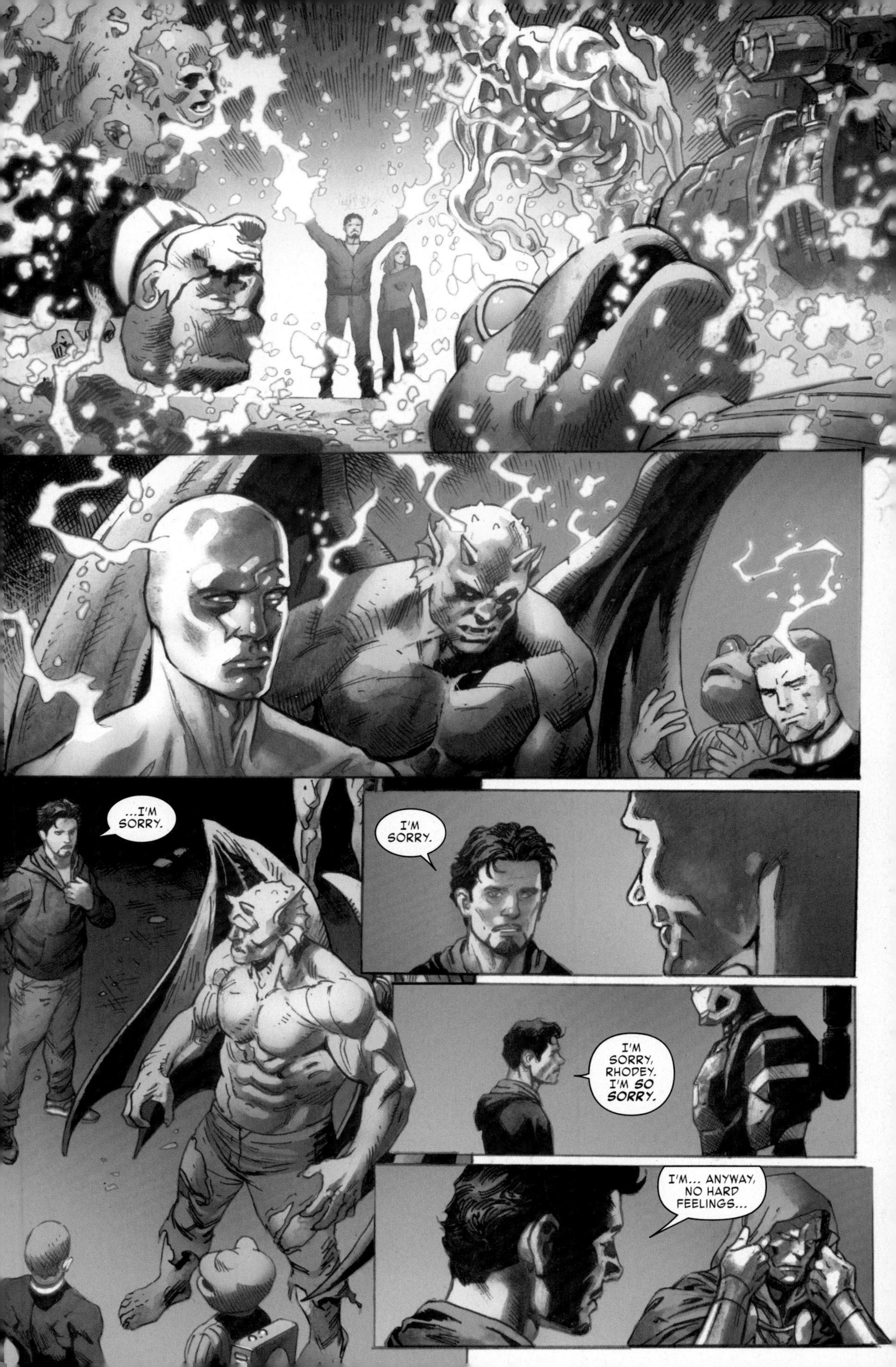
...I'M SORRY.
I'M SORRY.
I'M SORRY, RHODEY. I'M SO SORRY.
I'M... ANYWAY, NO HARD FEELINGS...

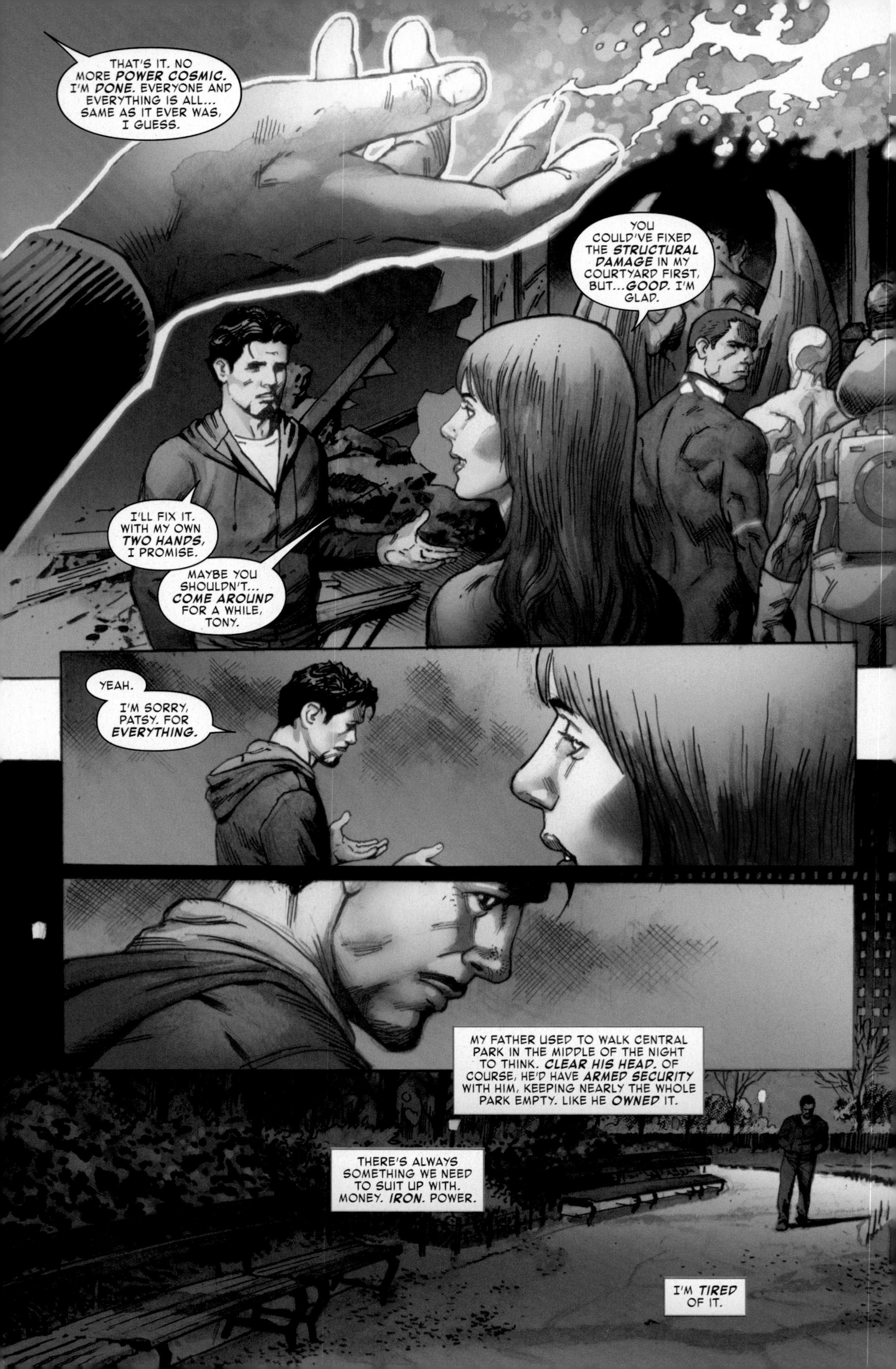
THAT'S IT. NO MORE POWER COSMIC. I'M DONE. EVERYONE AND EVERYTHING IS ALL... SAME AS IT EVER WAS, I GUESS.
YOU COULD'VE FIXED THE STRUCTURAL DAMAGE IN MY COURTYARD FIRST, BUT...GOOD. I'M GLAD.
I'LL FIX IT. WITH MY OWN TWO HANDS, I PROMISE.
MAYBE YOU SHOULDN'T... COME AROUND FOR A WHILE, TONY.
YEAH.
I'M SORRY, PATSY. FOR EVERYTHING.
MY FATHER USED TO WALK CENTRAL PARK IN THE MIDDLE OF THE NIGHT TO THINK. CLEAR HIS HEAD. OF COURSE, HE'D HAVE ARMED SECURITY WITH HIM, KEEPING NEARLY THE WHOLE PARK EMPTY. LIKE HE OWNED IT.
THERE'S ALWAYS SOMETHING WE NEED TO SUIT UP WITH. MONEY. IRON. POWER.
I'M TIRED OF IT.

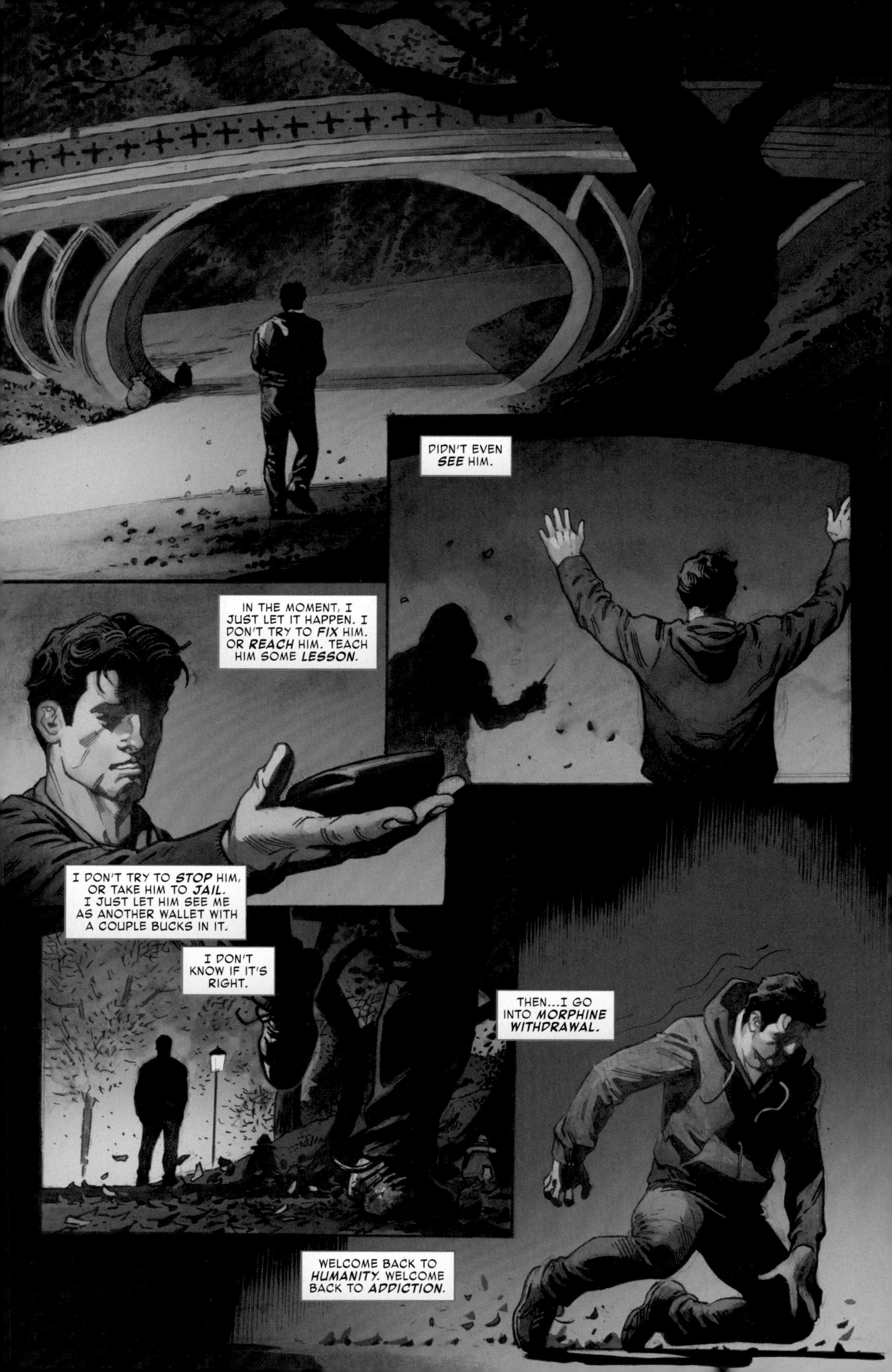
DIDN'T EVEN SEE HIM.
IN THE MOMENT, I JUST LET IT HAPPEN. I DON'T TRY TO FIX HIM. OR REACH HIM. TEACH HIM SOME LESSON.
I DON'T TRY TO STOP HIM, OR TAKE HIM TO JAIL. I JUST LET HIM SEE ME AS ANOTHER WALLET WITH A COUPLE BUCKS IN IT.
I DON'T KNOW IF IT'S RIGHT.
THEN...I GO INTO MORPHINE WITHDRAWAL.
WELCOME BACK TO HUMANITY. WELCOME BACK TO ADDICTION.

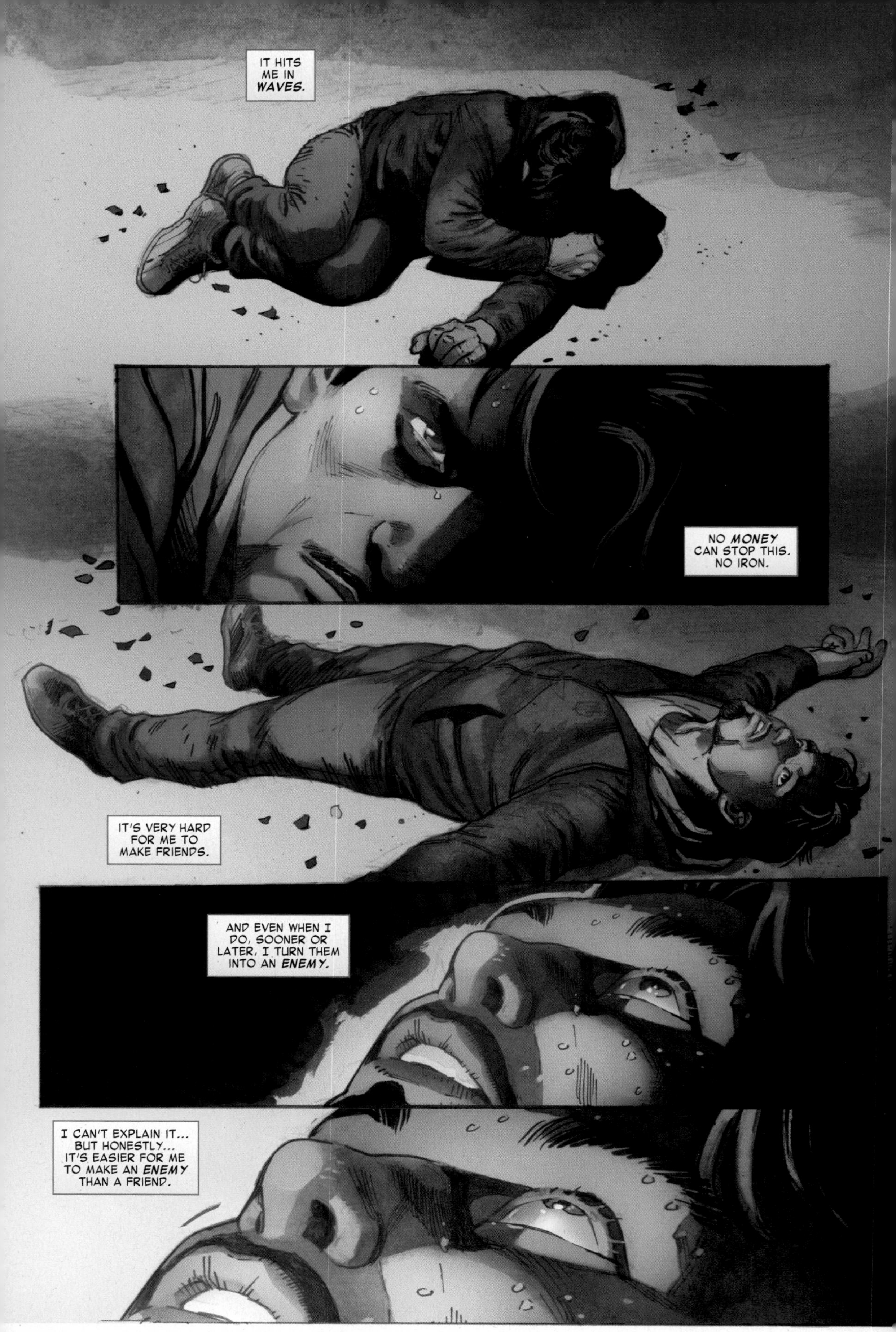
IT HITS ME IN WAVES.
NO MONEY CAN STOP THIS. NO IRON.
IT'S VERY HARD FOR ME TO MAKE FRIENDS.
AND EVEN WHEN I DO, SOONER OR LATER, I TURN THEM INTO AN ENEMY.
I CAN'T EXPLAIN IT... BUT HONESTLY... IT'S EASIER FOR ME TO MAKE AN ENEMY THAN A FRIEND.

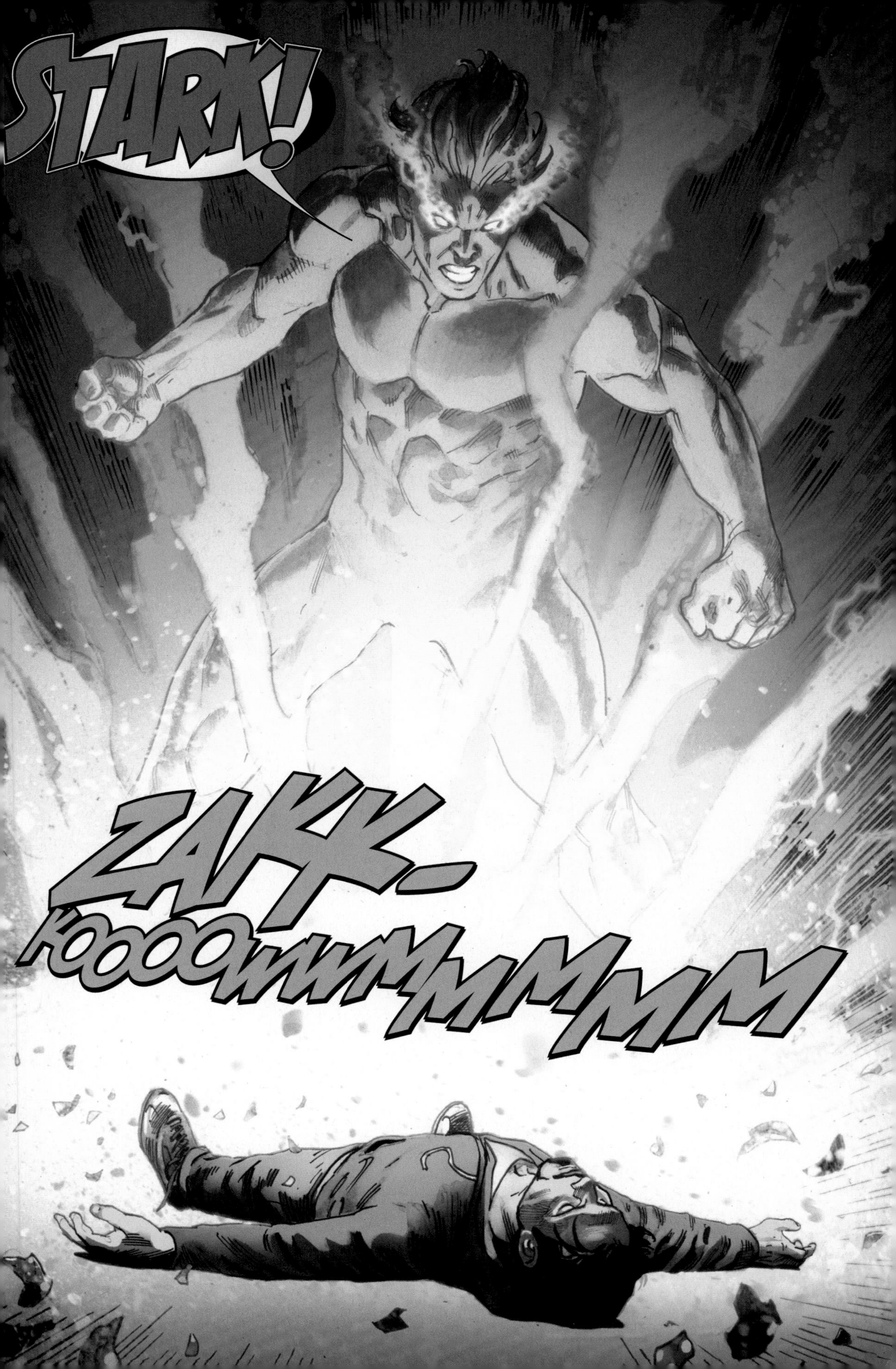
STARK!
ZAKK-KOOOOOWWWMMMMMM

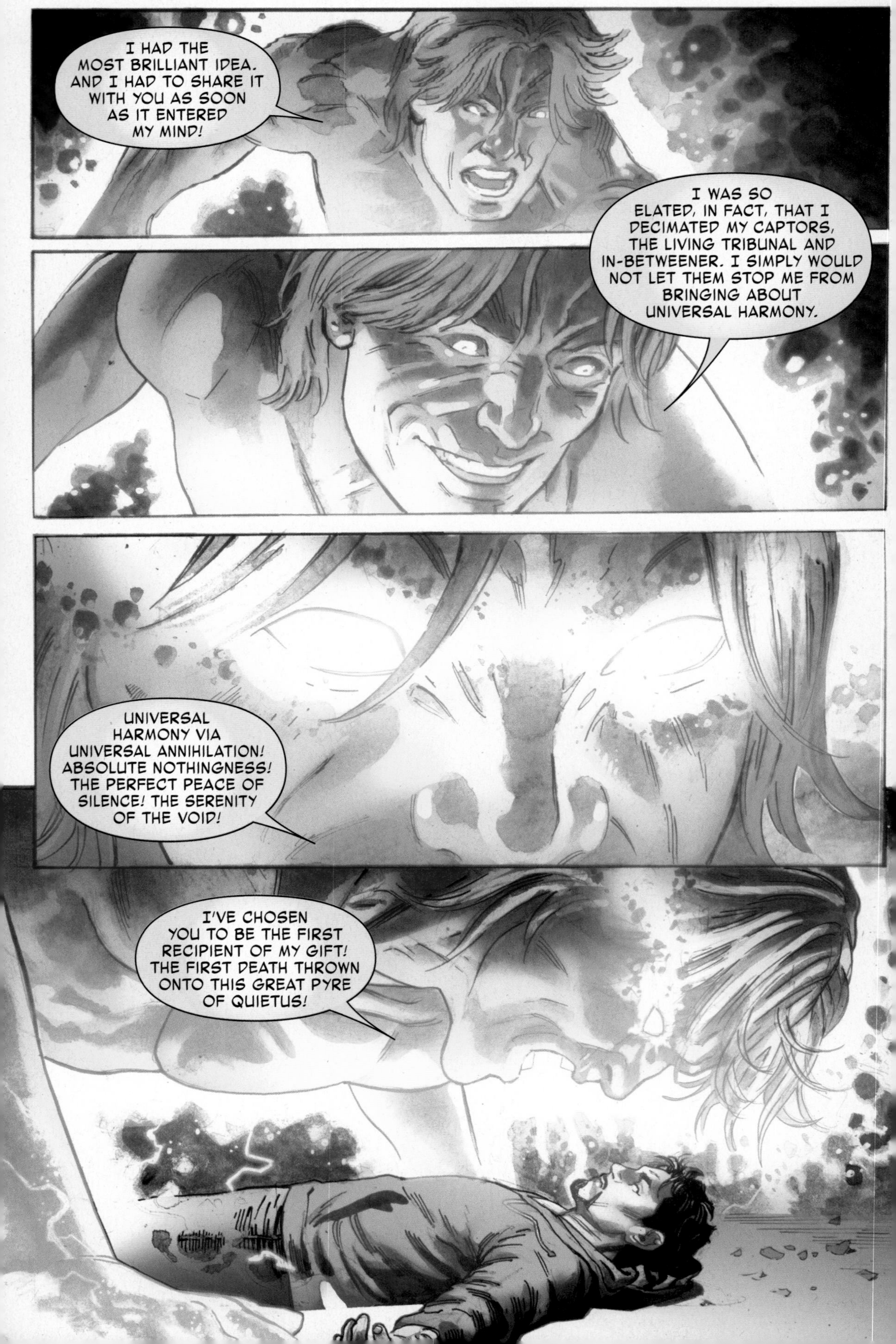
I HAD THE MOST BRILLIANT IDEA. AND I HAD TO SHARE IT WITH YOU AS SOON AS IT ENTERED MY MIND!
I WAS SO ELATED, IN FACT, THAT I DECIMATED MY CAPTORS, THE LIVING TRIBUNAL AND IN-BETWEENER. I SIMPLY WOULD NOT LET THEM STOP ME FROM BRINGING ABOUT UNIVERSAL HARMONY.
UNIVERSAL HARMONY VIA UNIVERSAL ANNIHILATION! ABSOLUTE NOTHINGNESS! THE PERFECT PEACE OF SILENCE! THE SERENITY OF THE VOID!
I'VE CHOSEN YOU TO BE THE FIRST RECIPIENT OF MY GIFT! THE FIRST DEATH THROWN ONTO THIS GREAT PYRE OF QUIETUS!

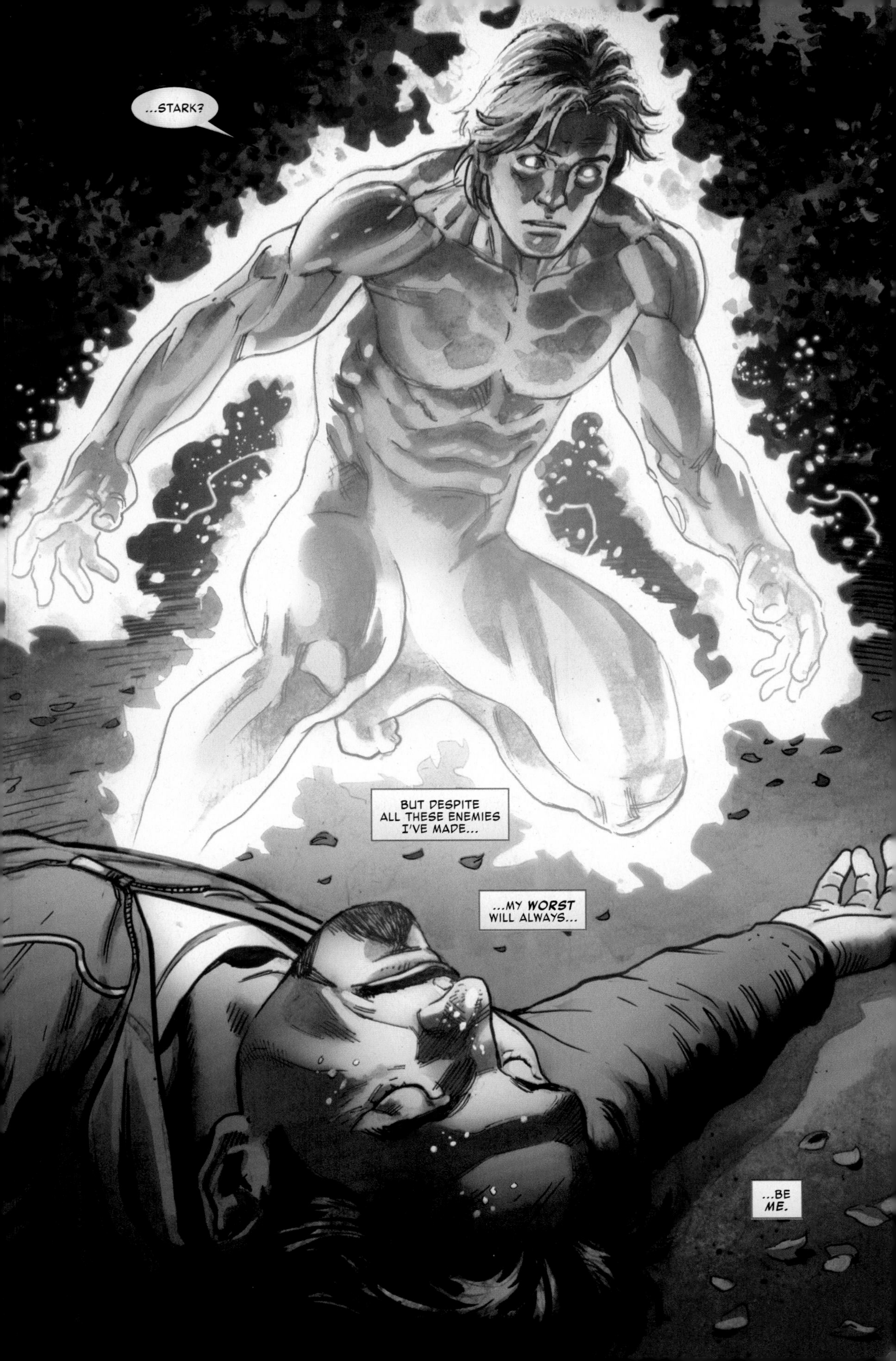
...STARK?
BUT DESPITE ALL THESE ENEMIES I'VE MADE...
...MY **WORST** WILL ALWAYS...
...BE **ME.**

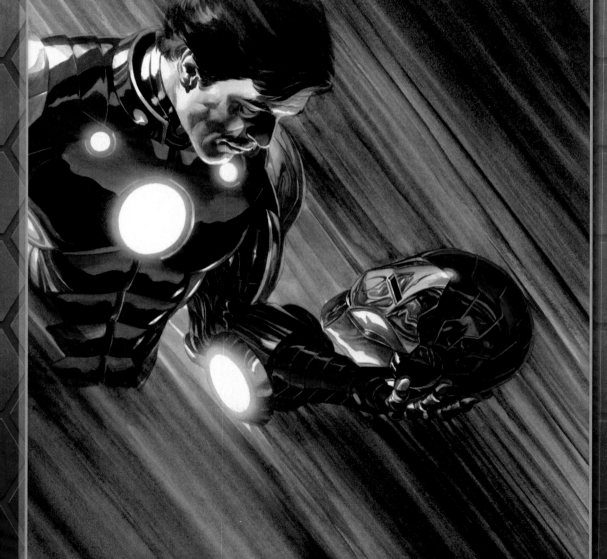

THE FINAL ENEMY

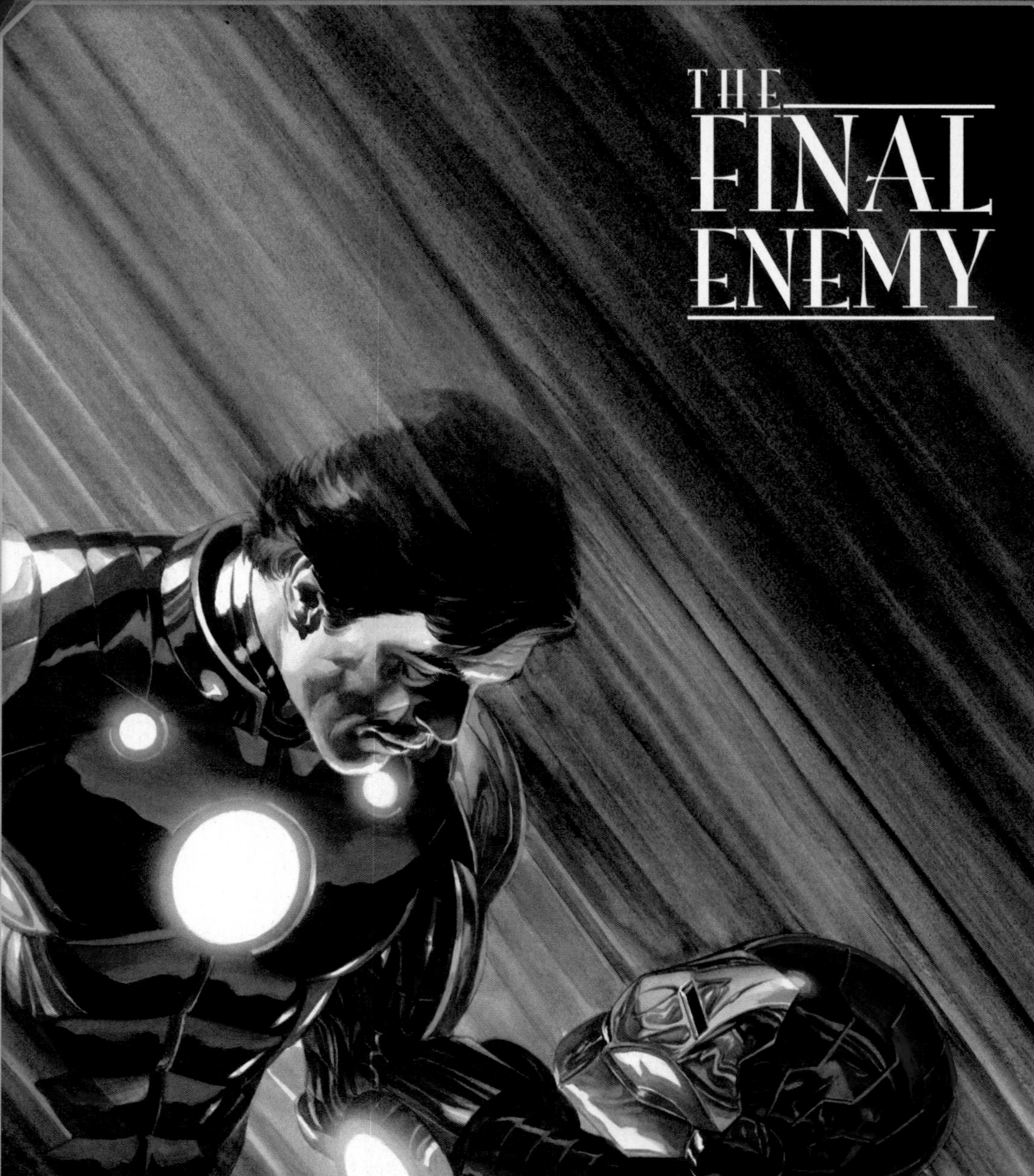

19

THE LAST MIDNIGHT

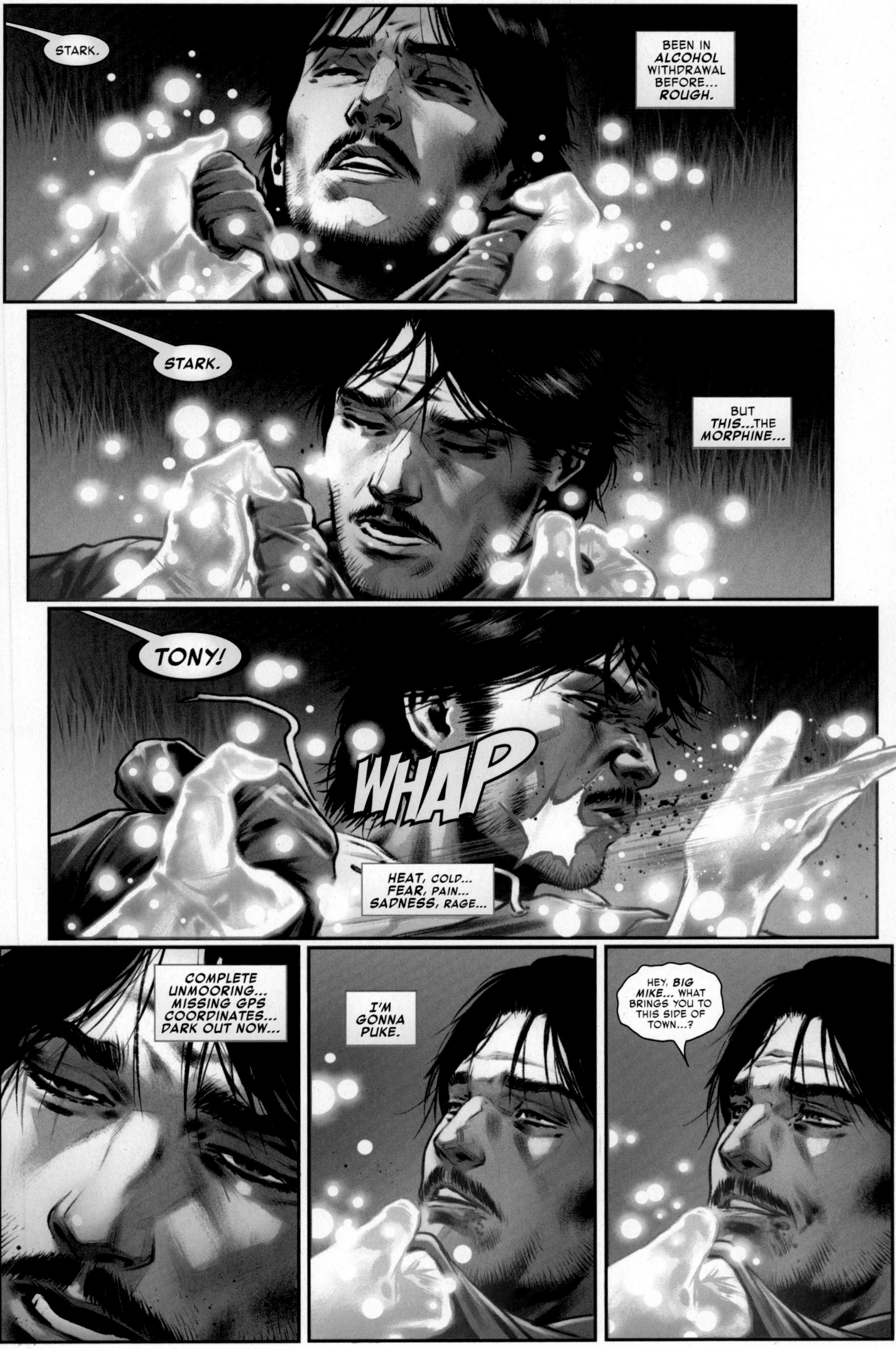
STARK.
BEEN IN ALCOHOL WITHDRAWAL BEFORE... ROUGH.
STARK.
BUT THIS...THE MORPHINE...
TONY!
WHAP
HEAT, COLD... FEAR, PAIN... SADNESS, RAGE...
COMPLETE UNMOORING... MISSING GPS COORDINATES... DARK OUT NOW...
I'M GONNA PUKE.
HEY, BIG MIKE... WHAT BRINGS YOU TO THIS SIDE OF TOWN...?

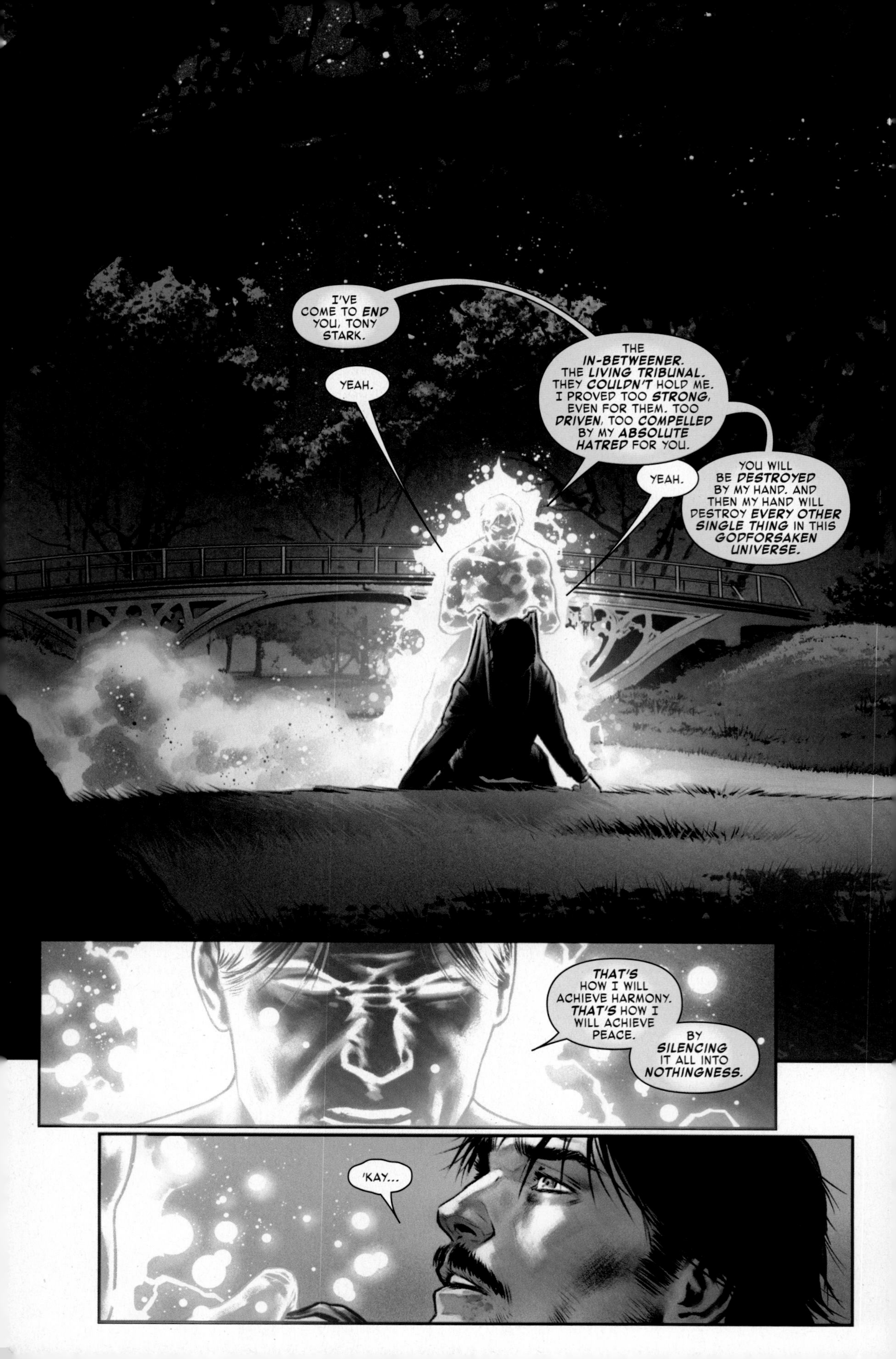
I'VE COME TO END YOU, TONY STARK.
YEAH.
THE IN-BETWEENER. THE LIVING TRIBUNAL. THEY COULDN'T HOLD ME. I PROVED TOO STRONG, EVEN FOR THEM. TOO DRIVEN, TOO COMPELLED BY MY ABSOLUTE HATRED FOR YOU.
YEAH.
YOU WILL BE DESTROYED BY MY HAND. AND THEN MY HAND WILL DESTROY EVERY OTHER SINGLE THING IN THIS GODFORSAKEN UNIVERSE.
THAT'S HOW I WILL ACHIEVE HARMONY. THAT'S HOW I WILL ACHIEVE PEACE.
BY SILENCING IT ALL INTO NOTHINGNESS.
'KAY...

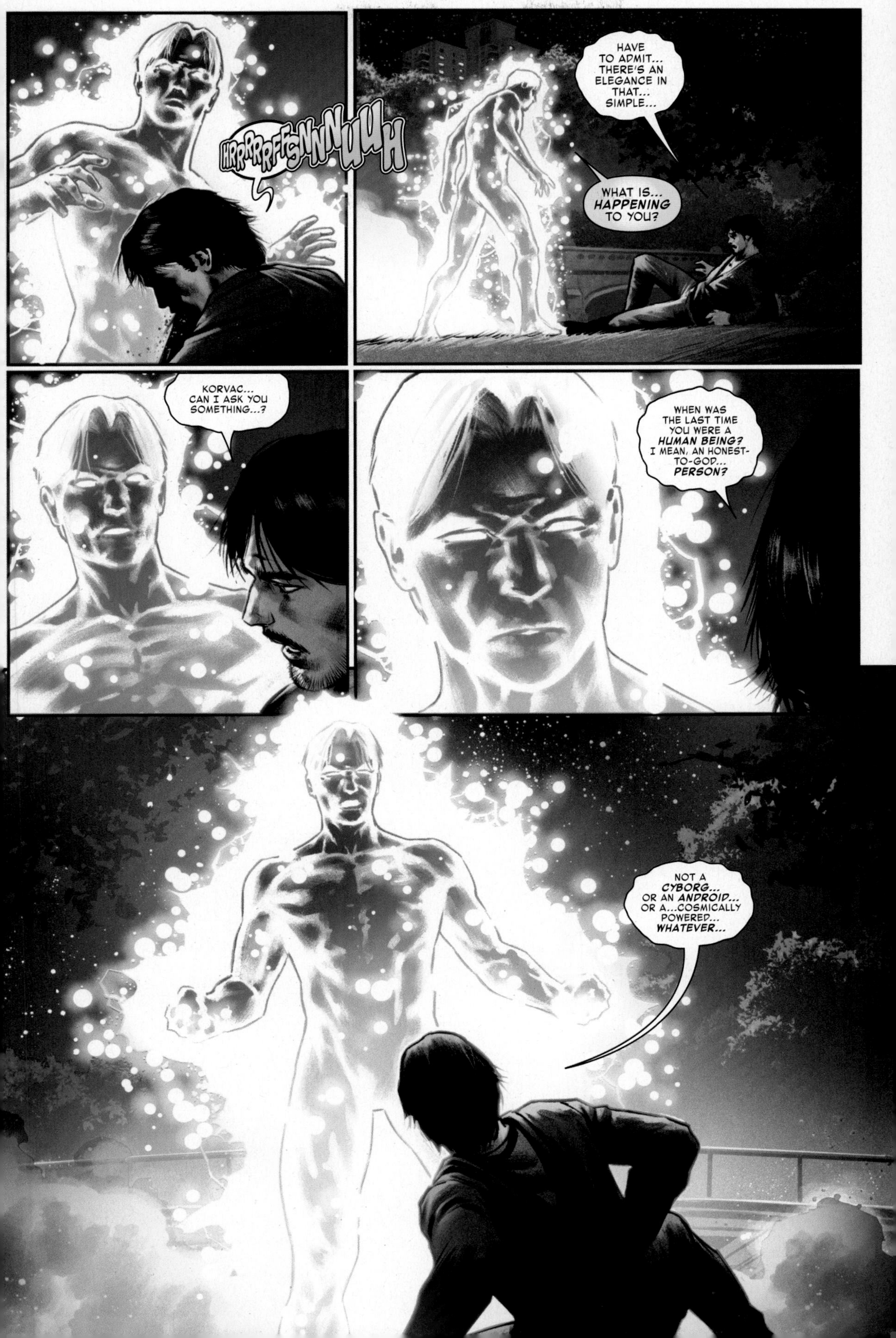
HRRRRRFFSNNNUUUH
HAVE TO ADMIT... THERE'S AN ELEGANCE IN THAT... SIMPLE...
WHAT IS... HAPPENING TO YOU?
KORVAC... CAN I ASK YOU SOMETHING...?
WHEN WAS THE LAST TIME YOU WERE A HUMAN BEING? I MEAN, AN HONEST-TO-GOD... PERSON?
NOT A CYBORG... OR AN ANDROID... OR A...COSMICALLY POWERED... WHATEVER...

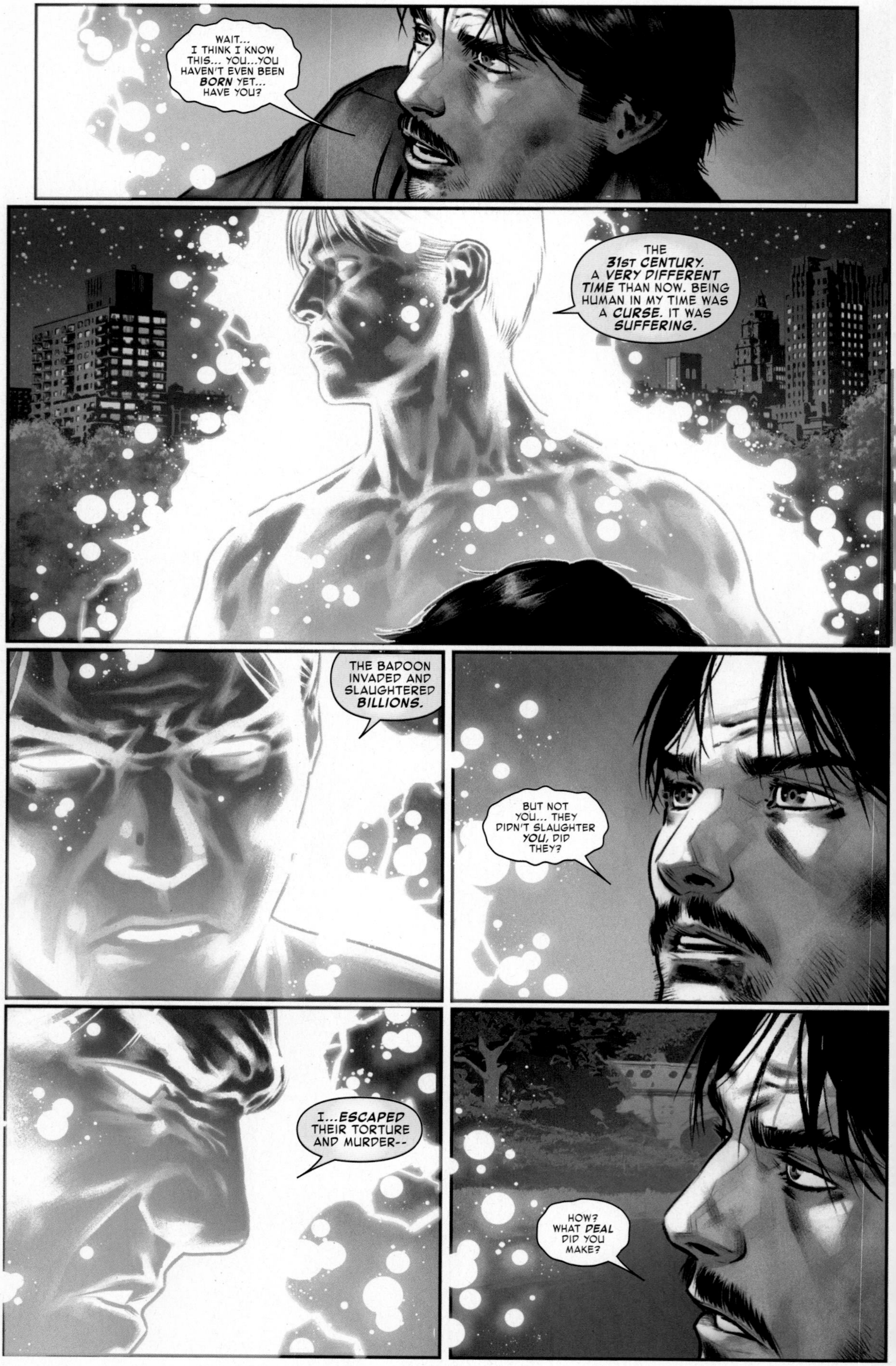
WAIT... I THINK I KNOW THIS... YOU...YOU HAVEN'T EVEN BEEN BORN YET... HAVE YOU?
THE 31ST CENTURY. A VERY DIFFERENT TIME THAN NOW. BEING HUMAN IN MY TIME WAS A CURSE. IT WAS SUFFERING.
THE BADOON INVADED AND SLAUGHTERED BILLIONS.
BUT NOT YOU... THEY DIDN'T SLAUGHTER YOU, DID THEY?
I...ESCAPED THEIR TORTURE AND MURDER--
HOW? WHAT DEAL DID YOU MAKE?

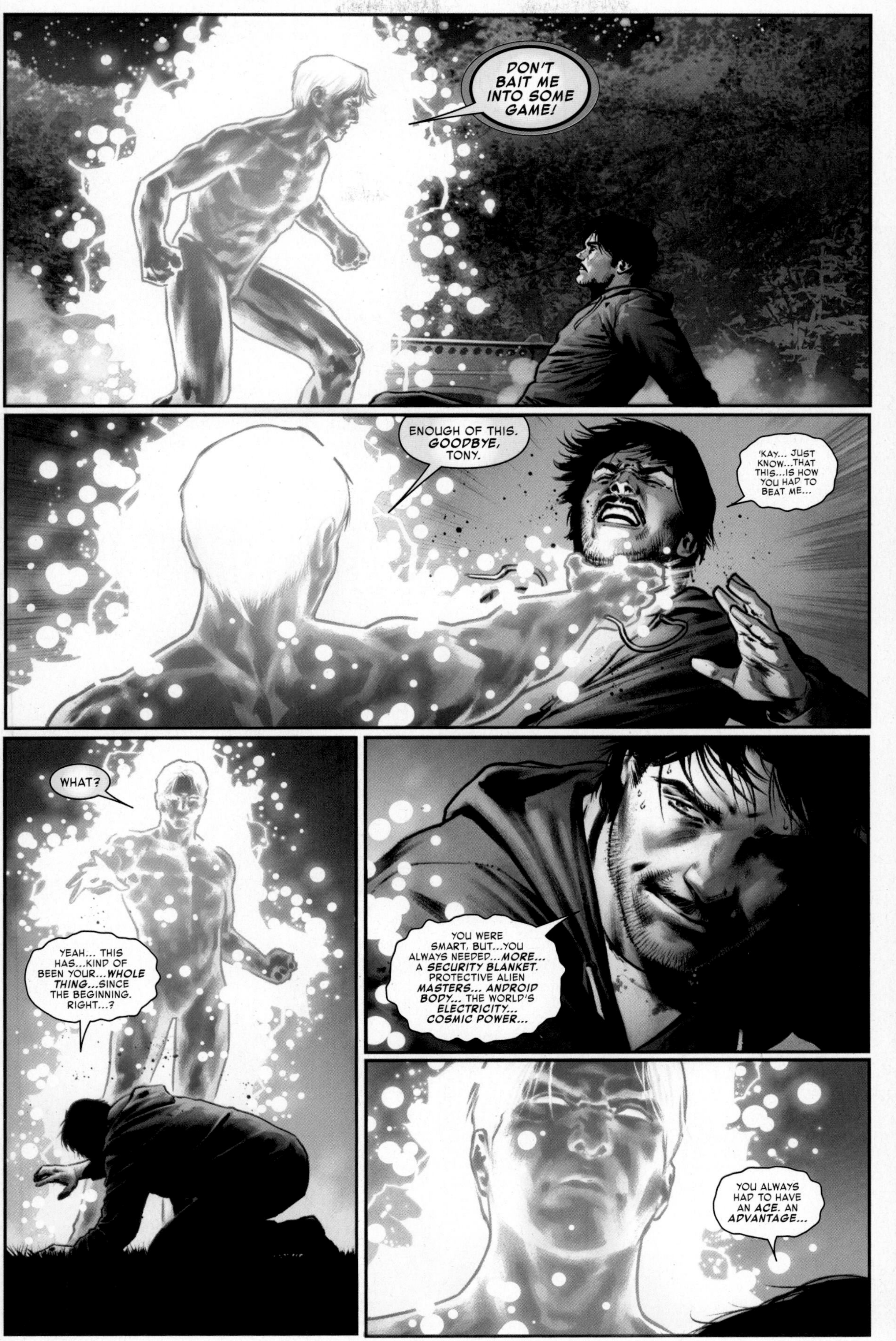
DON'T BAIT ME INTO SOME GAME!
ENOUGH OF THIS. GOODBYE, TONY.
'KAY... JUST KNOW...THAT THIS...IS HOW YOU HAD TO BEAT ME...
WHAT?
YEAH... THIS HAS...KIND OF BEEN YOUR...WHOLE THING...SINCE THE BEGINNING. RIGHT...?
YOU WERE SMART, BUT...YOU ALWAYS NEEDED...MORE... A SECURITY BLANKET. PROTECTIVE ALIEN MASTERS... ANDROID BODY... THE WORLD'S ELECTRICITY... COSMIC POWER...
YOU ALWAYS HAD TO HAVE AN ACE. AN ADVANTAGE...

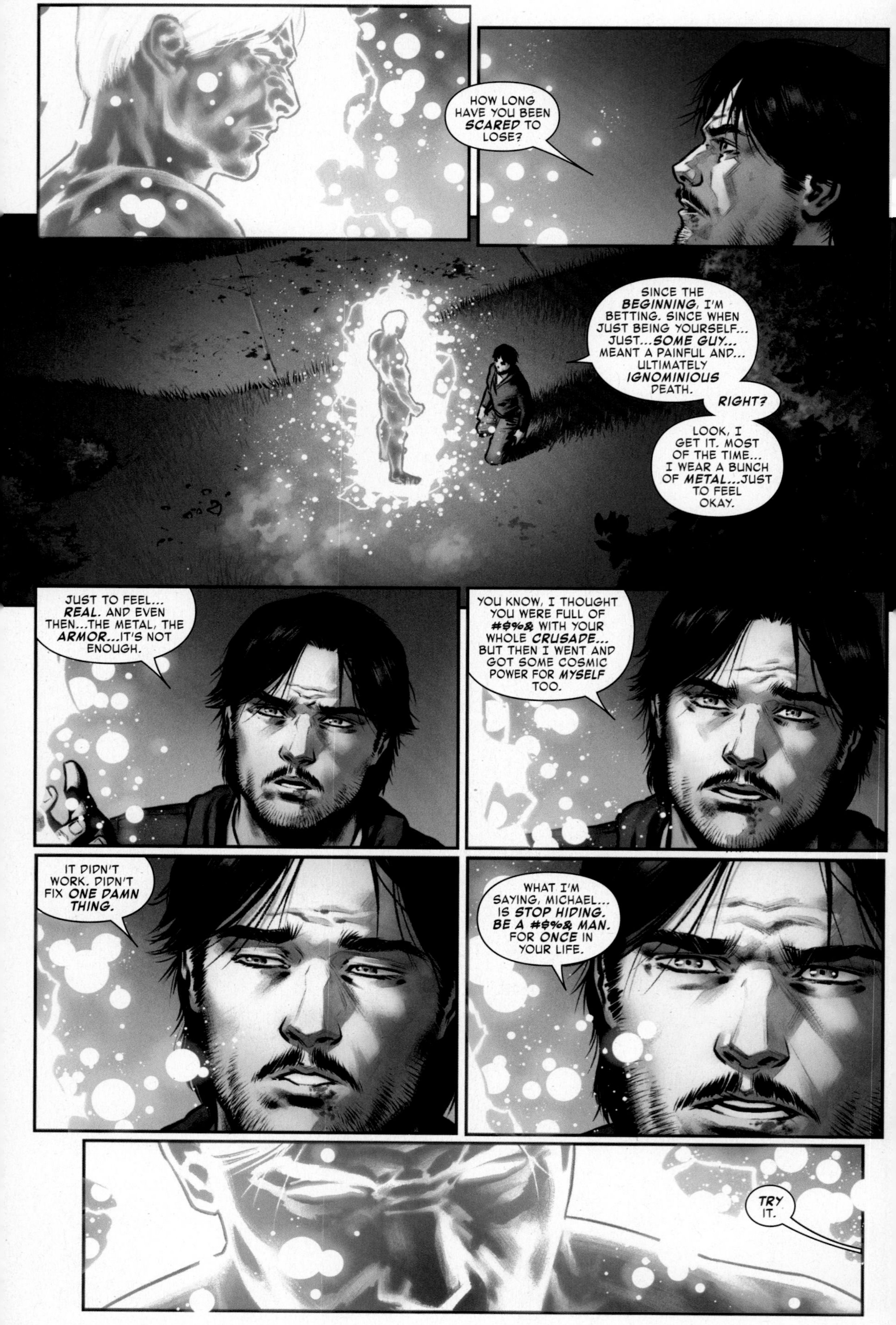
HOW LONG HAVE YOU BEEN SCARED TO LOSE?
SINCE THE BEGINNING, I'M BETTING. SINCE WHEN JUST BEING YOURSELF... JUST...SOME GUY... MEANT A PAINFUL AND... ULTIMATELY IGNOMINIOUS DEATH.
RIGHT?
LOOK, I GET IT. MOST OF THE TIME... I WEAR A BUNCH OF METAL...JUST TO FEEL OKAY.
JUST TO FEEL... REAL. AND EVEN THEN...THE METAL, THE ARMOR...IT'S NOT ENOUGH.
YOU KNOW, I THOUGHT YOU WERE FULL OF #$%& WITH YOUR WHOLE CRUSADE... BUT THEN I WENT AND GOT SOME COSMIC POWER FOR MYSELF TOO.
IT DIDN'T WORK. DIDN'T FIX ONE DAMN THING.
WHAT I'M SAYING, MICHAEL... IS STOP HIDING. BE A #$%& MAN. FOR ONCE IN YOUR LIFE.
TRY IT.

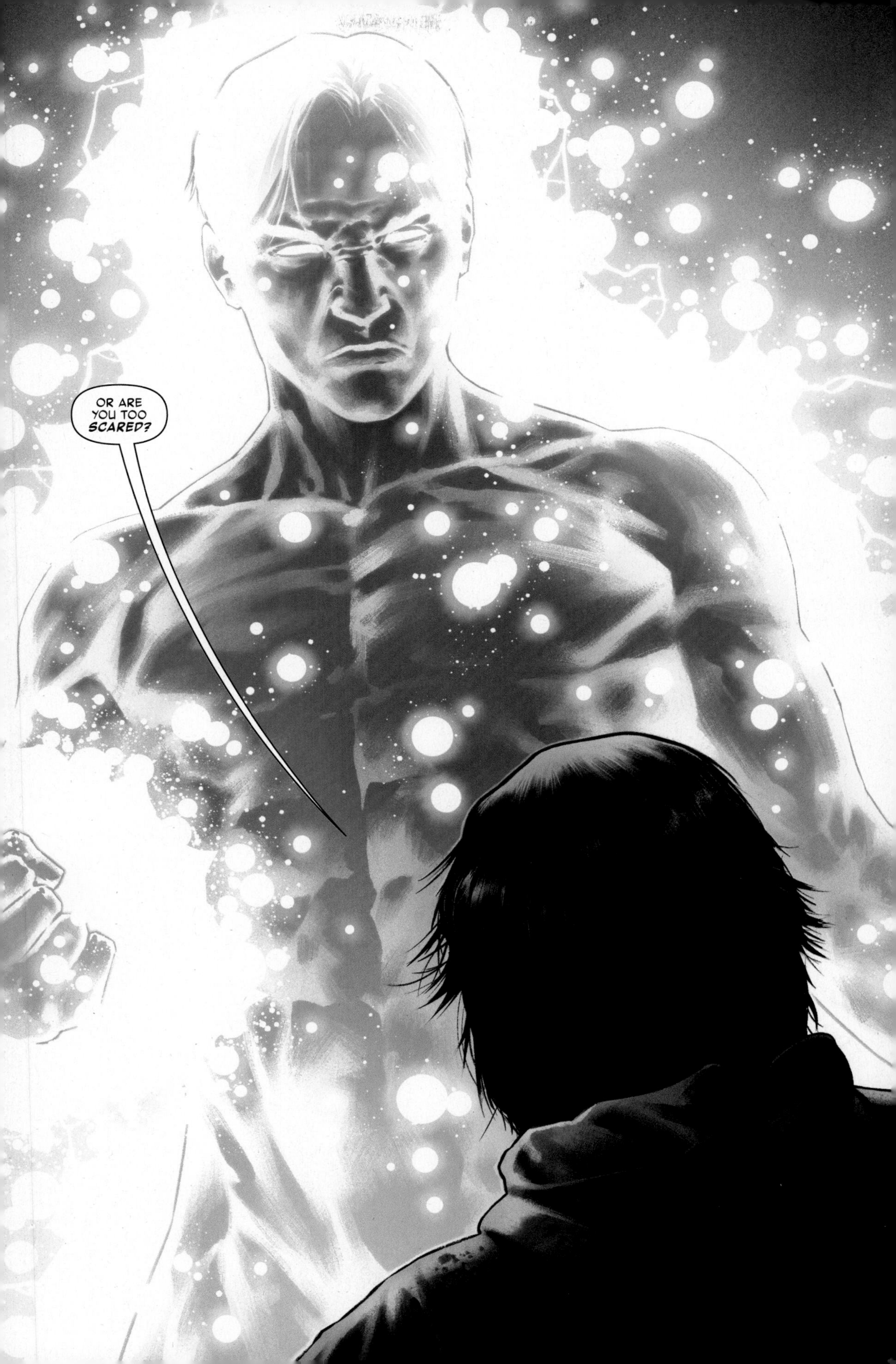
OR ARE YOU TOO SCARED?

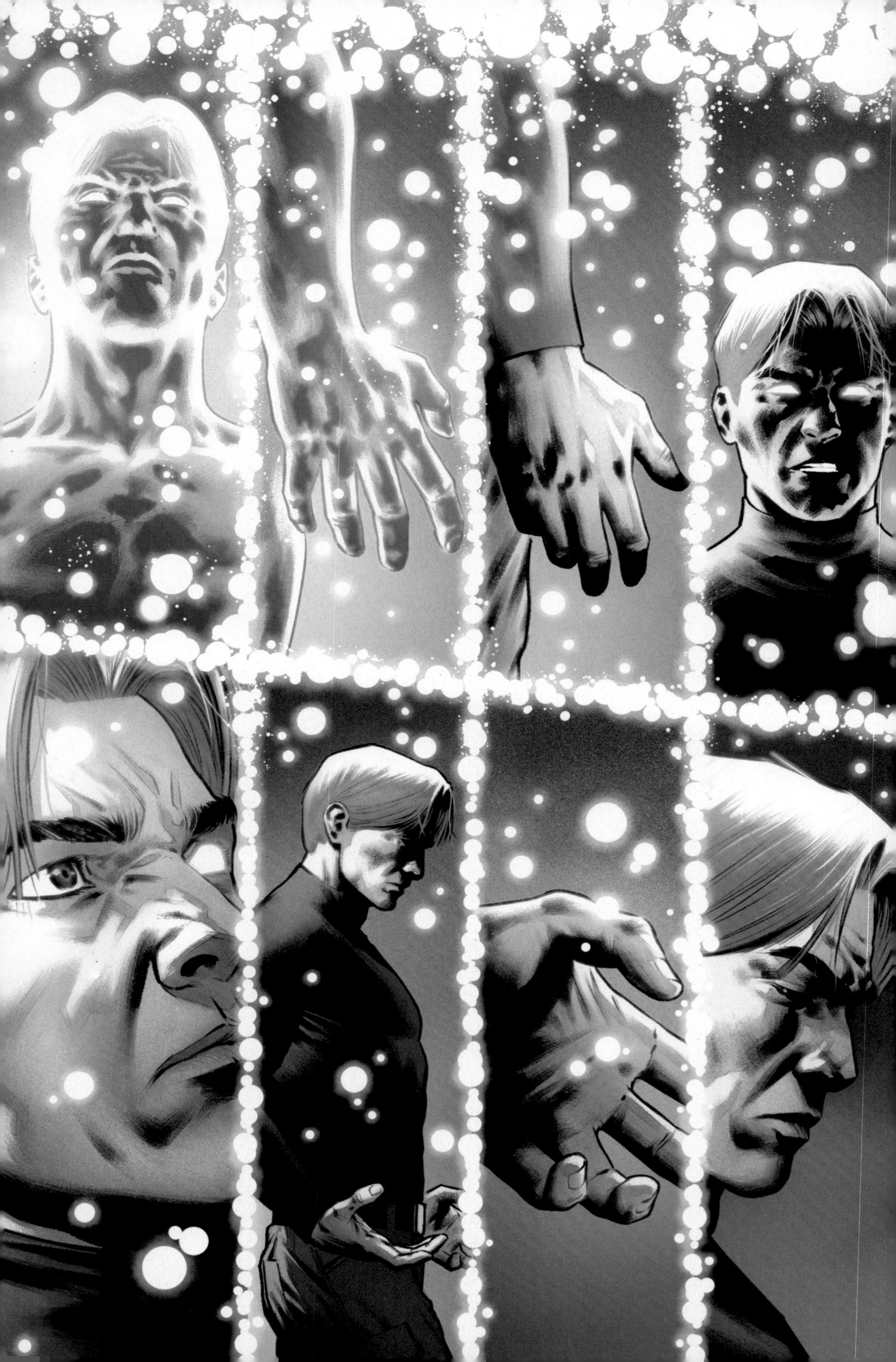

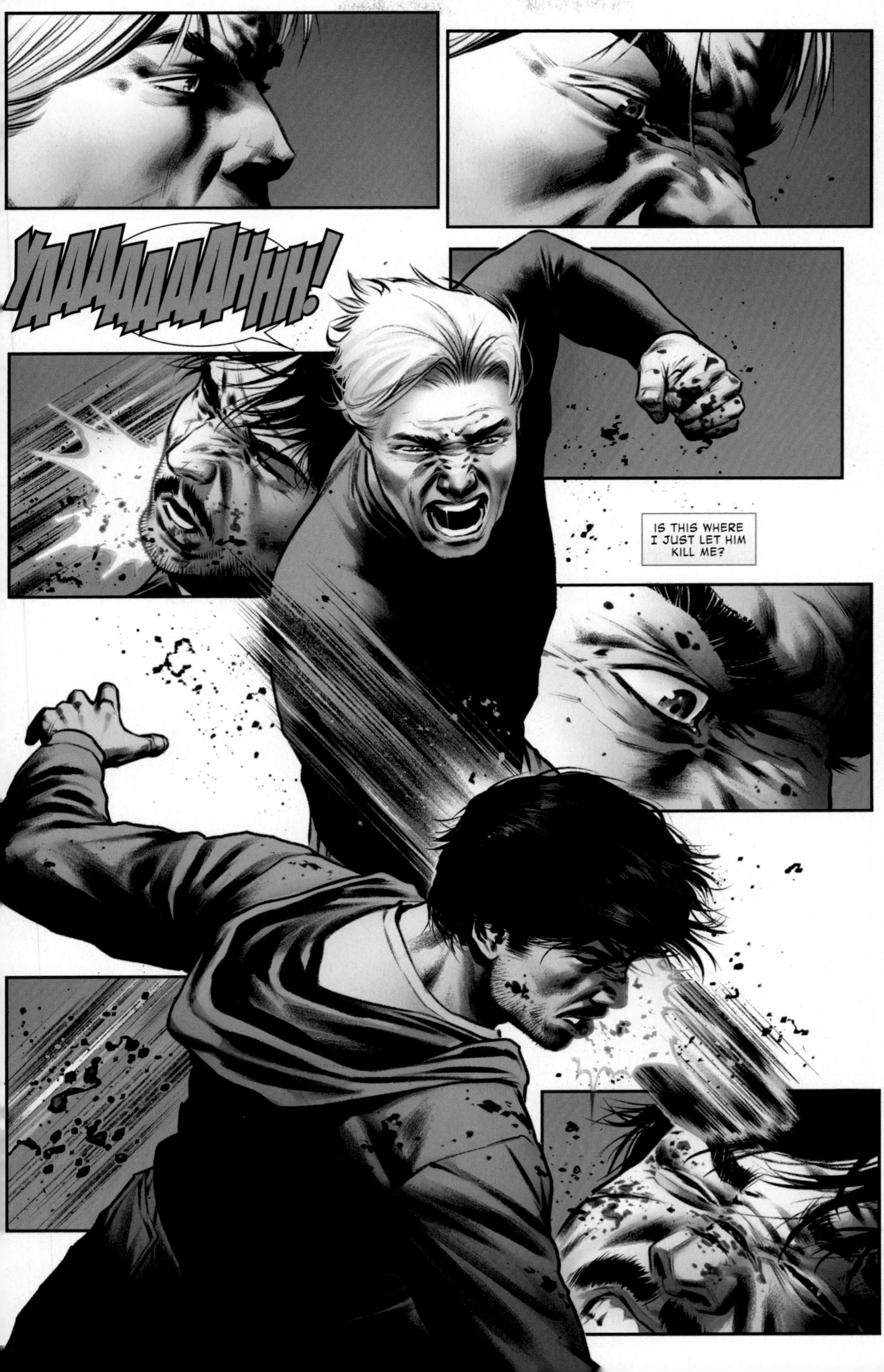
YAAAAAAAAHHH!
IS THIS WHERE I JUST LET HIM KILL ME?

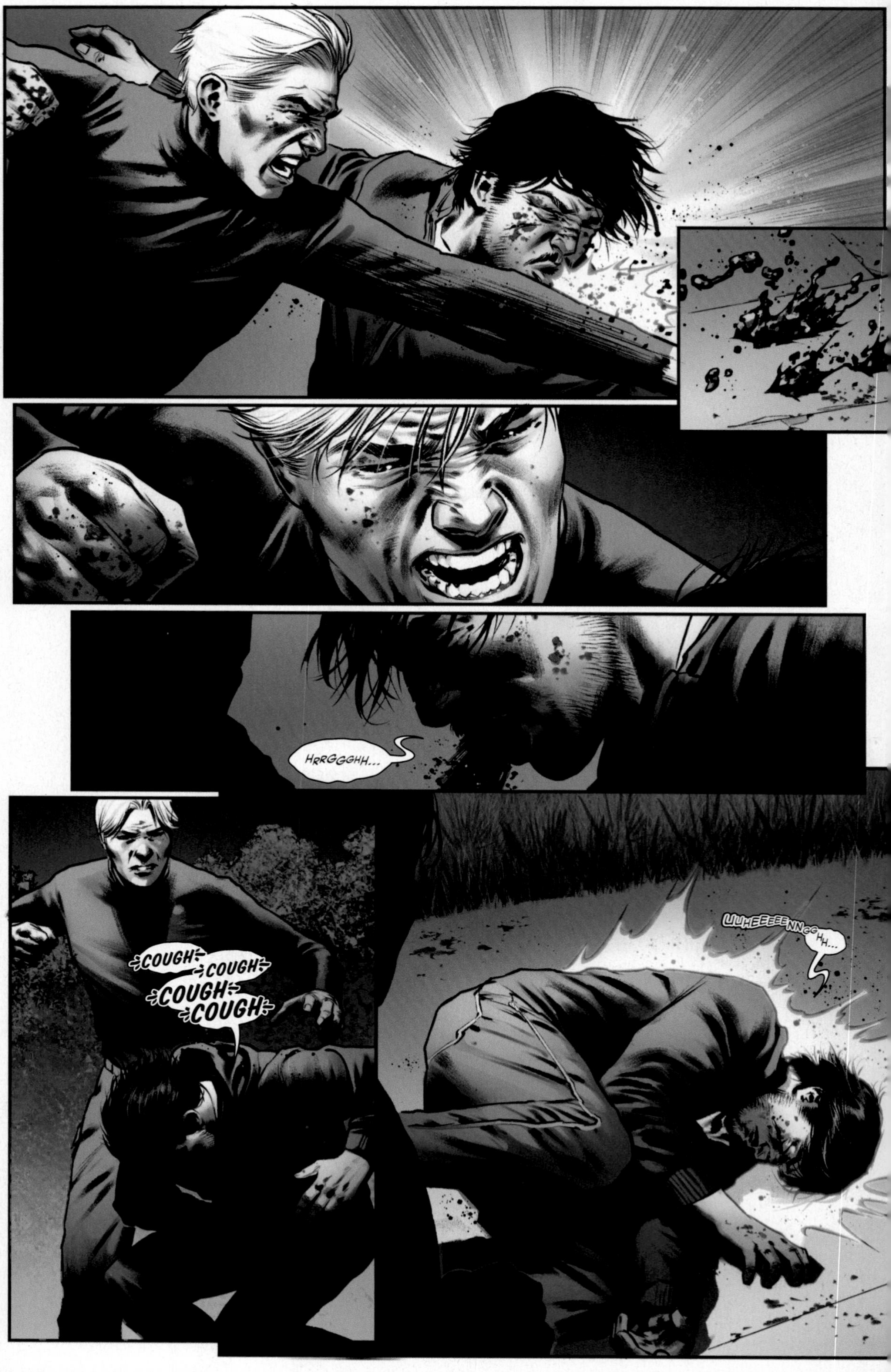
HRRGGGHH...
COUGH COUGH
COUGH COUGH
UUHEEEEEENNGGHH...

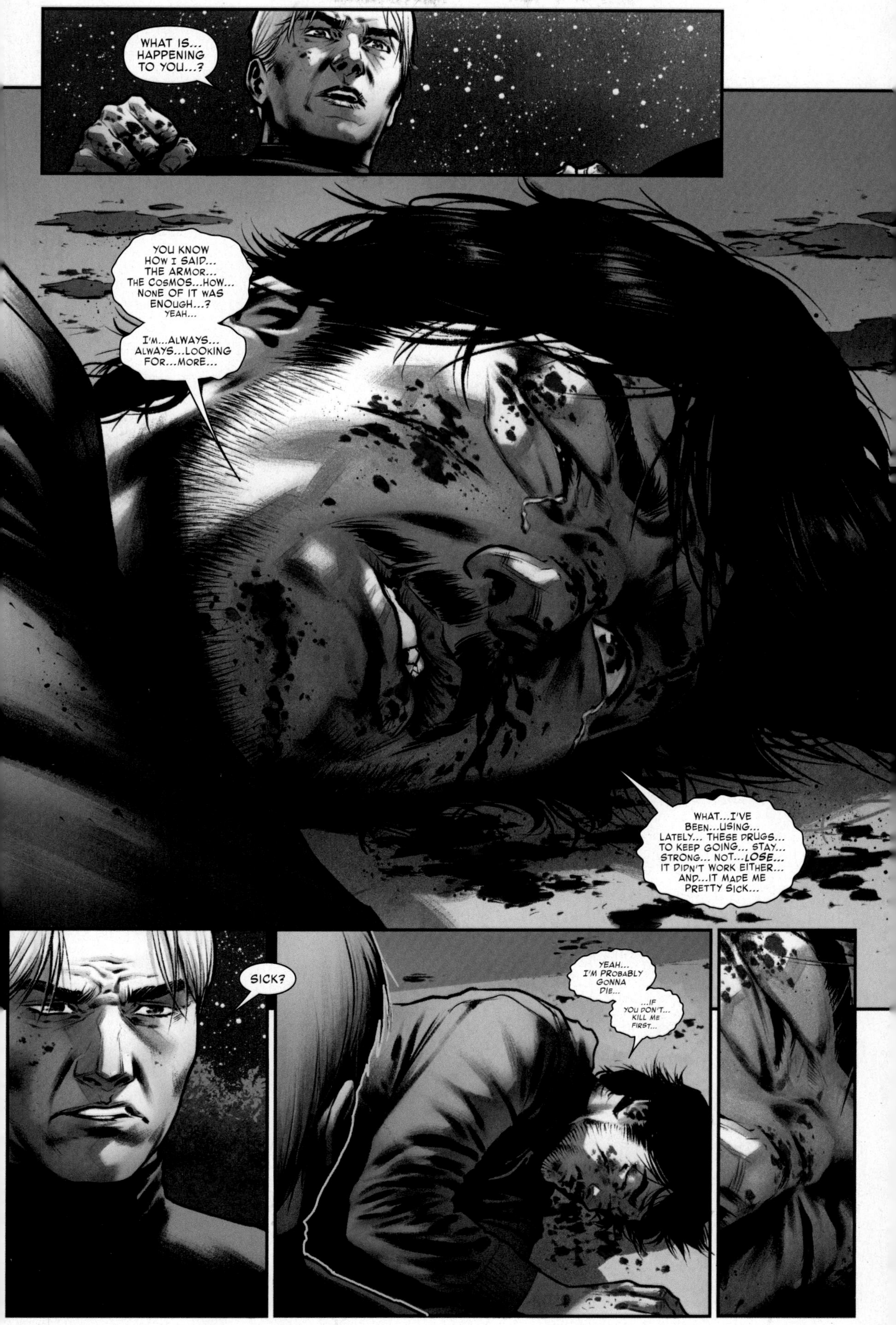
WHAT IS... HAPPENING TO YOU...?
YOU KNOW HOW I SAID... THE ARMOR... THE COSMOS...HOW... NONE OF IT WAS ENOUGH...? YEAH...
I'M...ALWAYS... ALWAYS...LOOKING FOR...MORE...
WHAT...I'VE BEEN...USING... LATELY... THESE DRUGS... TO KEEP GOING... STAY... STRONG... NOT...LOSE... IT DIDN'T WORK EITHER... AND...IT MADE ME PRETTY SICK...
SICK?
YEAH... I'M PROBABLY GONNA DIE...
...IF YOU DON'T... KILL ME FIRST...

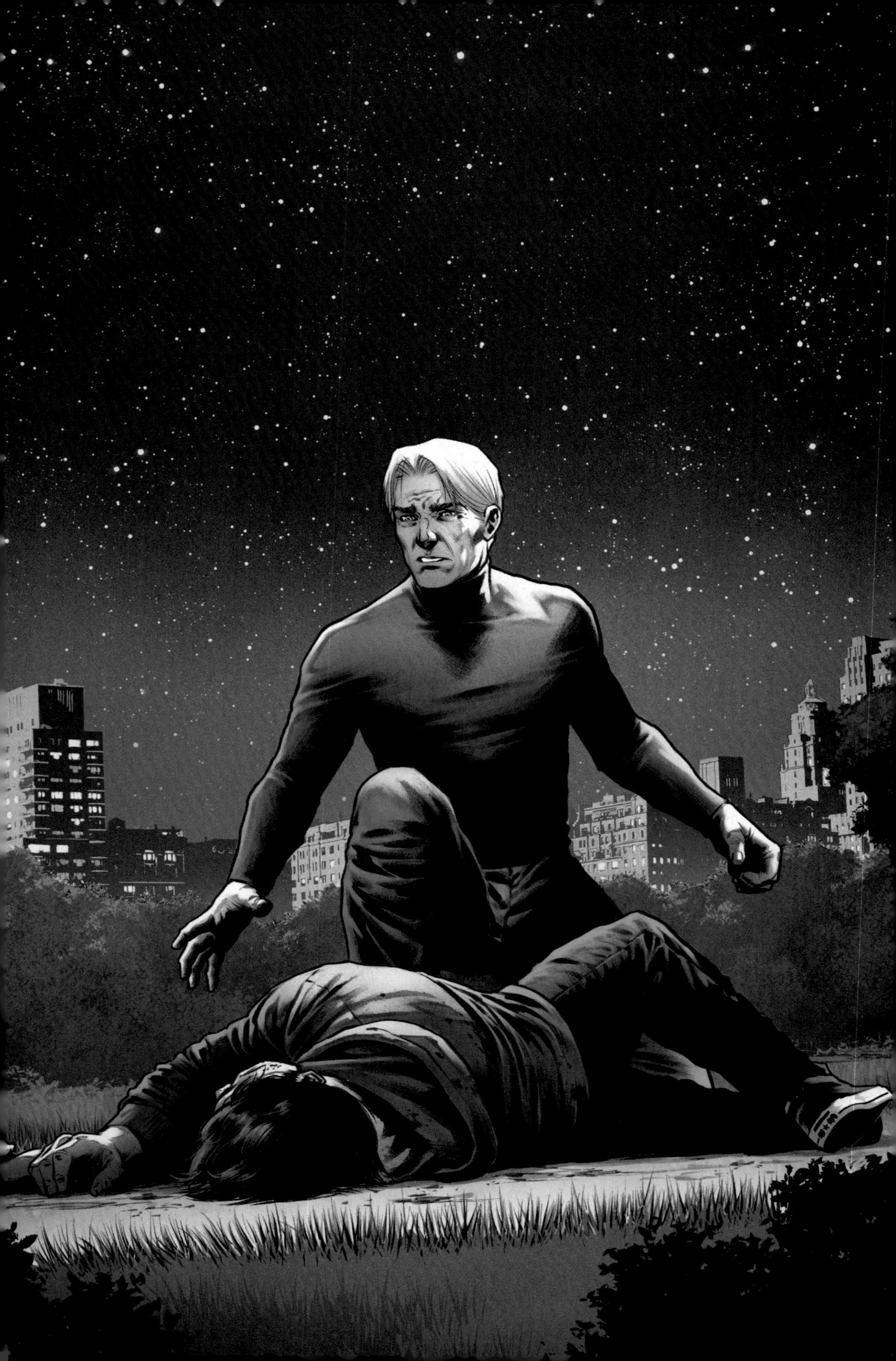

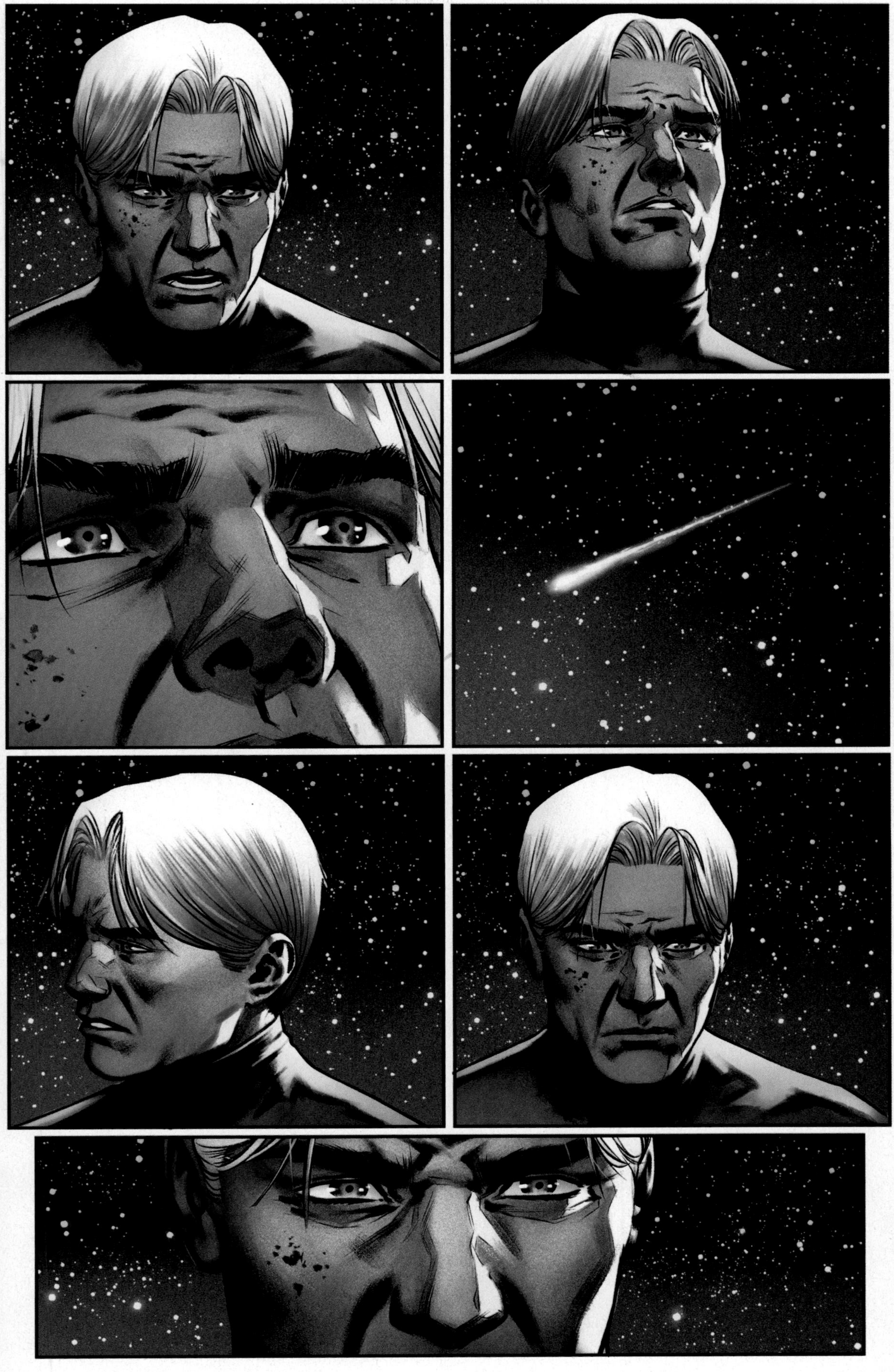

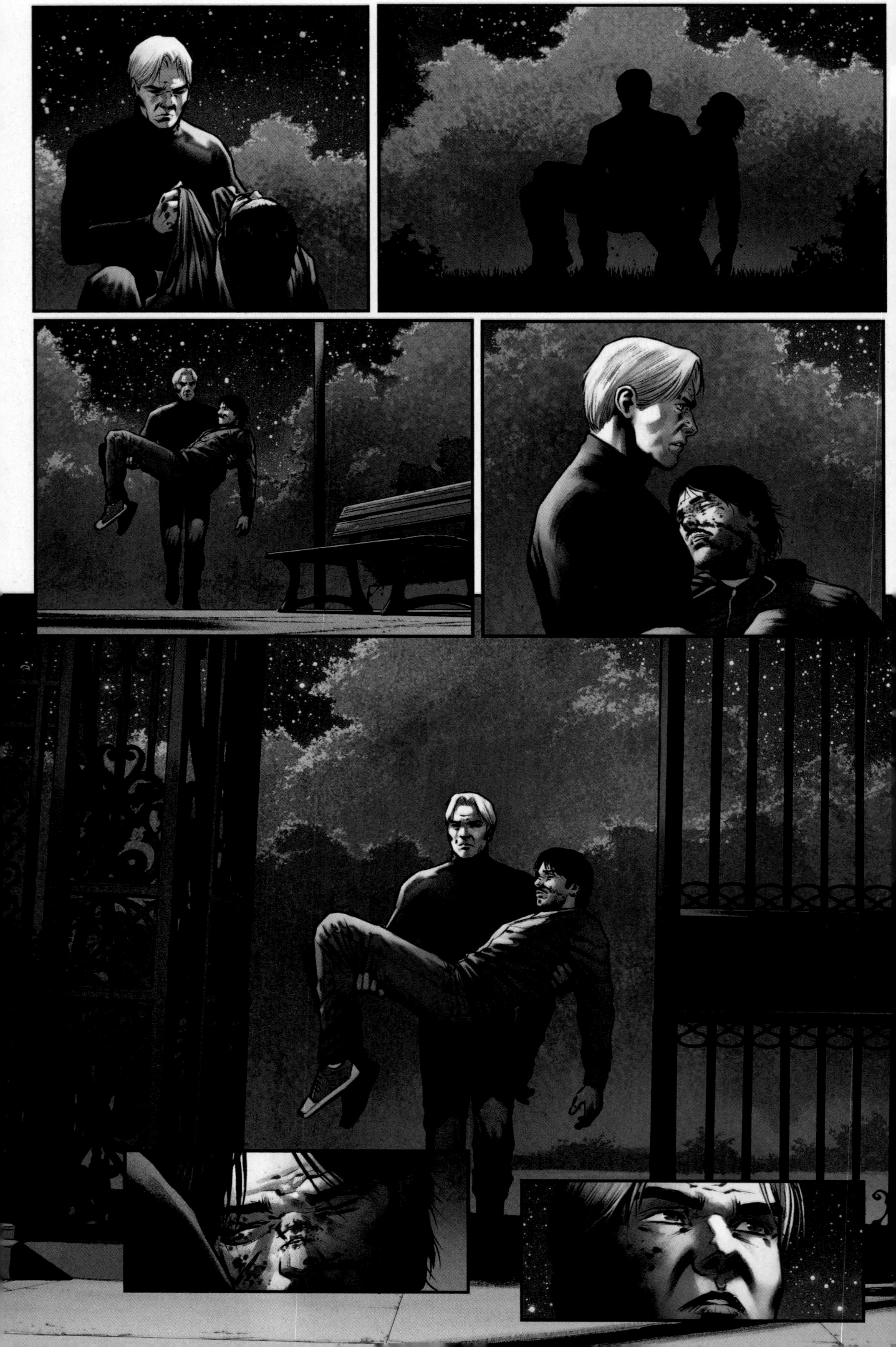

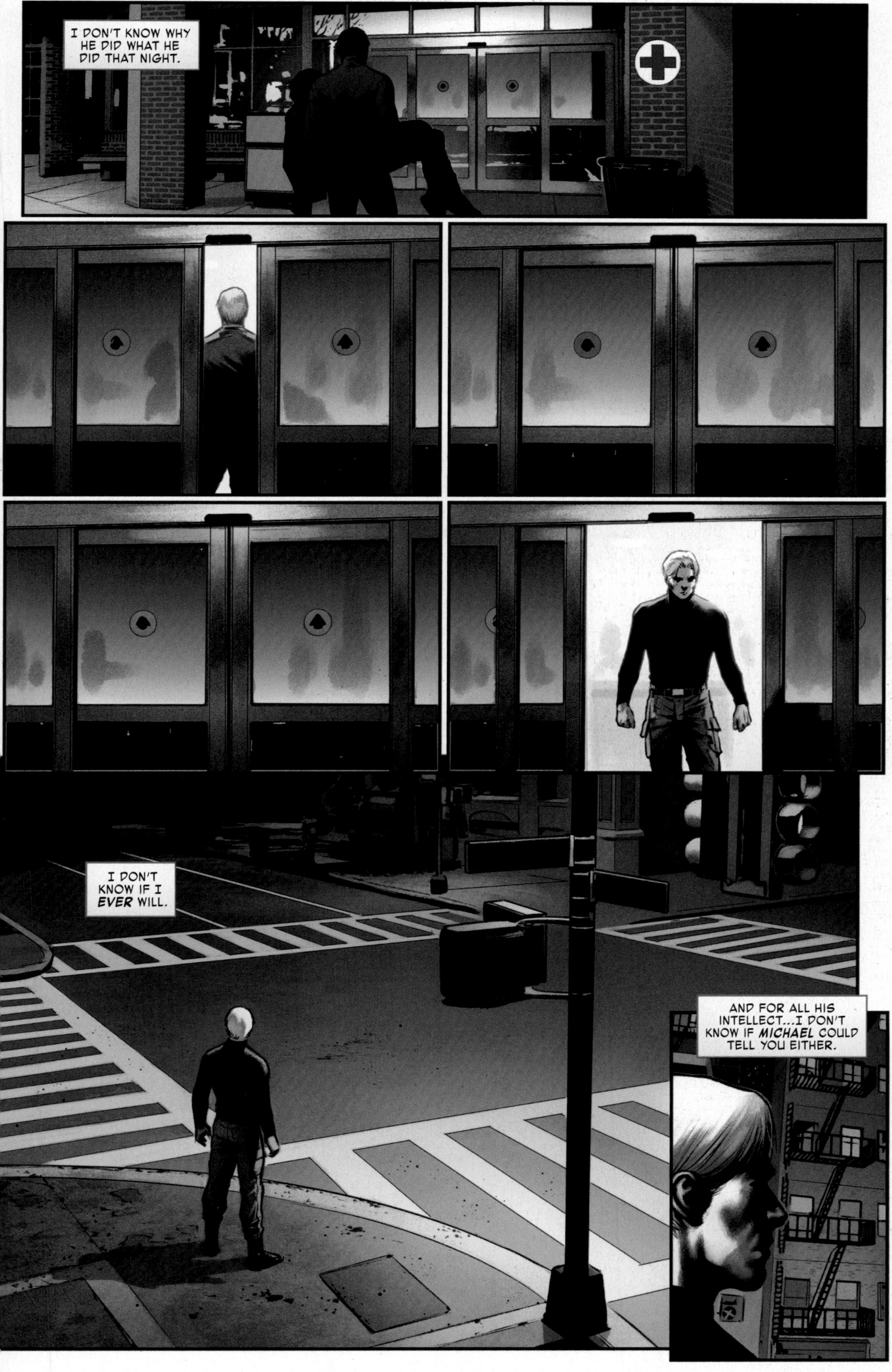
I DON'T KNOW WHY HE DID WHAT HE DID THAT NIGHT.
I DON'T KNOW IF I *EVER* WILL.
AND FOR ALL HIS INTELLECT...I DON'T KNOW IF *MICHAEL* COULD TELL YOU EITHER.

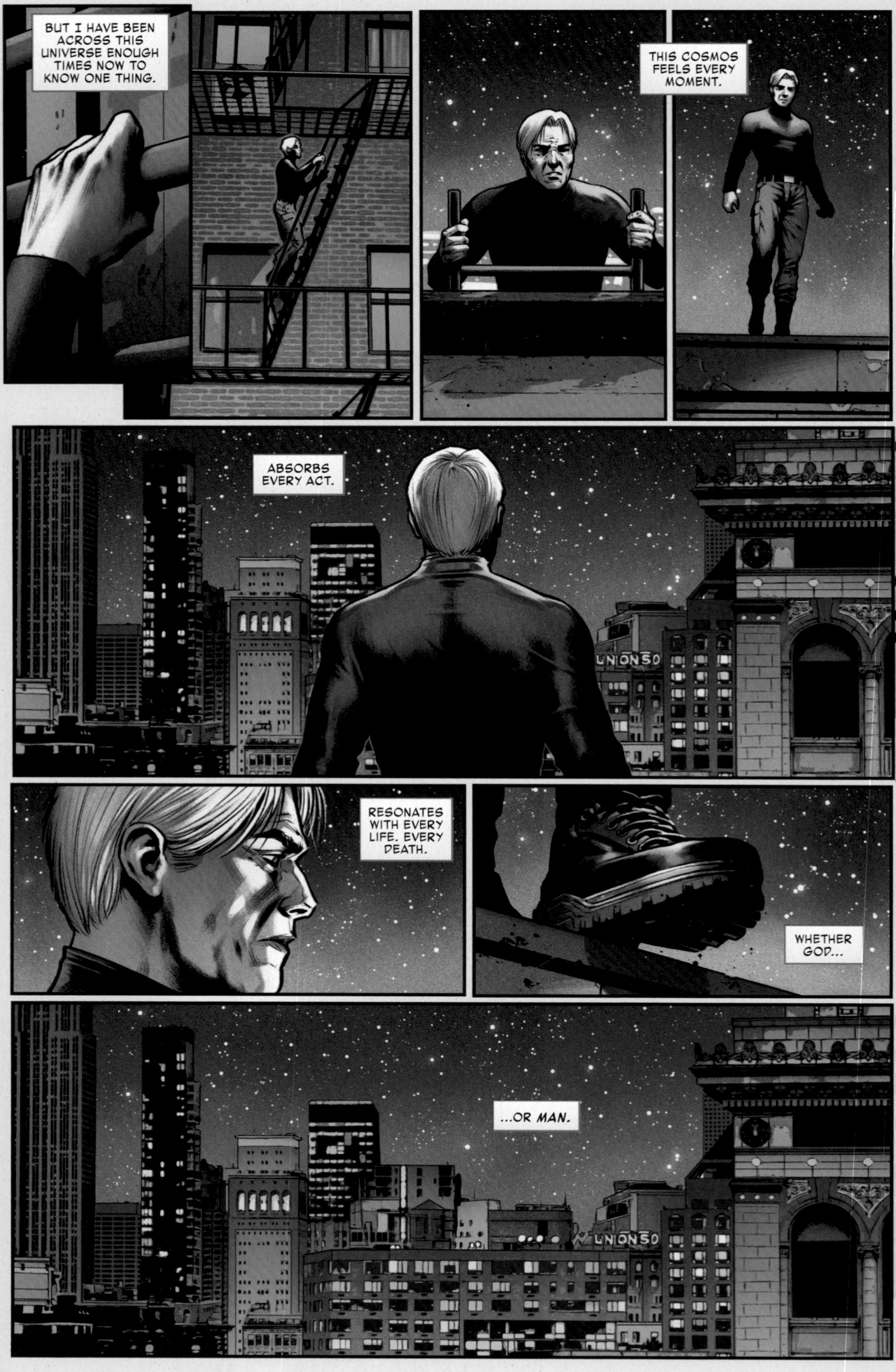
BUT I HAVE BEEN ACROSS THIS UNIVERSE ENOUGH TIMES NOW TO KNOW ONE THING.
THIS COSMOS FEELS EVERY MOMENT.
ABSORBS EVERY ACT.
UNIONSQ
RESONATES WITH EVERY LIFE. EVERY DEATH.
WHETHER GOD...
...OR MAN.

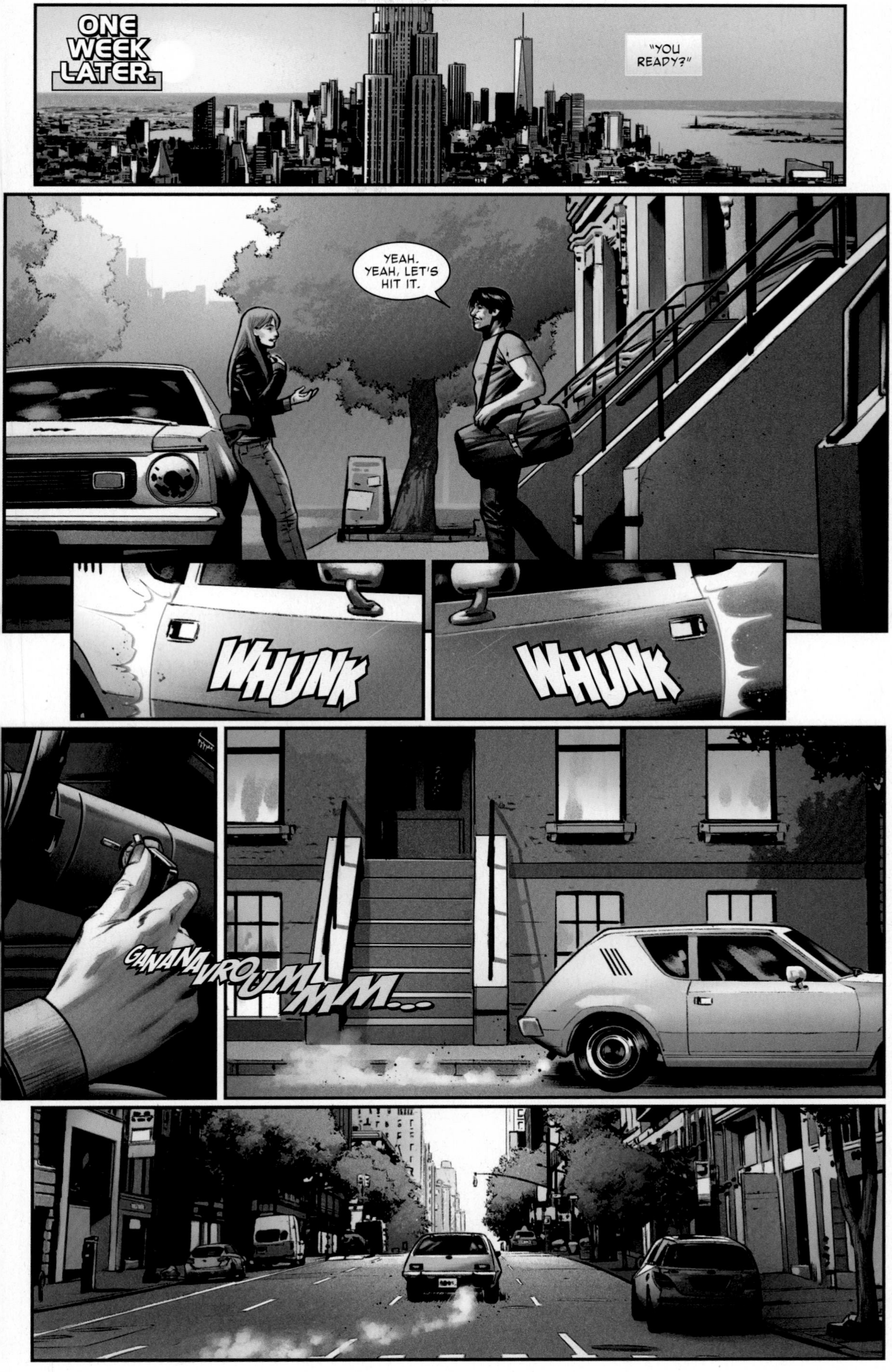
ONE WEEK LATER.
"YOU READY?"
YEAH. YEAH, LET'S HIT IT.
WHUNK
WHUNK
GANANAVROUMMMM...

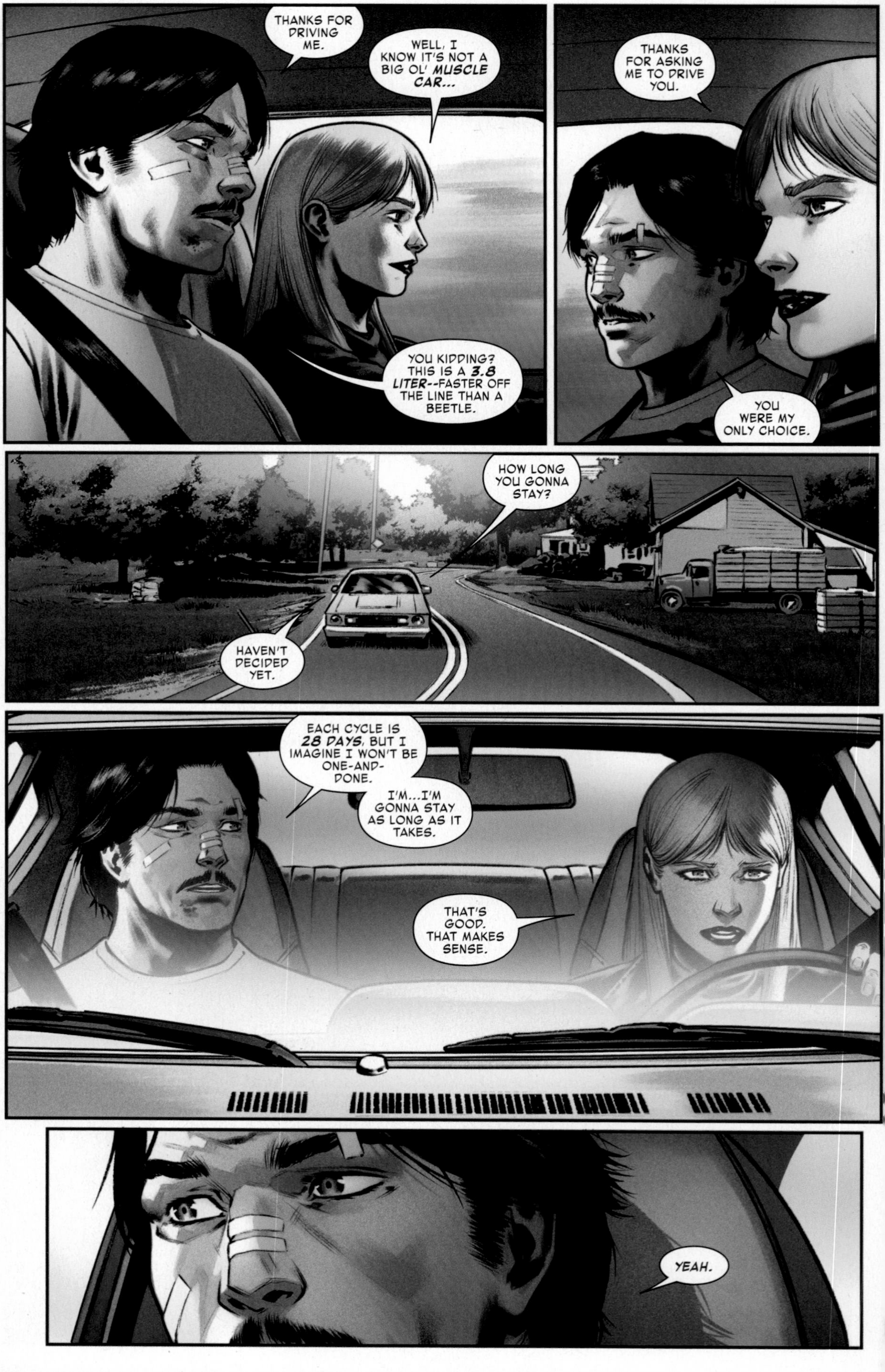

THANKS FOR DRIVING ME.
WELL, I KNOW IT'S NOT A BIG OL' MUSCLE CAR...
YOU KIDDING? THIS IS A 3.8 LITER--FASTER OFF THE LINE THAN A BEETLE.
THANKS FOR ASKING ME TO DRIVE YOU.
YOU WERE MY ONLY CHOICE.
HOW LONG YOU GONNA STAY?
HAVEN'T DECIDED YET.
EACH CYCLE IS 28 DAYS, BUT I IMAGINE I WON'T BE ONE-AND-DONE.
I'M...I'M GONNA STAY AS LONG AS IT TAKES.
THAT'S GOOD. THAT MAKES SENSE.
YEAH.

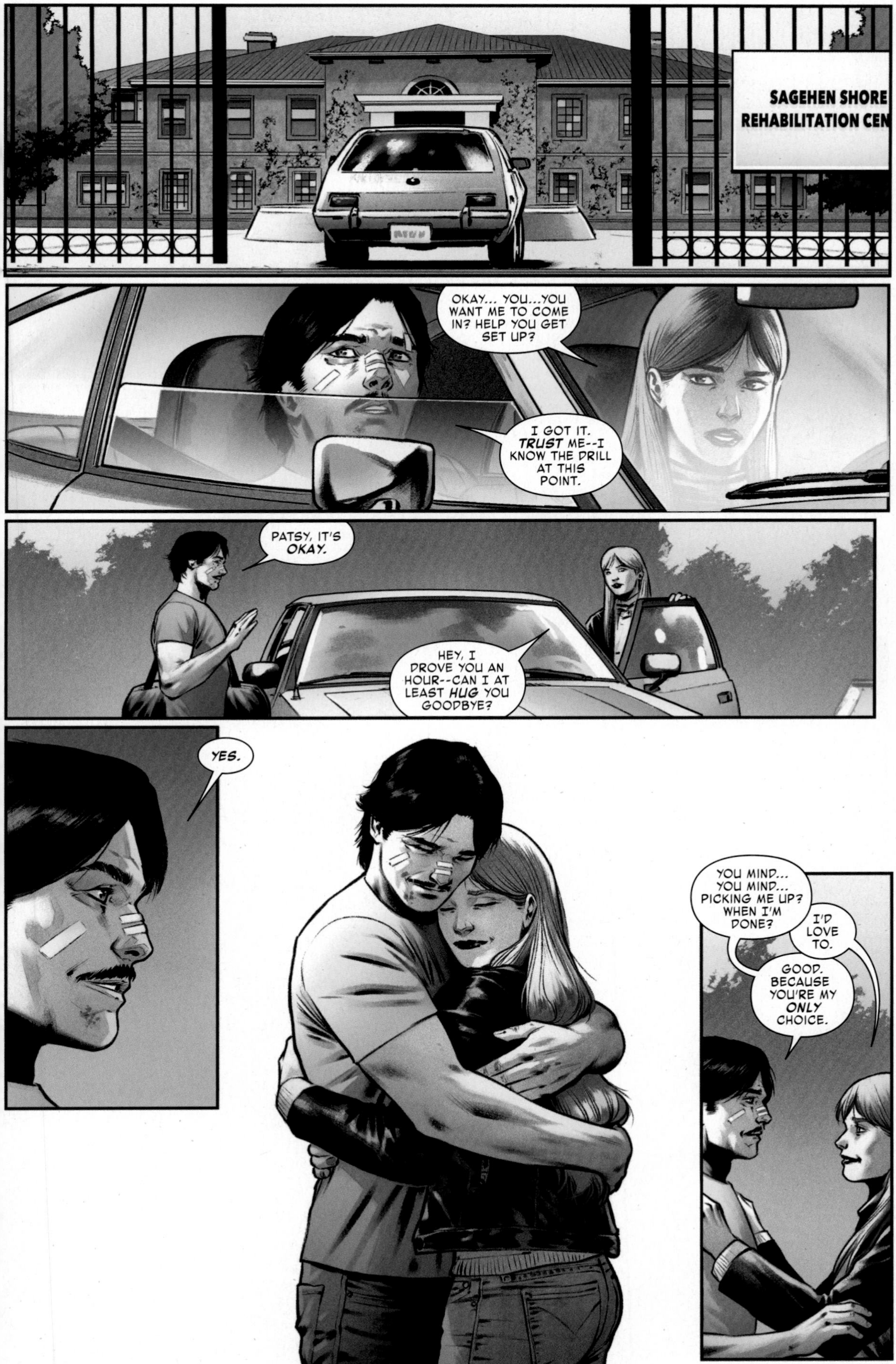

SAGEHEN SHORE REHABILITATION CEN
OKAY... YOU...YOU WANT ME TO COME IN? HELP YOU GET SET UP?
I GOT IT. TRUST ME--I KNOW THE DRILL AT THIS POINT.
PATSY, IT'S OKAY.
HEY, I DROVE YOU AN HOUR--CAN I AT LEAST HUG YOU GOODBYE?
YES.
YOU MIND... YOU MIND... PICKING ME UP? WHEN I'M DONE?
I'D LOVE TO.
GOOD. BECAUSE YOU'RE MY ONLY CHOICE.

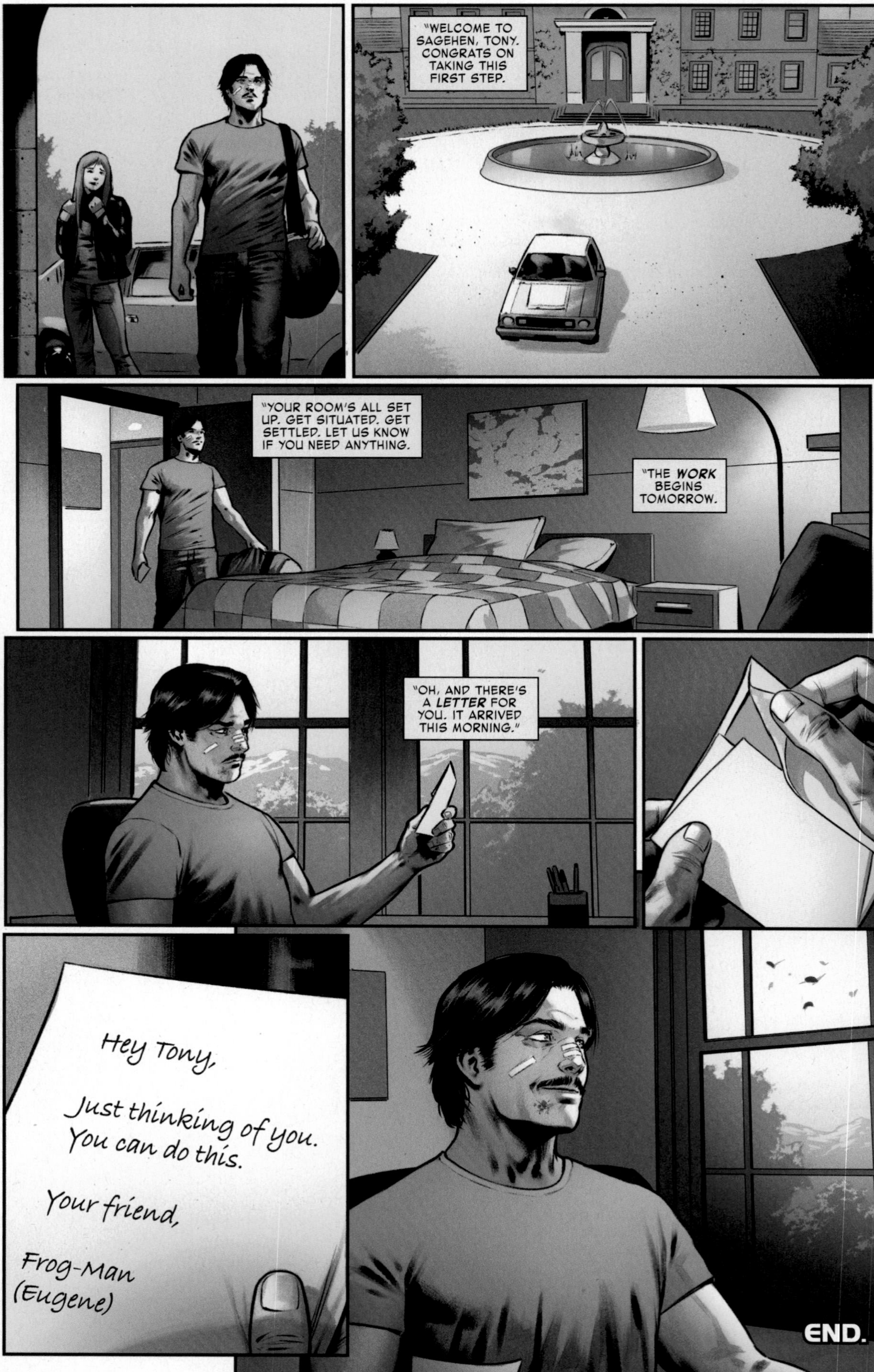
"WELCOME TO SAGEHEN, TONY. CONGRATS ON TAKING THIS FIRST STEP.
"YOUR ROOM'S ALL SET UP. GET SITUATED. GET SETTLED. LET US KNOW IF YOU NEED ANYTHING.
"THE WORK BEGINS TOMORROW.
"OH, AND THERE'S A LETTER FOR YOU. IT ARRIVED THIS MORNING."
Hey Tony,
Just thinking of you. You can do this.
Your friend,
Frog-Man (Eugene)
END.

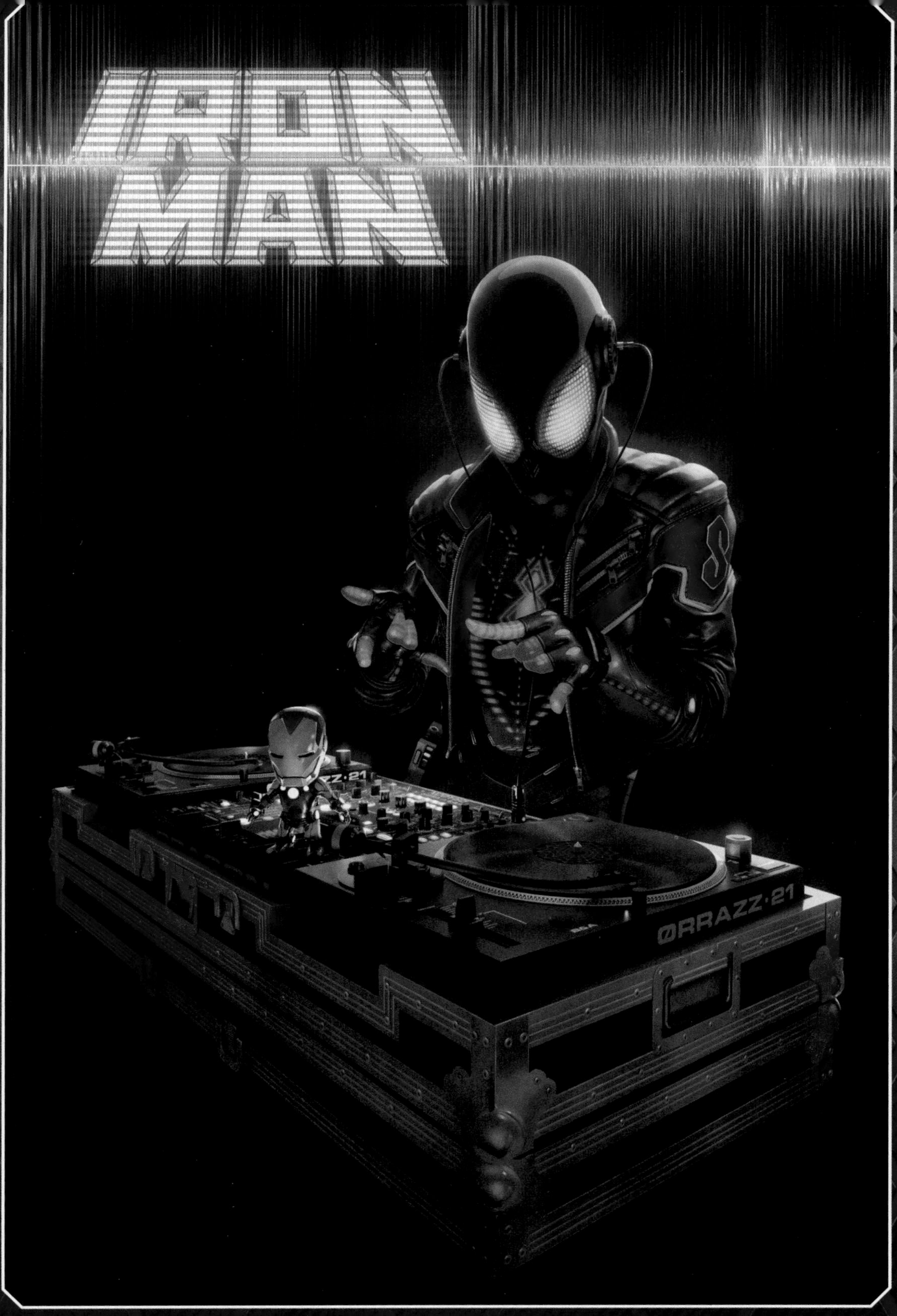
IRON
MAN
ØRRAZZ·21

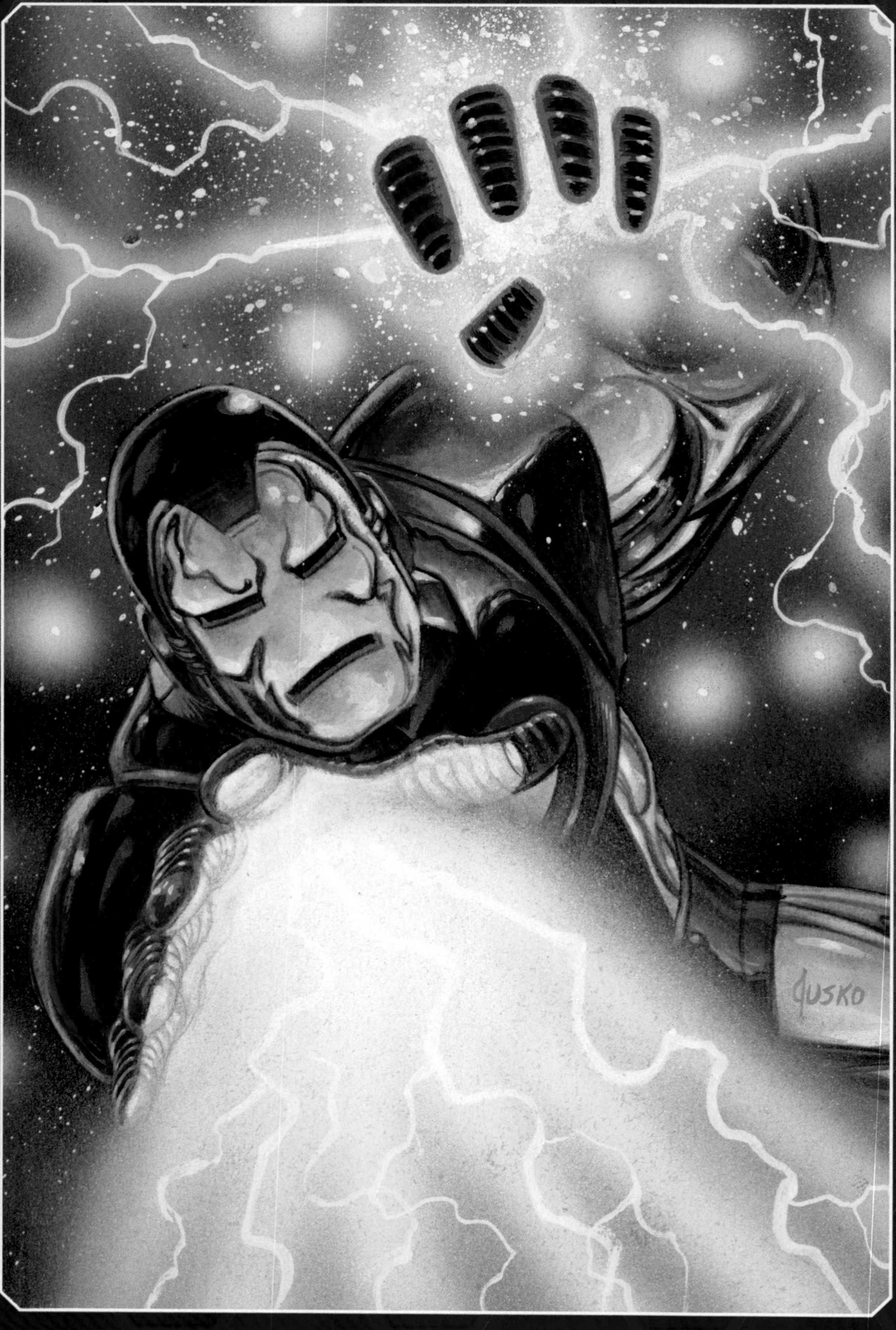
JUSKO

JOE JUSKO

#13 MARVEL MASTERPIECES VARIANT

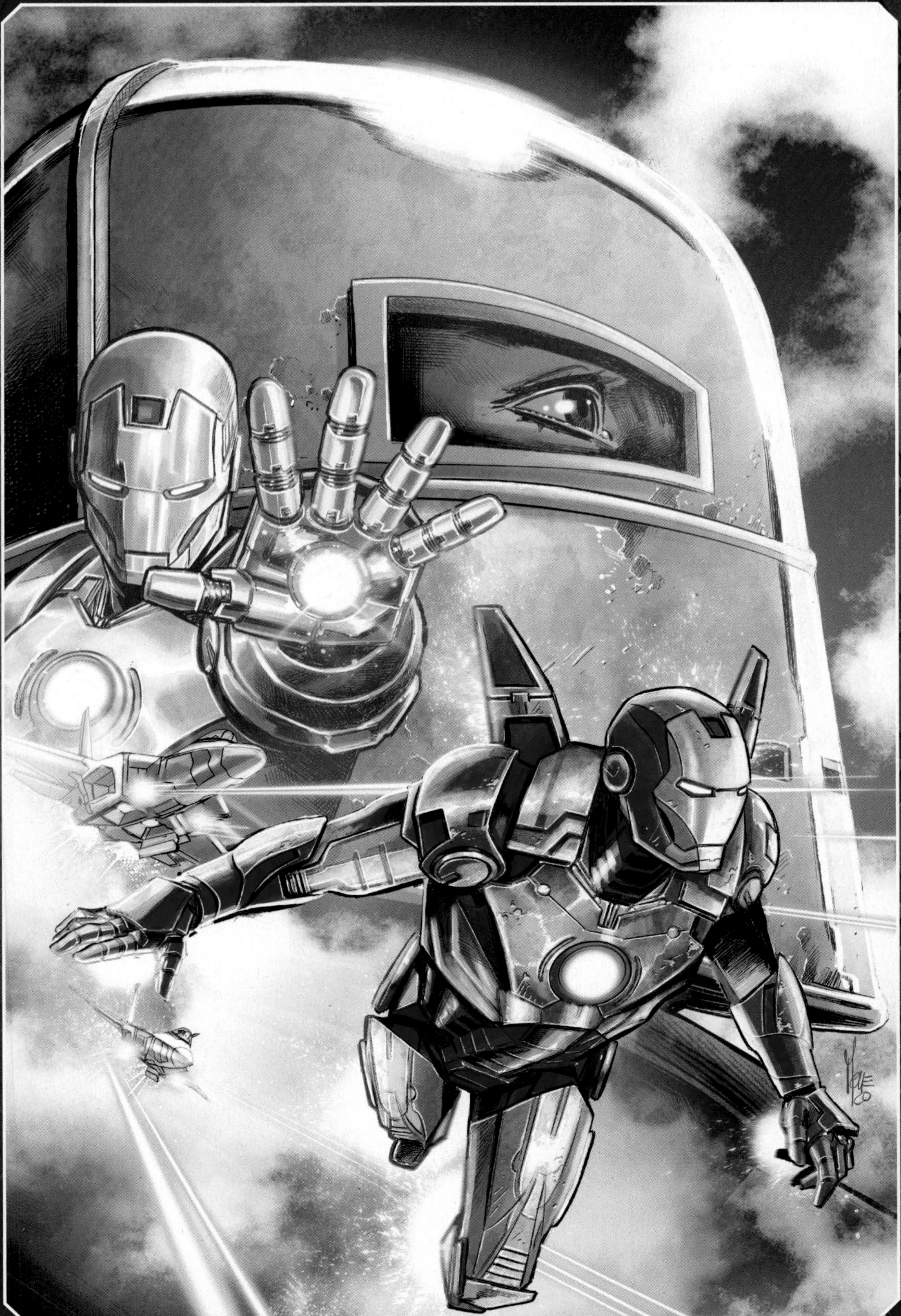

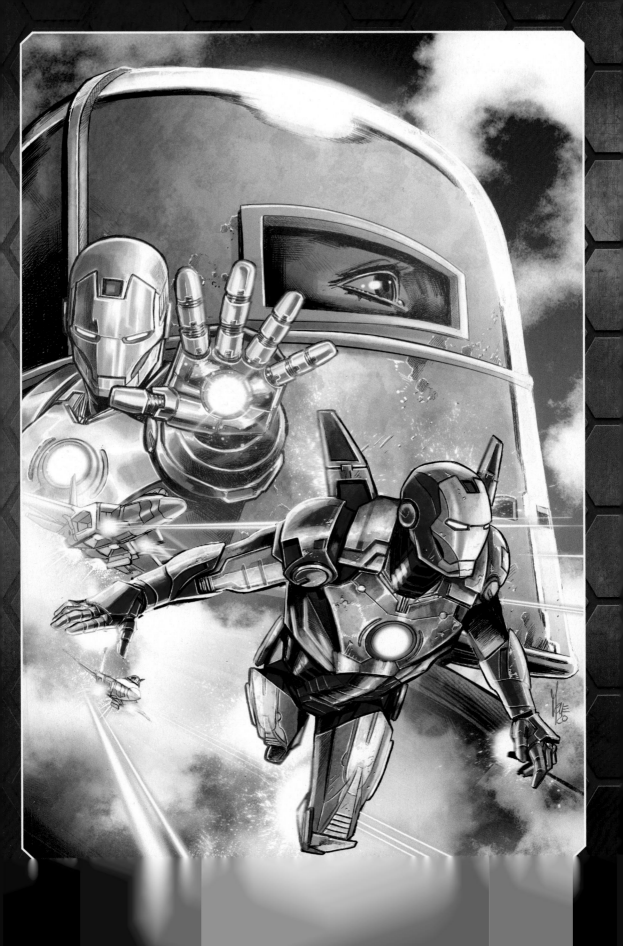

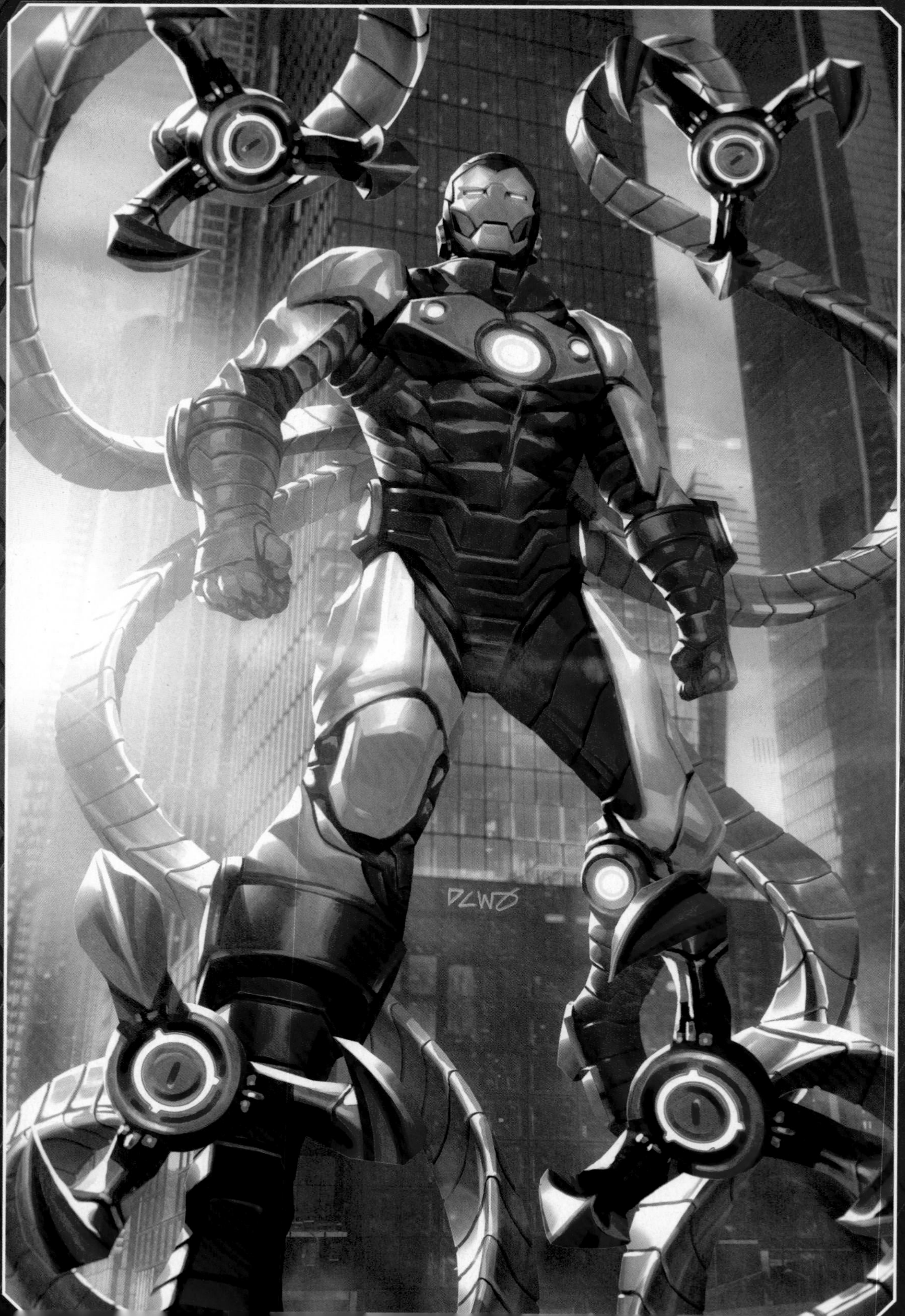

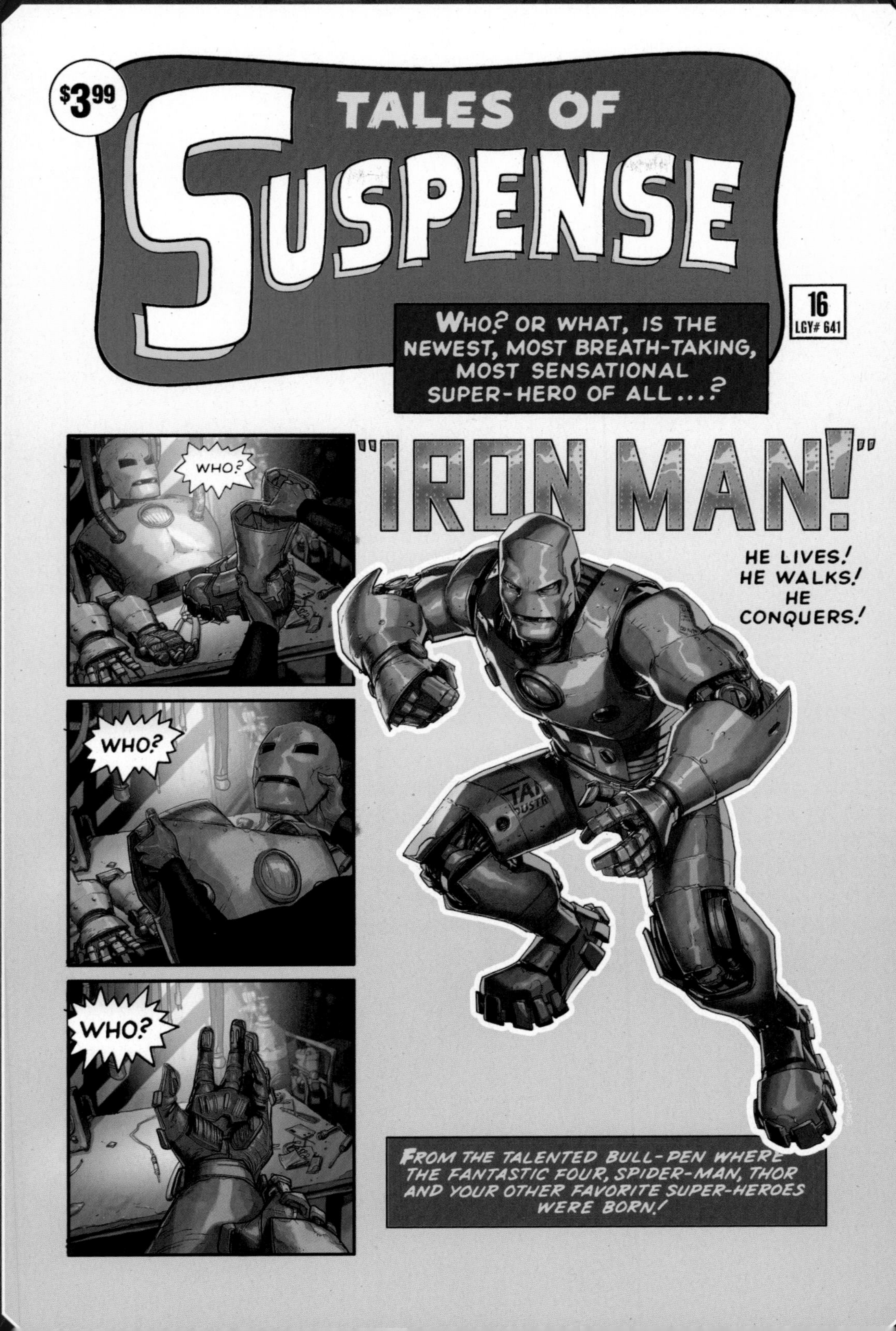
$3.99
TALES OF
SUSPENSE
16
LGY# 641
WHO? OR WHAT, IS THE NEWEST, MOST BREATH-TAKING, MOST SENSATIONAL SUPER-HERO OF ALL...?
WHO?
WHO?
WHO?
"IRON MAN!"
HE LIVES! HE WALKS! HE CONQUERS!
FROM THE TALENTED BULL-PEN WHERE THE FANTASTIC FOUR, SPIDER-MAN, THOR AND YOUR OTHER FAVORITE SUPER-HEROES WERE BORN!

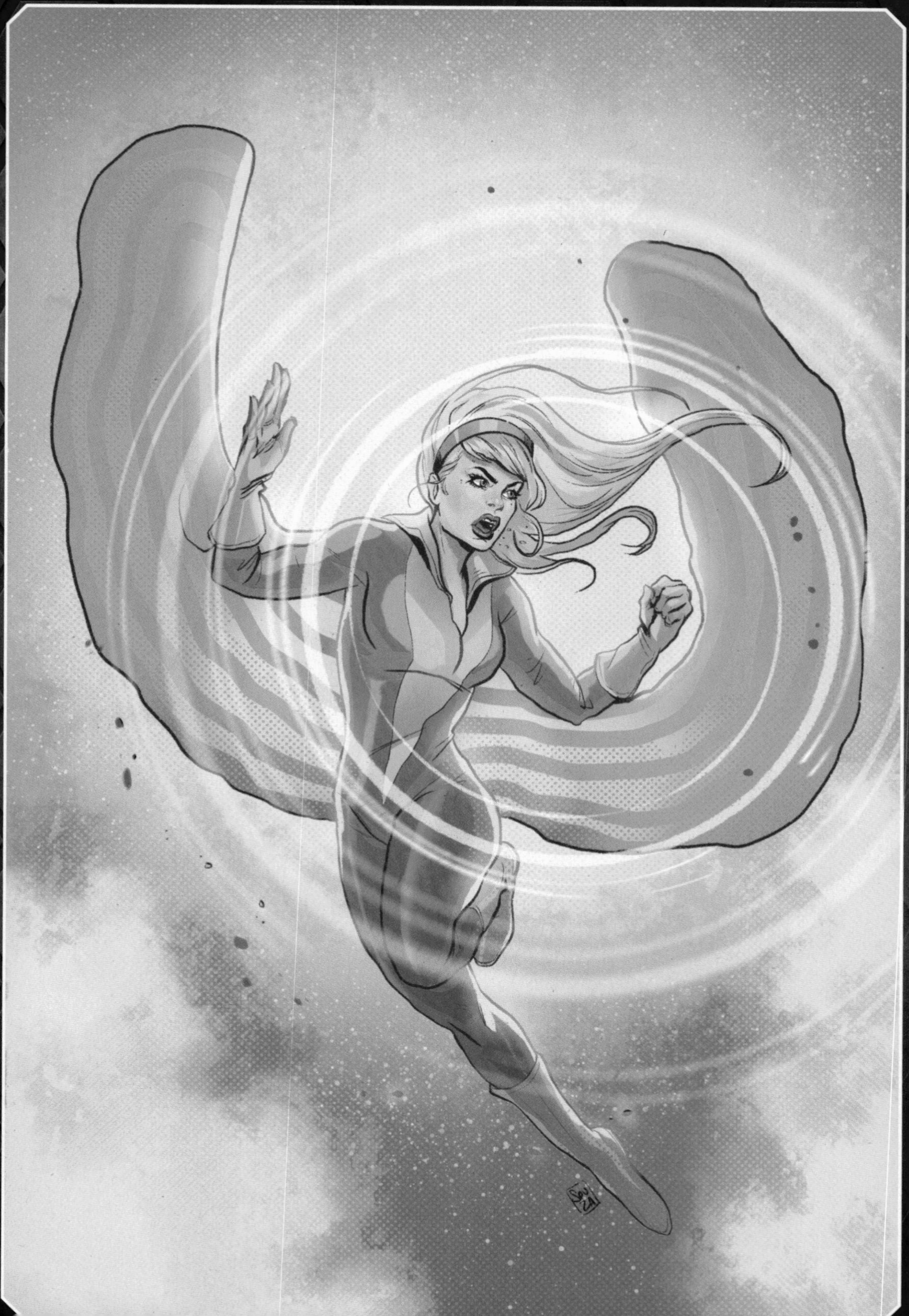

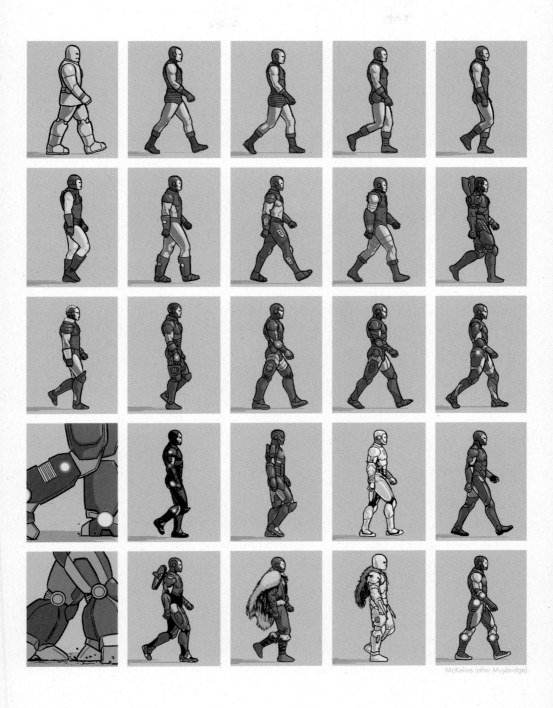

McKelvie (after Muybridge)

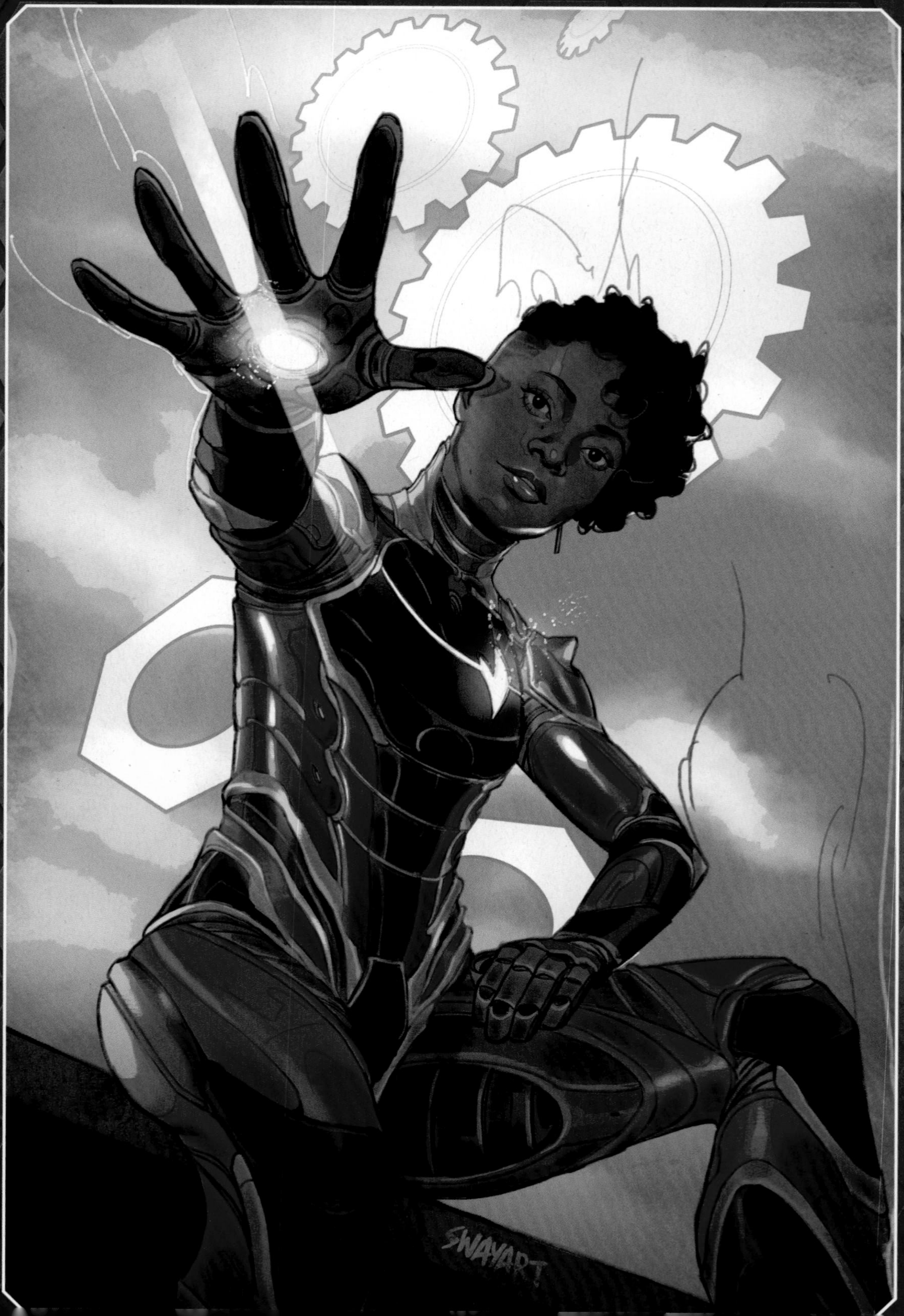
SWAYART

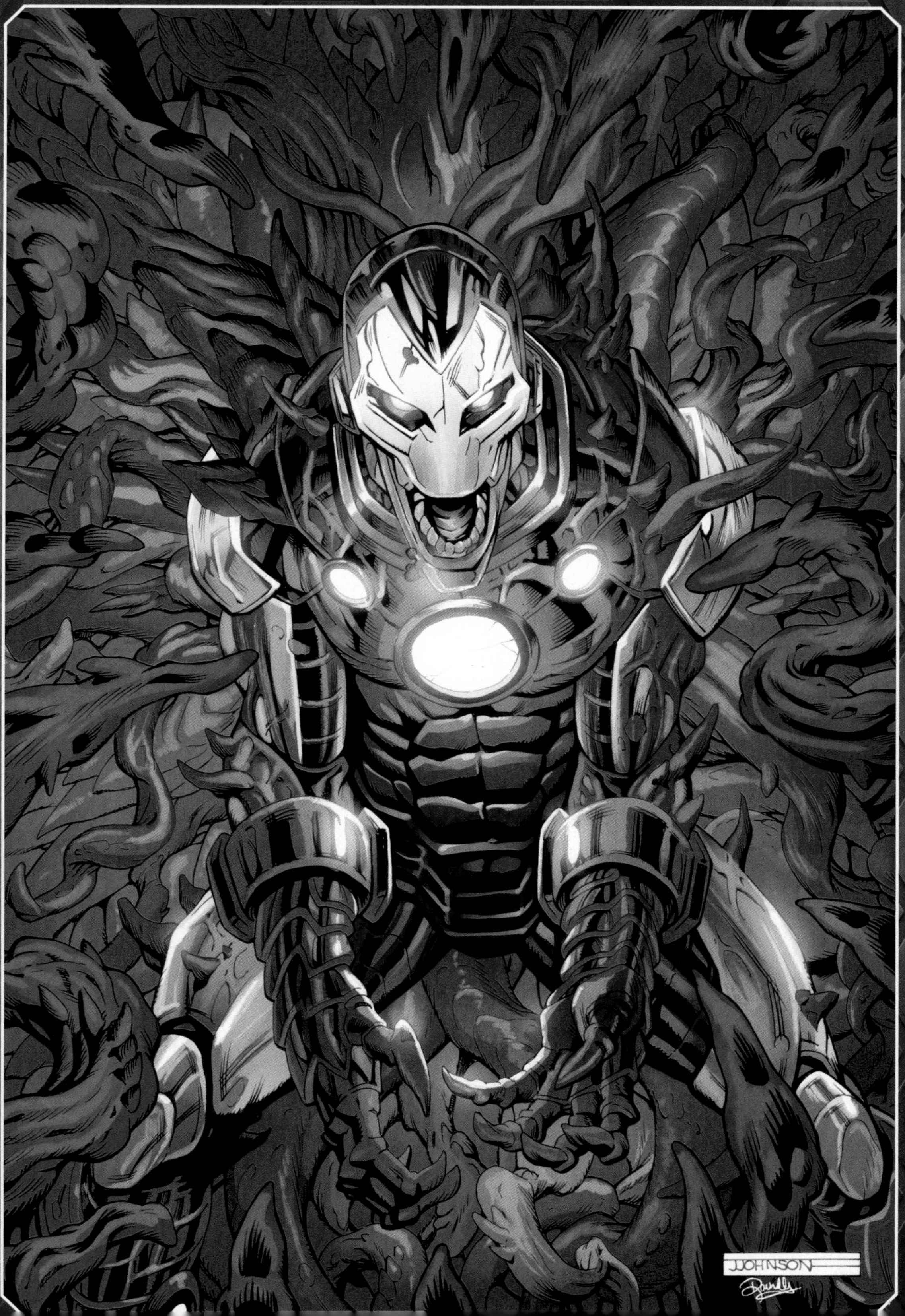
JJOHNSON

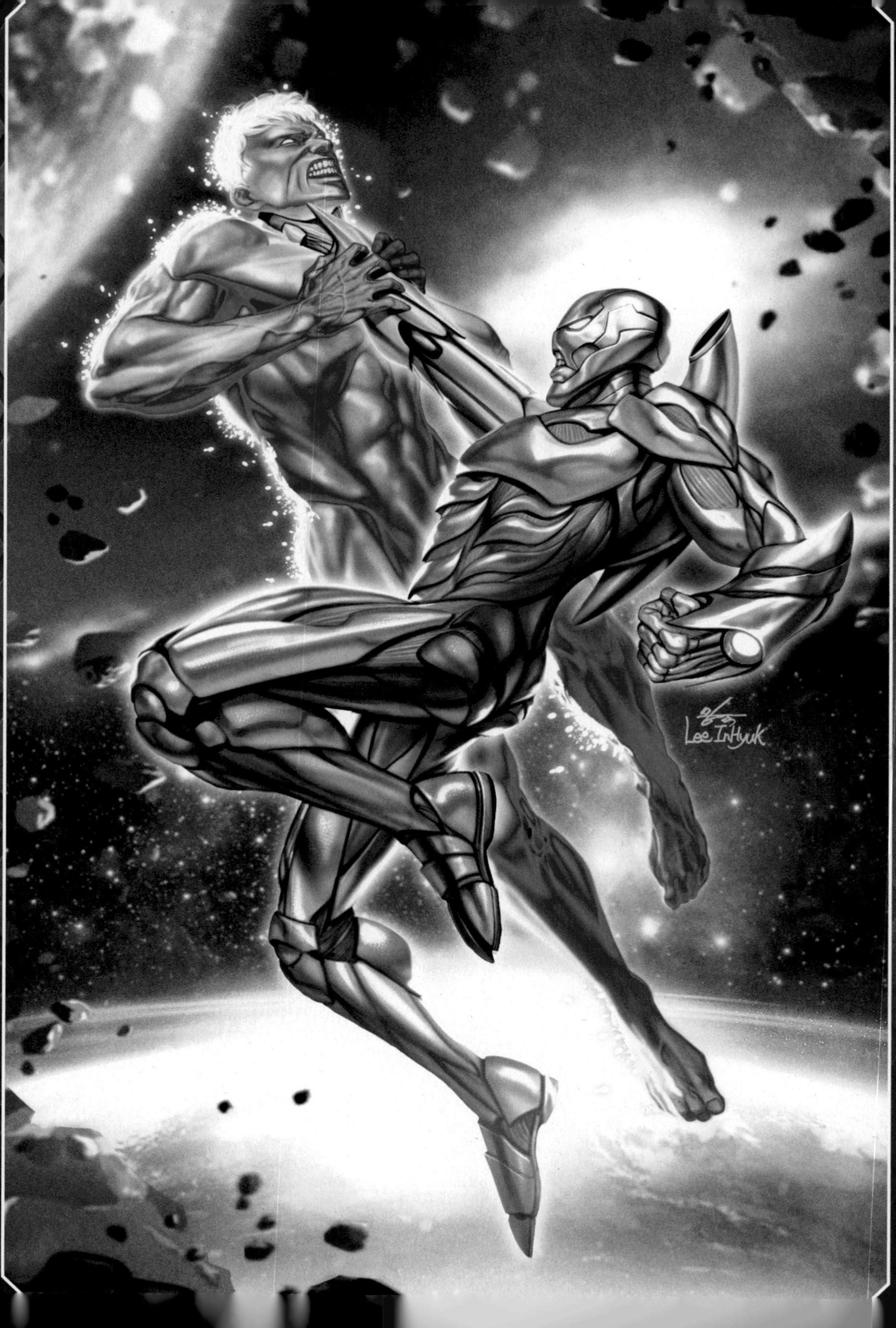
Lee InHyuk

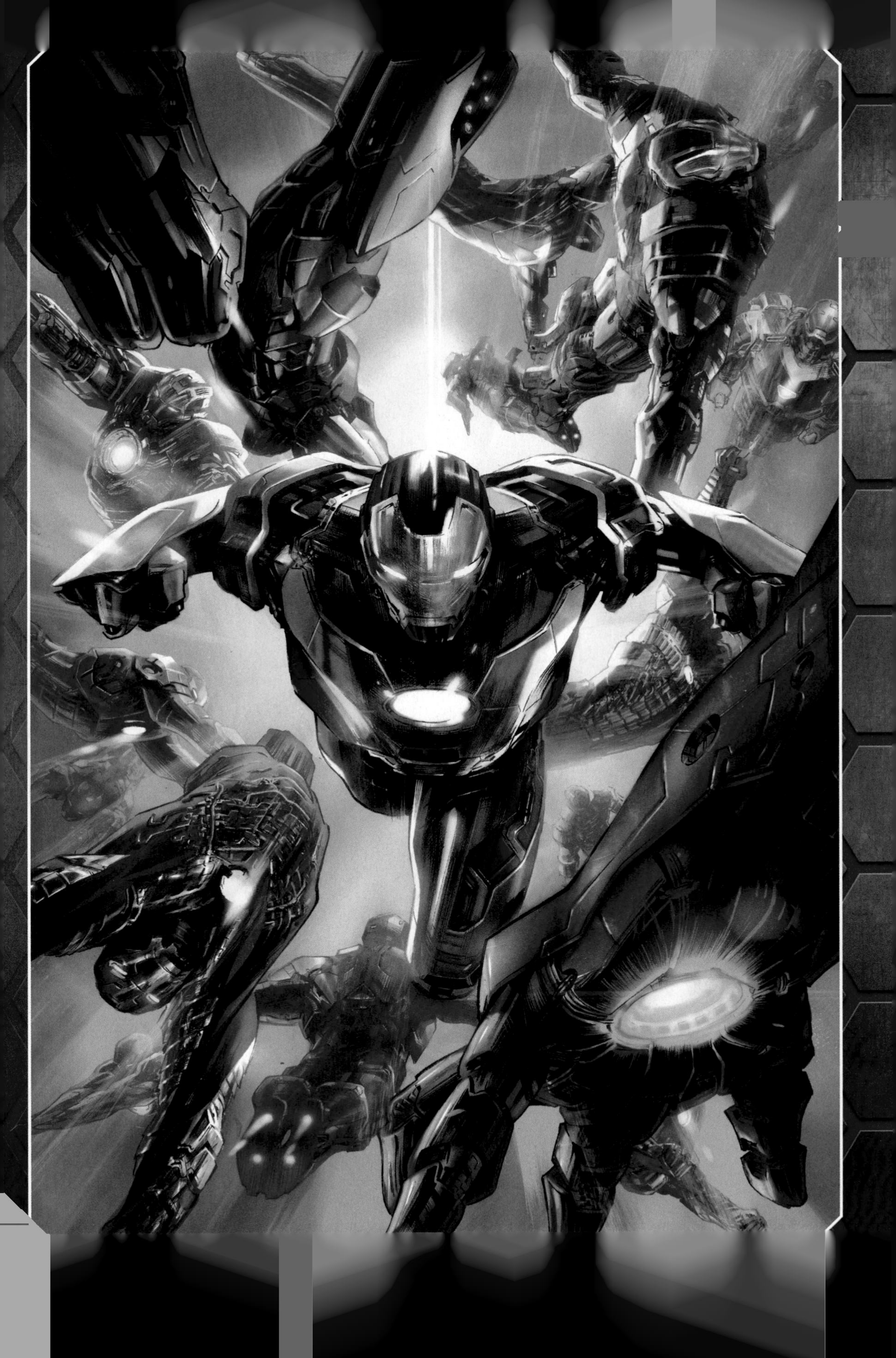

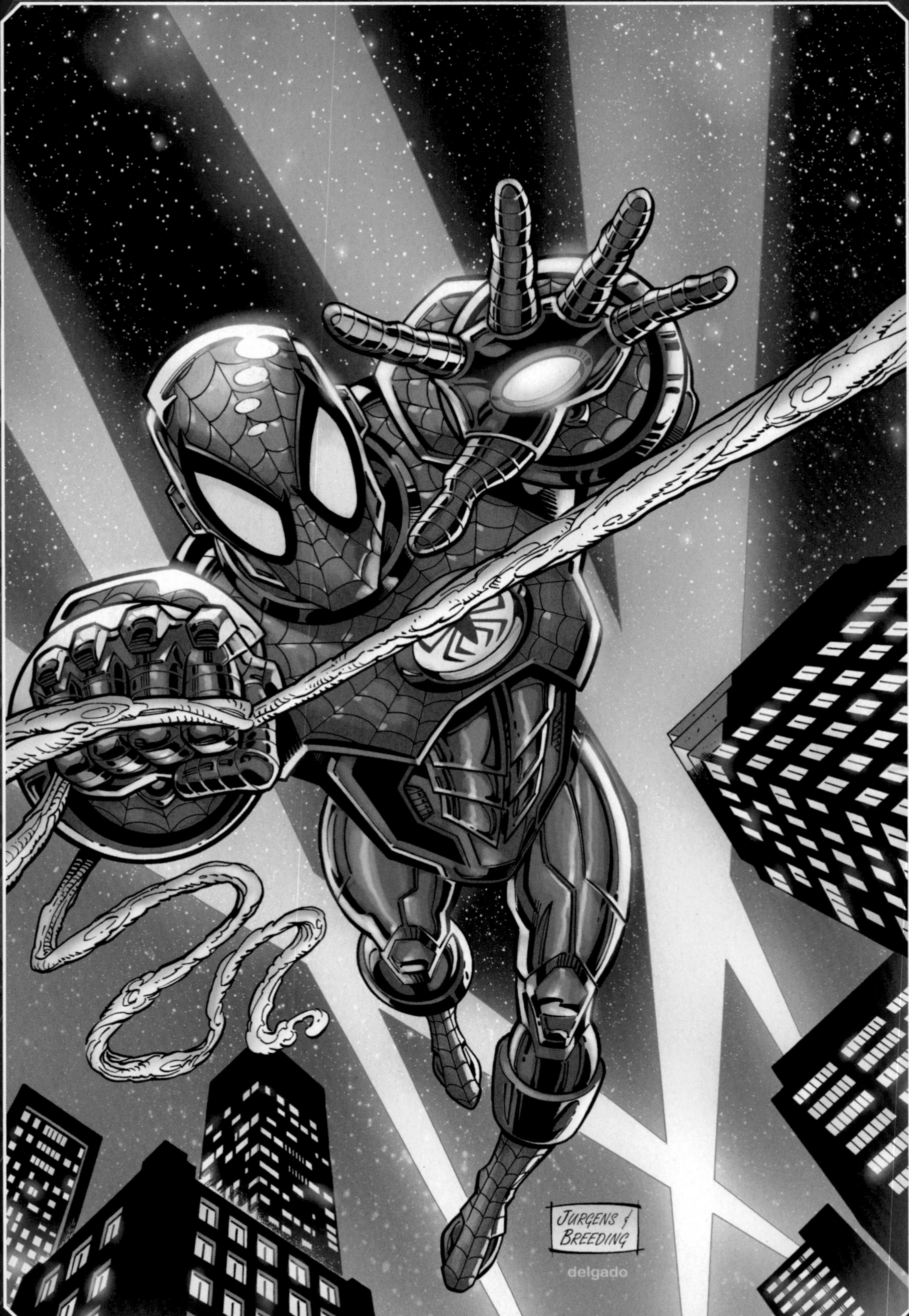
JURGENS & BREEDING
delgado

DAN JURGENS, BRETT BREEDING & EDGAR DELGADO
#19 SPIDER-MAN VARIANT

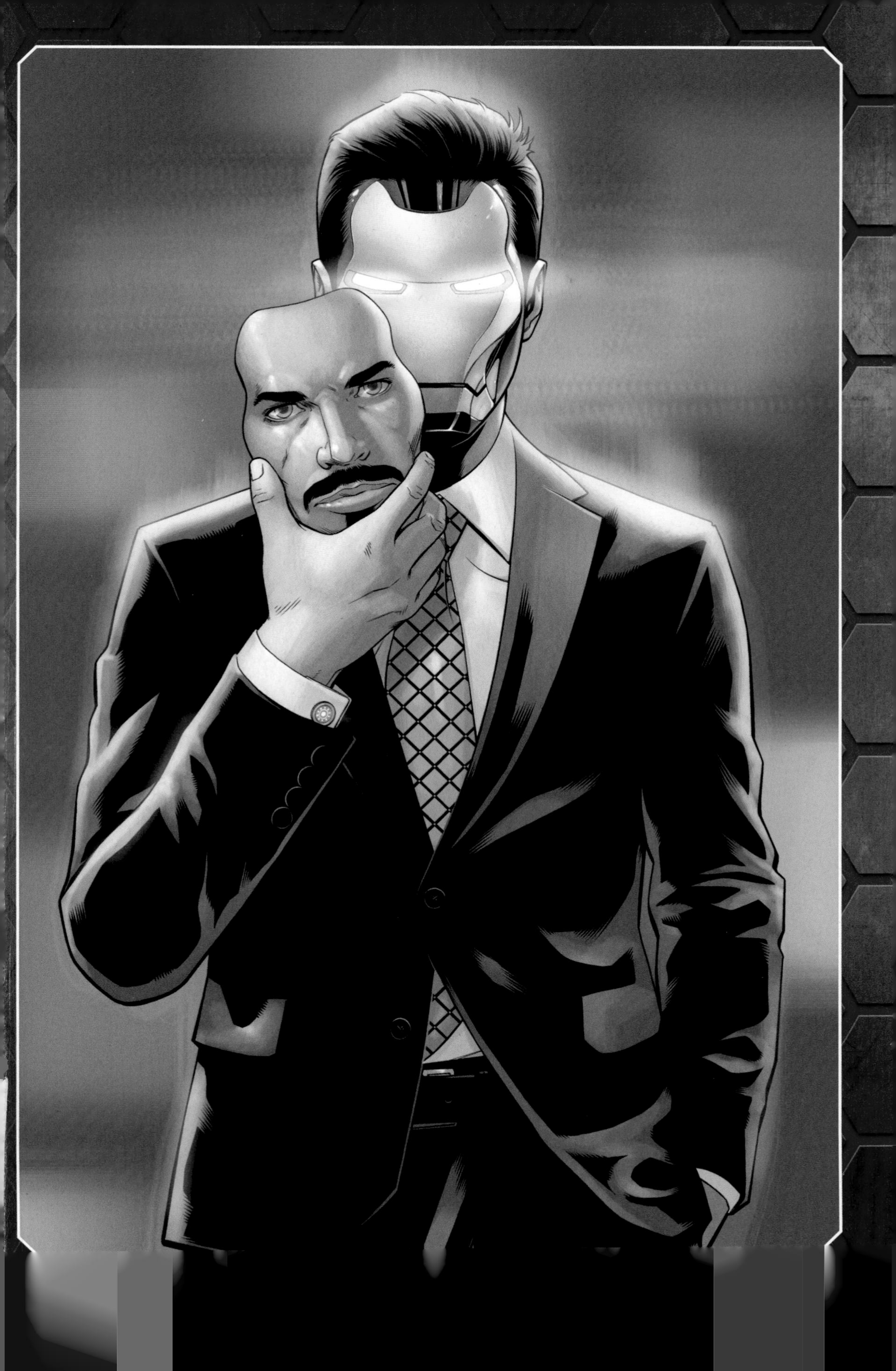

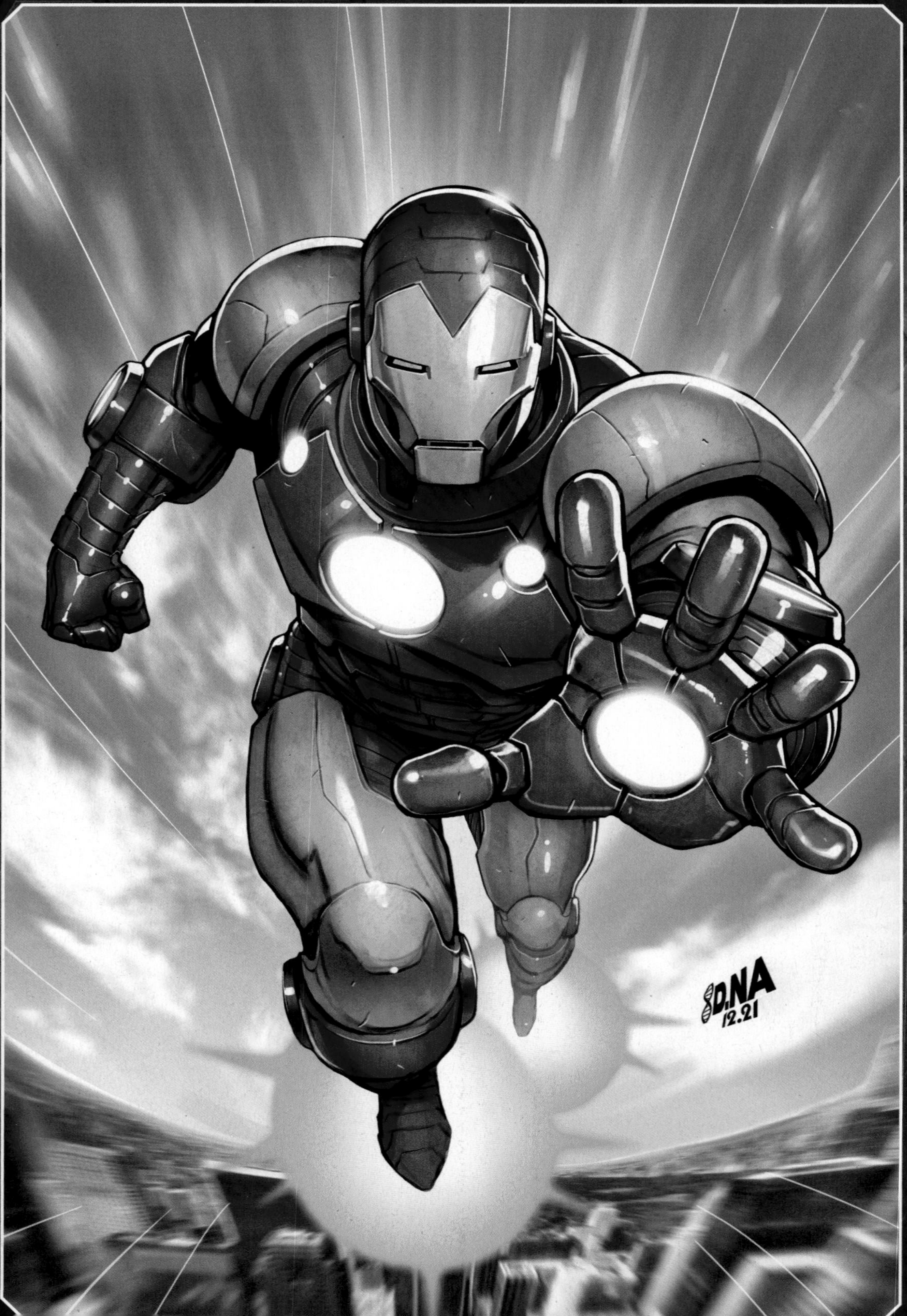
D.NA
12.21